The Closed World of East German Economists

The German Democratic Republic (GDR) was a unique experiment of creating socialism on German ground. In *The Closed World of East German Economists*, Till Düppe tells the story of a generation of economists whose entire careers coincided with the forty-one-year existence of the GDR. In a micro-historical fashion, he examines the world of East German economists through the formative episodes in the lives of five different economists from this "hope" generation. Using both the perspective of the actors as expressed in interviews and archival material unknown to the actors, the book follows East German economics from the early days of the acceptance of Marxism-Leninism through to its interaction with Western economics and its eventual dissolution following the collapse of the Berlin Wall. It is a fascinating insight into the challenges faced by economists working under the yoke of an authoritarian party regime.

TILL DÜPPE is a professor at the département des sciences économiques, and a member of the Centre interuniversitaire de recherche sur la science et la technologie, both at the Université du Québec à Montréal. For periods of this research, he was visiting researcher at the European University Viadrina Frankfurt (Oder) and at the Leibniz Centre for Contemporary History in Potsdam.

HISTORICAL PERSPECTIVES ON MODERN ECONOMICS

Series Editor: Professor Harro Maas, *Walras-Pareto Centre for the History of Economic and Political Thought, University of Lausanne*

This series contains original works that challenge and enlighten historians of economics. For the profession as a whole, it promotes better understanding of the origin and content of modern economics.

Other books in the series:

Erwin Dekker, Jan Tinbergen (1903–1994) and the Rise of Economic Expertise (2021)

Jeff E. Biddle, *Progress through Regression*: The Life Story of the Empirical Cobb-Douglas Production Function (2020)

Erwin Dekker, *The Viennese Students of Civilization* (2016)

Steven G. Medema, Anthony M.C. Waterman (eds.), *Paul Samuelson on the History of Economic Analysis: Selected Essays* (2014)

Floris Heukelom, *Behavioral Economics: A History* (2014)

Roger E. Backhouse, Mauro Boianovsky, *Transforming Modern Macroeconomics: Exploring Disequilibrium Microfoundations, 1956–2003* (2013)

Susan Howson, *Lionel Robbins* (2012)

Robert Van Horn, Philip Mirowski, Thomas A. Stapleford (eds.), *Building Chicago Economics: New Perspectives on the History of America's Most Powerful Economics Program* (2012)

Arie Arnon, *Monetary Theory and Policy from Hume and Smith to Wicksell: Money, Credit, and the Economy* (2011)

Jerry Evensky, *Adam Smith's Moral Philosophy: A Historical and Contemporary Perspective on Markets, Law, Ethics, and Culture* (2005)

Harro Maas, *William Stanley Jevons and the Making of Modern Economics* (2005)

Continued after the Index

The Closed World of East German Economists

Hopes and Defeats of a Generation

TILL DÜPPE
Université du Québec à Montréal

CAMBRIDGE
UNIVERSITY PRESS

CAMBRIDGE
UNIVERSITY PRESS

Shaftesbury Road, Cambridge CB2 8EA, United Kingdom

One Liberty Plaza, 20th Floor, New York, NY 10006, USA

477 Williamstown Road, Port Melbourne, VIC 3207, Australia

314–321, 3rd Floor, Plot 3, Splendor Forum, Jasola District Centre, New Delhi – 110025, India

103 Penang Road, #05–06/07, Visioncrest Commercial, Singapore 238467

Cambridge University Press is part of Cambridge University Press & Assessment, a department of the University of Cambridge.

We share the University's mission to contribute to society through the pursuit of education, learning and research at the highest international levels of excellence.

www.cambridge.org
Information on this title: www.cambridge.org/9781009233095

DOI: 10.1017/9781009233088

© Till Düppe 2023

First published 2023

A catalogue record for this publication is available from the British Library.

Library of Congress Cataloging-in-Publication Data
Names: Düppe, Till, 1977- author.
Title: The closed world of East German economists : hopes and defeats of a generation / Till Düppe.
Description: 1 Edition. | New York, NY : Cambridge University Press, 2023. | Series: HPME historical perspectives on modern economics | Includes bibliographical references and index.
Identifiers: LCCN 2022049625 (print) | LCCN 2022049626 (ebook) | ISBN 9781009233095 (hardback) | ISBN 9781009233057 (paperback) | ISBN 9781009233088 (epub)
Subjects: LCSH: Economists–Germany (East)–Biography. | Economists–Attitudes. | Germany (East)–History. | Marxian economics. | Germany (East)–Politics and government.
Classification: LCC HB107.5.A3 D87 2023 (print) | LCC HB107.5.A3 (ebook) | DDC 943/.10874–dc23/eng/20221205
LC record available at https://lccn.loc.gov/2022049625
LC ebook record available at https://lccn.loc.gov/2022049626

ISBN 978-1-009-23309-5 Hardback

What did you value most of the GDR?
That which it could become.

Volker Braun

Contents

Figures

Acknowledgments

I grew up in West Germany. Since adolescence, I could travel in the East and got to know a passing world that was never mine yet part of what happened to Germany in the twentieth century. It was thus part of my larger transgenerational history. The other Germany remained a strange thing to me, but I came to understand it as one possible, even if unlikely, and certainly intriguing answer to the disaster of mid-twentieth century. This book attempts to understand this answer.

I am grateful above all to the many witnesses who shared their invaluable memories as well as private archives with me. Above all Gisela Eckstein, widow of Arne Benary, Hannamaria Loschinski, daughter of Friedrich Behrens, and Siegrid Maier, widow of Harry Maier. I am equally indebted to the sharp comments and clear memories of Dieter Klein, the protagonist of Chapter 8, having just celebrated his 90th birthday in November 2021. Many other colleagues and friends of the protagonists of this book helped me in enriching their personal profile and seeing the archival materials in a different light. In particular, I thank Siegfried Apelt, Georg Aßmann, Ulrich Busch, Klaus Fuchs-Kittowski, Johannes Gurtz, Günter Krause, Thomas Kuczynski, Udo Ludwig, Siegfried Mechler, Heinz Paragenings, Günther Radtke, Jürgen Rambaum, Sibylle Schmerbach, Roland Sender, Klaus Steinitz, and Jürgen Wilke. I received comments at the many workshops and conferences at which I presented the work from, among others, Mario Bianchini, Ivan Boldyrev, Erwin Dekker, Yakov Feygin, Slava Gerovitch, Michael D. Gordin, Rüdiger Graf, Karl Hall, Dagmara Jajesniack-Quast, János M. Kovács, Harro Maas, György Péteri, Jean-Guy Prévost, Eglė Rindzevičiūtė, Reinhard Schumacher, Vítězslav Sommer, Liza Soutschek, Thomas Stapleford, André Steiner, Annette Vogt, and Hans-Jürgen Wagener. I thank Iris Winkler and Gudrun Wenzel for their invaluable help in the Stasi Record Archive. All quotations of archival material and of German references are translated by the author.

This research has been funded by the Insight Development Grant of the Canadian Social Sciences and Humanities Research Council (file number 430-2017-00439), and by the Bundesministerium für Bildung und Forschung "Modernisierungsblockaden in Wirtschaft und Wissenschaft der DDR." For ethics approval, please refer to the Comité institutionnelle d'éthique de la recherche avec des êtres humains at the University of Quebec, Montreal (project number 2097e2017). Previous versions of Chapters 3, 4, and 7 have been published as "A Science Show Debate: How the Stasi Staged Revisionism," *Contemporary European History*, 30 (1): 92–110 (© 2021 Cambridge University Press); "How Not to Be a Socialist Statistician: The Case of Ernst Strnad," *German Studies Review*, 45 (1): 43–63 (© 2022 German Studies Association, published by Johns Hopkins University Press); "How Western Science Corrupts Class Consciousness: East Germany's Presence at IIASA," *Isis*, 112 (4): 737–759 (© 2021 History of Science Society).

Introduction
East Germany's Hope Generation

The German Democratic Republic (GDR) existed for forty-one years. This gave time for a single generation to spend their entire professional lives in this state. Those born around 1930 made their vocational choices in the first years of the new state that was founded in 1949, were intellectually shaped during the years of the Thaw, built up their careers at the time of the consolidation of the GDR after the building of the wall, were at the peak of their careers in the 1970s, and allowed moderate but not radical reforms while retaining their posts in the 1980s. In 1989, they witnessed the ultimate reform that resulted in the end of their state. By then, they were close to retirement and could age with the unbroken belief in a better form of socialism to come. This book tells the story of this unique generation.

Generations are the rhythm of social history. Just as classes provide individuals with an economic identity and groups provide them with a social identity, generations give individuals a place in history. In his essay on the "sociological problems of generations," Karl Mannheim noted the importance of generational phenomena in the sociology of knowledge:

The fact of belonging to the same class, and that of belonging to the same generation or age group, have this in common, that both endow the individuals sharing in them with a common location in the social and historical process, and thereby limit them to a specific range of potential experience, predisposing them for a certain characteristic mode of thought, ... and a characteristic type of historically relevant action. (1952 [1928]: 291)

Generations constitute historical kinship by means of shared and negotiated experiences. They allow us to understand the stream of history in terms of collective aging, learning, remembering, forgetting, inheriting, and so forth. Nazism, World War II, its aftermath, the foundation of the GDR in 1949, the workers' protests in 1953, the so-called Thaw after Stalin's death, the building of the wall in 1961,

Ulbricht's New Economic System (NES), the succession from Ulbricht to Honecker, the period of détente, the rise of the reformist movement in the 1980s, the fall of the wall, and reunification are all events that took on a *unique* meaning for this generation – a "stratified" meaning, in Mannheim's terms (ibid.: 297). For other generations, even those born ten years before in the early 1920s or those born ten years later in the early 1940s, these events took on different meanings insofar as their experiences interacted more with regimes before and after the GDR. For those born in the early 1930s, they lived through these events with emotions, memories, values, and beliefs that were intimately tied to the state. They both were supported by the state and actively supported the state throughout their professional career.[1] It was they who took over the task of building up a socialist Germany, who stabilized and reformed it, and who resisted its degeneration. They are, as I propose to call them, the hope generation of the GDR.

In the literature on the GDR, this generation has been discussed in several terms.[2] In her important study on the preceding generation of "veteran communists," or Old Communists (*Altkommunisten*), Epstein speaks of the "Hitler Youth" generation.[3] In fact, they belonged to the small age group born between 1921 and 1934 that

---

[1] The centrality of this generation for the functioning of the state is best documented by Fulbrook, showing an "1929 anomaly": among all entrances in the "Who's Who" of the GDR, there is a significantly large share of those born between 1925 and 1935; see Fulbrook in Schüle et al. (2006: 113–130).

[2] In GDR research, the importance of generational experiences is well established. The most complete overview of the generational perspective in GDR research is the edited volume by Schüle et al. (2006). Niethammer (1994) suggested the first distinctions, while Land and Possekel (1994) analyze the different generational discourses in a Foucauldian sense. Another important generational study inspiring this book is the collective biography by Epstein (2003). For a historical discussion of Mannheim's original essay, see Niethammer in Schüle et al. (2006). I develop this notion of the preceding paragraphs in Düppe (2017).

[3] Epstein (2003) studied the generation of Old Communists born around the turn of the century, who were heavily influenced by their experiences as young communists in the 1920s and 1930s: the Weimar Republic, the rise of the Soviet Union, persecution during Nazism, and detention or asylum in the East and West during the war. She rightly calls them "veteran" communists for their emphasis on political struggle and the primacy of class conflict. Even if this generation indeed constituted the "strategic" political class in the GDR, the social coherence and incoherence of the socialist experiment cannot be understood without the impression they made on the generation at hand that carried their hopes without sharing the same experiences prior to 1945.

were obliged to partake in the German Youth (*Deutsche Jungvolk*) between age ten and fourteen, and then in the Hitler Youth (*Hitlerjugend*) or the League of German Girls (*Bund Deutscher Mädel*) between 1939 and 1945. As I argue in Chapter 1, one can indeed derive important elements of their values and beliefs from this uprising, even if (or because) it was often followed by an immediate switch, after the war, into the youth movement of the socialist party, the Free German Youth (*Freie Deutsche Jugend*, FDJ). The "amnesty" the socialist regime granted to their involvement in the National Socialist regime was correlated with the expectation of building up the state and thus the *burden* of hope projected onto this generation from the Old Communists.[4] This burden was reinforced by the sheer mythical status the Old Communists' sacrifices during Nazism gained as well as by the extent of their feelings of guilt for having taken part in the National Socialist regime. One could speak of a collective symbiosis between these two generations that is vital for understanding East Germany's history of experience. However, the title "Hitler Youth generation" applies equally to the many young men and women in the Soviet and Western sector who lived through this shared experience in a different fashion and did not become devoted to socialism. Also, the term reduces them to the blind spot of their historical awareness since their experience as National Socialist youth did not easily integrate into the highly stylized state narrative about Nazism in the GDR.

They could also be called the Thaw generation, since they acquired their professional ethos and set up their career during a period when Stalinism was put into question in discussions about a more democratic socialism.[5] As the only age group that was educated during the late Stalinism of the early 1950s, with its fierce logic of the enemy, the

---

[4] As the generation that build up what the Old Communists had created, the most common term used in the literature for what I call the hope generation is the "reconstruction generation" (*Aufbaugeneration*); see Schüle et al. (2006).

[5] The concept of the Thaw (Оттепель) stems from a novel written by Ilya Ehrenburg in 1954 and came to describe the liberalization of socialist society after Stalin under Khrushchev. In the Soviet context, it refers to the period until Brezhnev's ousting of Khrushchev in 1964. In the context of East Germany, there are several decisive turning points without a clear demarcation: the oppression of intellectuals during the revisionism campaign covered in part two in 1957, the building of the wall in 1961, or the 11th plenum in 1965 limiting freedom of expression in the arts. For a Soviet autobiography featuring "The Thaw Generation," see Alexeyeva (2009).

priority of the class struggle, and the tacit acceptance of state violence, the years after the 20th Party Congress represented a chance to appropriate and renew socialism on their own terms. A truly democratic socialism, whatever that might exactly mean, was indeed their shared object of hope. However, this task of appropriation was the task at which this generation ultimately failed. Stalinism was something they would battle against for the rest of their lives to the extent that they even considered the reforms of the late 1980s as the ultimate break with Stalinism. What then kept them from truly breaking with Stalinism much earlier? On the one hand, the cleansing waves of the first ten postwar years opened up significant career opportunities, which created strong bonds of gratitude that are often mixed up with the gratitude for free access to education. On the other hand, as I show in Chapter 3, Ulbricht's regime managed to transform Stalin's open violence into a subtler regime of control that appeared to be compatible with more democratic values. The Thaw thus created the hope that another socialism was possible while at the same time instituting a culture of self-censorship and party discipline.

One could also call them the generation of "reformers" to the extent that during most of their professional life in the 1960s and 1970s, they went along with and contributed to a row of economic and social reforms toward a more "modern" socialism. Once socialism was secured by the wall, Ulbricht's NES, Honecker's Unity of Social and Economic Policy, the policy of détente, and the beginning of the perestroika movement all renewed hopes and mobilized great efforts to change society. Considering that these reforms were paralleled by repeated disappointments in view of the increasing gap between East and West, their inexhaustible will to reform also reveals a future orientation that was essential for the GDR as a development project.[6] Hoping for the next reform of the next Party Congress implied being ready to excuse the shortfalls of the last reform of the last Party Congress, which is reflected in a lack of learning, the incapacity to tackle underlying structural problems, and also a certain conformism. Their flaunted reformist spirit, as I argue in Chapters 5 and 6, had rather the ideological function of placating and conciliating the lagging

---

[6] In 1950, East Germany's income per capita with respect to that in West Germany was 52.7 percent, a number that decreased despite moderate growth rates to 39.5 percent in 1960, to 35.7 percent in 1970, to 36.4 percent in 1980, and to 33.1 percent in 1989 (Judt 2000).

behind official goals and thus *reproducing* the hopes for a better future. In addition, they silently accepted that important strategic policies were rarely discussed in public discourse and subject to a network of secret activities that were hardly compatible with East Germany's official values, as we will see in Chapter 6 with the example of the so-called area of commercial coordination (KoKo).

Those born after the hope generation experienced the GDR in a very different fashion. Born in peace and stability, they had no memories of war or postwar reconstruction, had little experience with the importance of class and ethnic origins, did not have the same career opportunities once the important posts were blocked, had only an abstract understanding of the "enemy," and lived in a world of comparison between East and West.[7] As the so-called integrated generation that was "born into" the GDR, they were less emotionally dependent on their parents. The fact that the reform of 1989, at first supported by the hope generation, could lead to the dissolution of the state, reveals, among other things, a lack of understanding between these two age groups. As I argue in Chapter 8, while for the young perestroika meant a true *renewal* of socialism, for the hope generation it was an *undoing* of past mistakes, notably Stalinism. For those close to retirement who had invested their entire professional life in building up and improving socialism, the events leading to and following the fall of the wall were both the culmination and the disappointment of their hopes.

The term hope generation thus refers to a rich affective profile of a generational experience that is manifest in a specific set of values, beliefs, and actions. In short, it refers to an intimate bond, a symbiotic relationship with the Old Communists who projected a burden of hope onto them to make up for their sacrifices under National Socialism; it refers to the more or less vague hope for a peaceful, non-Stalinist, democratic socialism; it refers to their working ethos and reformist spirit to never stop building up and improving socialism – as if they never ceased being

---

[7] For an important study on the personality of the generation born into the GDR, see Vaizey (2014). Niethammer has pointed to the social mobility implications of the generational logic between the hope generation and those born into the GDR: "the career opportunities created by mass emigration in the 1950s, on the one hand, and the economic stagnation in the 1970s, on the other, resulted in a lack of career opportunities and the alienation of members of the younger generations. They constituted, as it were, the "working class" of late East German society" (1994: 104).

the "children of the rubble" (*Trümmerkinder*) they were in 1945; it refers to their basic future orientation that translates into an accepting attitude toward the problems of the present, and a forgiving attitude toward the fundamental shortcomings of the regime, including the subtle violence of the secret police, with whom they often cooperated.

* * *

Not everybody in this age group represents this generational experience. By focusing on economists, specifically academic economists in the capital of Berlin, I intend to exemplify the characteristic experiences of this generation.[8] Why them? Regarding other social groups, economists neither belonged to society's decision makers, who might appear as true believers but actually acted strategically (as those closer to the Old Communists), nor to the masses that mainly had to be kept in line, while not being vital to the state's continuance (as is true for many born into the GDR). Academic economists, like those of other mid-ranking professions, were located between the strategic class that had full insight into, and responsibility for, the party regime and those who lived under it passively without career ambitions. They belong to what Jessen has called the "value elite" of the society that represented, reproduced, and attempted to realize the state ideology of Marxism-Leninism (1998). Economists that were raised and instrumentalized by the strategic class, which is to say those at the semi-academic institutions that were

---

[8] In Mannheim's terms, economists could be called a "generation unit." (1952 [1928]: 307) One can be part of a generation that is characterized by a specific group (or generation unit) without being part of this group (ibid.: 288–290). Angela Merkel can be called part of the "green generation" without being a member of the Green Party. Yet the story of the Green Party can be telling about the generation she is part of. There are few global studies on economics in East Germany, but many treating specific periods, persons, or institutions. An early work on the early period is Becker and Dierking (1989). The most extensive overview of East German economic thought is the book by Günter Krause (1998b), including the short version (1998a), which is an invaluable source for understanding internal debates in economic theory, something which this book does not attempt to provide. More recent significant global studies on GDR economics are the works by Hans-Jürgen Wagener (1997, 1998), and more recently Wagener et al. (2021). The study by Caldwell (2003) is noteworthy for the English literature. Also the four-volume international comparison of economics in socialism edited by János Kovács sets new standards (2018, 2022, forthcoming a, forthcoming b). Unfortunately, there is a gap between this literature and that of GDR research in general, a gap that this book attempts to close.

founded and under direct control of the Central Committee (CC), are not the main focus of this book.[9] This applies in particular to economists at the CC Party Academy and CC Academy for Social Sciences. Even if this institutional line is not identical with the line between, say, dogmatists and intellectuals, the difference helps to reflect an important feature of the hope generation: they perceived themselves to be *less* dogmatic than other party members in higher ranks and *more* knowledgeable than those who needed to be educated. The hope they carried went in both directions.

Academic economists are also a telling group because running a socialist state is ideally a *scientific* undertaking. Economists were both the guard and example of this scientificity. While capitalist institutions are the mere expressions of power interests, East Germany's society was supposed to be governed by "scientific socialism." Being socialist in the GDR was therefore not only a matter of confession but of a scientific attitude. The very existence and prominence of all sorts of institutions for economic research and education shows that there was more to economic policy than the mere will of the party, as voluntarists in the Soviet Union of the 1920s thought. Economists were essential to the new socialist intelligence for representing the official state science. The Marxist belief in the unity of scientific knowledge, economic reality, and party politics was part and parcel of the intellectual ethos of East German economists. They were committed to scholarly virtues of honesty, argument, and evidence *in the name of* the party.

Economists are thus a telling group because they occupied a place at the crossroads of the main pillars of East German society. The professional values represented by academic economists were a resource for the stabilization of the society. Scholars studying the GDR have often employed dichotomies to describe its inner logic.[10] In this book, I focus

---

[9] Central Committee in the following CC. Also the term "at the Central Committee of the Socialist Unity Party" (*beim Zentralkommittee der Sozialistischen Einheits Partei – beim ZK der SED*), in the following CC. For an overview of the complex institutions mentioned in this book, see the Appendix.

[10] The most obvious dichotomy, which may apply to any social institution, is that between socialist ideals and reality. The hope generation held up the ideals of an inclusive, "democratic" socialism with liberty of expression and self-critique, and no personality cult, dogmatism, or self-adulation. Yet the reality was political mistrust, tutelage, surveillance, and uncritical acceptance of the Soviet model. Related dichotomies, discussed in the literature, include "paternalism and paranoia" (Fulbrook 1995), "repressions and beneficence" (Gieseke 2000),

on the value conflict between devotion and pragmatism, that is, between party loyalty and practical relevance. This tension applied to many mid-ranking professions but was particularly felt and known by economists (as Chapters 1–4 show) and was never resolved (as Chapters 5–8 show). It is manifest in two aspects of economic knowledge that are often noted in official documents: its *ideological* and *productive* function, both of which are deeply anchored in Marxist philosophy. On the one hand, ideological trust was central to institutional stability, such that academic economists help understand the persistence and stability of the GDR. On the other hand, since economists had to train teachers, bureaucrats, and functionaries fit for the administration of the Five-Year Plans on a local or national level, they help to understand the concrete application of Marxism-Leninism in the day-to-day reality of the socialist state. The focus on economists helps spell out, at an experiential level, a tension that permeated the GDR experiment in general.

The difficulty of balancing devotion and pragmatism is manifest in the contradictory *epistemic virtues* that economists had to represent.[11] More than others, economists were exposed to various value conflicts inherent in the socialist culture of knowledge. The perhaps most important virtue was that of honesty, which is also the most complex to understand because it seemed so little realized. As part of the first duties of party members, it derived from the confessional attitude that being a socialist is not simply lip service. In the words of the party statutes: "A party member is obliged to be honest and sincere toward the party and not to allow that the truth is concealed or distorted."[12] Honesty, and even liberty of expression, was the ideal, even if often

---

and "care and coercion" (Jarausch 1999). Their different emphasis depends on the respective profession that is analyzed, as does the one between devotion and pragmatism. Most of them reflect in one way or the other the complex relationship of the GDR population with the power of Old Communists.

[11] As an exercise in historical epistemology, I pay attention to the historical conditions of the success or failure of ideas in becoming academically and/or socially accepted knowledge. If the belief in empiricism or rationalism, for example, correlates with different beliefs regarding the good society, the explanation of this correlation would be subject to historical epistemology. Choices between methods and theories can be explained in historical terms. For the notion of epistemic virtues, and more on the historiography of this book, see Düppe (2011, 2017, 2019) and Düppe and Maas (2017).

[12] "Entwurf des Statuts der Sozialistischen Einheitspartei Deutschlands," *Neues Deutschland*, March 7, 1954.

visibly violated, of the many "personal statements" (*Stellungnahme*) and "conversational debates" (*Aussprache*) in which one was subtly forced to honestly admit one's own mistakes.[13] The virtue of honesty was informed by the question of trust and treason of Old Communists in a state of prosecution under National Socialism. Later, honesty fed into the very meaning of scientific truth as embodied by academia. This virtue notably translated into a commitment to a *nondogmatic* Marxism-Leninism that is nevertheless limited (or true) to the socialist party, a central term in several of the following chapters. The party itself repeatedly asked intellectuals to fight dogmatism and formal "bookishness" (*Buchstabengelehrsamkeit*). Following this call could put economists both in the role of the *party warrior* and the *defiant*, and they often played both roles at some point in their lives.

Anti-dogmatism also required embracing a plurality of opinions as well as an appreciation of an open and sincere debating culture (*Meinungsstreit*) that was essential to reproducing the democratic hopes embodied in the state of the GDR. Being open to debate and dialogue required the virtue of the acceptance of criticism (*Kritikfähigkeit*) and its correlating vice of sensitivity to criticism (*Kritikempfindlichkeit*). In the words of the party statutes: "Party members are obliged to develop self-criticism and criticism from below, to fearlessly expose shortcomings ... , to fight resolutely against any attempt to suppress criticism and to replace it with whitewashing and adulation."[14] But in reality, this virtue could foster humility toward the superiority of party decisions since economists were often required to change their opinions from Party Congress to Party Congress. An important central vice in apparent contradiction with the openness to debate was that of a conciliatory attitude (*Versöhnlertum*), that is, the lack of radicalism and the readiness to accept compromises with the enemy as social democrats do. Related was the vice of fickleness (*Wankelmütigkeit*) or a lack of clarity regarding one's basic Marxist-Leninist convictions. Both vices were a direct result of the priority of class conflict that the hope generation

---

[13] An *Aussprache* was an informal meeting of party officials, usually the party secretary of the party-group with one or several party members. In an attempt at "comradely influence" (*kameradschaftliches Einwirken*), they were used to talking things over face to face while showing openness for the point of view of everyone involved. In practice, as we are going to see, they were an effective tool for exerting informal pressure on party members.

[14] Ibid.

inherited from Old Communists. But above all, the open debate culture was in contradiction with the first duty of all party members, the unity of the party, which required consensus at all costs. The party statutes required that party members "protect in every way the unity and purity of the party as the most important condition for the power and strength of the party."[15] The necessity of the unity of the party, in turn, was justified by the most sacred virtue of East German socialism, that of peace.

The virtue of practical relevance (*Praxisrelevanz*) was equally multi-layered. It derived from the dedication of science to the progress of socialism and the productive function of economic knowledge. On the surface of the official image of knowledge, the belief was advocated that Marxist-Leninist litany alone would do the job. As Helmut Koziolek, a central economist of the hope generation, wrote: "The deepening of the Marxist-Leninist principles is essential for finding reliable, scientific and practice-effective solutions for the further development of our socialist economy" (1973: 13). Yet the proclaimed unity of Marxism-Leninism and the productive function of economic knowledge remained a promise that was never met. The virtue of praxis relevance, instead, was mainly a way to disqualify inconsequential science for its own sake that was associated with a bourgeois regime of knowledge. Evoking practical relevance was also a way to reinforce research control, link research to party decisions, and integrate individual research into closed collectives.[16] This often required compromises with academic liberty and in fact stalled scientific innovation that required individual initiative, but also speculation and abstraction. The rejection of any form of elitist bourgeois intellectualism impeded the individual creativity of the professorial profession. Rather than individual holders of knowledge, economists viewed themselves as part of closed collectives defined (and confined) by specific responsibilities. Intellectual collectivism thus helped in limiting academic liberty and increased the acceptance of subjecting one's research interests to a central plan. The integration of research into a central plan largely substituted the communication of research to a larger public discourse and thus inhibited the influence of public intellectuals.

---

[15] Ibid.

[16] Again, citing the party statutes: "It is not enough for the party member to simply agree with party decisions. The party member is obliged to fight for the implementation of these decisions" (Ibid.).

All of these scientific virtues and vices were intimately related to the moral virtues of the person. More openly than in other regimes, personal character in socialism is a condition for political credibility and scientific knowledge. The moral pressure that pervaded the profession of economists and society at large resulted in a rather conformist culture little inclined to intellectual creativity. It is for this reason that the Ministry for State Security, or the Stasi, which was in charge of inquiring into the personality and motivations of scientists, plays a vital role in understanding the role of economists and the constitution of knowledge in socialism at large.

* * *

By way of a collective biography, the following chapters follow the life paths of a handful of selected individual economists born in the late Weimar Republic. All the protagonists are related to one of the three research and teaching institutions in the capital of Berlin: the economics faculty (later section) at Humboldt University, the Central Economics Institute at the Academy of Sciences, and the Higher School of Economics. In a chronological series of microhistorical studies of key episodes of their lives, the following chapters paint a portrait of the formative events of East Germany's economists of the same generation. The selection of individuals was determined primarily by the availability of archival sources that allows the reconstruction of a rich and complex history of experience. But they were also chosen to capture the variety of existential options economists had and the different roles they played in various phases of their life without reducing them to stereotypical characters such as dogmatists versus reformers, ideologues versus dissidents, or perpetrators versus victims. The five individuals are thus chosen for being telling cases of the hope generation, be it for being representative cases and also for being outliers or leading figures.[17] Arne Benary (1929–1971) was an early intellectual avant-garde who became a political victim, Ernst Strnad (1928) was a party-loyal academic outsider, Erwin Rohde

[17] Having submitted a list of all major economists to the Stasi Record Archive (BstU), the selected episodes provide the most in-depth insights into the economists' profession. Many other economists of which one might suspect large Stasi files in fact had no files or the files no longer exist. In addition, the choice was determined by the availability of witnesses such as Dieter Klein and several others (see the list of interviews at the end of the book).

(1927–2010) was a mediocre specialist yet successful conformist, Harry Maier (1934–2010) was a scientific innovator and plaything of politics, and Dieter Klein (1931) was an intellectual reformer acting at the limits of the party. In addition, each chapter exemplifies one of the many fields in the complex mélange of forms of economic knowledge in the GDR.

Part I introduces these five protagonists by discussing their childhood and youth during and after World War II. What made them choose economics? What made them amenable to the ideology of Marxism-Leninism as taught in their undergraduate studies? Chapter 1 focuses on their experiences with Nazism, their socialization in the Hitler Youth, and the discrimination they were subjected to because of their ethnic or religious identity. It also highlights the postwar tumults that made them prone to the postwar propaganda on securing peace in the name of socialism and the opportunities to engage in ideological confrontation during the first cleansing waves at university. Chapter 2 discusses the important influence of the Old Communists, who taught them on the basis of very different, more violent memories of World War II and tended to consider Stalinism as necessary to force socialism into being. Regarding economic knowledge, the first part describes the historical situation that nourished the belief in the basic tenets of Marxism-Leninism: anti-fascism, anti-capitalism, class conflict, the single-party system, and historical determinism.

Part II tells of the formative period of their intellectual coming of age while writing dissertations and habilitations during the period of the so-called Thaw. The years after the Soviet break with Stalinism created hopes for a more democratic and decentralized socialism, which gave occasion for this generation to appropriate socialism on its own terms. These hopes were crushed by Ulbricht's so-called revisionism campaign. Chapter 3 focuses on the short career of Arne Benary, an economist related to Friedrich Behrens at the Central Economic Institute at the Academy of Sciences and a first chosen victim of Ulbricht's campaign. The field of knowledge at stake was the master discipline of the political economy of socialism, a thus far unwritten chapter in the Marxist tradition. What is a more "true" and less "revised" application of Marx? The top-down Stalinist centralism or more bottom-up approach to planning as ventured, for example, in Yugoslavia, Hungary, or Poland? The chapter shows how the Stasi, similar to the well-known show trials under Stalin, staged a *show debate* that, in spite of its forced character, allowed Ulbricht to both resist the reform of bureaucratic centralism and claim his policies to be a scientific undertaking. Many will remember this intervention as the beginning of a regime of self-censorship among East German economists, which would become a major obstacle to future scientific creativity.

As the flip side of this episode, during the same period of the Thaw, Chapter 4 shows how academia maintained relative autonomy in the face of party interests. A young academic outsider, Ernst Strnad, tried to mobilize, without success, his party relations against the most known senior economists in order to receive a doctoral degree. The question at stake was the status of political economy as an exact science, in particular the role of statistical methods. Considering the significant changes economics experienced in Western countries after the rise of the econometric movement in the 1930s, what would a socialist critique of "bourgeois" statistics look like and what would be the role of quantitative methods in political economy? Strnad's thesis tackled these questions, but it was written unsolicited and without supervision. Facing difficulties in finding academic approval, he mobilized high-party officials in his favor. Nevertheless, universities were not willing to give up their academic ethos and maintained the traditional mechanism of academic inclusion and exclusion. The chapter also shows that the transformation toward a Marxist-Leninist economic science left little space for appropriating, let alone contributing to, the simultaneous transformation of economics in Western countries.

Part III tells how, after the building of the wall, economists arranged themselves with the regime and developed a professional ethos of continuous reform. This included Ulbricht's attempt to modernize socialism through his NES, the so-called third university reform, Honecker's consumer-oriented Unity of Social and Economic Policy, and the détente policy of peaceful coexistence. Drawing on the example of Erwin Rohde, professor of public finance at Humboldt University, Chapters 5 and 6 describe the professional practices of university economists during the 1960s and 1970s, including engagement in party functions, teaching, and research subject to revised plans and institutional control. The organization of these practices, I argue, resulted in an increasing *turn inward* that was inherent in the epistemic regime of East German economists and deprived them of a critical role in social discourse. The ongoing reforms had to a large extent the ideological function of creating political stability through future promises, while the actual strategic activities that were little compatible with the official ideology were covered by a veil of secrecy. Erwin Rohde, for example, helped educate economists working in Western financial markets and secretly generating funds for the GDR.

The last part examines the decline of the identity of East German economists during the 1980s when confronted, first, with the cooperative spirit of Western science and, second, with the spirit of renewal of the younger perestroika generation. As a result of the period of détente, East and West German scientists interacted more frequently. Chapter 7 reconstructs the clash of cultures by focusing on East Germany's role at the International Institute for Applied Systems Analysis (IIASA) in Austria. IIASA was founded to bring together scientists from East and West to research shared problems and thus to build a bridge between the two opposing systems, with systems analysis referring to a set of technical theories of management, transport, and climate, as well as growth, innovation, and education. The underlying image of knowledge was in stark contrast to the intellectual culture that developed in the preceding decades in East Germany. Even if participation was considered important for displaying East German science, its contribution was caught up in the precepts of the Western scholar as a class enemy. The chapter presents the best-documented case, the economist Harry Maier, who was one of the few social scientists who visited IIASA for two years between 1978 and 1980, and then, in 1986, used a conference visit to escape from East Germany.

Chapter 8 tells the story of the hope generation's contribution to perestroika through the example of Dieter Klein, a progressive political economist of capitalism and science manager at Humboldt University. Welcoming the changes in light of the vision of overcoming Stalinism and inviting the young generation into the reformist movement against the Old Communists that stubbornly occupied the Politburo, the reform of socialism turned into a battle for its very survival. Klein contributed at first to the reformist perestroika research with a political economy of capitalism based on peace rather than class conflict, but was then increasingly disconnected from the civil rights movement due to his confidence in an inner-party reform. He was in the position of realizing his reformist ideas at the Party Congress in December 1989 when the party transformed from a force with constitutional power into a parliamentary opposition in the class enemy's political system.

The book concludes with the dismantling of East German economics after the reunification of Germany in 1990. The cleansing of the teaching staff was more radical than in any other reform seen in twentieth-century economics. During the shortest period, Western research standards and teaching practices were enforced. The economists of the hope generation, however, were spared having their careers cut and retired jointly with the GDR. They continued holding on to the hope that had endured throughout their career: that a future democratic socialism remains to be built.

* * *

In sum, these chapters describe the *closed world* of East German economists, which has no equivalent before or after. East German economics is historically closed by the beginning and the end of the state onto which its institutions were built. While witnessing instability before and after the foundation of their state, the protagonists of this book lived the majority of their professional life in a regime of astonishing political stability. There was only one major change of leadership, fewer upheavals than in other socialist regimes, and few so-called dissidents in their age group. Their world was also institutionally closed because of a "small-state attitude" and a local, inward orientation of East German economists toward their own hierarchies that created an *Eigensinn* beyond a mere cloning of the Soviet discourse. There were certainly many exchanges with other socialist countries all over the world, as well as some highly regulated contacts with Western economists. Yet, the way institutions were set up resulted in a working ethos of *small collectives* with distinct and limited responsibilities. Though their work was integrated through the hierarchy of planned research that generated a considerable density of discourse, the communication of research through the plan was rather a matter of being subject to political control than a contribution to the public sphere.

The historical, institutional, and political closure of East Germany's economics profession has to be kept in mind when thinking of their "contribution" to the history of economic thought. Preceding and parallel intellectual traditions of thought, such as Marxist economics, statistics, operations research, neoclassical economics, and so forth, did play a role in the GDR, but always through the lens of their own life-world. Economics in East Germany was, to a large extent, a genre of its own, and it fits uneasily into the narratives told in the history of economic thought classes.[18] Emphasizing the closed character of their life-world requires granting them the benefit of understanding their work on their own terms. It would be a historical blunder to subject their work to standards other than their own, as happened after the reunification in 1990. As seen from today's point of view, East German economics might have been intellectually mediocre, but this mediocrity had historical reasons that are equally interesting for the history of economics as the historical circumstances that favor the production of what counts as intellectual achievement today. Instead of subjecting their work to whatever standards, the story to be told here traces the events of the formation, stabilization, reforming, and degradation of their own standards.[19]

In trying to understand the closed world of East German economists from within, the following chapters give voice to first-person accounts, memories, and self-perceptions as drawn from in-depth interviews.[20] This voice helps understand the stability of more than four decades of GDR history from an experiential point of view. While individuals often present their perspectives in the language of the collective they were part of, they also reveal considerable tensions when trying to integrate their own biography into the social memory constructed by the party. Including the protagonist's voice also helps in understanding their sense of professional accomplishment, which they believe is often ignored in today's dominant (Western) image of the GDR. Many fear being seen as dupes, if not losers of history. Sullenness and distrust about any historical reconstruction, which is deeply anchored in their socialization, is omnipresent among them. In the course of the research undertaken for this book, this suspicion was felt at each point. At several points, I was told that those who have never set foot in the GDR have no right to write about it.

---

[18] In fact, some commentators even speak of the abolishment of economics after 1945; see for example Schneider (1997).

[19] It is thus an exercise in historical epistemology. For further remarks on the historiography of the present book, see Düppe (2011, 2017, 2019).

[20] Well established in general historical research on the GDR, the use of this source is less common in the history of the social sciences; see Bianchini (2020) and Wagener (1998) for exceptions; see also the early large-scale project on GDR oral history in the Hoover Institute Archives.

Considering the high level of secrecy associated with the late GDR, however, first-person accounts need to be supplemented by additional sources. The self-image of economists is to a large extent the result of a more complex institutional framework that was little understood by each individual. I thus also use sources of the strategic class, that is, archival sources that were *not* available to the protagonists themselves, such as the archive of the socialist party and that of the Stasi. As an object of half knowledge that hardly could be openly discussed, the Stasi's perspective adds both personal details as well as historical complexity to the careers of East German economists. The interplay of self-perceptions and archival materials previously unknown to the protagonists made the writing, and with some luck will make the reading, of this book a lively undertaking. It is history reaching into the present.

As rich and complex as these sources are, they still might be incomplete or even partial. As a result of the turbulences during 1989, precious Stasi files, among others those of the foreign espionage department, the *Hauptverwaltung Aufklärung* (HV A), were largely destroyed. Equally, as a result of its central role in the civil movement of 1989, the Stasi archive had a special legal status in comparison with the party archives at the *Bundesarchiv*, a status that was changed only recently in 2020. These events in the history of the archives of the GDR shaped the kinds of stories to be told in the following. They are thus as much the result of the present as they are of the past.

PART I

Growing into a Socialist Germany

1 | *Socialist Awakening*

In a spirit of great generosity, [the Communist Party gives] the younger generation, which had never enjoyed the right to organize itself freely and democratically, the chance . . . to cleanse their lives of fascist influence and to join together in shaping the future. (Erich Honecker, July 1945)[1]

When Stalin passed away in March 1953, the protagonists of this book were in their early twenties. They were about to graduate from university and ready to commit to careers as economists in a regime fully dedicated to following the Soviet example. This was by no means predetermined and was indeed an unlikely outcome of their childhood and youth during the two preceding decades – decades that rendered the twentieth century a time of extremes.

Born shortly before the National Socialist regime ended the short-lived democracy of the Weimar Republic, they grew up in a totalitarian and militarist state. Recalling the severe ostracism of several groups, they belonged to a cohort that was obliged to partake, at the age of ten, in the German Youth (*Deutsche Jungvolk*) and then, at the age of fourteen, in the Hitler Youth (*Hitlerjugend*). As adolescents, they witnessed (and possibly participated in) the ferocious final battles of World War II. At zero hour, they came of age as children of the rubble (*Trümmerkinder*) who faced poverty leading to malnutrition and disease, rebuilding efforts, revelations about the terror of Nazism, and a plurality of visions for what the proper response to it might be. The Soviet vision imposed itself more and more. They felt the increasing global conflict between the East and the West in their daily lives in the divided city of Berlin, notably during the airlift in 1948. When the GDR was founded in 1949, they entered university at a time when

---

[1] Speech titled "The Youth as an Active Participant in the Reconstruction of an Antifascist Order," cited in Buddrus (1995: 256).

higher education was formally subjected to the dictates of Marxism-Leninism and Stalin's personal cult, which guided the young state until 1955.

Growing up in these years of extremes, life presented itself as a continuous struggle between people with different political identities and ethnic origins. They thus learned what it meant to takes sides. As the only generation that partook in the Hitler Youth and the Stalinist mobilization of the early GDR, their childhood and youth would be decisive for the range of experiences they would be capable of in the GDR and thus decisive for their moral stricture and epistemic beliefs. Compared to the Old Communists, they did not form their political identity through resistance and battles against other political movements, the National Socialist movement in particular. Instead, their political identity was formed through the role models of those Old Communists, who continued seeing the GDR as an arena for a sustained fight between allies and traitor, between trust and suspicion. What made them amenable to follow Old Communists as examples?

Even if key events such as the participation in the Hitler Youth and the first Soviet-like institutions on German ground were unique to the age group of our protagonists, the outcome could have been different. In contrast to the subsequent generation that was "born into" the GDR, our protagonists did have a choice in where and how to live, and they made this choice in light of many who chose differently. The five postwar years were characterized by an open ideological clash between different ways to respond to the National Socialist regime and different visions regarding Germany's political orientation. The full range of political parties was still allowed in the early Soviet Occupation Zone. The first elections did not establish a full majority for the Communist Party (KPD), even after the forced integration of the social democrats (SPD) as the Socialist Unity Party (SED) in spring 1946. In addition, there were many for whom the end of the war meant the end of any social mobilization and a return to an apolitical private life. Many of those in the same age group, as Mannheim put it, "worked up the material of their common experiences" differently (1952: 304), acquired a lower political profile, chose a less ideological profession, or simply left the Soviet Occupation Zone and soon the GDR. Not so for our young men. What then explains why they, in contrast to others, were ready to commit to socialism and the Soviet example? Without searching for a general explanation, the reasons are individual and circumstantial. As much as the existing information allows, this chapter describes the contingent reasons for their emergent political beliefs. As multifaceted as their background was, however, for all of them the historical circumstances gave occasion to, and shaped, their commitment to the values of the emerging socialist state.

From a first-person perspective, the reason for their emergent socialist beliefs is obviously related with the simple persuasiveness of the Marxist principles they discovered in their late youth. As is common with the young, however, ideology is not the result of careful deliberation but a response to specific existential needs that makes them amenable (and vulnerable) to concrete role models. It was only at the end of their childhood and youth, which are described in this chapter, that they read Marx and got intellectually hooked on it. Being "betrayed" by the National Socialist regime that led to utter destruction and postwar poverty, their existential needs were related to their unstable family situation, loss of history, and lack of language and understanding, all of which resulted in a desire for safety and the notion that "this should never happen again."[2] While some found this safety by falling back on the religion of their parents and saying "never again will I devote myself politically" or "never again will I allow social exclusion," the five protagonists would follow the SED's catchphrase that socialism is the only legitimate anti-fascist regime that can secure peace and by extension prosperity. They would keep faith in the anti-fascist legitimacy of socialism for the rest of their lives. It would later be so strongly rooted in their social being that the similarities between the two regimes would never easily appear to them. In the words of Dieter Klein:

I was a loyal party member … without any doubts of its principles. In this early period, they [the principles] meant the opposite of fascism and offered the chance for an alternative. Whatever the nature of the party, it always stood for the idea of socialism, even if this idea became more and more damaged and distorted. Even in 1989, I did not want to get rid of the socialist party, but rather try to turn the SED upside down and turn this hardly socialist party into a socialist one. (Klein interview 2021)

---

[2] Regarding this diagnosis of the lack of fathers, history, and language, see the classic study by Bude on the career of the Hitler Youth generation in West Germany (1987); see also Buddrus (1995).

The political worldview of the hope generation grew from their basic belief in the anti-fascist character of socialism. This worldview, as we will see, resulted from a *symbiotic relationship* with the Old Communists as role models. Projecting their hopes onto the young men, they provided amnesty, orientation, and a sense of being.[3]

Reconstructing the path to their socialist dedication poses a significant historiographical challenge. Large parts of their childhood and youth would later be subject to both public and individual censorship. Whether it be the Jewish background of two of the five protagonists, the oppression of German minorities during Stalin's Great Purge, or the sentiments attached to their socialization in the Hitler Youth – both dear memories and a source of dormant guilt – each of these would become taboo given the official narrative of the socialist regime. While the regime was deeply invested in inquiring into the National Socialist past of the Old Communists in order to mystify it, to censor it, or to use it as a means to exert pressure, the National Socialist past of the young hope generation was left to them alone. The institutions of the new state did not allow them to come to terms with this past. Instead, they offered a highly stylized notion of an "anti-fascist" state nourished by the mythic battles of Old Communists as well as the opportunity to look ahead – that is, they offered amnesty by silence and oblivion. In this sense, Land and Possekel called their experiences in the Hitler Youth the "blind spot" of their generational memory.[4] Therefore, few sources tell us about their childhood and youth, be they official biographical documents or self-accounts. Much of the uncovering of the existential needs to which their socialist dedication was a response must be inferred from the circumstances of rather thin existing biographical information.

[3] This "symbiosis" explains the hope generation's unwillingness to challenge Old Communists, thus granting the GDR's institution its astonishing stability and lack of renewal despite the open and hidden violence and contradictions of the regime. The hope generation inherited a spirit of hostility and sacrifice that was rooted in war experiences and renewed in the context of the Cold War. The argument of a generational symbiosis was alluded to in Niethammer (1994: 108).

[4] See Land and Possekel (1994: 33). In Niethammer's words, anti-fascism "blocked the transfer of experience between the generations" (1994: 108). Also, Buddrus spoke of an "anti-fascism by decree" which "precluded a genuine catharsis" and lead into a "communal self-deception" (1995: 267)

Who then were the young men of this book when they arrived at university as the first cohort of East Germany's economics students? What were their memories, what were their needs, and how did their political consciousness take shape?

Dieter Klein

A first unchosen fact of life would be decisive for the childhood, youth, *and* professional career of all five protagonists: their family origin that associated them with a specific religious identity, a specific ethnic and national identity, or a specific profession and thus class identity. In contrast to those born after them, who grew up in a state where these identities officially no longer played a role, in both the National Socialist regime and the early GDR, identity mattered a great deal. Being Aryan, Jewish, half-Jewish, ethnic German (*Volksdeutsche*), resettler (*Umsiedler*), worker, bourgeois, close or distant to education, etc. determined the possibilities they were born into.

Dieter Klein, born in 1931, grew up in Prenzlauer Berg in Berlin in modest circumstances. His parents were both commercial employees, but his father lost his job during the Great Depression. The Depression offered promise for the socialist movement in Germany, and both the SPD and the KPD gained in popularity. Klein's mother was a member of the SPD, and his father a member of the KPD. In the years before National Socialism, the German left was increasingly jeopardized by the conflict between the reformist SPD and the Stalinization of the KPD. Communists considered social democrats to be the left variant of National Socialism. But by the time Klein would be able to understand anything of such debates, both parties were made illegal. When the parliament voted for the Enabling Act in March 1933, many communists had already been imprisoned and social democrats were a minority who would also soon be forbidden. Though Klein knew of the socialist background of his parents, they hardly spoke about politics at home in order to protect themselves and their son. They did not belong to the small minority of the two left parties who risked their lives for reform or revolution.

Another identity that played only a small role at home soon became important at school. According to the Nuremberg racial laws of 1935, Klein was considered a "half-Jew of the second degree" (*Mischling*), as the father of his father was Jewish, though not practicing.[5] Klein had fond memories of his grandfather, who died in 1937. The status of half-Jews during the National Socialist regime was undecided at first and hence precarious. Some wished to treat them like Jews, while others wished to "protect" their Aryan parts. The early laws discriminating against Jews did not apply to half-Jews, thus they were not branded with a Jewish star. However, marriage between half-Jews was forbidden, and marriage between Aryans and half-Jews was subject to permission but rarely granted. Later, the more the genocide advanced, the more half-Jews came under pressure. On German territory, they were subject to forced labor, and in Eastern occupied territories they were deported and killed.

Klein's father, a half-Jew of the first degree, was not drafted into the military as he was considered to "undermine military force" (*wehrkrafts-zersetzend*). Instead, he was forced to perform heavy physical labor in Berlin. Young Dieter Klein understood the reasons for the family's poverty. At school, no difference was made initially between him and Aryan children, though Klein did recall that he was not allowed to participate in the morning flag roll call.[6] His Jewish background did not prevent him from compulsory participation in the German Youth, the organization preceding the Hitler Youth. Starting in 1939, participation became obligatory, and in 1941, Klein, age ten, had to take part. The German Youth was used for war purposes such as collecting scrap metal for military production. They also had to swear an oath of obedience to the *Führer* and to National Socialist ideas, an oath that might have meant little at this young age. They were old enough, however, to develop their first role models and acquire a sense of sociality and affective bonding to a larger *Volk*. Considering the political orientation of his parents and the discrimination he faced as a half-Jew, Klein recalled, at age ninety, a certain reluctance regarding the German Youth:

My reluctance simply resulted from the fact that I saw at home how threatening the system was when my grandparents said cautiously, "on the second floor, they were picked up again." For me, this youth organization was included in this system. I also had [negative] experiences of my own. For

[5] Two Jewish grandparents would count as a half-Jew of "first degree." See on the status of half-Jews, Ehmann (2001).

[6] Klein (2009) as part of a video series produced by Roland Sender showing autobiographical accounts of about one hour, presented in front of former colleagues. I thank Roland Sender for the permission to use these videos. See also Rohde (2009) and Kolloch (2008).

example, it was a popular practice to put two chairs on a table, and two of the young people had to slap each other until one fell off. I had the feeling that this wasn't for me though this feeling was not backed by explicit beliefs … This experience made me dislike organizations of any kind. It took a while until I got over it and was gradually able to become active again in [political] organizations. (Klein interview 2021)

Compared to other children of his age group, Klein's experience with the German Youth was shorter than expected. In March 1943, when Klein was twelve years old, the first Allied attacks poured down bombs on Berlin. While many young children were sent into camps in the countryside in so-called children evacuation campaigns (*Kinderlandverschickung*), half-Jewish children were forbidden to join until November 1943, and then they were often excluded. When several of the houses on Klein's street were bombed out, the family looked for a place outside the city and found a room northeast of the city in Werneuchen. In this small village, his obligatory participation in the German Youth was no longer reinforced, and Klein was spared the National Socialist propaganda during the last violent years of the war. On the contrary, in Werneuchen he had a group of friends that rejected the National Socialist regime and were all glad not to be forced to be involved in any way, though they still sensed the danger of the regime and the war. It turned out that the landlord of the room the family rented was the local village leader of the National Socialist party (*Ortsgruppenführer*), and the room was close to a military airport base that would also soon be bombed. Having attended at first a one-class village school, Klein's parents wanted him to attend a high school (*Gymnasium*). His half-Jewish identity could have prevented this, yet the director of the school granted him a special permission. But this also meant that the family had to pay the significant fees levied for attending the *Gymnasium*, though these were not specific to the National Socialist regime. Many of the same generation emphasized the sacrifices the payments required. Access to education was a privilege, and the free access once provided in 1949 would be welcomed with gratitude and seen as proof of the anti-fascist legacy of socialism.

In May 1945, Klein was thirteen years old and would be turning fourteen in October. Thus, he was just months too young to be obliged to join the actual Hitler Youth, which was involved in the battles around Berlin. At zero hour, he returned with his family to an occupied, divided, destroyed, and close to anarchic Berlin as a so-called child of the rubble (*Trümmerkind*). As all children did, Klein experienced postwar poverty, particularly during the cold winter of 1946–1947. Note that the full meaning of fascism was openly revealed to the masses only after the war when the crimes of the National Socialist regime were shown to the population through public displays of posters with images of dead bodies in the concentration camps. The population was blamed for being complicit (*mitschuldig*).

Schooling mattered. Continuing his education at Schinkel Gymnasium in Prenzlauer Berg, Klein recalled the peculiar mixture of teachers after the removal of members of the National Socialist party (NSDAP), including returning prisoners of war. Some of the teachers openheartedly expressed their support for the "democratic system," as socialism was propagated at the time. But his actual politicization during school time was caused, first, due to the presence of a separate school class dedicated to workers' children:

There was a special class [*Aufbauklasse*] at the Gymnasium with all working-class children who were led to the Abitur by special measures. They all had very sensible views, were cheerful people, and yet were still very committed. The whole manner of their appearance was attractive to me. You could tell they knew what they wanted, and they were visibly quite tough with themselves and with others. I liked them. And they were all in the FDJ. (Klein interview 2021)

Thus, in the last years at the Gymnasium, Klein also became a member of the FDJ, something he did not associate with his experiences in the German Youth. Among his schoolmates, FDJ members were in a minority. In Berlin, only 5 percent of those between age fourteen and twenty-five joined the FDJ (Ohse 2009: 76).

Another influence on Klein turning toward the socialist movement were certainly his parents. They both became member of the SED and no longer had to hide their orientation at home. In addition, Klein recalls an encounter with a friend of his father:[7]

My father had a good friend who I liked to visit. He showed me Marx's *Capital*, which he had saved from the Nazi era. My father pushed Engel's *Peasants' War* to me across the table. So my politicization happened through

---

[7] Klein's father held no official party function. Later, he was a staff executive at the German Investment Bank and then at the opera (*Volksoper*).

my head and not through an organization. The friend encouraged me to say that if one lived in the GDR, the country that one hoped embodied the future, then one should also do something political for it. (Klein interview 2021)[8]

This family friend one day was arrested for his involvement in the black market trade between the zones. His wife warned Klein not to visit him in prison as this might have negative consequences. Later, Klein blamed himself for following her advice. He could neither imagine that his friend did anything wrong, nor that the regime arrested him without good reason. "By then I was so socialized in a way that I couldn't imagine the administration doing anything wrong. That was the Stalin era . . . It took me a while to get used to the idea that injustice could exist in that system, too." (ibid.). The anti-fascist profile of the FDJ was so dominant in his political mind that he did not easily associate the two regimes. It would remain the basic conviction that would nourish his being socialist until the end of the GDR. "Anything that was the alternative to (fascism) was to be supported . . . That was the starting point for me and my family, and that dominated also my evaluation of the system." (ibid.) in addition, Klein appeared to have no difficulties associating his own experiences during National Socialism with the anti-fascist propaganda driven by the Old Communists and Soviets' war against fascism, even if his memories of being discriminated against as a half-Jew were little acknowledged by the Soviet administration.[9] This was possible because Klein experienced comparatively less indoctrination into Nazism, knew of his own and his family's discrimination, and, above all, because it was simply not the time to ruminate with his new friends about personal memories. What mattered was building toward a brighter future.

I don't think that was a delusion, but we were . . . so filled with what had to be done now and what had to be worked on that in our conversations about

---

[8] According to Land and Possekel, such an encounter with an old comrade is typical for the biographical narrative of the hope generation: "An 'old comrade' appears again and again in their stories who, in view of the sudden loss of their orientation in 1945 . . . , pointed out the way toward the action of reparation, toward a humanistic action in the context of the SED" (1994: 34).

[9] "What I had observed with my parents and grandparents, how I myself did and did not get along in the Nazi era, and what the older generation had experienced, definitely went hand in hand for me. I did not see any breaks there" (Klein interview 2021).

ourselves we were absorbed by the presence ... We did not sit down and discuss how the years before had been for us. The crucial question was always: What to do now? (Ibid.)

In 1951, at the age of eighteen, Klein graduated from high school. By then, his desire to become politically active had been formed, and he decided to study economics at Humboldt University where he would remain until the end of his career. He recalled that the majority of other students were older than himself, such as soldiers returning from Soviet war prisons, members of the socialist party that were delegated from the industrial Ruhr area in West Germany, and devoted socialists who had been illegally active until 1945. Being a student also carried with it a feeling that many members of his generation shared when sitting in their first lectures: the feeling of *gratitude* for having been given access to higher education. By *showing* gratitude, the young students were prone to the indoctrination that awaited them, namely indoctrination into Stalinism. As Klein said of himself and his fellow students:

We were fully convinced that our studies were a kind of gift from those who earned the money in the society, a gift, as it were, from the working class. We were thus greatly motivated during this strange time between the rise of new hopes and hopeless dogmatism. We were convinced that things had to be as they were and sometimes wondered what was being offered to us, but by and large we passed our studies in deep faith; it was only now and then that I was held back by my wife, who was more down-to-earth than I was with my aloof principles. (Klein 2009)

The gratitude for having been given the opportunity to gain an education and later have a career would remain a central virtue for this generation. They judged, for example, the many who had left the country in the years preceding the building of the wall as lacking gratitude for what they received from the state. Their gratitude, in turn, would also feed into a very forgiving attitude toward the short-comings and contradictions of the regime.

Klein's undergraduate education ended in 1955 with a diploma thesis on trends in the Berlin retail trade. His thesis had to be based on Stalin's ideas, which was not an easy task for such a specific subject. Nonetheless, his performance was sufficiently convincing that he received the position as assistant for writing his doctoral dissertation at the chair for political economy. He wrote his thesis under the supervision of Heinz Mohrmann, yet the institute was headed by the most doctrinaire Stalinist at the university, Robert Naumann, who is discussed in Chapter 2. It was then, at the end of his undergraduate education, that Dieter Klein became a formal member of the party.

Arne Benary

Arne Benary, born in 1929, did not come from a worker's or farmer's family. His father was a medical doctor, which would later count as being "close to education" (*bildungsnah*) because of the elevated income associated with a bourgeois milieu. Born in Greifswald, Benary grew up in his father's hometown of Erfurt in Thuringia. His father worked as a surgeon and women's doctor. Arne was his first son, and two years later his second son was born. Though his father's workplace changed several times, the family remained in Erfurt until the end of the war. Also, Benary's father was considered a "half-Jew of the first degree" such that Arne counted as a "half-Jew of the second degree." A combination of his profession and racial status may have prevented his father from being drawn into the military. The increasing demand for medical doctors during the war must have given the family more security than other half-Jewish families at the time.

Benary's political memberships are documented. Starting in 1939, he was obliged to partake in the German Youth, and in 1943, at age fourteen, in the Hitler Youth. At this point, the Hitler Youth had turned into a paramilitaristic organization that was preparing for active battle. In August 1944, the leader of the Hitler Youth, Arthur Axmann, called on those sixteen years and older, those born in 1927 or 1928, to volunteer for military service. Within six weeks, 70 percent of this age group had signed up (McDougall 2008: 30). Some of Arne's friends who were one year older than him thus served in the dangerous role of anti-aircraft auxiliaries (*Flakhelfer*).[10] Erfurt experienced more than twenty-seven British and American air raids. Benary instead was most likely used for manual work related to these battles, and possibly was actively involved. The city was taken by US forces on April 12, 1945, and in July it became part of the Soviet Occupation Zone.[11]

---

[10] Between January 1943 and the end of the war, approximately 200,000 German teenagers (including tens of thousands of girls) served as *Flakhelfer*; see Kater (2004: 198–199, 235–237) and Buddrus (1995).

[11] See the Stasi files on Benary, in particular MfS AOP 1012-57 (1): 134.

Immediately after the war, Benary's father became chief medical doctor of a regional hospital in Meiningen, a small town in Thuringia. Benary's family thus possibly suffered less from postwar poverty than others. In spring 1946, at age seventeen, Benary graduated from high school (*Oberschule*). Up until this point, he had not experienced any formal socialist education at school, and there is nothing on the surface of his biographical background that would indicate his inclination to become dedicated to the socialist cause. On the contrary, his father appeared to be critical of the regime.[12] However, something must have drawn him into it. In 1946, he became one of the first members of the FDJ, the youth organization of the socialist party, just like hundreds of thousands of other young East German men and women who switched, in a matter of months, from the Hitler Youth and the League of German Girls respectively to the FDJ. We can only speculate on the reasons, the ease, and the tensions that might have accompanied this astonishingly quick switch between two ideologically opposed youth organizations.

The FDJ was founded in March 1946 and was open to everyone between the ages of fourteen and twenty-five.[13] Membership was particularly attractive for the younger cohort aged between fourteen and eighteen, or those born between 1928 and 1932, that made up more than 60 percent of the first FDJ members. Having just been "betrayed" by the National Socialist regime, one would not expect to immediately join another social movement with dedication to yet another party that required significant party discipline. Political disillusionment and critical distance from big political ideas was a natural reaction among the older generation but equally among the majority of the younger generation. However, while in Berlin only about 5 percent of the young joined the FDJ, in the rest of the Soviet zone about a third joined, according to Ohse (2009: 76). What made it so easy for some to take a fascist and an anti-fascist oath one after the other?

There were several concrete differences in the two youth organizations that might have been essential for the young who are more

---

[12] His father is reported to have withdrawn from participation in the political organization of the hospital. In 1949, his father was moved to a different working place "for political reasons." He had taken old furniture from his office, thus violating public ownership (MfS AOP 1012-57 (1): 23; 134).

[13] The following reflections on the relationship between Hitler Youth and the FDJ are informed by McDougall (2008), Ohse (2009), and Buddrus (1995).

sensitive to practical details than big ideas. In contrast to the later years, the early FDJ was a nonmilitaristic organization. There was no uniform to be worn and no parades to be walked. More importantly, in contrast to the separation between the Hitler Youth and the League of German Girls, the FDJ was a unisex organization and thus presented an opportunity to meet with the other sex. Also, since the FDJ was known for its evening dances, many wanted to seize this rare occasion to have fun during the poverty of the postwar period. Some more politically minded members even complained that dancing seemed to be the only reason why many came to the meetings. The mixture of individual motivations also gave the early FDJ an aura of inclusiveness. At the beginning, the FDJ presented itself as more of an umbrella organization of other youth organization, including Christian groups, in order to attract as many young people as possible. "Everybody was heard," one witness recalled, as in principle everybody could be part of the socialist movement. In December 1945, Erich Honecker, who would become the head of the FDJ (to be founded some months later), declared: "Differences of belief and *Weltanschauung* should, in our view, not be a source of dissension. We believe in total tolerance in such matters."[14] This sense of inclusiveness was indeed an essential part of the ethos of this generation and would later nourish trust in an open debate culture. On a deeper level, the young certainly looked for a place to belong. A natural need for those going through puberty, this longing might have been reinforced by the fact of having grown up in a society with a rigid order, possibly having lost family members in the war, and the anarchic state in postwar cities. However, this need could have been met by any other youth organization.

The underlying reason that might explain the smooth ideological switch is related to what McDougall has called an "amnesty alliance" between the Old Communists and the Hitler Youth generation (2008: 35). The Soviet administration did not have much choice but to "forgive" the Hitler Youth when mobilizing the young for their

---

[14] Cited in McDougall (2008: 38) and in Buddrus (1995: 252). Buddrus describes well the subtle transition from political inclusion to political indoctrination in the first years of the FDJ. In the early Soviet Zone, the less political Protestant Church or even the Esperanto movement were still allowed, but soon put under control of the FDJ before being openly repressed in the early 1950s. This was also manifest in the rhetorical choice to speak of "democracy" rather than "socialism."

cause. Considering that participation in the Hitler Youth was obligatory and that this exact cohort would be crucial for building up new
institutions, it was not possible for the Soviet administration to dismiss
an entire cohort of the population through their "denazification"
policies: 8.7 million of 8.87 million young people between the ages of
ten and eighteen were members of the Hitler Youth and the League of
German Girls. The administration thus drew the line at a high Hitler
Youth rank: those who ranked *Unterbannführer* and upwards, the
"paid" Hitler Youth, were excluded from the FDJ (McDougall 2008:
30). But that was only a very small number, and leadership experience
in the Hitler Youth below these positions could actually be a resource
for higher positions in the FDJ. Indeed, even some dedicated socialists
did not join because they perceived "the same rabble" as in the Hitler
Youth taking part (ibid.: 24).

Though there was no official amnesty directive, the attitude was
clear. The young were generally "excused" due to their age; that is,
they were considered *victims* of fascism. As Otto Grotewohl, one of the
heads of the SED, said at the first FDJ parliament in June 1946, the
party did consider the young "not for a single day or hour" responsible
for the regime (in McDougall 2008: 30). The FDJ thus offered political
amnesty of the collective guilt, of the "complicity" (*Mitschuld*) that
was heavily communicated by the denazification campaign to the rest
of the population. This amnesty might have been attractive to those
who came out of the war with actual feelings of guilt, feelings that
emerge more easily among the young but are less easily recognized as a
driving force of their actions. Thus, while the Old Communists took on
the ethos of the fighters against fascism, the young were put into the
role of misused *victims* of the Nazi regime. The psychological twist
inherent in this role was the basis of their emotional dependency:
"Communists hoped," as Buddrus argued, "that by extending an
amnesty to the young, declaring faith in them and yet simultaneously
reminding them of their guilt, they would induce young Germans to
seek absolution by throwing themselves whole-heartedly behind the
new order" (1995: 256).

Amnesty came at the cost of censoring one's own past. The young
could not or certainly were not encouraged to openly speak about their
life in National Socialism. Despite the inclusive and light atmosphere of
the early FDJ, there was a taboo of not speaking about the tragic events
of war. Memories were held back. McDougall argued that "a pragmatic

pact of silence between regime and young allowed the Hitler Youth generation to participate actively in the political and socio-economic reconstruction of East Germany after 1945 ... Private thoughts and memories of the Third Reich – whether positive or negative, defiant or remorseful – remained powerful. They were simply given no public outlet in the GDR" (McDougall 2008: 27, 45). It is this pact of silence that created a symbiotic bond, an emotional dependency between Old Communists and the hope generation. The hopes put onto the young, involving the bright future they were to create, were to make up for the sacrifices of their role models in their fight against fascism, a burden that granted authority to the Old Communists' historical version of fascist Germany in contrast to their own past.[15] This lack of integration of their own biography into that of the state can be understood as an initial form of self-censorship in the name of higher ideals. Accepting this silence led to a "conservative alliance" between these two generations, an acceptance that gave the older generation room to maneuver and allowed them to paper over apparent contradictions between the GDR's ideals and the reality that the following chapters describe. In particular, their alliance would manifest in the fundamental ambiguity of a simultaneous acceptance and rejection of Stalinism and the presence of subtle state violence. It is for this reason that this generation, as we will see in Part II, did not achieve a renewal or appropriation of socialism in its own non-Stalinist terms, but fell back into self-censorship and party discipline.[16] On the surface of their self-awareness, this pact between the two generations would be manifest in the basic belief held as a dogma until the end of the GDR, that only socialism, in contrast to capitalism, is entitled to guarantee peace.

---

[15] Regarding the tension between public and private memory, see the oral history study by Moller in Schüle et al. (2006: 399–410).

[16] In Niethammer's words: "This large class of (mid-rank) leaders ... seems to be a key to the structural history of the GDR since the 1960s: a relatively homogeneous generation with state-related career experience and executive activism, whose fate was indissolubly linked to the state and whose experience was not repeatable for younger generations. This class of leaders needed the aging Old Communists at the top, whose politics – derived from the 1920s and from the Soviet Union – they implemented without being able or willing to renew it, and who at the same time, like a praetorian guard, shielded this younger generations from their own experiences and perspectives" (1994: 105).

In addition to the amnesty regarding their past, the hope projected onto the young, as we have seen in the case of Klein, was an attractive feature of the FDJ. It helped them to look ahead instead of back. The FDJ offered a source of overt optimism regarding the building up of a new socialist state as well as opportunities for personal advancement. Being a socialist, until the end of the GDR and beyond, meant believing in the *future* of socialism, as if they never grew out of being a child of the rubble. This future orientation deeply fed into the belief structure of our protagonists, and it would become manifest in both the belief in Marx's historical determinism as well as the trust in the party's claim to modernism. With this future orientation also came an elevated work ethos typical of the hope generation. Hard work was an important source of satisfaction in its capacity to deal with difficult emotions. In addition, the language of sacrifice and effort that echoed the propaganda of National Socialist militarism (as well as Prussian Protestantism) was certainly something they were able to recognize from their earlier socialization.

All of this might not have been apparent to the young men, including Arne Benary. What was present in their mind was rather the postwar struggle that made them relive on a smaller scale the larger class struggle the older generation experienced in the Weimar Republic and during Nazism. Those in the FDJ comprised a minority of all youths. For others, the parallel between the Hitler Youth and the Free German Youth might have been too obvious, as their distrust in political devotion was too great or religion was more important. But there was also an actual enemy of the FDJ, the so-called werewolves that continued the Führer's struggle. They distributed anticommunist leaflets, sang old Hitler Youth songs, and interrupted FDJ meetings. The existence of werewolves was a welcome excuse for the Soviet administration to arrest whoever they saw necessary. Thus, in these first years, the young learned their ABCs of political agitation, with the language of veteran communists on their lips. In this sense, the war was not over. Peace had to be fought for.

In short, the FDJ was attractive because it offered a combination of the old *and* the new, of "the reassuring familiar alongside the fresh and exciting" (McDougall 2008: 41). For those who joined the FDJ, the differences might have been present to their mind, while the subtler similarities and unrecognized emotional needs might have remained unrecognized. For the many young men and women in the Soviet zone who did not join the FDJ, the contrary appeared to be the case.

Figure 1.1 Third Youth World Festival, Berlin, August 1951.
© DEFA-Stiftung/W. Pawlow, W. Mikoscha, J. Monglowskij.

There are no documents that allow a reconstruction which of these motivations led to Arne Benary joining the FDJ at the earliest occasion possible in 1946. Neither his professional choice after school gives an indication. He decided to train as a banker between 1946 and 1948, a profession that would be subjected to a socialist transformation but at the time was still practiced as before. Working at a bank and learning about socialist ideas at the FDJ easily explains his choice to enroll in the economics program at University of Jena. After his first year, in 1949, he moved to a bigger department at the University of Leipzig. There, he would encounter his single most important role model and tutor for the remainder of his career, Friedrich Behrens. He graduated in 1950 and became Behrens' assistant in writing a dissertation and teaching classes in political economy (where he met his future wife). For half a year in 1952, he had to work in industry to gain experience as a worker (*Stahlwerk Brandenburg*). While also teaching at a school for finance in Brandis, in 1954, he graduated with a doctoral thesis on "current problems of the agrarian theory of Marxism-Leninism" that discussed a central problem of Stalin's political economy, specifically, how industrial progress depends on agricultural development.[17] He then became Behrens' higher assistant (*Oberassistent*) to write his habilitation. The two became friends and engaged in activities outside of their professional relationship. It was then, in 1954, that they moved together to Berlin to the newly founded Central Economics Institute at the Academy of Sciences. It is there that we take up his story in Chapter 3.

Erwin Rohde

The other three protagonists of this book were either born in Germany's Eastern territory such as Eastern Prussia, East Pomerania, and Silesia that would become part of Poland or Russia after World War II, or belonged to the German minorities in Eastern states (*Volksdeutsche*), such as Czechoslovakia or specific Soviet regions. Their move to the later territory of the GDR had several causes. Some of the *Volksdeutsche* were expelled from Soviet territory after the German army invaded the Soviet Union in 1939, while others were resettled by Hitler's campaign to bring German minorities abroad back "home" (*Heim ins Reich*). Others were taken by the withdrawing German army or fled from the arrival of the Soviet army, and most of the remainders were expelled after 1945 from the Soviet, Czech, or Polish national forces. Once they settled in the Soviet-occupied zone after the war, they would all be called "resettlers" (*Umsiedler*). The political will was to quickly integrate them into society without consideration of their migratory past, but their different background also led to tensions with the existing population. Starting from nothing, resettlers stuck out due to their accents and were often looked down upon, both in West and East Germany. The reason why they settled in the Soviet instead of the Western zone might have been related to personal circumstances or was the result of administrative allocation but was only in exceptional cases a matter of political preference.[18] Compared to the Old Communists, who knew the capitalist West from

---

[17] MfS AOP 1012-57, I: 23.

[18] Around 12.5 million Eastern refugees had to be integrated in the new frontiers of the Eastern and Western occupied zones. By 1948, around 4.5 million of them were in the Soviet zone, which constituted around 25 percent of the entire population (see Wille 1991: 6). Already in 1950, after the foundation of the GDR, there was no special legal status attached to resettlers.

exile or prewar activities, none of the five economists in this book knew West Germany or Western Europe from their own biographical background, as did very few of East Germany's hope generation.

Erwin Rohde was born 1927 in Insterburg in Eastern Prussia, East of Königsberg, a town of 50,000 inhabitants that is today called Chernyakhovsk in the Russian province of Kaliningrad.[19] Rohde's family, he recalled, would later be considered "distant from education" (*bildungsfern*). His father, Richard Rohde, was a tailor, and his mother, Emma Rohde, née Sternberg, was a salesperson.[20] Thus, it was not obvious how the family would pay for their son's high school fees. His father received a disability pension, which helped. In his hometown, Rohde witnessed not only the oppression of the large Jewish population but also, after the attack on Poland, the oppression of the Polish population, who were subject to forced labor. In 1937, he had the option, and in 1939 he had the obligation, to become a member of the German Youth, while in 1941 he was required to be a member of the Hitler Youth. He does not mention this in his short biographical notes, but his membership in both organizations is documented for the years between 1937 and 1944.

Beginning in 1941 with the attack on the Soviet Union, the region came under crossfire with the first Soviet air attacks on Königsberg. Close to Insterburg, a war prison was built. In 1942, Rohde witnessed the deportation of the Jewish population. In summer 1944, the region was surprised by British air raids, which they thought they were protected from by distance. The center of the city was largely destroyed. It was then that the Hitler Youth, Rohde included, were summoned to volunteer for military service. As mentioned, 70 percent of this age group signed up, and they were often assigned as anti-aircraft auxiliaries (*Flakhelfer*). The closer the Red Army came, the more people were evacuated. There is no documentation indicating to what exact extent Rohde was involved in the war activities at the end of 1944, but considering his age, he must have participated to some extent.

---

[19] See his papers in the University Archive of Humboldt University (hereafter NR). The following information is based on his curriculum in NR 1 and 2, as well as 4, 12, 16, and 72. In the Stasi files, there is but a travel cadre file in MfS HA/AKG RK, 521–540.

[20] Despite the Jewish maiden name of her mother, no religious aspect of his life is reported. Rohde also had two sisters, who are unknown to the author.

When the Soviet offense in East Prussia began in January 1945, including repeated air attacks on the city, only about a fifth of the population was left. In Rohde's oral account, he mentioned that his family decided to await the Red Army, welcoming them as liberators. He added that his family feared he would become a prisoner of war and disguised him as a woman (Rohde 2009). Since it is documented that the Hitler Youth was very involved in defending the Königsberg area, Rohde indeed could have taken part in the final fights against the Red Army. However, according to the documentation in the archive, he had already enrolled in November 1944 in a high school close to Berlin at a time when the Red Army had not yet arrived in Insterburg. The family may have wished to stay but were not allowed to, or some other reasons may have caused them to move. It is difficult to imagine the origin of the Soviet-friendly attitude of the family, but in any event if they had awaited the Red Army, their attitude would not have made a difference. Once the Kaliningrad area was annexed, the remaining population fled, was expelled, or was subject to violence and later forced labor. The family went to Falkensee close to Berlin where one of the family's aunts was living. The choice of a place to settle could not have been political since the end of the war and the territorial organization were not yet clear in November 1944. They might have expected, as was the case with many other refugees, that after the war they would be allowed to return to their hometown. But it soon became clear that this would not happen. It was a new beginning.

Arriving in Falkensee on the outskirts of Berlin in November 1944, Rohde was enrolled in the local high school, where he remained until April 1946. It is documented that his father became a member of the KPD. Regarding his own politicization, Rohde recalled that he shared his room with an "uncle" who had been a communist imprisoned during Nazism and thus was an actual veteran communist. Having learned to see the immediate past as well as the present situation through his eyes, before the end of 1945 Rohde too became a member of the KPD and actively engaged in its cause. In 1946, he became the founder of the youth section of the FDJ in Falkensee. Rohde thus has the longest party experience of the five protagonists discussed in this book. The speculations mentioned above regarding Benary's adherence to the FDJ apply equally to Erwin Rohde. Sticking out at school due to his Eastern accent as well as the organization he adhered to, he decided, in April 1946, to move to Berlin. The same month, he witnessed the forced unification of the SPD and KPD as the SED, of which he fully approved. His party membership gave him access to a special educational class (*Sonderlehrgang*) that soon gave him a high school degree and access to university. Thus, in 1947, he enrolled in economics at Humboldt University, which was then still called Berlin University. Like Klein, Rohde would remain at this university until the end of his career.

Rohde acquired his political identity as a young party warrior during the years of open struggle for the political identity of East Germany. Even after the forced unification of the SPD and KPD, the united left did not win the majority of votes in the first democratic elections. In 1948, the Nationalist Party and the Farmers' Party were formed to weaken the Liberal Party and the Christian Democrats (CDU). These "bloc parties" (*Blockparteien*) remained in existence until the end of the GDR but without actual political influence. The official plans of Stalin were to prepare a political order for a unified neutral Germany. Only in 1949, after the long months of the Berlin blockade, was the power of the SED constitutionally secured. Rohde would later comment that at this time the SED was "hindered by other parties from being effective" (2009). Also, at the university, those dedicated to the Soviet example were still the minority until 1950. Rohde built up his party profile through the hostility and struggle over Stalinization with other academic groups. Only a small minority of one or two dozen were comrades from the party as compared to 600 students – a "small banner of the honest," as Rohde called them in a 1986 speech (*Fähnlein der Aufrichtigen*).[21] The pioneering spirit shared by them created important bonds and heightened their shared intellectual experience when reading Marx on their own. As Hans Wagner, one of the other comrades, recalled: "We studied 'The Capital' alone in 1948. There was no one who could teach it. But it

---

[21] See his talk in 1986 to graduates of the year 1961 about the history of the faculty ("Zur Geschichte von Lehre und Forschung an der wirtschaftswissenschaftlichen Fakultät/Sektion der Humboldt-Universität zu Berlin," October 1986, in NR 16). Rohde used the term "Fähnlein" (small banner), willingly or not, that was used by the German Youth as a (para)military unit referring to four "Jungzüge" of three "Jungenschaften" each of fifteen young scouts.

was the best teaching we could have. I have always told my students: it would be best if you read 'The Capital' on your own."[22]

The socialist cause found little echo among the majority of students that did not come, as was traditionally the case, from lower-class families. Also, those coming back from war prisons wished to quickly get a degree and were not interested in socialism, as Rohde recalled in the same speech. A poster that announced a meeting of the party students was forbidden, and their meetings had to take place outside the faculty. The first official FDJ groups at the faculty were not founded before 1949. Rohde was also active in battling so-called bourgeois economists, notably in business economics (*Betriebswirtschaftslehre*), which was still a dominant element of the curriculum but considered bourgeois by socialist dedicates. Rohde put up flyers opposing the prominent business economist Konrad Mellerowicz.[23] As with many FDJ students, he took part in leaflet actions in West Berlin. Later in 1955, he was even put under arrest for a day or a night, which was not uncommon in these years. "Studying and political struggle constituted a unity," he commented in 1977 (NR 15: 9).

It should be noted that during Rohde's undergraduate studies, the curriculum had not yet been adapted to the doctrines of Marxism-Leninism. He was thus trained in an economics curriculum that did not differ much from that of the 1920s. He became interested in finance and taxes in particular, a subject taught by the aged Oswald Schneider, who had been trained in a bourgeois tradition by Gustav Schmoller. Already as a student, Rohde worked part time at the Central Finance Administration (later Ministry of Finance) as an associate of Ernst Kaemmel, a later professor of finance at Humboldt University.[24] The field of finance was a surprising choice, since the status of finance, comparable to that of business economics, had been put into question. In the early GDR, the financial system was downplayed considering the overall importance of "use value" and the decreasing importance of

---

[22] Hans Wagner Interview, *SED-Reformdiskurs*, TB Wagner.

[23] See documents related to his studies in NR 3 and the remarks in Hesse and Rischbieter (2012). For his arrest, see NR 16.

[24] Kaemmel, after a formal divorce from a Jewish woman, was employed by the Reich Ministry of Finance during Nazism. In July 1945, after remarrying he began working for the German Central Finance Administration and moved from West to East Berlin. See Rohde's talk in honor of Kaemmel's 100th birthday in September 1990 (NR 31).

monetary terms when counting in "material balances." As a party warrior, Rohde put himself in an ambiguous position in which he would remain until late in his life.[25]

As more and more teaching staff that did not wish to follow the Soviet example left the scene, party members such as Rohde were ideal candidates for an academic career. He graduated in 1949, the year before Marxism-Leninism became the foundation of higher education in the so-called second university reform, which is described in Chapter 2. Though he expected to have a career at the Ministry of Finance, in May 1950, he was called back to the university. In response to the enforcement of Marxism-Leninism, Oswald Schneider left for the West and the department was vacant. Finance experts with a socialist dedication in teaching and administration were rare and in high demand. Thus, at age twenty-three, Rohde acquired a position as assistant at the Institute for Finance, which he was to run almost solely, since Martin Schmidt, head of the institute, also had a part-time post at the Ministry of Finance.[26] Rohde's career advanced through his dissertation and early publications on a new system of public accounting (Rohde 1956a; Rohde et al. 1951). He studied how to control the expenses of local administration with respect to the national budget. When Stalin died in 1953, Rohde was twenty-six years old and well on his way to a future academic career. By 1955, he had already received national recognition for his early work. His quick career rise exemplifies the career opportunities that the early GDR created for Soviet-loyal teachers in economics.

Harry Maier

There is more documentation available on the biographical background of the fourth protagonist of this book, Harry Maier. In 1986, he applied for treatment as a political refugee in West Germany and had to explain in this context the complex history of his family before 1945.[27] In the many files on him at the Stasi, this past never appeared

[25] For early debates on the financial system in the GDR, see Krause (1998b: 275).

[26] Martin Schmidt, who was the head of a section of the Ministry of Finance until 1958, became department chair without a doctoral degree, which he received only in 1956. In 1958, he became president of the State Bank.

[27] See further details in a letter from September 14, 1986, in N 2693-14. For more biographical background information, see Harry Maier's papers (N 2693-17,

in detail. Maier lived without public recognition of the difficult years leading up to his career as an economist.

Maier was born 1934 in Feodosija, a small town on Soviet territory on the Crimea. His family origin goes back to rich farmers that had moved to the Crimea from South Germany in the early nineteenth century. Once the Red Army took possession of the Crimea in 1922, the family was expropriated. While most of the German farmer families were sent to the north of the Soviet Union, his father, Klaus Prieb, was permitted to stay because he found employment as a bookkeeper for the local administration in the nearby city of Tokmak, where he met his wife, the schoolteacher Wally Maier. During the Great Purge of Stalin in 1938, however, when Harry was four years old, his father was arrested and sent to a Gulag in Siberia. The young Harry must have recognized the worries of his mother anxiously waiting for his father's letters, which at one point simply ceased. Her own letters were sent back to her, and she never received an official statement of his death. Harry thus grew up with his mother, his grandmother, and his sister.

At the age of seven, in September 1942, Harry was supposed to begin schooling, but this was not to happen. When the German army broke through Sevastopol and quickly approached the city, the Soviets tried to relocate the remaining population. The German army, however, arrived earlier than expected, the city became occupied territory, and school was interrupted. Between 1942 and 1944, the *Volksdeutsche* on the Crimea were naturalized as German citizens, which later gave them the name "administrative Germans" (*Administrationsdeutsche*). Starting in September 1943, these new German citizens were sent to the German territory as part of a campaign that had been run since 1939 in several Eastern regions called "back home to the Reich" (*Heim ins Reich*). He, his mother, his sister, and his grandmother thus left Tokmak to be transferred to several cities before arriving more than a year later, in January 1945, in Belzig close to Berlin. Maier was not even eleven years old, and his situation in the last years of the war had likely been too unstable for him to be subject to a systematic National Socialist indoctrination.

Peace did not mean peace for the "administrative Germans" from the Soviet territory. The Soviet military administration in Germany forced them to return to the Soviet Union as they did not accept the

N 2693-4); for a list of his publications see N 2693-20; see also MfS HA XVIII 16682, MfS U 25-89, MfS HA XVIII AP 46049-92, and MfS 58363-92.

naturalization of the National Socialist regime as legitimate. Maier's mother was afraid that, upon returning to the Soviet Union, the same fate of her husband during the Great Purge would await them. Therefore, she changed her name from Prieb to her maiden name, Maier, and went into hiding at a friend's place in Schöneberg in Berlin. Once she found a job as a teacher, the family became legal residents of Berlin. It was only then, in 1946, that Harry began regular schooling at Prenzlauer Berg. He was put into fourth grade based on his age instead of his proven education, yet he performed well. In 1949, he entered high school, skipped a grade, graduated in 1953, and enrolled in economics as one of the first cohorts at Higher School of Economics in Karlshorst. Without any activity in the FDJ being documented, even before finishing high school, in 1952, he became a member of the party. After his first year of studies, he changed to Humboldt University, which had more prominent teachers in economics. He met his future wife, who was also enrolled in economics, as well as the future sociologist Helmut Steiner. Together, they visited the rehearsals of Berthold Brecht. As a party member at the Higher School of Economics, he was an organizer of the student party-group (*Gruppenorganisator*), and at Humboldt University he was secretary of the student party-group. Party-groups gathered all party members and existed in every organization. The activity of these groups was vital for how political power was employed on a local level, as we will see at several points in the following chapters.

It is difficult to reconstruct these political choices after Maier's arrival in Berlin. Being in a highly unstable situation regarding his national and geographical identity during the war, the peace agenda and the support for worker and farmer families might have been factors in his choice. And yet, how must he have felt about the Stalinist education he received considering what happened to his father, his family, and himself? In 1953, once the danger of being sent back to the Soviet Union was over, his mother legally applied to use her maiden name Maier. She was right in trying to evade the resettlement. As Maier notes, Germans that returned to their prewar location in the Soviet Union continued to be oppressed.

Maier graduated eight years later in 1961 with a doctoral thesis on a socialist critique of bourgeois Christian socialism (1965). He then received a post at the Central Economics Institute at the Academy of Sciences to write his habilitation. He then decided to change to the intellectually less stable but more challenging field of the political economy of socialism.

Ernst Strnad

There is little documentation about the last of the protagonists, Ernst Strnad, who also came from an Eastern territory to Berlin.[28] He belonged to a small and little-researched minority of Germans in Czechoslovakia that were part of the Czech Communist Party (KPČ).[29] Strnad was born in 1928 in Mikulášovice, called Nixdorf in German, a small town close to the German border that was part of the contended Sudetenland. His father, born in 1889, was a steel worker (*Stahlschleifer*) and active for the KPD in the city council.[30] During the economic crisis, his father had to work in road construction for some time. After 1933, his father hosted political refugees that fled Nazi Germany to the Czech Republic. In this time, his father had been in touch with Florian Schenk, a famous communist from the same region who had been a member of the KPČ in the Czech parliament between 1935 and 1938 and later became a famous unionist in the GDR.

In September 1938, after the threat of a military conflict, the region was annexed by Hitler's Germany, and much of the Czech population fled or was dispelled to other regions. The so-called *Henleinpeople*, the party of Sudeten Germans run by Konrad Henlein in favor of the annexation, surrendered his father and around fifty other communists of the region to the fascist authorities for their political identity. After imprisonment in 1938, he was relocated in 1939 first to the concentration camp in Dachau and shortly after to Buchenwald, the same concentration camp where in 1944 the famous communist leader Ernst Thälmann was killed. From then on, there were only few letters to the family, and Strnad would learn about the truth of his father's camp experience only after the war. After pleas from the local population in

---

[28] Biographical information about Strnad is limited to the documentation regarding his doctoral thesis in SAPMO-BArch, DY 30 83342. There is also the account he published about his father jointly with his brother (Strnad and Strnad 1994). His father published some of his concentration camp memories in 1966, shortly before he passed away in 1967, in short articles in the local party newspaper in Bernau ("Mein Weg," *Bernauer Wochenzeitung*, February 12 and 19, 1966).

[29] For the German-Czech context between 1945 and 1950, see Zimmermann (2010) and Kučera (1992), as well as the book by Douglas (2012).

[30] "Josef Strand was never in high offices and central bodies, but as an elected city councilor in old Czechoslovakia for many years he was a democratic parliamentarian who stood up for the interests of the people, regardless of their nationality" (Strnad and Strnad 1994: 49).

Nixdorf, including pleas from his sons, Josef Strand was released from Buchenwald before its liberation in May 1944. This liberation suggested both high esteem at home and some recognition of his person among the authorities in the concentration camp.

We do not know how Ernst Strnad, as the son of a communist, had been treated after the annexation of the region in October 1938, but it is likely that he, with or without formal membership in the Hitler Youth, had also been involved in war labor. Whatever he contributed to the war, the political sacrifice of his father might have evoked profound feelings of guilt, gratitude, and also vengeance that accompanied his becoming a socialist. In any event, his father wished his children to continue his struggle. "He and his wife and comrade-in-arms," as his father wrote about himself, "raised their children to be good socialists and patriots ... They continue the revolutionary tradition in the new situation of national struggle."[31] Jointly with his brother, Ernst Strand would study and write a book about what happened to his father in the concentration camp, which was self-published in 1994 once the biographies of Old Communists were no longer censored. While for the other protagonists, the symbiotic relationship with Old Communists might have applied more on a level of historical experience, for Ernst Strnad, it applied on the individual level of his own family.

In the book on their father's struggle in the concentration camp, the two brothers depict a schematic image of the humanist morale of his father and other prisoners and the unhuman crimes of the Nazi regime. He described the constant fear of death, the heavy physical labor in the stone quarry, the struggle for survival in finessing SS order, the severe and unpredictable punishments, the solidarity among communists, questions of trust, and the threat of denunciation. He recounts how his father lost his teeth when being whipped for declaring his anti-fascist attitude; he noted the public denigration when marching in chains through the city of Weimar; and he emphasized the industrial sabotage in the Gustoff-Werke II where prisoners were used for weapon production; half of the rifles would not work, according to his father's account (Strnad and Strnad 1990: 109). But they also emphasized the plurality of prisoners, such as the presence of Sinti and Roma, a plurality which was absent from the public mind during socialism.

---

[31] Josef Strnad, "Mein Weg," *Bernauer Wochenzeitung*, February 19, 1966.

After the war in 1945, the family was again the object of suppression, this time from the Czech authorities regardless of their role in fascism. Informal and formal expulsions of the German population in the Czech Republic, and the Sudetenland in particular, were carried out. Some were also subject to forced labor or internment. About one and a half million went into the Soviet zone and another one and a half million to the Western zones. Even the KPČ, not yet the governing authority, was in favor of the expulsions. Josef Strnad does not report about these events in his short biographical account. He only mentions that "I was employed by the Czechoslovak city administration as a representative of the Nixdorf anti-fascists. My main task was to protect the rights of the German anti-fascists until they moved to Germany." In June 1946, the Strnad family then was relocated from their home town to Bernau close to Berlin. Here, they again played the role of a cultural minority as they did in their hometown.

Immediately after their arrival, Ernst Strnad began studying economics at Berlin University. There, he witnessed the difficult struggles regarding the Sovietization of the university described in Chapter 2. He graduated in 1950 and found employment as a lector of foreign languages in the publishing house *Die Wirtschaft*.[32] There, he became a member of the socialist party, the same year his father became a mayor in the suburbs of Berlin. Although he had no academic employment, Ernst Strand wished to contribute more to the Marxist-Leninist transformation of economic knowledge that was officially called for after the foundation of the GDR. He thus wrote, without supervision, a dissertation on the critique of the use of statistics in bourgeois political economy and its proper use in socialist political economy. He would finish it in summer 1955, the months after the 20th Party Congress that broke with Stalinism. His story is the subject of Chapter 4.

* * *

There is no single answer to the question of what put the five future economists on the socialist path to which they would remain loyal for the remainder of their careers. Indeed, they would develop rather different attitudes toward the virtues and vices of the socialist state. Ernst Strnad and Erwin Rohde would show great faith in orthodox party

---

[32] One of the translations still in the library system is a book on business trade by Smirnov (1954).

discipline, Klein would slowly develop increasing doubts about the party line but not act against it until the last minute, and Benary and Maier would come into conflict with the party but never gave up hope for future reforms. They certainly had different notions of what socialism was supposed to be, but they agreed until the end of their lives that socialism was the only answer to the horrors of fascism and the only system that guaranteed peace. By implication, and nourished by the political struggle over the Stalinization of East Germany, they considered West Germany to be the continuation of "monopolistic capitalism" of which fascism was an extreme variant. This is the existential source of what in their economic philosophy would be stylized as the notion of class conflict. It is also the existential source of accepting the oppression of inner-party criticism and anything else alluding to factionalism in the name of peace. As we have seen, they held these beliefs in contradiction with some aspects of their own biography to the extent that their experiences with Nazism were not solely negative and their experiences with Stalinism were not solely positive.

What made this stylization of their beliefs possible was that their own individual memories of the National Socialist regime and World War II was never actually reflected upon and thus remained open to reinterpretation by others. The underlying existential needs and sentiments of a growing personality – such as a sense of belonging, perspective, security, and vision, and also the relief from guilt attached to the National Socialist regime – were less present in their minds than the idolization of the role models of Old Communists and the heroic myths attached to them. Nazism was a past that had been "present in a condensed, implicit, and virtual form only," as Mannheim wrote with regard to the phenomenon of inherited and appropriated memories (1952 [1928]: 295). The belief in the state of the GDR was nourished by the conviction that the way back was blocked by the struggle and sacrifices of their role models during Nazism. Despite apparent tensions between their individual memories and the official narrative about the National Socialist regime in the GDR, it was their generation that granted the regime the most credit for representing the legitimate anti-fascist agenda of the GDR.

Who then were their role models as burgeoning economists at university? What were the debates and struggles they witnessed during the institutional transformation of university between 1945 and 1955?

2 | *Socialist Role Models*

It is one of the noblest tasks of our party and our state to convey to our growing youth the life and battle experiences of the proven revolutionary fighters who struggled for decades for the rights of the working class. (Josef Strnad)[1]

One of the party slogans after the foundation of the GDR was "learning from Soviet men is learning to win." The victory that the Soviet incorporated was less the abstract victory of a socialist society as such, but the victory of the Red Army over fascism. The slogan thus referred to the strong link that existed since 1945 between socialism and antifascism. But it also referred to the psychological twist that the Soviet forces demanded from the East German population: to respond to a defeat by turning it into a victory. As tempting as this solution might have been to the disaster of World War II, the obvious self-denial the slogan offered could only be a temporary defense mechanism regarding a past that continued impacting the political mind of the people. In addition, the slogan also came at an immediate cost: learning to win means, first of all, not to stop fighting. That is, following the Soviet example, it was as if the war had not ended at all. The new institutional structure of East German society, including that of the academic economists surveyed in this chapter, was nourished by precisely this temptation to turn, following the Soviet example, loss into victory.

The First University Reform

The students that arrived at Berlin's university in 1946 and 1947, such as Rohde and Strnad, witnessed what later would be called the first university reform: the denazification carried out according to a law shared by all occupied sectors, which went along a slow but steady

---

[1] "Mein Weg," *Bernauer Wochenzeitung*, February 19, 1966.

Sovietization in the Eastern sector.[2] In the Soviet zone, the denazification of the faculty was carried out by individual committees on behalf of the German Central Administration for National Education (*Deutsche Zentralverwaltung für Volksbildung*). Former members of the NSDAP were, in principle, excluded from further employment. Those who sought to stay filled out a questionnaire about their past relationship with the regime and their future plans regarding research and teaching. "I presume that the members of the teaching staff," the head of the selection committee wrote, "will take into account the new political circumstances when choosing topics for their courses."[3] In Berlin's university, around 80 percent of staff were immediately affected. In Leipzig's economics faculty, where Arne Benary would study, all the economists had to leave university immediately. The economics faculty at Berlin's university received eight applications, while the large majority of the teaching staff did not claim their continued existence as economists. Three out of the eight applicants were approved, but none of them as actual professors. In other disciplines, denazification was carried out less severely, such as in medicine, where all professors were reemployed after formal exclusion. In West Germany, however, in what became a shared belief among East German citizens, the cleansing was not carried out nearly as strictly as in the East.[4]

---

[2] Humboldt University has always valued its preservation, equally during its socialist period. Compare the works prepared at the occasion of its 150-year celebration in 1960 (Berthold 1960) and its 200-year celebration in 2010 (Tenorth 2010–2012). For the socialist period, see the excellent volume edited by Jarausch (2012). For economic sciences, see in particular Zschaler (1997) and Hesse and Rischbieter (2012). For the Sovietization of East German academia in general, see Connelly (2000). All in all, in this book there will be more emphasis on Humboldt University than the Higher School of Economics because the former existed before and after the GDR, thus the historical frictions before 1950 and after 1989 are more visible and better documented.

[3] Spranger, Archive Humboldt University, WiWiFak Dekanat 1872: 115. For a more extensive discussion about the changes at the faculty after 1945, see Nötzold (1996), as well as Hansen (2012).

[4] "After 1945," Ash observed, "the number of politically based dismissals was more than twice as high as after 1933" (1999: 333). However, in 1954, 28.4 percent of all university teachers in East Germany were still former NSDAP members, which amounts to the same percentage as that of SED members (1999: 334). For the survival of former National Socialists in the GDR as compared to the FRG, see for example Bösch and Wirsching (2018). While in administration,

Regarding new appointments, the preference was for communists, preferably those trained in the Soviet Union, and otherwise scholars returning from exile in the West or those who had been active in the resistance.[5] The most important new appointment was the economic historian Jürgen Kuczynski (1904–1997), who was the main character of the reconstruction of the faculty and an important role model for the young.[6] Born in Berlin in a Jewish family, Kuczynski was part of an educated middle class (*Bildungsbürgertum*). He had studied philosophy, finance, and statistics in Berlin, Erlangen, and Heidelberg. Between 1926 and 1929, he visited the Brooking-School in Washington and was the head of the research department of the American Federation of Labor. Kuczynski's intellectual profile was that of a labor economist of the 1920s with a strong matter-of-fact orientation and emphasis on empirical detail using descriptive statistics. On his return to Germany in 1930, he became a member of the KPD, editor of the communist journal *Die Rote Fahne*, and teacher at the Marxist Workers' School. After Hitler's takeover, he was involved in illegal activities for the KPD before immigrating to England in 1936. There, he was head of a group of German communists, supported German scientists in British exile, and also worked for the Soviet military intelligence. In 1944 and 1945, he was a researcher for the United States Strategic Bombing Survey.[7] After the war, he returned to Germany and became head of the Central Finance Administration before becoming a professor of economic history at Berlin's university. Kuczynski was a veteran communist with

---

denazification could be considered more radical in the East than in the West, the same did not apply to industry, as Niethammer argued (1994: 104).

[5] The regime preferred those returning from Soviet exile over those returning from Western exile since the latter were suspected to be corrupted by their capitalist experiences. This idea that communists returning from Western exile had greater democratic tastes than those returning from the Soviet Union has been shown to be false by Epstein (2003).

[6] As one of the most important East German intellectuals, Kuczynski has received considerable attention from historians; see Haun (1999), Kessler (2005), and Fair-Schulz (2009).

[7] About his secret service activities, see Stibbe (2011). John Kenneth Galbraith reports on Kuczynski's role in the US Strategic Bombing Survey activities, notably regarding the abduction of statistician Rolf Wagenfuehr, who worked for the Soviets in Berlin. Kuczynski apparently worked for both fronts at this time, though with little strategic relevance (Galbraith 1981: 222). Later, in 1953 during the anti-Zionist campaign, Kuczynski was subject to the suspicion of cooperating with Western intelligence.

rare experiences in the Western sphere. His biographical background was well known by his students, including Rohde, Klein, Strnad, and Maier.

At first, Kuczynski was the only teacher presenting economics from a communist point of view. To his students, he represented traditional scholarly values with an appreciation for the complexity of empirical research and presenting socialist ideas within the context of broader European cultural history. In 1948, he finished the seventh volume of his major work of forty volumes on the history of labor in capitalism. Later, Kuczynski would become a member of both the Soviet Academy of Sciences and a fellow of the Royal Statistical Society and was thus one of the few East German economists to gain an international reputation. He was also central to the first institutional changes in economics at the later Humboldt University before the formal introduction of Marxism-Leninism, notably the integration of the business school into the university. Though he brought forward mainly financial reasons, this integration would diminish the role of "bourgeois" business economics in the future socialist regime. He succeeded, and the new faculty of economics thus was founded in 1946. Outside the university, Kuczynski was a central intellectual figure of the early GDR. Until 1950, he was head of the Society for the Study of Soviet Culture and became an early member of the People's Chamber (*Volkskammer*). At the same time, he became repeatedly subject to party inquiries, be it before Stalin's death because of Trotskyism, or after Stalin's death because of revisionism, as we will see in Chapter 3.[8] The example of Kuczynski shows that being an Old Communist was not equivalent to being a Stalinist, which made him an ideal role model for the younger generation and their desire for intellectual autonomy.

But in the first postwar years, there were not enough of Kuczynski's kind, and the university had to employ what were considered bourgeois economists. Several social democratic–oriented economists hoped for a future at Humboldt, such as Bruno Gleitze, director of the Central Statistical Office, and Friedrich Lenz, who did research on planning methods while upholding the principles of a market economy. Sixty-two-year-old Oswald Schneider, a student of Gustav Schmoller who had already been put into forced retirement during the National

---

[8] For his investigation of "Trotskyism," see MfS AOP 338-55.

Socialist regime, was reestablished as a professor of finance. But business economists also expected to continue their long tradition at Berlin's university. Bruno Rogowsky, who was banned during Nazism as a Freemason, became director of the business school that was integrated in the university. In 1947, Konrad Mellerowicz was reestablished as professor of business economics. Rogowsky and Mellerowicz still hoped for a future for business economics at Humboldt as they tried to hire, without success, the father figure of German business economics, Eugen Schmalenbach (Hesse and Rischbieter 2012).

As mentioned, the curriculum did not change in the first postwar years. Kuczynski was the only one who represented Marxist thinking in his classes, while other classes were differently and certainly less politicized. Social democrats and business economists that had no inclination to teach the Soviet literature reacted with a retreat into politically neutral teaching. The first debate about the new form of economics therefore took place on these terms: to what extent should a university professor show political dedication? Against those who defended a neutral scholarly ethos, Kuczynski responded with an article published in 1947 entitled "Shall University Teachers Make Propaganda?" "To the lecterns of our universities belong professors that are confessors of a democratic Germany" (1947: 62). The term democratic was used in contrast to capitalist and thus meant socialist. Those who defended less politicized notions of economics were soon reproached with the label of "objectivism." With this label, the regime could both reproach all sorts of existing "bourgeois" approaches in economics and get Marxists in line with a "voluntarist" notion of economic policy: saying that there is no objective obstacle to the creative power of the will of the workers' class, that is, the party.[9] It should also be noted that the shared opposition to the remaining bourgeois intellectuals was not favorable for debates by party-loyal socialists, in spite of their very different experiences of the war. Marxism came to postwar East Germany with an aura of self-evidence.

There was also considerable variety among the students. Since the university was the only one in postwar Berlin, students from all sectors and political orientations, including many homecoming soldiers, traveled to Unter den Linden. Clearly only a minority of them enrolled with a socialist dedication, and the majority would never acquire it. There

---

[9] On the objectivism campaign, see Feige (1995).

were surely also those who simply wished to receive a professional education without being involved in politics at all. One kind of student stuck out, though. A new schooling institution in Berlin integrated in the university was created right after the war that gave workers and farmers without a high school degree access to higher education. Since 1946, students could attend a "pre-study institution," which in 1949 was transformed into the so-called Workers' and Farmers' Faculty (ABF), which was modeled after the Workers Faculties, the *Rabfak*, in the Soviet Union. For three years, workers' children received a stipend to prepare for university, to which they would be granted privileged access. Note that in order to break the established bourgeois privilege of having access to higher education, young students often had to break with their proletarian parents. Without a higher education themselves, parents tended not to support the educational ambitions of their children and preferred vocational training. All the greater was the influence of the teacher role models at the ABF. In fact, the ABF, mostly a boarding school, was known for its strict ideological education. Once students joined other students at the university, they stood out because of their mature socialist beliefs.

While universities were not yet subjected to Marxism-Leninism in the immediate postwar period, the party founded two major academic institutions following the Soviet example. In 1946, the Party Academy Karl Marx (*Parteihochschule Karl Marx*) was founded with the task of training the political and administrative class.[10] The academy was part of a network of regional and district schools related to the one in Berlin, while Berlin's Party Academy was related to the one in Moscow. Though the school was, as the name suggests, subject to the party, in particular the department of agitation and propaganda, it was considered a higher school (*Hochschule*) and thus an academic institution. The primary task was to form higher party functionaries in a curriculum ranging from six months to three years, but it also had the task of doing "research" and thus had the right to issue doctoral degrees. It had four departments: the history and philosophy of Marxism-Leninism (history of the labor movement, the Communist Party of the Soviet Union, and the SED); the political economy of

---

[10] For a participant account of the history of the Party Academy, see Möller and Preußer (2006). More recently, a short history has been written by Orlow (2021).

capitalism (Marx) and socialism (starting with Stalin); industrial and agrarian economics (as discussed during Stalin); and the teachings of the Marxist-Leninist Party, that is, the interpretation, justification, and application of party decisions. To respond to the increasing demand for party-loyal academics in the history, philosophy, and economics departments, in 1948 the Party Academy began offering lecturer classes for becoming university teachers. Among others, Eva Altmann, later rector of the Higher School of Economics, was born as an economist from these classes without other academic qualifications. Even if the Party Academy was an important channel through which the party influenced the public university system, universities, as we will see, would maintain a different ethos compared to that of the Party Academy. While education at the Party Academy prepared for a career in the strategic class, a degree from one of the academic institutions that hosted the protagonists of this book would usually not suffice for a career in strategic higher party functions.

A second institute founded equally according to the Soviet example in 1949 was the so-called Marx-Engels-Lenin Institute (in 1953 called the Marx-Engels-Lenin-Stalin Institute, and in 1956 the Institute for Marxism-Leninism). The main task of the institute was the editing of the classics, in particular the works of Marx and Engels and the history of the communist party.[11] The first director was another key figure and role model that was equally active as head of the research department at the Party Academy as well as professor at Humboldt University, the prominent Old Communist, Joseph Winternitz.[12] Born in England to a Jewish family and raised in Prague, he had been a member of the KPČ since 1920 and of the KPD since 1922. As editor of the communist journal *Vorwärts*, he was in close contact with Walter Ulbricht and headed the party training of the KPD until 1933 as well as the KPD propaganda department until 1931. In 1933, he immigrated to the Czechoslovak Republic and remained active in similar functions for the KPČ. After the attack by the German army, as a British citizen he moved to England but continued working for the KPČ from a distance. After the war, he disagreed with the KPČ's approval of the expulsion of the Sudeten Germans to Germany. In 1948, he returned to Berlin as a

[11] The institute also hosted the party archive. See Müller-Enbergs et al. (2010: 1095).
[12] See the recent biography by Keßler (2019).

university professor, head of the research institute of the Party Academy, and in 1949 the founder of the Marx-Engels-Lenin-Stalin Institute. Still before the national unification of the economics curriculum, he coordinated the change of the curriculum regulations in favor of socialism and marginalized business economics.

The rising global conflict and the politicization of universities increasingly divided students into camps for and against the Soviet orientation at the university. When students were excluded from university for political reasons, large protests took place in April 1948 that resulted in several arrests and also the abduction of students. Also, in June 1948, the Berlin blockade isolated Berlin's Western sectors such that provisions for the entire population were flown in by an ingenious military airlift system, which lasted for almost a year. At the same time, the Berlin Senate forbade the so-called counter-revolutionary student associations, which resulted in flyers at the faculty against teachers coming from the Party Academy: "Red professorship on the march! In a three-and-a-half-month course, professors are fabricated at the Party Academy of the SED in Klein-Machnow! Twenty-two loyal party communists get ... their lectures prepared for the coming winter semester!" (in Schneider 1997: 220).

The increased division between students, professors, and administration, paralleled by global politics, resulted in the foundation of a second university in the Western part of Berlin called the Free University.[13] At the economics faculty, several professors, most notably Bruno Gleitze, left under protest during the summer of 1948. Students, Rohde and Strnad included, could learn on a local level what it meant to engage in a global class conflict. The crisis ultimately resulted in the foundation of the two German states in summer 1949 when the Soviet administration turned over control to the single-party power of the SED. In the last elections months before, despite electoral fraud, the SED gained no more than 66 percent of the vote. The first version of the constitution still aimed at a unified Germany without anchoring the "leading role of the party" constitutionally. Though practiced ever since, this did not happen officially until 1974.

Days after the foundation of the GDR, a lecturer in political economy and assistant to Joseph Winternitz, Eva Altmann, permitted a vote

---

[13] For the foundation of the Free University, see Lönnendonker (1987); for the difficult beginnings of its economics faculty, see Rieter (2010).

on the legitimacy of the GDR after an intense debate among FDJ
economics students. The majority voted that it was not legitimate (in
Zschaler 1984: 162).

The Second University Reform

It was only after the foundation of the GDR that universities were
formally subjected to a socialist regime, a nationwide reform that in
retrospect would be called the "second" university reform (the first
being denazification). It was propagated under the motto "Storming
the Science Fortress" (*Sturm auf die Festung Wissenschaft*), meaning
that the university was considered a strategically important and
strongly anchored institution of bourgeois societies.

The reform had three cornerstones that formalized the tendencies
seen since 1945. The first was the break with the bourgeois privilege of
education. Universities were to break down the class differences that
are created in a capitalist society through education. Thus, farmers,
workers, and also women received privileged access to universities in
the form of special funding and lower entry requirements. Some of the
students were actively recruited while at work, being promised student
stipends and accommodations. The idea of the already-existing
Workers' Faculties was thus generalized. At the same time, students
had to partake in workers' and farmers' activities, as Benary did after
he graduated for several months in industry, but more notably during
the seasonal harvest (*Ernteeinsätze*).

Second, as with all other institutions, universities were formally
subject to a foundation in the doctrines of Marxism-Leninism.
The reform required an introductory year for students of *all* disciplines
with a social science curriculum (*gesellschaftswissenschaftliche
Grundstudium*) consisting of courses in Marxism-Leninism, political
economy, and dialectical and historical materialism, as well as sports
and Russian. Several teachers of this introductory curriculum came
from the so-called faculties of human sciences that had existed since
1946, notably at the universities in Leipzig, Jena, and Rostock. The
goal of these faculties was the quick training of party-loyal bureaucrats
and teachers for the new institutions on all levels of society. The influence of the party was institutionally enforced by party representatives
in all university levels, the so-called party-groups, that intervened in
dialogue in research activities. In addition, universities were subjected

to a central ministry that played an increasing role in the further history of the national centralization of the scientific and disciplinary culture, the so-called State Secretariat for Higher Education (*Staatssekretariat für Hochschulwesen*) founded in 1951. The State Secretariat, like the Party Academy, also held short classes to shape loyal university teachers.

Third, universities became committed to the aim of building up socialism. In a Marxian world, science is a productive force (*Produktivkraft*). The socialist politicization of science meant that science was to be useful *for* politics, and in turn that politics was founded in science. The two spheres, in contrast to other totalitarian regimes, are therefore supposed to be distinct but nevertheless dependent on one another. This translated, first of all, into an antagonistic attitude toward pure theory: science for its own sake was considered bourgeois indulgence. The regime thus fostered, as the postwar debates against the remaining social democrats anticipated, the "battle against objectivism in scientific work."[14]

The second university reform greatly increased the demand for teachers of political economy, which became, as it were, *Erste Wissenschaft* in the socialist state. But this imperative also created a deficit of interpretation: how could Marx's writings, by then already more than a hundred years old, carry entire academic disciplines? The challenge was serious. Some years before, Stalin had already made a contribution to the meaning of Marxist linguistics (1950). In economics (which by that time consisted of techniques and issues on which Marx never had anything to say), what, for example, would a Marxist theory of statistics, insurance, or accounting look like? Some traditional elements that stood for pluralism in the larger social sciences fell: sociology as well as business economics was no longer taught as a discipline. Sociology was considered a bourgeois construct since it presupposes that social regularities exist independently of the economic base as described by Marx. It was fully banned and rehabilitated only in the late 1960s.[15] Business economics was replaced by so-called industrial economics (*Industrieökonomie*).

For those not yet committed to the Soviet regime, the university reform was an apparent renunciation of academic liberty. Thus,

[14] Cited in Wollmann (2010); on objectivism, see Feige (1995).
[15] On sociology, see Wollmann (2010).

the "bourgeois" faculty left for universities in West Germany. Bruno Rogowsky, Oswald Schneider, and Konrad Mellerowicz protested against the new curriculum with an unsuccessful petition to the State Secretariat for Higher Education. They argued in particular for the comparability with West German universities, an argument warranted by the official aim of the party to prepare for a unified Germany. Students of the FDJ were also implied. Erwin Rohde together with Waltraud Falk, head of the FDJ group, and Hans Wagner, a future economics professor at Humboldt, would hang up provocative wall posters against the remaining business economists.[16] They were successful. In spring 1950, Rogowsky, Schneider, and Mellerowicz left the faculty, such that only one of the founding professors of 1945, Jürgen Kuczynski, remained at the faculty.[17] While Erwin Rohde and Ernst Strnad were in the midst of this struggle over the Stalinization of the curriculum, Dieter Klein and Harry Mayer arrived only after.

The bourgeois economists left a large gap to be filled that was difficult to replace with qualified academics who were fully committed to the party line. This resulted in a trade-off, easily felt by students, between political loyalty and academic quality at the cost of formal academic qualifications. Jessen spoke of a "revolutionary rebuilding of the (social science) disciplines by a nonuniversity alternative elite, which was installed on a wide scale by ignoring the access standards typical of the (academic) profession" (1998: 38). The majority of those who became university professors during the 1950s did so without a formal degree of a "habilitation," the official qualification written after a doctoral dissertation.[18] Also, quality standards to receive a formal degree were lowered. Fritz Behrens in Leipzig had granted a "diploma," an undergraduate degree required for writing a dissertation, to Alfred Lemmnitz, a teacher at the Party Academy, for his illegal activities during fascism. He thus received a doctorate and later in 1952 a professorial title without ever having studied economics. Yet, he was in a central position to carry out the structural change after the

---

[16] Regarding Mellerowicz's protest, see Schneider (1997), and regarding the students' protests, see Hesse and Rischbieter (2012).

[17] For a comprehensive assessment of the situation at the entire university during the 1950s, see Vogt (2012).

[18] Requirements for assistant posts were (including the stipend-financed *Aspiranten*), as Vogt observed for the 1950s, rather liberal with respect to both grades and disciplinary background (2012: 226).

second university reform as dean of the economics faculty at the University of Rostock. All the new hires at Rostock after his arrival in 1952 received their academic degrees from Lemmnitz.

Compromises with traditional requirements were also necessary at Humboldt University. In 1950, Heinz Sanke's habilitation in economic geography was pushed by the party-group, and Otto Reinhold, then only twenty-six years old, was named professor in 1951, being one of the first profiteers of the hope generation. Reinhold would have a fast career as an economist in party-close institutions and, as we will see, would be an important reference point for several of our protagonists. But the full-blown dogmatist of the socialist regime, who stood for this trade-off between political loyalty and academic quality and arrived at Humboldt University after the second university reform in 1950, was Robert Naumann (1899–1978). Naumann's chair for the political economy of socialism became the center of power for the faculty and formed a certain antidote to the somewhat more liberal intellectualism that prevailed in the lectures of Jürgen Kuczynski.

Born in Berlin, Naumann left for the Soviet Union during its very first days in 1920 in the context of a workers' aid program. He learned the skills of a toolmaker, passed classes at the German party school in Moscow, and since 1922 had taught himself political economy at the German section of the Communist University of the National Minorities of the West. In 1926, he studied for four years at the Institute of Red Professors, the cadre university of the party. Between 1930 and 1943 he was employed in the propaganda section of the Executive Committee of the Communist International, the governing authority of the Comintern. From the end of the war until 1950, he taught political economy as the head of several schools for prisoners of war in the Soviet province. Naumann was one of the first German-Soviet communists who stood for the Soviet imperialist agenda to draw Western countries into their undertaking. He was the representative of Stalin's views on political economy in the early GDR.

Returning to Berlin after thirty years in 1951, he became professor and head of the chair for political economy at Humboldt University. He was also the head of the nationwide council for basic studies in social sciences at the Secretariat for Higher Education. As vice-rector between 1951 and 1964, Naumann was responsible for designing the introductory Marxist-Leninist curriculum that became obligatory after the second university reform. Naumann co-authored the German translation of the "textbook of political economy" initiated by Stalin and published in 1955 (Autorenkollektiv 1955). His solidarity with Stalin became manifest in his essay on "Stalin as Economist" (Naumann 1953). In 1954, Naumann became a member of the CC. He received all these powerful positions in East Germany's academic education system without any academic credit. It took him until 1959 to write his dissertation at Humboldt University on the critique of West German "neoliberal" policies (Naumann 1959). Having spent the years of the war in the Soviet Union, he had forgotten much of his German, to the extent that he could only read his manuscript aloud in an awkward accent. He proclaimed "as if from the pulpit" (Klein 2009) the history of the Communist Party of the Soviet Union. Though intellectually he was hardly inspiring, he had the highest authority.

Naumann was important for me because he was a deterrent from the very beginning. I was still a very Stalinist young man when I came to the university and continued to be influenced in that way in the first years. At the same time, the manner of his appearance was so off-putting and his reasoning was at times so irrational. As word got around, without being officially discussed, he sought out agents ... and also found them. He was a dangerous man ... Thus, it was clear to me that I will not continue in the political economy of socialism. In the political economy of capitalism, people came together who at least could think objectively and to some extent even critically. (Klein interview 2021)

Naumann's Stalinist dogmatism was something the burgeoning economists would struggle against for the rest of their lives – a "primary stratum of experience" in Mannheim's terms (1952: 298). Naumann became an example of what students would learn to associate with being dogmatic, a mere preaching of what had been already written in contrast to the creative application of Marxism-Leninism to the current historical situation. In other words, cases such as Naumann made clear the important generational differences between them and the Old Communists and thus helped them break with the symbiotic relationship established in the first postwar years. As a future professor at Humboldt said about Naumann in a rare dissociation to the Old Communists: "He was an outsider, but also powerful and dangerous. He got stuck in the past. I had the same experience with other anti-fascists, too. They continued where they stopped during the Weimar Republic" (Apelt interview). However, when trying to explain why they did not resist more than they did, once again, they would point to their experiences with National Socialism, adopting the position of "victim" given by the Old Communists. As Dieter Klein said about Naumann's teaching of the history of the Communist Party:

People like me who came out of the Nazi era with some conscience and had experienced liberation by the Red Army, who would then be fibbed to about the history of the party that was not put in the context of other information, could do nothing but believe it. Everyone around me threw themselves into the breach with full conviction, even if one had just come out of the Gulags. For a long time, I just did the same. (Klein 2009)

The experiences with the National Socialist regime as children could both explain their beliefs in socialism and excuse their susceptibility to its dogmatism. It should be noted, however, that during the 1950s, 15 percent of the GDR population that had also lived through Nazism, more than two and a half million people, including many of their fellow students, left the country.

It was the conflict between these two intellectual styles, Naumann's dogmatism and Kuczynski's intellectualism, that formed their intellectual identity. The liberal policy of granting academic positions on the basis of political loyalty increased the tensions between the loyalists among the academics and those holding up the professional ethos of an academic marked by vision, inspiration, and rigor. The meaning of being academic was up for reevaluation. One early case of this conflict was the prominent Joseph Winternitz. As a central link between the party and the educational and academic sphere, already by February 1950, Winternitz was heavily criticized for his nuanced comments on the rising conflict between Stalin and Tito in an article "Learning from Stalin" in *Einheit* (1950). Without even mentioning Tito, he wrote about the use of the spontaneity of labor with respect to conscious planning, which supposedly supported Tito's so-called imperialist campaign against Stalin.[19] While the editor of the journal lost his job, in March 1950 Winternitz was appointed dean of the economics faculty at Humboldt University. Yet a lurking arrest in 1951 made him move back

---

[19] See Keßler (2019: 60–67) for more on this episode of the critique of Winternitz.

to England, where he died in 1952. Having identified with Winternitz's ethos, the students would learn to what extent party discipline was relevant for an academic career.[20]

There were some others like Kuczynski and Winternitz who inspired lived socialist ideas. One was the Hungarian László Radványi, alias Johann Lorenz Schmidt (1900–1978). Schmidt returned from Latin American exile after he had been sentenced to death in Hungary. With the air of glamour of his wife and famous novelist Anna Seghers as well as a handful of assistants from Latin America, he taught the theory of imperialism in the spirit of Georg Lukács, who would soon be considered "revisionist." His international insights put the doctrinaire narratives in a larger context. In a 1954 article, Schmidt criticized the overly Soviet orientation as irrelevant to the GDR economy, an issue many students would raise for the rest of their lives.

There were also those who were intellectually inspiring but had a less heroic political profile than Naumann and Kuczynski since they had managed to slip through the denazification campaign. Though considered bourgeois, they had to be employed in the new regime in light of the high demand for teachers. Without being critical of the regime, they represented an old way of thinking that was little informed by the current needs of the party or Marxism-Leninism in general. One who was central for Erwin Rohde was Ernst Kaemmel, professor of finance (1890–1970).[21] He moved from West to East Berlin out of political conviction, but since he had previously worked for the National Socialist finance administration (*Reichsfinanzverwaltung*) until 1941, he had less influence in setting the socialist agenda. As the head of the tax department at the Central Finance Administration, Kaemmel was criticized by the economist elite of the Old Communists, Fred Oelßner and Alfred Lemmnitz, for his "humanistic" emphasis on tax justice and opposition to the discrimination against bourgeois businesses and professions. Although the criticism of Kaemmel's bourgeois position persisted, in 1953 at the age of sixty-three he became professor at Humboldt University. His major work would be a history of finance that would be the starting point of Rohde's Marxist interpretation of bourgeois finance in the eighteenth and nineteenth centuries in

---

[20] See Müller-Enbergs et al. (2010).
[21] See Rohde's talk in honor of Kaemmel's 100th birthday in September 1990 (NR 31).

particular (Kaemmel 1966). But these applied fields had little influence on the overall agenda and were even considered dangerous in their relative independence and bourgeois origins, statistics being one example examined in Chapter 3. Rohde recalled:

With Naumann having established the faculty, there was a great preponderance of political economy. During his reign, political economists had considered themselves the guardians of the Holy Grail of Marxism-Leninism. And we others – statisticians, industrial economists or financial economists – were ideologically weak and had to be controlled if we were hostile or hurtful to the party line. (Rohde 2009)

Apart from the influence of role models, the moment when the young economists felt themselves awaken to their socialist being was an experience they fondly recalled: the reading seminars of Marx's *Capital* became an obligatory exercise for all students. Whatever happened, the belief in Marx's critique of political economy was never questioned, despite the repeatedly frustrated attempts to derive protocols for running the socialist state. Reading Marx was an eye opener not only because of the ideas themselves, but because it introduced students to a highly valued debating culture that came with his "dialectical materialism" and was lacking in the orthodox lectures of Naumann. It was there that not only knowledge was transferred, but intellectual attitudes and argumentative patterns were shaped. Marx's texts are sufficiently rich that they allow for both an interpretive intellectualism and the authority of expertise, such that the ongoing question of what is true to Marx would accompany the young economists for the rest of their intellectual life. The creative application of Marx, however, as we will see, could be applied to both critiquing *and* justifying party decisions. Therefore, Marx's texts, as important as his ideas were for East German economists, do not help in understanding the shape of its epistemic regime. As we will see, Marx's historical determinism also helped bear the very contradiction between the reality created by the party and the ideals expressed by Marx. Being Marxist was a balm for bearing the reality of socialism.

Three More Institutions, and the Three Economic Laws

It might have been against the background of the open struggle at Humboldt University and the foundation of the Free University that the need for yet more institutions of economic education and research in Berlin emerged, institutions that were truly born out of the womb of the revolution.

First, but least important to our protagonists, in 1951, the party founded the CC Institute for Social Sciences (*Institut für Gesellschaftswissenschaften beim ZK der SED*), which was renamed, in 1976, the CC Academy for Social Sciences (*Akademie für Gesellschaftswissenschaften beim ZK der SED*).[22] Next to the Party Academy and the Institute for Marxism-Leninism, this was the third institution for economic knowledge under the lead of the party. Activities resembled those at the Party Academy, though with a slightly higher level of abstraction. The first director was the Old Communist and Soviet returner Helene Berg, followed by Otto Reinhold in the early 1960s, who occupied a central role among East German economists. Apart from Otto Reinhold, there were few interactions between economists at the Academy for Social Sciences and university-based economists. The latter economists often demarcated themselves from those in the party-based institutes by being more "critical" and less "dogmatic," a demarcation that was important for maintaining their scientific ethos.

Second, founded in 1950 during the second university reform, the Higher School for the Planned Economy (*Hochschule für Planökomie*) would be the only university that specialized in economics in the GDR. Compared with the economics faculties at already-existing universities, its profile was closer to the party regime and yet was not a party institution such as the Party Academy.[23] The share of party members among the academic employees was higher than in other universities. The university was run as a boarding school, which soon gave it the nickname the "red monastery" (*rote Kloster*). Before enrolling in one of its programs, students were selected through personal conversations according to their political potential. As Harry Nick, a political economist born in 1932 who was one of the first students, recalled: "This university was indeed something very special in the university landscape

---

[22] For a history of the Academy for Social Sciences, see Mertens (2004: 61–110).
[23] The Higher School of Economics is much less researched than Humboldt University. The only archival-based research is that of Alisch (2010). There are several personal accounts of the school, for example Kupferschmidt et al. (2013), or the report of the alumni meetings (https://treffen-hfoe.de/).

of the GDR. Without any tradition, it was created specifically for the purpose of training leaders for the socialist economy" (2003: 38).

Eva Altmann, the first director, was the role model for the first cohort of students. Altmann was one of the few females among the Old Communists. Born in 1903, she had been a member of the KPD since 1923, studied economics from 1924 to 1927, and then worked among others for the communist journal *Rote Fahne*. In 1930, she was imprisoned for nine months for the preparation of high treason. During the first years of the National Socialist regime, she was again put in prison several times and placed under surveillance for her communist activities, but then soon worked as a secretary in industry. After the war, she was at first hired by the Greater Berlin Magistrate in the administration for education and then, in 1948, took the first lecturer course at the Party Academy. Joseph Winternitz was involved in this course and took her on as an assistant to Humboldt University, and he might have also supported her career leap as director of the Higher School for the Planned Economy. It was only in 1952 that she received her doctoral degree from the University of Halle.[24]

In the course of the further academic reorganization in the 1950s, the school gained importance. In 1956, the school was joined with the Higher School for Finance in Potsdam and was now called the Higher School for Economics (*Hochschule für Ökonomie*). Eva Altmann was replaced by Alfred Lemmnitz, the director of the school in Potsdam, a position he held until 1958. Also, Helmut Koziolek, born in 1927, came from Potsdam and became vice-rector of the school at the age of twenty-nine. He had only received his PhD in 1955 and would have a fast-rising career in the political economy of socialism. When, in 1958, the University of Foreign Trade in Berlin-Staaken, founded in 1954, was incorporated into the school, the Higher School of Economics became the most important university solely dedicated to economics in the GDR.

---

[24] Other higher party intelligentsia were involved in the foundation of the school, such as Ernst Hoffmann, who had been the responsible party agent of the second university reform at the CC department for agitation and propaganda. While teaching the philosophy of historical and dialectical materialism in 1952, equally without a dissertation, he became professor after a decree of the State Secretariat for Higher Education. Hans Mottek, born in 1910, upon returning from British exile, took over the department of economic history after a dissertation written under the supervision of Kuczynski at Humboldt University.

The faculties at Higher School of Economics present an apt image of the structure of economic knowledge in East Germany. There was "socialist economics" (*sozialistische Volkswirtschaftslehre*), which was the study of the institutions of planning; industrial economics, which replaced business economics; financial economics, which was largely of an administrative kind, as we will see; international economics; economic governance (*Wirtschaftsführung*), which dealt with public policy; and statistics and later computer science. While these were considered specialized fields, the two fields that united economic knowledge were the political economy of capitalism, which taught Marx and applied it to the current state of Western capitalism, and the political economy of socialism, which entailed the application of Marx to the development of socialism. While the past achievement of socialism was the least debatable part of the political economy of socialism, its theoretical foundations with respect to the degree of the permitted market categories was the sensitive weak spot of this new discipline. It should be noted that important parts of Marxism, such as historical materialism, were also the subject of philosophy, such that economists did not hold a monopoly on the state-founding ideology.

The reputation as a "red monastery" did not prevent the party from intervening. On the contrary, the closer an institution was to the party, the more intervention was possible since the party could rely on the cooperation of its members. An early occasion was the reception of Stalin's publication on the *Economic Problems of Socialism in the USSR* (1972 [1952]), as well as the official textbook *Political Economy* that was ordered and controlled by Stalin and published at the end of 1954.[25] This text came as a surprise to many economists since Stalin accepted the existence of "basic economic laws" of socialism, which appeared to limit the will of the party.[26] What they indeed entailed was the simple negation of the vices of capitalism and they were thus of a normative character. There were three laws, which would remain a point of reference of all future discussions in the political economy of socialism. The first refers to what in Western

---

[25] See Stalin (1972 [1952]) and the contextual accounts in Pollock (2006) and Düppe and Joly-Simard (2020).

[26] The voluntarist notion of planning following the slogan of the "dictatorship of the proletariat" was widely accepted among socialist economists in the post-war Soviet zone. "The plan is the basic economic law of socialism," Behrens wrote in 1949 (cited in Becker and Dierking 1989: 321).

vocabulary is called welfare maximization as an objective function: saying that socialism amounts to a steady growth of economic well-being. The second is the law of the balanced proportionate development of the economy, an idea going back to Stalin's industry-based, and industry-interdependent, approach to planning, and later giving rise to the use of input–output analysis. The third is the contested "law of value" that implies "commodity production," that is, the use of prices to capture socially necessary production costs to be used in proper accounting methods.[27]

The extent to which the third law requires "decentral" planning describes the orthodoxy-reformist axis around which theoretical debates in the political economy of socialism evolved. The discussion centers on the extent to which Marx's political economy of capitalism applies to the political economy of socialism – value theory, commodity production, cost accounting, profits, demand, etc. If so, these categories would constitute the objective scientific foundation that should be used for, but also limit, economic planning. The other extreme is to deny the application of these terms. While the latter results in a voluntarist notion of planning without scientific foundation, the former tends toward a stateless socialism without private ownership of capital. Negotiating something in-between, one rhetorical move stems from Stalin's textbook that the meaning of the laws of capitalism "transform" in socialism, which resulted in tedious conceptual sophistry that went on until the end of the socialist regime. But these debates remained largely theoretical, while the actual institutional organization of economic planning was discussed in the subfield of "economics" that was considered independent from the political economy of socialism.[28]

The party ordered that in all relevant institutions Stalin's work had to be discussed during two weeks by the respective party-groups of the

[27] Accounting was the frame within which statistics should be used, according to Stalin. "No construction work, no work for the state and no planning is imaginable without correct accounting. But accounting is inconceivable without statistics" (Stalin 1972 [1952], cited in Strohe 1996: 4)

[28] About these laws and foundational issues of the political economy of socialism, see Becker and Dierking (1989: 407–474), Krause (1998b: 121–138, 161–170), Wagener et al. (2021: chapter 3), and also the discussion in Müller et al. (1999). These debates have evoked interest among Western scholars ever since the 1970s, notably in response to the Soviet discussion. See most extensively Ellman (1973).

schools. However, at the Higher School of Economics the discussion took place only in two meetings. In April 1953, the CC Secretariat (*Sekretariat des Zentralkomittees der SED*), the more executive version of the Politburo, published a "personal statement" (*Stellungnahme*) critiquing the Higher School of Economics in *Neues Deutschland*, entitled "Against the Conciliatory Attitude (*Versöhnlertum*) in Ideological Questions." Thus, Eva Altmann was equally subject to the label of Trotskyism and received a party rebuke (*Rüge*).[29] The Stasi informant wrote about Altmann that she "has not yet shed her bourgeois background despite long party membership ... She has organizational talent; however, it is questionable for whom the organizational talent is used." She reveals an attitude of "conscious opacity," and "discredits skilfully trustworthy comrades." In her theories, she "underestimates practical experience" and "treats Marxism-Leninism as a dogma, ultimately in a metaphysical fashion." The informant concludes: "I have the impression of deliberate parasitical efforts."[30] In addition to Altmann, scholars that were critical of Stalin's text were labeled "Trotskyist," which became the placeholder for every criticism of the Stalinist regime. This objection was raised against Bruno Warnke, who was fired from the school and excluded from the party.

In the course of reforming and appropriating the old institutions of knowledge in the GDR, the old Prussian Academy of Sciences was central.[31] Going back to members such as the brothers Grimm and the brothers Humboldt, the research emphasis at the academy was on the natural sciences and it was missing a politically oriented department. Thus, the party decided on the foundation of the Central Economics Institute at the Academy of Sciences of the GDR (*Zentralinstitut für Wirtschaftswissenschaften*), the first institute at the academy that was fully based on Marxist-Leninist doctrines. As a symbol of the socialist adoption of the bourgeois bastion of knowledge and inspired by the Soviet model, the institute was supposed to be the main academic research institution for economics.[32] The initiative came from Fred

---

[29] There were four party penalties: warning (*Verwarnung*), rebuke (*Rüge*), strict rebuke (*strenge Rüge*), and party ban.

[30] MfS AP 2493-63 Berlin, February 18, 1953.

[31] The most detailed and well-researched edited volume on the Academy of Sciences is that by Kocka et al. (2003).

[32] See the yearly report of 1957 in Krause (1998a: 88) and Bichtler (1986: 159). For a history of the institute until Honecker, see Steiner (2000).

Oelßner, the economist among the Old Communists' Politburo members who chose Gunther Kohlmey as first director who in turn chose Fritz Behrens as vice-director. All three economists were important role models for the hope generation of economists.

Fred Oelßner, born 1903, the son of a known social democrat, had been a member of the KPD since 1920 and in 1924 was imprisoned for this reason. In 1926, he was delegated to Moscow where he studied and taught at the Lenin school before becoming an assistant at the economics department of the renowned Institute of Red Professors, the central Marxist party institute. He returned to the KPD's agitation and propaganda department in 1932, teaching at the party school "Rosa Luxemburg." During Nazism, he was part of the KPD leadership in exile in Paris and was personal secretary of Walter Ulbricht, but he returned to the Soviet Union to teach again at the Lenin school as well as at the Communist University of the National Minorities of the West. There, in 1936, during the Great Purges, he was fired for alleged ideological diversion and had to work in industry and as a free journalist. Being a naturalized Soviet citizen, in 1940 he took part in designing the KPD plans for postwar Germany, and in May 1945 worked for the Soviet army in the Occupied Zone. Being well connected, he was the ideal candidate to become the head of the department for agitation and propaganda of the KPD in 1945. His intellectual profile shows little in his biography, but he became the Politburo member responsible for the theoretical party journal *Die Einheit*, head of the commission for the production of consumer goods, and professor of political economy at the CC Institute for Social Sciences.

Fred Oelßner suggested Gunther Kohlmey as the director of the institute, who had a more pronounced profile as an economist. Kohlmey, born in 1913 in Berlin, graduated with a diploma in economics in Freiburg in 1936 and in 1939 with a dissertation in Berlin that was, under National Socialist governance, considered of sufficient quality to give him an assistant position at Berlin's university until 1943. At the end of the war, however, he had to engage in active battle on the Eastern front against the Red Army. He decided to defect to the Soviet forces, and was held for some time as a prisoner of war in Moscow before he became a teacher at the Central Antifascist School in Krasnogorsk for other prisoners of war. Returning to Germany in 1947, his activities up until 1943 were forgotten, and he became the founding dean of the economics faculty of the German Academy for Administration in

Forst-Zinna and then professor at the German Academy for State and Legal Sciences (*Staats- und Rechtswissenschaften*) in Potsdam. Teaching also at Humboldt University, Kohlmey, like Kuczynski, became one of the role models for several of our protagonists. In 1955, after the foundation of the institute at the academy, he received a national prize.[33]

Kohlmey was to set up the heads of the departments of several institutes, being further divided in working groups (*Arbeitsgruppen*). He himself became the head of the political economy of socialism. For the political economy of capitalism, he instead chose Johann Lorenz Schmidt, who had come from Humboldt University, and for the history of economic doctrines (*Lehrmeinungen*) he chose Rudolf Agricola, who had been rector of the University of Halle-Wittenberg. This department soon joined with the political economy of capitalism, as the history of economic thought was congruent with the ideological development of capitalism. For the department of the economy of the GDR as well as vice-director of the institute, Kohlmey chose Friedrich (or Fritz) Behrens from University of Leipzig.

Behrens could not be considered a veteran communist, though he had been a member of the party before 1933.[34] Born in 1909 in Rostock to a worker's family at a shipyard, Behrens was to become a marine engineer. Until 1931, he was active in the SPD. After a special talent exam (*Begabtenprüfung*), he studied economics and statistics in Leipzig between 1931 and 1935, graduating with a dissertation. This may have led him to change, in 1932, from the SPD to the KPD. He must have kept his communist identity to himself when in 1935 he became a scientific assistant at the Statistical Office in Berlin (*Statistisches Reichsamt*). He remained in this institution and worked, after the occupation of Czechoslovakia between 1941 and 1945, at the Central Statistical Office in Prague, where he also taught statistics at the university.

---

[33] About Kohlmey, see Steiner (1996) and MfS AP 1710/53.

[34] For Behrens' biographical background, see his papers, the *Nachlass Behrens* (thereafter NRB), in *Archiv der Berlin-Brandenburgischen Akademie der Wissenschaften* (thereafter ABBAW). See also the collection of essays edited by Müller, Neuhaus, and Tesch for memories of former students, evaluation of his work and list of references (1999). See in particular the article by Steiner in that volume as well as Steiner (2000). For an English presentation of Behrens' work as an economist, see Caldwell (2000). Keßler (2005) compares the political profile of Behrens and Kuczynski, arguing that Behrens did not have the same attachment to the party as Kuczynski.

In 1946, as a new member of the SED, he became a professor of statistics and political economy at University of Leipzig, a faculty that after the first university reform had no economists left. Similar to Kuczynski at Humboldt, Behrens had made his name by reconstructing the economics faculty from scratch. He was friends with the philosopher Ernst Bloch and the literary scholar Werner Krauss. In 1947, he wrote his "habilitation," which under normal circumstance was a condition to become professor, on a "theoretical and statistical study on productive labor in capitalism" (Behrens 1948). Just like Kuczynski at Humboldt, he was actively involved in the marginalization of business economics, criticizing other economists as "objectivist."[35] As head of the university party-group in July 1949, Behrens defended the notion of a "bolshevist strictly scientific objectivity" while critiquing "bourgeois objectivity." At the same time, after he critiqued the state-bureaucratic character of the new socialist society, he himself was criticized as objectivist by higher party functionaries, Fred Oelßner in particular.[36] Nevertheless, in 1954, he received a third-class national prize for his work in Leipzig, making him the third economist to receive this prize after Fred Oelßner and Jürgen Kuczynski.[37] Confidence in him was so strong that at the same time he was made head of the Central Office for Statistics (*staatliche Zentralverwaltung für Statistik*) as well as a member of the Council of Ministers of the GDR. Arne Benary, his assistant, came with him to Berlin.

In July 1954, the doors of the institute opened. It was soon filled with young assistants writing their dissertations and habilitations. Among them was Karl Bichtler, who would play an important role for both Arne Benary and Harry Maier. Bichtler, born in 1929, was a horde leader in the Hitler Youth at age fourteen. Documents report that his uncle was involved as a police officer in the prosecution of communists. In 1944, he received training as a glider pilot, and then in 1945 he was part of the *Volkssturm*. Some months after the war, he assisted a short course at the KPD school in Camburg, which led him to decide to join the party in November 1945 and in 1946 to join the

---

[35] See the article on "Marx as critique of business economics" written by his student Wolfgang Berger (1949).

[36] On the anti-objectivism campaign against Behrens, see Feige (1995: 1074–1083).

[37] See his newspaper article "Mein Weg in die Wirtschaftswissenschaften," *Tägliche Rundschau Berlin*, 18, October 10, 1954 (also in ABBAW, NRB, 223).

FDJ. He was apparently one of the cases of those who profited from their leadership experience in the Hitler Youth. A report written about him by an informant of the Academy of Sciences exemplifies the general attitude to excuse the National Socialist involvement of the young, even if half-heartedly. The report refers to the dilemma that excusing the young for their Hitler Youth involvement implied that their decision to join the KPD and the FDJ months later could equally not be taken seriously.

One could say that he changed his political conviction (_Gesinnung_) like a dirty shirt. His entry into the KPD was not made out of persuasion (_Überzeugung_); he was sixteen years old. Other motives may have led him to it, in particular when considering the fact that he was a horde leader in the Hitler Youth. It may be that over the years and the attendance of many schools, as well as dealing with real anti-fascists has shaped him into a real and convinced comrade who, with great love, is fully committed to our party.[38]

After studying economics in Jena, Bichtler became a "scientific aspirant" to write his dissertation at the CC Institute for Social Sciences. In 1956, Bichtler joined the economics institute at the Academy of Sciences as an assistant to Kohlmey to finalize his dissertation. He became the head of the party-group of the institute.

In terms of economic research, the most urgent question after the foundation of the institute was related to the party's program to build the socialist foundations of the new state. The 2nd Party Congress in July 1952 called to create "the foundations (_Grundlagen_) of the socialist state," and Ulbricht asked to "boldly tackle the new tasks."[39] Apart from applied economics (_zweigökonomische Forschung_) on specific economic sectors and observation of the West German economy, one central question at the institute was the "transitional period" from capitalism to socialism.[40] This is what was meant by basic research

---

[38] MfS AIM 3238-71: 17

[39] Cited in Bichtler (1986: 160). The institute also hosted the nation-wide Section of Economics that consisted of economists and state functionaries and was to be a central administrative hub for East German economics. The section published the first research plan for economics in 1954, but in the further existence lost importance; see for example Krause (1998b: 281).

[40] Other issues were that of ownership, notably the difference between nationalization and socialization, which is surveyed in Krause (1998b: 270), and yet more extensively in Kovács (2018). The institute also focused on questions of

in the political economy of socialism. The new institute members were encouraged to question deeply and critically all the more, as it was apparent that the second Five-Year Plan, after the first of 1951, would need much improvement.[41] Next to the question of the functional relationships between the different economic sectors, notably agriculture and industry, the hot issue was the extent to which the state would play a role. It was on this topic that Arne Benary would soon take position, as we will see in Chapter 3.

One of the first big events organized by the institute, and thus a key event for the new elite of economists in the GDR, took place in March 1955, and discussed "the transitional period from capitalism to socialism in the GDR."[42] Four-hundred and fifty participants were present at the conference, which included not only academicians but also the political class. That is, the entire economic intelligentsia gathered to discuss the foundations for the future development of the GDR. Economists in the GDR knew each other. In his final speech, Fred Oelßner was optimistic regarding the vivid debate:

That is exactly what we urgently need, a real free exchange of scientific opinions. We will not make progress in our development if we restrict our discussions to reproducing what has already been printed somewhere or what an authority has already said. We will only progress if we treat our questions freely, openly and critically, if everyone expresses his opinion as he thinks, and if in this way – through unavoidable mistakes – the core of truth will ultimately emerge. (1955: 299)[43]

---

the productivity of labor, and the critique of West German "state monopoly capitalism" and West German economics (see Krause 1998b: 280).

[41] About the economic situation of the early GDR, see Steiner (2004: chapters 2 and 3).

[42] See the proceedings, Oelßner (1955).

[43] Anti-dogmatism was also a catchword of Stalin's science policy. Famously intervening in a debate on linguistics, in 1950, he wrote about those who simply repeated Marx's writings: "As a science, Marxism cannot stand still ... In the course of its development, Marxism cannot help but be enriched by new experience, by new knowledge; consequently, its individual formulas and conclusions must change with the passing of time, must be replaced by new formulas and conclusions corresponding to new historical tasks. Marxism does not recognize immutable conclusions and formulas, obligatory for all epochs and periods. Marxism is the enemy of all forms of dogmatism" (Stalin 1950).

Figure 2.1 Conference of the Central Economics Institute at the Academy of Sciences of the GDR, January 26–29, 1956.
First row, second from the left: Johann Lorenz Schmidt, Speaker Siegbert Kahn, last in first row Alfred Lemmnitz; second row starting third from the left: Robert Naumann, Friedrich Behrens, Jürgen Kuczynski, Kurt Vieweg, Martin Schmidt, Otto Reinhold, Fred Oelßner, and the last in the row Werner Mussler. All major institutions discussed in this chapter were present. Photo: Bundesarchiv, Bild 183-35886-0003/Fotograf: Weise.

* * *

In March 1953, Stalin passed away. Among the young economist intelligentsia, this might have caused the same sorrow as everywhere in East German society. But Stalin's death was followed by a first wave of resistance among East German workers. In June 1953, workers' strikes took place everywhere for more self-governance and more democratic influence. Shortly after, on June 17, Soviet tanks shot down the strikes. It was then that the belief system of the hope generation experienced its first test: the regime, according to the Old Communists' logic of political struggle and confrontation, could do no other than blame the class enemy, saying the strike was the result of a Western conspiracy. Having no political agency yet, most young economists indeed believed in this explanation. "Our youth friends and comrades stood firmly by the policy of the party and government in the attempted coup on June 17, 1953," Erwin Rohde stated in 1977 (NR 16: 9). Deeply enmeshed in Stalinist beliefs, the young economists did not have the larger perspective needed to reflect on their newly acquired beliefs. Others in the same age group, and certainly those who threw stones at the Soviet tanks, were capable of such reflection.[44]

The struggle against dogmatism became a catchphrase of the so-called new course politics after the workers' strikes. Showing the ability of self-criticism, which is one of the foundations of being anti-dogmatic, the party declared itself to be opposed to all kinds of "letter punditry" (*Buchstabengelehrsamkeit*) in July 1953.[45] In light of Chapter 1, we may interpret this call for anti-dogmatism in generational terms. For Old Communists, speaking of truth is always a confessional matter related to trust and loyalty – the trustworthiness of those exposed to pressure in Gestapo cells or of spies that claimed to be communists but actually were not. Since suspicion was thus omnipresent among communists, strictly obeying party discipline remained the only way to prove trustworthiness. Remaining in a state of "class conflict" after the war, Old Communists required party discipline, suppressed doubts, and showed mistrust toward their own population – reminiscent of the Germans of 1933. For the younger generation, however, having blindly taken Hitler oaths in their youth, speaking of truth was associated with a commitment to deep honesty and the trust that the reality of their socialist utopia would emerge from the honest, open debates that the party called for.

The different visions of a scientific foundation of East Germany's economics profession came to the fore after a major change in the Soviet Union, the 20th Party Congress. The period of the Thaw, once Khrushchev broke with Stalin's "cult of personality," was a formative time for the status of economic knowledge in East Germany, an occasion for young economists to appropriate socialist society on their own terms. The Thaw period between Khrushchev's "secret" speech in February 1956 and the building of the wall in 1961 would be the period in which the five young economists presented in Chapter 1 were to establish their academic careers and complete their dissertations and habilitations. This required a difficult balancing act between the

---

[44] Regarding a full account of the intellectual response to the 1953 crisis, see Herzberg (2006: 61–121).

[45] "Der neue Kurs und die Aufgaben der Partei ... " (*Neues Deutschland*, July 28, 1953). At another instance in November 1955, still before the 20th Party Congress, the party lamented that mere "bookishness" (*Buchstabengelehrsamkeit*) is not a sufficient condition of the success of the construction of socialism (*Neues Deutschland*, January 11, 1955).

academic and the political. Not all of them would manage to pass this stage of their career, as Chapters 3 and 4 show. The most important source of the intellectual independence of the future economics professors was the new openness resulting from de-Stalinization. Dissertations and habilitations represented for many an attempt to negotiate the boundaries between Stalinism and a more democratic socialism. This experience of being liberated from one's early indoctrination into Stalinist ideas, combined with debates about the nature of a socialism specific to the GDR, was constitutive for the future professors' intellectual identities. Seizing on the differences between (Stalinist) dogmatism and the real issues of building up socialism in a divided Germany was this generation's major task for ensuring socialist prosperity in peace.

Among the many cases of inner-party oppression during this period, one early case that was significant for the entire profession of economists was that of Friedrich Behrens and Arne Benary at the Central Economics Institute at the Academy of Sciences. It would later be recalled as the first major lost chance at true reform.

PART II

Coming of Age during the Thaw

3 | *Staging a Scientific Debate*

Aunt Minna from West Germany writes to her relatives in East Germany and concludes the letter: "I hope the letter will reach you – I heard there is strict censorship." After four weeks, the letter comes back with the remark: "Could not be delivered because of defamation. There is no censorship here."

When Khrushchev broke with Stalin at the 20th Congress of the Communist Party in January 1956, new hopes for a truly socialist society were revived everywhere in the Eastern bloc states. Regarding the execution of state power, one hope was the end of the regime's open state violence (which Berlin's citizens had witnessed 1953 when Soviet tanks crushed the workers' strike). But looking back from today, what followed was a shift toward subtler measures of executing state force, notably the increasing use of large-scale surveillance methods by the Stasi. As the "shield of the party," the Stasi was supposed to stop class enemies from acting against the state before the army had to be called in. The more subtly it operated, the more democratic (and benevolent) the state would appear to its people and other states.[1]

The second hope that the 20th Party Congress nourished, which was central for the intellectual ethos of GDR economists, was the idea that socialist societies would come closer to the ideal of being a *scientific* undertaking – in contrast to the arbitrariness under Stalin or the reign of blind class interests under capitalism. Also, scholars at the Central Economics Institute at the Academy of Sciences hoped for more occasions to provide the party with sound reasons for a better economic policy. However, this hope was crushed during the so-called *revisionism* campaign that First Secretary Walter Ulbricht launched against large parts of the intelligentsia in the wake of the 20th Party Congress.

---

[1] For a general introduction to the Stasi, see Kowalczuk (2013) and Gieseke (2015). Regarding the transformation of the Stasi during the Thaw, see Engelmann and Schumann (1995).

Dismissing other socialists who were not true to Marx's doctrines, the notion of revisionism had a long party history going back to the First International, the conflict with Eduard Bernstein, Lenin's polemics against the syndicalists of the German Labor movement, and Stalin's rejection of Tito.[2] To "revise" Marx was to question the inevitable, law-like, and "scientific" historical course of the Communist Party.[3] Ulbricht managed in the late 1950s to create a campaign against those reformist ideas from within the party, which claimed the intellectual heritage of the Marxist-Leninist tradition but were critical of his bureaucratic state apparatus. He managed not only to mark them as revisionists, but also as dogmatists, such that his own policies appeared to be the manifestation of scientific socialism. This is the context of the dismantling of the Academy's Department for the Economy of the GDR, led by the prominent economist Friedrich Behrens, a dismantling that marked the moment when economists, as a profession, withdrew into a regime of self-censorship. This chapter reconstructs this episode.

In 1956, Behrens and his assistant Arne Benary wrote a small booklet about the diminishing role of the state in socialism entitled *The Economic Theory and Politics of the Transitional Period*. The draft was finished in summer 1956 and the printed booklet was ready to be shipped out in fall 1956. After the Hungarian uprising that November, however, the booklet was perceived as a threat to Ulbricht's regime. Since there was considerable sympathy for the authors' ideas among the members of the Institute of Economics at the East German Academy of Sciences, mere censorship would have undermined the relationship between the ruling party and the institute. Between January and April 1957, the party, with the help of the Stasi, therefore staged what I call a *show debate*, that is, a public condemnation staged in the form of an academic debate. The term show debate suggests an analogy with the well-known show trials under Stalin.[4]

[2] For an overview, see Labedz (1962). See more recently Kolar (2016: 223–237).
[3] Kolar emphasized the link between historical determinism and scientificity (thus anti-dogmatism) as one of the characteristic elements of the post-Stalinist regime (2016: 7).
[4] One of the best known show trials against economists was that against Nikolai Bukharin that ended in execution, as well as the imprisonment and later execution of Nikolai Kondratiev. On show trials, see the classical study by Hodos (1987); and on show trials in East Germany, see Beckert (1995). Though the transition from show trials to show debates corresponds to the shift from open

Just as the show trials took the form of adherence to law and legal proceedings, including defense and prosecution, but de facto served political aims, so did the show debate take the form of adherence to scholarly virtues of intellectual honesty and openness to evidence and arguments, but de facto served political aims. Just as show trials were a way of appropriating the legal values of justice in socialism, so was the show debate a way of appropriating the scientific virtue of truthfulness in socialism and, by extension, appropriating the Academy of Sciences as the old bourgeois bastion of knowledge. Whereas Stalin's show trials featured confessions and executions, the aim of the show debate was to persuade the institute's council of party members at the institute, the party-group (*Parteigruppe*), to drop their support for Behrens and Benary and publicly announce the dogmatic and revisionist character of the booklet. This would result in Behrens being stripped of his higher functions and the end of Benary's academic career. This chapter shows how the show debate was organized, researched, and staged.

The show debate took place at the bimonthly meeting of the party-group at which the close to fifty party members of the institute discussed relevant political issues.[5] At the occasion of discussing Behrens and Benary's booklet, one or more major CC representatives were, unusually, also present, increasing the political pressure on the group. These representatives included Karl Kampfert and Otto Reinhold, head and vice-head of the CC Department for Science and Propaganda (*Abteilung Wissenschaften und Propaganda*); Gerhart Ziller, CC economy secretary; and Kurt Hager, CC science secretary and friendly acquaintance of Behrens. The two main Stasi informants at the meetings were "contact person" KP Karl Bichtler, code name "Bischak," party secretary of the institute, and "secret informant" GI Günther Ulisch, code name "Walter," assistant of Gunther Kohlmey, the head of the institute.[6] The two main Stasi officers in charge were Captain Roland

---

violence to more subtle state force, show debates did have their precedent in Stalin's regime; see Pollock (2006) and Düppe and Joly-Simard (2020).

[5] Günther Ulisch lists forty-nine institute members, of which there were at least four without party membership. See his report in MfS AIM 2981-62-2-1, 8, 165.

[6] For Bichtler, see Chapter 2 and MfS AIM 3238-71; for Ulisch see mainly MfS AIM 2981-62. Ulisch had studied at Humboldt University and was one of Kohlmey's first student assistants in 1954. There were several other informants who reported less frequently (GI Anna, GI El(l)i, GI Gisela, and GHI Toback), who have not been identified. See their reports in MfS AOP 1012-57, MfS AIM 3238-71.

Kießling and Lieutenant Klaus Seiß.[7] After the meetings they met personally with the informants and prepared meeting reports (*Treffberichte*). In addition, Kampfert sent reports on the meetings directly to the CC Secretariat. The multiple reports largely complement each other.[8] Although the party-group was the immediate audience of the debate, the entire community of East German economists would later read the published "consensus" to dub the booklet revisionist.

The importance of the marginalization of Behrens and Benary for the future of East Germany's intelligentsia has long been recognized in the literature, but the nature of the debate has been viewed as a matter of the party imposing itself.[9] Without taking the Stasi into consideration, a key element of the party's success in the debate is missing: the claim to a scientific foundation of the party's policies, including the claim to represent anti-dogmatism. While the party, and Ulbricht in particular, held political responsibility for conducting the revisionism campaign during the Thaw, it was the Stasi who staged the debate to

---

[7] They worked under their superior major, Paul Kienberg, the department head of HA V in charge of state apparatus, culture, churches and underground. None of them were trained economists.

[8] Though one might expect differences between the handwritten minutes, the reports written for the CC by Bichtler or Kampfert, and the reports written in reported speech by the Stasi officers after meeting the informants (*Treffberichte*), this does not appear to be the case. They are consistent and complementary. The principal Stasi records are the Benary files, MfS AOP 1012-57, 1 and 2. In the party archives, most records are to be found in one file only (SAPMO-BArch, DY 30 83342), which must have been created ex-post to collect all information about Behrens (possibly by Kampfert). Surprisingly, in the official protocols of the meetings at the Academy of Sciences there is hardly any mention of the debate; see ABBAW: NSchn, 680.

[9] The literature on the revisionism debate against Behrens and Benary began almost immediately after the debate took place, focusing mainly on the underlying economic ideas that are less covered in this chapter; see for example Jänicke (1964: 104–110). Without access to the archives, the published materials were treated by Becker and Dierking (1989: 407–489). For other studies based on published materials, see for example Krause (1996). An early article in English was written by Sanderson (1981). The party archives (SAPMO-BArch) were first used in Steiner (2000), and then in Caldwell (2000), which also used the Behrens archives (ABBAW NRB). Regarding the campaign against Kuczynski, see Haun (1999). For a recent account of economists of this period using interview materials, see Bianchini (2020). The most complete study using the party archives is Herzberg (2006). This chapter adds the important perspectives from the archives of the MfS and the personal views of contemporary witnesses, in particular Heinz Paragenings, a debate participant, Hannamaria Loschinski, Behrens' daughter, and Gisela Eckstein, Benary's former wife.

such an extent that this political intervention in the academic sphere did not appear as censorship. The Stasi was key for legitimizing the party's intrusion into the Academy of Sciences. With subtle force, as the following shows in detail, the Stasi managed to establish the belief that dogmatism is that which is actually *against* the party line, and that free scientific debate is that which practically *advances* the cause of the party. A show debate can obviously be considered as a form of censorship, rather than an alternative to it. Whatever terms one prefers, the debate paved the way for how censorship would later work in East Germany, that is, on the one hand through self-censorship, and on the other through the acceptance of submitting one's research to a central (party) plan. Both minimized the apparent conflict with an open debate culture and with a constitution that guaranteed freedom of expression. "There is no censorship here," Ulbricht would proclaim at the 30th Plenum of the CC in January 1957.[10]

To be sure, the state power that was being executed was subtler than that during Stalin's famous Moscow show trials. "The revisionism debate was not a Stalinist method," debate participant Heinz Paragenings, a historian born in West Germany, reminded me in a personal conversation. But he also added that the consensus that emerged to call Behrens and Benary "revisionist" had in fact been a matter of force. It took from the end of January until April 1957 to reach this consensus. But first, what was the booklet all about?

The Draft

After Khrushchev's speech became public, the air at the Institute for Economics was thick with hopes for change. Behrens' team – young economists in their early twenties – were enthused about possible changes. They included, next to Arne Benary, his assistant at the statistical office, Dieter Mann, Heinz Paragenings, and about ten other

---

[10] See Herzberg (2006: 463); on censorship, see Darnton (2014). Throughout the existence of the GDR, censorship continued to exist in the form of print permissions (*Druckgenehmigung*), which was accepted as normal. Also, the control of access to Western literature and specific authors, closed library sections, publications and translations abroad, international conference participation, and so forth became normal. Textbook production was subject to the approval of higher-level party authorities, such as the Party Schools or the Politburo itself. Topics such as the decision-making of the party, military economics, or the role of the Soviet Union were taboo.

young scholars.[11] Their official task was to inquire into the foundation of the new state, that is, the transition from capitalism to socialism, which included the difficult question regarding to what extent state and market categories were needed for state planning that hitherto was run as a rigid bureaucracy of norms. How should production costs enter the plan, and how should the plan account for (changing) demand? In the hope of a renewed debate about such questions, Behrens wrote a programmatic piece deploring the lack of creativity among East German economists titled: "About the State of Economic Science" (Steiner 2000: 111–115).[12] He linked the dogmatism of his colleagues with the phenomenon of bureaucracy, both bourgeois holdovers:

Dogmatism is a form of bourgeois ideology ... Dogmatism occupies the same class-hostile place in our ranks as bureaucracy – both belong together like base and superstructure. For can we imagine the bureaucrat who thinks, that is, who is not a dogmatist? And can we imagine a dogmatist who does not cling to what makes the bureaucrat's life dear and worthwhile: regulations, paragraphs and citations?[13]

Regarding the self-criticism of past mistakes – the epistemic virtue Khrushchev highlighted at the congress – Behrens concluded, in a Kantian fashion, that "we, ourselves, have to battle against our past mistakes. If we forget this, then we forget the most important lesson of the 20th Party Congress: *to think for yourself.*"[14] Behrens sent the text to the party newspaper *Neues Deutschland* in order to reach a large audience, but it was not to happen. The editors who acted like referees rejected it for "both its tone and content."[15] The meaning of dogmatism was still to be decided.

In the same free-thinking spirit, Behrens and his assistant Benary finalized the draft of their booklet, getting it ready to print in the summer of 1956. They again took serious issue with the bureaucracy of planning. In the light of apparent problems with the first Five-Year Plan, Behrens and Benary contrasted mere administration with "economic governance" using economic "levers." As Benary argued, economic governance meant that the "spontaneous labor force," which was at the heart of Marx's thought, should be taken into account when defining the domain of

---

[11] For a complete list see ABBAW: Zentralinstitut für Wirtschaftswissenschaften, file 284.
[12] See ABBAW: NRB, file 77.   [13] Ibid.: 113.   [14] Ibid.: 115.
[15] May 5, 1956, ABBAW: NRB, file 268.

"conscious planning." This also put forth the question of cost accounting and the criteria of efficiency. Decentralization in the form of self-administration could be a means of using the "law of value" under socialism, because only under socialism do prices actually reflect value and thus lead to efficiency and, by extension, growth. By contrast, under capitalism allocation was distorted by capital interests. In Behrens' chapter of the booklet we read:

Just as centralization is not the obligatory form in which the socialist state is run, the central directive is not the obligatory form by which the socialist economy is managed. As the economic laws of socialist production take hold, i.e. as socialist production relations consolidate themselves, management of the economy by central directive must decrease in proportion, otherwise it will become an obstacle for further development. (1957: 117–118)

In this way, Behrens and Benary critiqued the orthodox voluntarist notion of the economy and the stark contrast with the inner dynamic of a capitalist economy that results from competition and profit maximization. Benary criticized the state of the debate about planning methods for not yet being scientific.

If up to today, the fact that the political economy of socialism has not yet become what it should be, ... is not least due to the fact that we have excluded the methods of planned economic management ... from critical analysis, ... and thus did not escape the danger of limiting ourselves on the one hand to the catechizing treatment of political-economic doctrines, and on the other hand to the mere interpretation of the economic policy of the government. (1957: 3)

Note, however, that this ambition of being more scientific meant merely to freely treat ideas that were taboo in the last decades of Soviet discussions. There is very little actual detailed analysis of the institutions that coordinate between the spontaneous labor force and the conscious plan. In today's terms, their argument remains on the level of political philosophy rather than economic analysis.

Their inspiration for the practicability of decentral planning was the Yugoslav model of workers' self-governance in contrast to the Soviet model. In Behrens' group at the academy, Edvard Kardelj's famous Oslo speech that had informed Tito's reforms was discussed. In May 1956, Behrens and Benary traveled to Milan to meet a Yugoslav economist, possibly Kardelj himself. Later in the fall of 1956, Benary traveled to Yugoslavia and Bulgaria with his friend and Kohlmey's assistant, Kurt Zieschang. For Benary, Stalinism was a system rather than a personal cult. Ulbricht, however, had already played down the question of Stalinism in March 1956, first by reducing Stalinism to a personal cult and then denying that there ever was a personal cult in East Germany.[16] Behrens also demonstrated distance from the party's blind Soviet faith. He inquired about the reparations payments to the Soviet Union that he learned were much higher than had been officially reported. In a mid-November trip that was organized by Benary, Behrens sent his assistant, Dieter Mann, to see Fritz Baade at the Kiel Institute for the World Economy to retrieve data on the payments.[17]

Critical of Soviet-inspired centralization, Behrens and Benary's most provocative thesis in the booklet revived Marx's notion of the "withering away" of the state as part of the bourgeois superstructure – an Old Communist utopia almost forgotten in the future envisioned under Stalin:

The view that the state can do everything, and that every affair, even the most private, has to be managed and controlled by the state, is not socialist, but "Prussian," that is Junker-monopolistic. Socialist, that is, Marxist-Leninist, is the view of the withering away of the state as soon as the socialist relations of production solidify and the capitalist threat becomes ineffective; but this means that the self-government of the working masses by the state must find its complement in the self-government of the economy. (Behrens 1957: 125)

Behrens knew how provocative the booklet potentially was but hoped that it might steer discussions in the right direction: "I am aware that my remarks touch upon some dogmas. I am sure that I will be 'forgiven' if these remarks provide the impetus for a discussion that brings us closer to solving some of the problems I have indicated" (ibid.: 122). Until the fall of 1956 it all seemed to happen just like that. The booklet, ready in print at the popular publishing house *Die Wirtschaft*, potentially could reach a large audience. One Stasi informant at the institute reported discussions dating from February and July 1956 about drafts

---

[16] Ulbricht's reaction to the 20th Party Congress in March 1956 is published in *Neues Deutschland*, March 4, titled "Über den XX. Parteitag der Kommunistischen Partei der Sowjetunion."

[17] See for example SAPMO-BArch, DY 30 J IV 2-2-549, 12–14.

of Benary's chapter. The general attitude was positive and engaged: "it was a good manuscript, thus the discussion was vivid," Kohlmey had concluded.[18] Indeed, according to a later witness, Johannes Puhlmann, an editor of the publishing house, and Karl Kampfert, who would become the fiercest critic of Benary and Behrens, were at this time in favor of their booklet, believing that it would be in line with the party's direction in the near future.[19]

Things changed when Soviet troops shut off Nagy's democratic-oriented government in Hungary on November 4. Even if the Hungarian uprising was hardly led by intellectuals, let alone economists, First Secretary Ulbricht clearly feared that the same could happen in East Germany. In addition, the so-called Harich group was imprisoned in early November.[20] Led by Wolfgang Harich, a professor of philosophy at Humboldt University, the group proposed ideas for which the label revisionist might actually be appropriate: they proposed free elections, a German path to socialism independent from the Soviet Union, the reunification of a neutral Germany, and collaboration with West German social democrats. Thus, at this point Ulbricht changed gears in order to maintain power.[21]

At the same moment in the institute, there was a large consensus that democratic change would happen. Still in November, the party-group sent a joint letter to the party leaders (Steiner 2000: 120). In the name of the consolidation of power and better communication with the people, they lamented the lack of information – some listened to the forbidden United States sector radio – and demanded economic reforms. But this letter was the beginning of an intervention of the party apparatus jointly with the secret police that would reverse this consensus in a matter of months. During the same period, the show trials against the Harich group took place.

---

[18] Reported by Ulisch GI "Walter," MfS AIM 2981-62-2-1, 99.
[19] Reported by Zieschang, MfS AOP 1012-57-2, 147.
[20] On the Harich group, see Hoeft (1990) and Brockmann (2019).
[21] For a study of the overall factors that helped Ulbricht to maintain power, see Granville (2006), Connelly (1997), and Herzberg (2006). A wave of protests spread through the country. Veterinary medicine students at Humboldt University, to give but one example, wished to abolish the Marxist-Leninist basic studies. Supported by senior physicians, they went to the sector border for a demonstration (Vogt 2012; Wolle 2006).

A Necessary Debate about False Theories

The first round of events took place in December 1956 and January 1957 when the party came to terms with the fact that mere censorship would not resolve the issue and that it needed to stage a debate.

It began harmlessly enough. On November 13, Behrens received a letter from the publishing house *Die Wirtschaft* informing him that they had asked Kampfert from the CC Department for Science and Propaganda if quoting Georg Lukács, a member of the Hungarian Nagy government, was a good idea at this moment.[22] During the following weeks, Kampfert (or maybe Hager or even Ulbricht himself) made up his mind. On December 13, the CC Secretariat accepted Kampfert's proposal that the "revisionist" booklet should not be shipped (it must have been Ulbricht who used this word for the first time). "Some of the arguments in the booklet currently present the grave danger of politically disorienting the reader and demobilizing the necessary measures to consolidate our state power," the minutes of the CC Secretariat say.[23] All dozen members of the CC Secretariat now knew exactly what Ulbricht thought of the booklet. At the same meeting, the CC learned of Behrens' attempt to get the reparations payments data from Kiel, which launched a party trial against him, Mann, and Benary.

As decided by the Secretariat, the party-group of the publishing house had to discuss the party's decision in Kampfert's presence. The group did not unanimously agree to withhold the booklet. Heinz Brandt, the engineering editor, wanted to release it. It was this decision of the publishing house, rather than the one by the Secretariat, which was communicated in a letter to Behrens and Benary. In the same week, on December 21, the party-group meeting of the institute had to discuss this letter from the publishing house.[24] Behrens and Benary were angry and said that they would neither change the text nor wish to see it published by *Die Wirtschaft*. They also speculated rightly that the publishing house was asked by the Politburo to write the letter. The institute's party secretary, Bichtler, objected and asserted that the publishing house had acted on its own. The discussion was heated.

---

[22] Puhlmann to Behrens, SAPMO-BArch, DY 30 83342, 38–39.
[23] Secretariat minutes, SAPMO-BArch, DY30 56214, 3.
[24] See report Ulisch, GI "Walter," MfS AIM 2981-62-2, 55–61.

After the meeting Bichtler reported to the CC Secretariat that "the majority of comrades in the party-group shared strong sentiments against the party apparatus and the 'regulation' of scientific work."[25] Another Stasi informant pointed to the risk that if the party refused to release the booklet, Behrens and Benary would use that against the Politburo.[26]

Indeed, there was a great deal of confusion regarding proper behavior among the economists at the institute. On January 7, Kampfert informed CC science secretary Hager about the current discussions.

How should the scientist behave if the results of his investigations contradict the views of the party leadership or party decisions? How does a scientist behave when his research results cannot be published due to the political situation? ... Can there be a scientific debate if the scientist cannot publish his research results? What role and tasks does the party apparatus have in connection with the above questions?[27]

The party leadership clearly saw that the integrity of its relationship with the academy was at risk. The booklet had to be released, but in a different form. And so, on January 15, the Secretariat decided that a revised version of the booklet should be printed in the more specialist journal *Wirtschaftswissenschaften*, but should include counter-statements written by other economists. "Since the views contained in the booklet are widely used in academia and other circles," say the minutes of the CC Secretariat, "it is necessary ... to have a debate about these false theories."[28] The debate was necessary not because it was unclear if the theory was true or false, but because those who believed it was true had to be convinced that it was actually false. Behrens and Benary should be beaten at their own game and on their own ground so that the political intervention would appear as the result of a genuine debate and not censorship plain and simple.

For Behrens and Benary, the game that was being played was obvious. They demanded that their text should not be published at all. They wrote to the editors, pointing out that Behrens "had no intention to be marked as a revisionist." But their demand was simply ignored.[29]

---

[25] Report in SAPMO-BArch, DY 30 83342, 47.
[26] GI "Elli," MfS AOP 1012-57-1.
[27] Report in SAPMO-BArch, DY 30 83342, 48.
[28] Secretariat minutes, SAPMO-BArch, DY 30-J VI 2-2-522, 7.
[29] January 24, SAPMO-BArch, DY 30 83342.

A discussion of their booklet was put on the agenda for the following party-group meetings, discussions that were decisive for the party not to lose touch with the community of economists. It was then that the Stasi came into play.

Operation Theory

In January 1957, it appeared that only a minority of the institute's party-group supported the party's point of view that the booklet was revisionist. The exceptions were Bichtler and Turley, respectively the secretary and manager (*Parteigruppenorganisator*) of the party-group. What could the Stasi do in order to turn around the consensus?

Considering that the majority of scholars were upset with the party, it was not clear whom the Stasi should target. Until December, Captain Kießling had no real focus in his explorations. "At first it was not immediately possible to assess which comrades took an unclear position because of their mere petty-bourgeois attitude and who was actually damaging for the party," Kießling wrote, probably in early January.[30] But on January 19, Kießling and Lieutenant Seiß met with Bichtler, who delivered a first clue. He reported that there were rumors that a *second booklet* authored by Behrens and Benary, more outspoken in its political implications, had been circulating among Behrens' assistants. He also reported a conversation with Zieschang, Kohlmey's assistant and Benary's friend, who claimed to know of the second text: "Zieschang said in a drunken state that Behrens and Benary wanted to wind up (*aufrollen*) the GDR. When the KP wanted to know more about [what Zieschang knew], he turned silent."[31] The second booklet does not appear in any of the archives, but it might have been destroyed by Benary at the first signs of state intervention. "If there had been a second text, my father would have mentioned it at some point sooner or later," his daughter Hannamaria Loschinski later commented.[32]

This rumor about the existence of a second text allowed the Stasi to single out Benary and cast him in a light that could potentially create division in the institute. "The past few weeks have provided evidence

---

[30] Benary file, MfS AOP 1012-57-1, 17; see also Ulisch's, GI "Walter," reports in MfS AIM 2981-62-2, 18.
[31] Zwischenbericht, January 24, 1957, MfS AOP 1012-57-1, 80.
[32] Hannamaria Loschinski. Interview by author.

that Benary is the spokesman in the party-damaging discussions in the Academy of Sciences, who uses his position and scientific status to foster party-damaging beliefs," Kießling wrote.[33] In contrast to Behrens, who might have been too central to the institute, Benary was the ideal victim, one who could be made a showcase for what happens if one diverges from the party line. By polarizing the institute members, the Stasi could create division in the debate and thus dissolve the subtlety of the existing arguments. And what polarizes more than confidential personal defamation? Thus, the Stasi opened "observation operation 37/57" with the code name "Theory." Its mission, in its own terms, was to acquire information about the true beliefs of the institute members and Benary in particular. But what this mission actually meant in the academic context was to develop ad hominem arguments that should undermine Benary's political credibility, resulting in his dismissal from the institute. Thus, the express aim of Operation Theory was "to isolate Comrade Benary and to support the work of the party-group such that Benary, with our help, would be ultimately removed from the institute."[34] The Stasi, as police, brought in a logic of reasoning about persons into the academic sphere. The difficult balancing act was, however, that despite this logic, the academic sphere had to maintain its autonomy without appearing as the mere mouthpiece of the party.

Kießling thus rolled out the full Stasi machinery. They looked into Benary's entire past, his private life, and his family; they interrogated his former student colleagues in Leipzig and his neighbors, surveilled his apartment, read his letters, and recorded his telephone calls. His secretaries were asked to work as informants reporting about telephone calls in the office. But these make for less interesting documents as there was a gap of expertise. They also considered recruiting a "slim" woman to pry information from him; Benary was known to "have no firm attitude about the opposite sex" and so he might reveal his true beliefs to a female informant. But there is no evidence that such a woman was ever recruited. After several weeks of inquiry the Stasi found little evidence in his past that could discredit him, apart from his participation in the so-called nepotistic "Brandis circle," a "petit-bourgeois group" of Behrens' assistants at University of Leipzig who knew each other from teaching at the same school of finance in Brandis. They

---

[33] MfS AOP 1012-57-1, 17.   [34] Ibid.: 16.

supposedly denied jobs to other comrades, and thus prevented that "class-conscious and reliable comrades could initiate a progressive development at the institute."[35] Benary was considered a "favorite" (*Günstling*) of Behrens, became party member merely out of careerist reasons, and was responsible for a petit-bourgeois atmosphere in the academy institute.

Clearly that was not enough, and the first meeting of the party-group, on January 23, indeed went in Behrens and Benary's favor. Ziller, Kampfert, and Reinhold from the CC were present. They openly claimed that the booklet did not merely contain false opinions but also revisionist conceptions. Behrens, however, defended the booklet, arguing that the CC members had not properly read it, nor were they in a position to judge. He claimed his right to do basic research independent of the current political situation, as the party had asked him to do. He also addressed the nature of scientific debates when he contested that his opponents used the argument of preserving the unity of the party against the possibility of scientific debates. He again opposed the idea of publishing the booklet. After the meeting, Behrens' assistants also discredited the CC members' scientific judgment, as Ulisch, GI Walter, reported:

Paragenings stated that the staff of the CC, in particular Comrade Reinhold and Comrade Kampfert ... were not entitled to discuss scientific questions. They were not scientists and have no publications. Their abilities would not be enough to judge such questions; he thinks their only task in the entire discussion is to defend Comrade Ulbricht's line.[36]

That is where matters stood until a few days later First Secretary Ulbricht himself intervened.

Not Authority Only

The first turning point in the debate was an intervention from above. At the 30th Plenum of the CC at the end of January, in front of the

---

[35] See Benary file, MfS AOP 1012-57, 126. In addition, the Stasi identified a connection with Kurt Vieweg, in particular with his assistant Marga Langendorf, who was arrested for a revisionist agricultural reform programme (MfS AOP 468-59-4). Vieweg apparently tried to hire Benary as an assistant. For the entire Stasi case against Vieweg, see Scholz (1997).

[36] Benary file, MfS AOP 1012-57-1, 136.

entire East German public, Ulbricht intervened directly in the debate. After announcing a major shift in German–German policy that West Germany first needed to develop before unification, he cited and critiqued Behrens and Benary's still unpublished booklet, along with the Petöfi Club in Hungary, Kardelj's ideas in Yugoslavia, and the Harich group – all put in one and the same box of revisionism-feeding imperialist forces. He thus watered down the meaning of "revisionism" to a mere catchword for party enemies. Ulbricht singled out Benary for being "at war with Marxist theory" (Ulbricht 1957: 50). With reference to Mao's Hundred Flowers Campaign of pluralist criticism as an engine of progress in socialism, he said: "The weed of revisionism is … neither a flower nor beautiful, nor a useful plant" (ibid.: 53). And he added his version of the crux of all Marxist political epistemology:

> For us Marxist-Leninists, the pursuit of objective truth serves to elaborate that political direction, which … enhances the power of the workers and peasants, and which strengthens the party's leading role, influence and connection with the masses. Any scientific debate that serves this purpose is valuable and welcome. (Ibid.)

Ulbricht dedicated an entire section of his speech to the struggle against dogmatism and thus claimed political authority regarding the meaning of scientific debate. He called to fight against the "simple reproduction of dogmas without connection to life and praxis" (ibid.: 72). The further battle over economic ideas would take place on this very epistemological ground. After Ulbricht's speech, it was clear that the result of the debate at the institute would attract the attention of the entire political, academic, and also public audience.[37]

The Stasi officers hoped that with Ulbricht's backing they could undermine the consensus at the institute. Some days after the speech, the officers planned the upcoming meetings of the party-group.

> Next week, another party gathering on the booklet will take place. They will discuss the theory of spontaneity and the market mechanism. According to Comrade Morgenstern, this will force Behrens and Benary to take a position regarding freedom of expression. At the same time, this meeting will serve to show the other comrades that the theories are wrong and can lead to

---

[37] Immediately after Ulbricht's speech, hardliners Robert Naumann and Alfred Lemmnitz, the president of the Higher School for Economics, were the first to blow the horn of the revisionism campaign to come. See Naumann (1957) and Lemmnitz (1957).

dangerous political conclusions. To this end, the existing GI and KP must take an offensive position and, above all, stress the danger of such ideas in order to isolate Behrens and Benary. In the second meeting, which would have to take place in two to three weeks, the GI and KP should openly address the fact of Behrens and Benary being against the party and call for removal from the institute and the initiation of a party trial.[38]

But this was not to happen. Ulbricht's authority was not enough to force consensus. The two meetings of the party-group in February did not settle the debate. At the first meeting on February 15, Hager and Kampfert were present, Behrens had to be at the statistical office, and Benary, in response to Ulbricht, gave a long personal statement (*Stellungnahme*) blaming and defending himself. His theory wrongly presumed, he said, that the party wished for fast and fundamental change. He insisted he had made only theoretical mistakes, thus showing loyalty to the party. But when it came to accepting the label of revisionism, he candidly expressed his doubts:

It is particularly difficult for me to gain clarity about the question of revisionism. Nobody will expect me to condemn right now as false all my theoretical ideas that I have developed over a long period of time. Above all, nobody will be served if I engage in "general self-criticism," without being really convinced. Some things have become clear to me, some not yet.[39]

Benary's statement proves his continued commitment to honesty in the face of an increasingly fake debate. But it had little success. Hager and Kampfert repeated that Behrens and Benary's ideas were not merely theoretical but ideological mistakes. The strategy was clear: if the issue was theoretical, the party would have to allow pluralism of opinion; if it was ideological, it would be possible to use ad hominem arguments provided by the Stasi in order to discredit Behrens and Benary politically.

Ulbricht's speech left his mark on the discussion, and some switched sides. Zieschang, who basically repeated Ulbricht's speech, exercised self-criticism for his previous support of Behrens and Benary. Their mistakes, he said, went back before the 20th Party Congress, that is, they were not historically contingent but were more deeply anchored in their personal attitudes. But not everyone felt obliged to change sides. Paragenings said that *some* aspects of the booklet were wrong while

[38] Kießling, February 5, 1957, MfS AOP 1012-57-1, 123.
[39] Benary statement, SAPMO-BArch, DY 30 83342, 155.

others were right, which made the informant describe his attitude pejoratively as conciliatory (*versöhnlerisch*). If one showed an understanding for both sides of a conflict, an attitude that is valued in bourgeois intellectual cultures, one revealed oneself to be shaky in one's attitude and to lack class consciousness. Also the sluggish work of the party-group, that is, Bichtler, was blamed, who in turn blamed the lack of unity among the party leadership.[40] In the end most institute members agreed that the text contained mistakes but was not revisionist. Therefore, Hager concluded, more discussion was necessary.[41]

At the next meeting on February 27, Hager, Kampfert, and Reinhold were present, as was Behrens. This time the counter-statements to be published jointly with the two articles of the booklet were discussed, written by Kampfert, Hermann Scheler, Humboldt (a philosopher of historical materialism), Helmut Richter of the CC Institute for Social Sciences, and Herbert Luck, an economist from Rostock. Marx's withering away of the state, so ran one argument, consisted in a gradual disappearing of the compulsory character of the state rather than of its central economic function. Behrens was enraged. As if the historical meaning of revisionism would still matter at this point, he refused the label and explained why his ideas did not question Marx's basic principles. He did not elaborate on the positive role of the state because that was simply not the topic of the booklet. He called the counter-statement written against him a "defamation" and openly said what others must have felt, that "at present a campaign is run against him ... They try to plant things on him ... What happens has nothing to do with a scientific debate."[42] This was Behrens' last intervention in the debate, as he did not attend another meeting. He must have believed that everything he said would be turned against him, and so gave up believing in the rules of the game.

Trying to plant things on them was exactly what the Stasi planned for the coming meeting. The decisive testimony that would supplement Ulbricht's authority came from Zieschang, Benary's friend who turned out to be the informer. During February, Stasi Officer Kießling set up three meetings to talk things out (*Aussprache*) that were carried out first by Bichtler and Morgenstern, the party organizer of the institute at

---

[40] In Ulisch's report, GI "Walter," in MfS AIM 2981-62-2, 79.   [41] Ibid.: 89.
[42] Bichtler KP "Bischak," MfS AOP 1012-57-1, 160.

the CC, then by Kampfert and officers Kießling and Seiß themselves. First with hesitance, but then with increasing assertiveness and confidence, Kurt Zieschang spread all sorts of half-truths and discrediting private information. He put forth class arguments, arguing that Benary became a party member out of career interests rather than conviction, while describing Behrens as a bourgeois intellectual: "Behrens wants to represent his own doctrine, as every bourgeois scientist wants to have a theory associated with his name."[43] He said that Behrens had contacts with the enemy such as the West German social democrat Viktor Agartz (which would have indeed shown a revisionist attitude). He testified that Benary, in a drunken state at a garden party after a sailing trip, spoke of the Polish intervention as "red fascism." He claimed, "Behrens said that the time of changes in the GDR had been missed. One should better bury it and rebuild socialism from anew."[44] And yet he assured the Stasi that Behrens was less radical than Benary. Regarding the second booklet, Zieschang presented details of its actual contents: Behrens and Benary claimed that workers in East Germany were exploited and should be considered as state wage-labor just like workers in capitalism. But the most critical piece of information was the following:

Some weeks ago Zieschang walked into Benary's room; [another comrade] was also present, who had several pages in his hand and behaved very secretively. Zieschang, who wanted to read them, did not get them, so he tore them from [this] comrade. However, they were immediately taken away by Benary, who pocketed them. Zieschang said he had recognised, because of the lettering and a few sentences he could read, some sort of program that entails slogans such as "freedom of expression, freedom of the press" and the like.[45]

These were the slogans of the Harich group. In later meetings, Benary would deny that this had happened. Paragenings recalled in a personal conversation that the program did in fact exist. But if the program had really existed, recalled Benary's former wife, also a trained economist, they would have discussed it at home.[46] If discussed at home, however,

---

[43] Zieschang "Aussprache," MfS AOP 1012-57-1, 120.   [44] Ibid.

[45] Ibid.: 112. Ernst Wollweber, head of the Stasi, also received a separate report about this meeting (SAPMO-BArch, DY 30 47840, March 6), in which the program was referred to as the second booklet – which thus might have been identical.

[46] Heinz Paragenings. Interview with author; Gisela Eckstein. Interview with author.

Benary might also have expressed the wish to keep it confidential. Whether or not it really existed, the program soon began to exist as a matter of fact within the debate (and Paragenings might have remembered this fact rather than the program itself). In any event, he and many at the institute did not agree with these claims made in "the program." As Marxists-Leninists, everyone thought that democratization had to come from below, from economic reform, and not from above, from political reform. The Stasi knew of this disagreement well and now hoped to finally break through the stubborn sympathies for Behrens and Benary.

Events outside the institute also played in favor of the Stasi. On March 9, a verdict was reached about Harich: guilty, with a punishment of ten years in prison. Steinberger, for a short time the assistant of Behrens, was also put in jail.[47] Benary now understood what was at stake and also the risk that Zieschang represented to him. As Kießling reported, Benary "recently called Comrade Zieschang by telephone and begged him to keep quiet about the conversations they had. As Comrade Zieschang pointed out that all things had to be clarified by the party, Benary retreated noticeably."[48] At home Benary dealt with his one-month-old second child, adding to the fatigue caused by the discussions. The pressure left its mark. He got sick and left for his father's town. His wife began seriously worrying: "I hoped they would not arrest him," she recalled:

After the thirtieth plenum, the situation turned severe. He once came home, dropped into the chair, still wearing his hat and coat. "Can you imagine what a crazy day I had today?" ... To get home, he first drove to S-Bahn Friedrichstraße before taking the train to Niederschöneweide. The S-Bahn

---

[47] In addition to Zieschang's testimony, Captain Kießling gained another point by organizing, on January 31, a special interrogation of Bernhard Steinberger in prison about Behrens (MfS AOP 1012-57, 162). Between his release from prison in the Soviet Union in October 1955 until renewed imprisonment because of involvement in the Harich group, Steinberger was an assistant in Behrens' department. Steinberger mentioned that they would put Behrens in charge of economic affairs once their democratic reforms, without Ulbricht, were put into place. Behrens would not have liked to be associated with their entire program, but this mention could clearly stoke the ad hominem attacks in the debate.

[48] Kießling report, MfS AOP 1012-57-1, 148.

was still running normally in West Berlin as there was not yet the wall. At the first stop, it flashed in his head: "If I now, here, get off, all the trouble is over!" I was shocked, and I realised what pressure he was under. But he did not get off.[49]

The Showdown

The showdown was planned for March 13. All the information acquired by the Stasi, in particular from Zieschang's testimony, was revealed. Two meetings were scheduled, both dedicated solely to Benary: a department head meeting followed by a party-group meeting. When Zieschang repeated his testimony in the first meeting, Benary was stunned, as GI Elli reported:

Comrade Zieschang has talked about many of the details he knew through his close personal connection to Benary from the past. Obviously, Benary had not expected that and was very scared and became increasingly insecure. During the break, he said: "Now you get to know people." That referred to Comrade Zieschang . . . After the meeting, Benary was extremely nervous and insecure. For the first time we have managed to unsettle his arrogant position.[50]

As if in court, Behrens' other assistants were also called into the room and were asked separately about Benary's program. As had Benary himself, they denied its existence. Bichtler reported that he believed that Benary and the other assistants coordinated their statements beforehand. Indeed, the telephone calls of Benary and other assistants were reported in which it became clear that they prepared for the party-group meeting.[51] But their discussion was theoretical, and they did not mention a "program." At the end of the department head meeting it was decided that Benary would be dismissed as vice-director of Behrens' department. But the more important party-group meeting was to follow.

At this meeting, party secretary Bichtler presented the evidence acquired by the Stasi mainly from Zieschang. However, nobody really reacted to it. It all seemed so constructed. Paragenings felt offended: "He (Paragenings) refuses constructing artificially (political) *factions*."[52]

---

49 Gisela Eckstein. Interview with author.
50 Report "Elli," MfS AOP 1012-57-2, 182.   51 Ibid.: 189–194.
52 KP Bischak, MfS AOP 1012-57-1, 201.

Mann referred to the general confusion in the institute after the 20th Party Congress. And Johann Lorenz Schmidt, former head of the history of economic doctrines group, said that it was wrong to judge comrades only one-sidedly. Bichtler proposed that Benary be removed from the institute, but to no avail, as a consensus had not been achieved:

At the end of the speech, the KP [Bichtler] demanded that Benary be removed from the institute. The discussions in the group meeting, however, had no success ... Most of the comrades said nothing about it, some said that what the party leadership says is of course very bad, but one should check this all first. Not a single comrade said anything about the KP's demand to remove Benary from the institute. It was agreed to hold another group meeting next week and continue the discussion.[53]

In his further report, KP Bichtler asked the Stasi officers for more evidence to discredit Benary but there was nothing more to deliver. One option was left: in the final meeting on March 26, as Paragenings recalled, there were two officers keeping records in addition to the members of the Politburo. Their identity was not revealed but everyone knew that it must have been the Stasi. Most likely it had been the two officers Kießling and Seiß themselves. Paragenings always felt free to say what he thought. But then no more, he recalled.[54]

Kampfert opened the meeting by increasing pressure: the CC expected the institute's position in writing by the next day. He, instead of Bichtler, proposed the resolution to declare the booklet revisionist. Everyone understood that, as the Stasi planned, "the aim of the meeting was to force everyone to take a position."[55] Party loyalty seemed to leave no choice, and yet, some did not speak out, and some were still against the resolution, which shows how profound was the trust in the party's appreciation of truthfulness and honesty. Nevertheless, nobody voted against the resolution. Ulisch GI Walter added, as if the Stasi would not know, that those from Behrens' group had only agreed on the resolution because they saw no other way out for themselves.[56] The resolution was presented, it says, as the result of a "thorough, severe, and serious discussion."[57] It declared Behrens and Benary's booklet revisionist because of the opposition of administration and (scientific)

[53] Ibid. [54] Heinz Paragenings. Interview with author.
[55] Kießling, March 12, 1957, MfS AOP 1012-57-1, 185.
[56] Walter report, MfS AIM 2981-62, 138.
[57] Benary file, MfS AOP 1012-57-2, 28.

economic method, and a general disregard for the leading role of the party. But, moreover, it stated that Behrens and Benary behaved in an *unscholarly* manner; in other words, in an astonishing and duplicitous feat of reasoning, the party's claim to the scholarly virtues that make for a scientific debate was maintained.

Just as we reject the content of the work, so do we reject the method ... Both comrades had to be aware of the nature of their views. For example, although Comrade Benary knew there were others in the Institute who did not share his views ... a general discussion of their views was bypassed. Such a method is all the more strange because both comrades repeatedly and urgently demanded the development of scientific debate and they had to be clear that such fundamental issues would first have to be discussed at the Institute.[58]

Everyone knew that this resolution would mean Benary's removal from the institute and the end of his academic career. He was to be sent into industry. The resolution was instantly published in the third edition of *Wirtschaftswissenschaft*. The Stasi had attained its goal.

In May, the party-group of the institute sent another statement to the CC Secretariat, not published, in which they explained why they initially supported the ideas of Behrens and Benary. They blamed a "petty-bourgeois atmosphere" that fostered an "individualist work ethos." Behrens' notions of self-governance were too "theoretical" and "too far from practice," and the mistake was that they were not thoroughly discussed, and thus were treated dogmatically. Dogmatism, "being alien to life," and "fetishism" were all equated with that which is not in the current interest of the party. Thus, the Marxist commitment to practical relevance was mobilized against anything beyond the status quo.

It is imperative that the party-groups watch over an open, factual, undogmatic and comradely atmosphere that includes, however, ruthlessness against deviations from Marxism-Leninism. Petty-bourgeois sensitivities must be persistently fought. We must convince ourselves that we can only live up to our political-ideological obligations if all important issues are discussed to the end.[59]

A scientific debate, therefore, was that which furthered the cause of the party. The link between dogmatism and revisionism, and thus the party–knowledge nexus, had been forged.

[58] Ibid.: 29.   [59] Party-group statement, SAPMO-BArch, DY 30 83342, 97.

The Debate after the Debate

In the spring of 1957, the texts of the booklet were published in *Wirtschaftswissenschaft* jointly with the counter-statements.[60] The "debate" and its resulting "consensus" were made public. But this was only the beginning of further rituals against revisionism. For Behrens, what followed was a series of repeated self-incriminating "personal statements" (*Stellungnahmen*) that were supposed to show that he himself admitted his errors and changed his mind in the course of the debate. The first was written in June 1957 as a letter to the Politburo, which decided to publish it in *Wirtschaftswissenschaft*.[61] He responded to the counter-statements mentioned earlier, but still pointed to the contradictions between the economic base and East Germany's state superstructure that hindered economic growth:

One might say that my answers are wrong. But if one does not agree with an answer to a scientific question, one has to give another answer. Of course, the admissibility of my question can be questioned. This would mean, however, that the admissibility of dealing with objective contradictions regarding the growth rate of a socialist society is called into question. (Behrens 1958: 36)

Hypocrisy, for Behrens, would mean giving up his deep trust in a socialist society, which he never did. Thus, his statement was again published jointly with other articles showing that his amendments to his original ideas were not sufficient. One of them was written by the two direct allies of the Stasi, Karl Bichtler and Kurt Zieschang (Bichtler and Zieschang 1958). The pattern was clear: suspicion against Behrens was operational in keeping up revisionism as a watchword against internal party critiques.

The official party penalty for Behrens came in July 1957 for his acquisition of the reparations payment data from Baade in Kiel. He and Benary received a "rebuke" (*Rüge*) and Dieter Mann a "warning" because all three "lacked vigilance ... that Baade used them [these statistics] for campaigning against the Soviet Union," the verdict

---

[60] See the entire issue of *Wirtschaftswissenschaft*, 3. Sonderheft (1957). Comparing the printed but unshipped versions of fall 1956 (Behrens and Benary 1956) and the published version, I did not find evidence of any revisions.

[61] Behrens (1958: 31–38); see also SAPMO-BArch, DY30 47889. The other statements were Behrens (1960: 650–651); Behrens (1961).

said.[62] Only then was it officially decided that Behrens had to be removed as director of the statistical office, and that "because of the bad influence that the comrade exerted on the younger scientific staff of the Institute for Economics, he can no longer remain deputy head of this institute."[63] The change in his career was thus presented as *not* being the result of his "revisionist" position. Behrens would remain at the academy, first in the group on the history of economic doctrines, then as the head of a small group on labor productivity.

But Behrens and Benary were not the only ones who had to change careers in the wake of the events. Paragenings stayed for one more year and then was likewise sent into industry.[64] Dieter Mann remained for two more years and then left for West Germany. Ulbricht also asked Kohlmey personally to publish a statement regarding his responsibility for the events at the institute (Kohlmey 1958).[65] Fred Oelßner then replaced him as director of the institute. This was a curious choice, since Oelßner had lost all his CC functions as a consequence of the dismissal of other political victims of the revisionism campaign, notably Politburo member Karl Schirdewan.[66] The academy's institute thus became the "parking lot" for those diverging from the party line. Founded according to the Soviet model as the highest authority in academic ranks, the Central Economics Institute at the Academy of Sciences was scientifically downgraded and lost its leading function in economic sciences. Bichtler, instead, was awarded 150 DM from the Stasi for his successful collaboration, and was soon promoted to party secretary of the entire Academy of Sciences and later director of the

---

[62] Secretariat minutes, SAPMO-BArch, DY 30 J IV 2-2-549, 12–14.   [63] Ibid.

[64] Paragenings later had a comeback in academia, receiving a doctoral degree in 1969 in applied economics, publishing until late in his life; see Wolf and Paragenings (2004).

[65] For his own later account of this text, see Kohlmey (1992). Kohlmey's role in the context of the debate described in this chapter is complex and would require a separate treatment. Suffice to say that putting him on equal terms with Behrens does not do justice to his role; see Steiner (1996).

[66] Politburo member Schirdewan was considered a potential successor to Ulbricht but fell into disgrace. He considered Ulbricht's response to the 20th Party Congress as too soft. Next to Schirdewan and Oelßner, Wollweber, the head of the Stasi, and Ziller, the economy secretary, were also victims of this final attack against revisionist factions of the party. Ernst Wollweber, in Ulbricht's eyes, did not support sufficiently the new course of the Stasi's increased role. See in detail Epstein (2003: chapter 6).

institute.[67] Ulisch was awarded 100 DM, and left the institute in 1962 to continue his career at the Stasi.[68]

What happened to Behrens and Benary after these months of defamation? With fewer responsibilities and fewer obligations to participate in the institute's meetings, Behrens had more time to write, but turned toward less contested fields such as the history of economic thought and empirical studies on labor productivity. Nevertheless, he was under the continuous surveillance of the party apparatus and the Stasi. He was often denied travel to international conferences and he struggled with long refereeing processes, unqualified referees, and slow publication processes.[69] He felt blackballed, as he complained in a letter to Hager in 1961: "Such treatment is not only daunting, it is also unworthy and harmful, and I cannot believe that this is in the interest of the party."[70] In 1959, Günther Mittag suggested that Behrens should be sent into industry, a suggestion that was even supported by the institute's party-group. But this did not happen.[71] As so often in socialist regimes, Behrens' family also suffered from the affair. His daughter studied economics at Humboldt University during the reign of Naumann. Though she knew little of the debate involving her father she was called to the party-group of the students to distance herself from her father's views. The partner of his other daughter, Christin, when becoming a candidate of the party, was advised to end the relationship.[72] Behrens' wife suffered more severe consequences. She was mayor of Zeuthen, a small town outside of Berlin where the family lived, and was asked to resign from her post.[73]

Behrens continued to operate on the margins of the party line by critiquing bureaucracy and centralism. In a private meeting with Ernst Bloch, he supposedly said, according to a Stasi report: "In reality, I'm a

---

[67] Bichtler file, MfS AIM 3238-71, 12. He defended his doctoral thesis at the Academy for Social Sciences in 1957; cited in Mertens (2004: 350).

[68] Ulisch file, MfS AIM 2981-62-1, 151.

[69] See SAPMO-BArch, DY30 56227; SAPMO-BArch, DY30 56244; SAPMO-BArch, DY 30 83342.

[70] Letter, ABBAW: NRB, file 171.

[71] See letter in SAPMO-BArch, DY 30 83342. Roesler speculates that Wolfgang Berger, a personal referent of Ulbricht and one of Behrens' first students in Leipzig, might have saved Behrens from industry. In Müller et al. (1999: 39–53).

[72] Hannamaria Loschinski. Personal interview. See also GI "Walter," August 9, 1957, MfS HA IX 11 ZUV 76-6, 163.

[73] Family statement, ABBAW: NRB, file 326.

deeper revisionist than they know!"[74] In September of 1967, at the occasion of a conference on one hundred years of Marx's *Capital* in Frankfurt, West Germany, Behrens delivered a different version of a speech that had been agreed with the institute. Another lengthy discussion at the institute and party expulsion awaited him; thus he chose to retire.[75] He continued to analyze the East German state but without publishing his thoughts. He criticized the GDR as a continuation of a bourgeois order in which the state became a class of its own. He thought of the East German state as a form of monopoly fostering hypocrisy and a lack of integrity among state functionaries who form their own class interests against the working class.[76] Though he soon became known in the West as a progressive economist, he never wished to leave East Germany.[77]

As for Benary, the Stasi mistakenly worried that he would leave the country.[78] Instead, he fully embraced his new position at a cable plant (VEB Kabelwerk Oberspree). There, he could breathe fresh air, his wife recalled:

That was the best thing that could have happened to him … When he came home from the cable plant on his first day, on 1 August, 1957 – I remember that very well – he said: "You know, I think that's the right place for me." When he introduced himself to the new party-group the comrades said: "We do not at all care about the affair at your institute, and your party's punishment! Now you belong to us, and you have to fully commit yourself to solving our problems." What a reception! That encouraged him.[79]

Kampfert, however, did not give up mistrusting Benary. In 1959, he asked Benary to write a statement admitting his revisionist position back in 1956 to be presented at the party-group meeting, and to be

---

[74] July 1, 1959, MfS HA IX 11 ZUV 76-6, 92.
[75] Behrens file, MfS HA XX 9-23, 99. For the speech, see Behrens (1968: 288–299), and for the uncensored speech see Müller et al. (1999: 142–145).
[76] This work would be published after the fall of the Berlin Wall by his daughter; see Behrens (1992) and Steiner (1992: 1160–1168); see also the fictitious interview with Behrens that Behrens wrote himself, and his diaries, ABBAW: NRB, file 326, 285.
[77] The first references in the West go back to Croan (1962).
[78] Benary file, MfS AOP 1012-57-2, 148.
[79] Gisela Eckstein. Interview with author.

published jointly with Behrens' statement mentioned earlier.[80] It is unclear with what kind of emotions he wrote this statement: with humiliation, indifference, irony, or honest conviction. But at this point, Benary appeared to care less about intellectual honesty and simply went along with what the party wished him to do. In a personal letter to Behrens, with whom he remained good friends, he wrote on November 14, 1959:

Thursday was the planned conversation with Kampfert. It took an hour and was very friendly. My job assessment was quite good ... and my wish to stay in the plant for the time being was met. However, I cannot get out of making a last statement. It would be necessary and time to finally draw a line ... It's not about a theoretical statement, but about a political one – well, so be it![81]

His statement reads in fact like a bow to the party. Yes, his text from 1956 was revisionist, and yes, he could have become "a mouthpiece for irresolute elements inside and outside the party."[82] However, for Kampfert, the struggle against Benary appeared to become a life mission. On January 21, 1960, he returned *again* to the party-group of the plant for another occasion to talk things over.[83] Benary's statement was still not sufficient, and he explained to the party-group that Benary was still not yet fully honest. He argued that Benary had developed his own "factionist" conception against the party.

These last attempts by Kampfert led nowhere. Benary wished for and also had an impressive career, rising from a worker in the organization department to become the economic director of the plant. Paragenings met him once during these years on a professional occasion. Paragenings had the notion that Benary wanted to come back to academia, which contrasts what his wife recalls from these years. Whatever his future plans, they were not to be. On October 10, 1971, at the age of forty-two, Benary committed suicide.[84] According to the criminal investigations and according to his wife, the circumstances were unrelated to his professional career. But to some they left this impression, as Paragenings speculated in a personal conversation.[85]

---

[80] See letter Kampfert, SAPMO-BArch, DY 30 J IV 2-2-696, 15–60; Behrens (1960); Benary (1960: 651–652).
[81] Letter Benary, ABBAW: NRB, file 247–241.   [82] Ibid.: 652.
[83] Kampfert report, SAPMO-BArch, DY30 48131.
[84] Criminal record in MfS AS 152-74.
[85] Heinz Paragenings. Interview with author.

Figure 3.1 Arne Benary, December 1958.
Photo courtesy Gisela Eckstein.

Self-censorship

The affair surrounding Behrens and Benary was deterring and has been called "traumatic" for the entire profession of East German economists, as Krause argued. It "burdened the atmosphere for open dialogue."[86] The atmosphere at the institute became dull and intellectual enthusiasm vanished behind a veil of self-censorship. The political economy of socialism was browbeaten, mediocre, and reduced to commentary on party decisions. In the wake of the events described in this chapter, for the entire community of political economists, a genre of writings against revisionism emerged. Debunking revisionism became part of the plan for economic research and a standard lesson in the basic studies of the social sciences taught for every discipline at all universities.

---

[86] See Krause (1998b: 291).

Meißner, head of the department of the history of economic doctrines at the academy institute, witnessed the turn inward among many economists, reporting to the Stasi as "GI Rolf Hansen."[87] In September 1961, shortly after the wall was built, he openly expressed his notion of the "stagnation" of economic science at the institute:

At present, there is a great deal of disapproval among all important economists, reluctance at work and no assurance how to get out of the current stagnation in economics ... One often demands to pose bold questions when new research projects are announced. This demand is no longer taken seriously, because in a number of cases their realization has led to rather serious consequences for the respective authors. Many economists now ironically say in internal conversations: Yes, bold, but careful.[88]

The publishing houses would accept manuscripts only if there were official approvals from one of the CC institutions, he wrote, even if the approval came from someone without scientific qualifications. In an attempt to justify his critical attitude, Meißner explained, not without desperation:

This overall situation ... leads not only to reticence in scientific research, but also reinforce those who are eager to spread pessimism and like to take advantage of difficult situations in order to oppose the policies of the Party and government. They have enough undeniable facts to go peddling with. That is dangerous. In addition, it is very difficult for us to distinguish in this situation if someone who spreads such facts does so out of concern for improvement or because of the joy of spreading a negative atmosphere.[89]

That was enough for the Stasi to stop working with Meißner.

The consequences of the revisionism campaign were also felt at Humboldt University. Next to the well-researched case of Kuczynski,

---

[87] See MfS AOP 2540-63, I and II. See also the letter from Harry Nick to Behrens that testifies to the same frustration among economists at the institute, April 10, 1965, ABBAW: NRB, file 324. See also further reports by Ulisch in MfS AIM 2981-62, Teil 2: 3. The importance of the debate as the beginning of self-censorship in East Germany has been noted in the literature, in particular by Steiner (2000).

[88] MfS AOP 2540-63, I: 190.   [89] MfS AOP 2540-63, I: 203.

Erwin Rohde, the protagonist in Part III, was made complicit in an intervention of Naumann against Kohlmey as a revisionist:[90]

One day I was called to Robert Naumann's office as a vice-rector in the main building. He said that our Institute finally had to make a reasonable contribution to the revisionists' standpoints and gave me this task. Thus, I sat down with two colleagues, and we wrote an article that led to consensus among the leading comrades. I am ashamed of this article, until today. I am ashamed because we cut off a very reasonable person like Kohlmey. He was a good comrade who deserves better. I am even more ashamed because we did so in complete ignorance of his ideas. We did not know what a central bank policy was, and how it could intervene. We simply argued against Kohlmey because the party leaders wished to favour the views on fiscal policy of the Ministry of Finance. If I were to meet Kohlmey someday, I would tell him this face to face.[91]

It is difficult to pinpoint the phenomenon of self-censorship historically, as it is hardly ever directly expressed, has many forms, and often takes place unconsciously. Erwin Rohde is one of the few who openly regretted, in the 1990s, the common practice of self-censorship resulting from the events in the 1950s:

In the first years of the GDR, we could publish quite freely. But year after year, this became ever more difficult; there clearly was a lot of censorship. But as time passed, many, and I count myself among them, habitually anticipated censorship and asked themselves: "Am I allowed to write this or that? Is this going to cause me trouble?" After all, we no longer needed any state censorship, as we applied more and more self-censorship. And self-censorship is the death of all science and scientific progress. (Rohde 2009)

---

[90] In addition to what would be stamped a "revisionist" book about the origin of World War I, published in summer of 1957, Kuczynski too lost his position at Humboldt University as head of the economic history department, though he was allowed to teach. From then on, the young and dedicated Waltraud Falk took over the department, which lost its intellectual aura (see in detail Haun 1999; Keßler 2005).

[91] Rohde (2009). For the mentioned article, see Rohde et al. (1958). In retrospect, Rohde agreed with Kohlmey that the Soviet model could not be applied to an East Germany that already had a developed fiscal and financial system. "The attempt to transfer the Soviet findings of a rather backward country to us has led to our ultimate failure. We had no chance to build a decentralized control system. We should have involved the central bank policy as an instrument of planning and management of the national economy" (Rohde 2009).

Note that self-censorship, from the first-person perspective, not only results from the fear of consequences but also from the desire to contribute to politics and thus to behave strategically. As Klein explained:

One had to try to formulate results in such a way that one's critique could be heard, and possibly be included in politics ... That is quite common with scholars who work for a political authority, even if this is especially relevant in state socialism. Of course, I have often tried to formulate [my thoughts] in such a way that they were commensurable. And in this process, my own thoughts were certainly kept back. You could choose to either say what you think and already know in advance that you put yourself out of the range of influence. Or you want to make a difference and have to adapt your strategy accordingly. (Klein interview 2021)[92]

Another form of self-censorship is the simple acceptance of the presence of the party and its power within the academic institutions. The revisionism campaign in fact instituted the leading role of the party in academic life. The young assistants clearly understood that their careers would depend on party approval.[93] With the addition of peer pressure, there was a shrinking possibility of anyone who was not a party member at this point becoming a professor. Conversely, without career ambitions, one could easily avoid frictions with the party system. Those who did not aim to become professors were left alone, and were thus free to conduct research in tenured middle-ranking positions.[94] But the acceptance of the influence of the party in universities also had its limits, as I show at the case of Ernst Strnad in Chapter 4.

The revisionism campaign could have been the end of the intellectual activity of economists. However, as we will see in Part III, the party

---

[92] The same attitude can be found among the generation of Klein's students: "I actually always wrote and said what I thought. The language I chose was of course strategic, but not the content. I think that I never have written anything that I actually thought was wrong. Maybe I left out a few things, knowing that saying so leads to problems" (Michael Brie, interview, *SED-Reformdiskurs*, TB Brie).

[93] Since the late 1950s, party representatives sat on most university committees; see Vogt (2012: 145–157). The university-wide average of party members of all new professors increased in the 1960s to 76 percent; in Middell (2012: 382).

[94] "For many scientists, the post of a professor [...] was by no means attractive, because in a politically pervaded university, having the responsibility of a leader came with the necessity of compromises with the agenda of the dominating party and thus a time-consuming diversion from teaching and research" (Middell 2012: 376).

again and again managed to reawaken the belief in a harmonious and productive relationship between the profession and the party. In 1963, Ulbricht managed to revive interest among economists when he announced the so-called New Economic System of Planning and Government. Though there was no mention of the diminishing role of the state or self-governance, the reform introduced market categories of profit and decentralization very much in line with the ideas of Behrens and Benary. Wolfgang Berger, Helmut Koziolek, and Otto Reinhold, scholars who knew Behrens' work very well, were at the origin of Ulbricht's new policy. In other words, the current needs of the state apparatus overshadowed scientific ideas to the extent that what was considered unacceptable in the wake of the Hungary uprising could become acceptable later when the storms calmed down.

* * *

The case of Arne Benary and the dismantling of Behrens' research group was but one example of the many subtle forms of political control in East German economics. It exemplifies well a general pattern of mixing repression with offers of integration for those willing to submit.[95]

Instead of direct intervention, as in Stalin's show trials, the means of oppression and censorship were manifold and increasingly subtle. The most open means to exert political pressure were party trials, which potentially exposed the party to public criticism. There was also formal censorship in terms of party approval of textbooks, for example. More personal pressure was exerted through career interruption, as in the case of Benary, or removal from higher positions, as in the case of Behrens, but also intervention in professional liberty such as travel and publication bans. These measures could also apply to family members or friends, such as the case of Behrens' wife or Benary's friend Zieschang, pressure that could be used for denouncing or revealing discrediting information about others. But more subtle pressure that was not even perceived as such was the most preferable: the nudging of consensus.

---

[95] Among the many studies regarding oppressive Stasi measures, see regarding economists, Alisch's study on the Higher School of Economics, in particular the activities of informal collaborators (IMs) and of so-called secret officers on special employment (*Offiziere im besonderen Einsatz*) (2010: chapters 6 and 7). The Stasi presence at Humboldt University has been critically and thoroughly studies by Kowalczuk (2012).

On the individual level, there was the discussion called *Aussprache*; on the level of firms, there were so-called brigade deployments, that is, visits by CC members talking with those on the shop floor.[96] And on the academic level, as we have seen in this chapter, intervening in debates were ways to enforce consensus.

The responses to such measures were equally manifold. While in the early years deterrence was necessary for introducing this culture, the mere anticipation of these measures resulted in fear and self-censorship. Considering that most of these measures presume professional ambition, the hope generation with high career opportunities were particularly sensitive to these measures. This applied less to those "born into" the GDR, since they had from the start lower career opportunities. Accepting the lack of a career, and thus not having the opportunity to be heard as potential critique, allowed for a relatively free petty-bourgeois lifestyle. Another response was to develop strategies that circumvent political control in presenting one's ideas in a way that does not evoke suspicion among party authorities, which was perhaps the most common way of censoring oneself. This resulted in a discourse of economics that was heavily canonized and full of jargon, citatology, and phraseology. "So one began with a Honecker citation. So what? That does not cost me anything," the political economist Hans Wagner witnessed.[97] One could also choose a low institutional visibility in order to have more freedom, such as clandestine seminars in informal networks, or simply private discussions as they continued between Behrens and Benary.[98] The lowest and most common form of self-censorship was to accept as normal the presence of surveillance, ignoring the open contradictions between the ideals of socialism – social justice and individual development – and its reality: stagnation, lack of rationality, political tutelage, and surveillance.

But then, there was also the fundamental forgiving attitude that I pointed to in Part I that granted the Old Communists the range of maneuver to act against the values they represented. Paragenings,

---

[96] Brigade deployments have been analyzed by Bergien (2012).

[97] Hans Wagner interview, *SED-Reformdiskurs*, TB Wagner.

[98] There were certainly also national differences. As compared to other countries, such as Poland or Hungary, the GDR was more conservative, which explains the fact that there were less "big debates" in economics, and also less celebrities that stand for an intellectual creativity of the rank of Oskar Lange, Leonid Kantorovich, or Jànos Kornai; see Kovács (forthcoming a).

looking back, explained away the behavior of the party apparatus by the early state of socialism when remnants of bourgeois state force remained necessary.[99] The belief remained that the party would in the end be open to the truth. And this belief was nourished by a strong conviction shared by East Germany's hope generation: that socialism was the only alternative to the totalitarian regime of fascism. The memories of the World War II made them both believe that there would never again be victims of the state and simply accept as normal that there were in fact victims of the state.

Note that these responses do not exclude each other, and many mid-ranking professionals might have played several roles at various points of their career. There was also no determinism to the extent that once fallen out of favor, one could be reestablished when the political situation has changed, and once established on the highest level, a change of political situation could end this trust within a minute. The option of leaving was hardly conceived by anyone. Simply imagining life in a Western capitalist country made most academics of the hope generation feel uneasy. It should also be noted that most of the violence that happened in prisons or through psychological measures of the Stasi were kept secret. Those who were not affected by it, as is often the case in authoritarian regimes, did in fact not know, or did not want to know, the extent of the violence the regime they supported was capable of. As Klein said in 1996: "I might not have believed that the system was capable of doing the harm that many already knew."[100]

It was through the experiences of the revisionism campaign that the intellectual ethos of young economists gained shape. The lasting effect for the remainder of the East German state was that the party could continue to claim the epistemic values of a scientific debate despite their obvious oppression. What is obvious to us, having access to more archival sources, might not have been obvious back then. Thinking of the perspective of the actors, the show debate would have been an utter failure if all had understood its show character. For those who did not, Behrens and Benary's notion of decentralization was indeed revisionist, and their party loyalty made them trust in the scientific organization of the state apparatus. As demanded by the party until the end, this larger audience of political economists continued putting major

[99] Heinz Paragenings, interview with author.
[100] See interview Klein, *SED-Reformdiskurs*, TB Klein.

intellectual efforts into further reform proposals. But we should also point to those who did understand the show character of the debate and considered it an appropriate measure of the party against class enemies. For them, the idea that the party is founded in scientific knowledge boiled down to mere faith in the law-like future development of socialism, that is, it boiled down to a point where knowledge and ideology fused. Being an intellectual, for them, became mainly a matter of personal devotion – a devotion for which the Stasi, rather than the Academy of Sciences, was the ultimate judge.

But then there were also many people who did understand the show character of the debate, did not give up their basic socialist beliefs, and began living in an inner exile. For them, the show debate was in fact political deterrence. It is for them that the dismantling of the academy's institute in 1957, and post-Stalinism at large, was a missed opportunity for a better GDR. Many of them might have agreed with what Behrens' daughter said when summarizing the lesson of the revisionism campaign: "Never wear your heart on your sleeve!"[101]

[101] Hannamaria Loschinski. Interview with author.

4 | *Negotiating Socialist Statistics*

The Communist Party does not fear criticism, because we are Marxists, the truth is on our side . . . Inner-Party criticism is a weapon for strengthening the Party organization and increasing its fighting capacity. In the Party organization of the Red Army, however, criticism . . . sometimes turns into personal attack . . . This is a manifestation of petty-bourgeois individualism . . . Anyone, no matter who, may point out our shortcomings.[1]

When trying to understand how scientific cultures change at times of political upheaval, the historian does well in treating the winner and loser symmetrically. And this applies equally to the transformation of science in the young GDR. While Chapter 3 considered a case of an academic contribution that was considered vital but was politically suppressed, this chapter considers a case of an academic contribution that was considered marginal but had the highest political support. While Chapter 3 made a case for the loss of academic autonomy, this chapter proves the relative autonomy that academia could maintain in state socialism.[2]

In concrete, this chapter covers a debate between leading statisticians, economists, and the party apparatus that took place equally during the revisionism campaign in the wake of the 20th Party Congress. The concrete occasion of the debate was a doctoral thesis written by Ernst Strnad about the socialist critique of statistics and its use in political economy. What makes the situation surrounding the thesis unusual is that Strnad wrote it on his own, without supervision, and not as a doctoral student in any program. He then set about finding readers for the thesis who would formally approve it, thereby

---

[1] Quotations from Mao Tse Tung, "Criticism and Self-criticism."
[2] As Shapin and Schaffer argued in their classic study on the scientific revolution, the academic loser is as telling about the social constitution of a new knowledge regime as is the winner (Shapin and Schaffer 1985).

earning him a doctoral degree. For reasons explained later, the thesis, and Strnad's efforts to secure readers for it, drew the attention of high-party officials and became part of the ongoing battle between the party and the academy.

In these early years of the GDR, as we saw in Chapter 2, "bourgeois" scholarly standards and academic customs were open to political reassessment. In 1950, following the founding of the state, the second university reform gave privileged access to higher education to students from the working class and imposed Marxism-Leninism as the basic foundation of all sciences. The increased scarcity of academics under this new constraint forced universities to award professor titles on the basis of party biographies without the necessary academic degrees. Moreover, the dissertation examination rules were reassessed on a national level.[3] This situation created the opportunity for scholars at the margins to influence the newly emerging socialist academic landscape. As an external doctoral candidate with little academic but considerable political credentials, Strnad's case was an occasion to negotiate the extent to which the socialist party could exercise academic authority.

Given the striking synchronicity of events surveyed in Chapter 3 and the negotiation about Strnad's doctoral thesis, this chapter sheds another light on the nature of Ulbricht's intervention in the academic sphere that stabilized his rule after Stalin. Precisely because Strnad was an outsider, his case provides a "lower bound" at which academic autonomy and self-governance in the face of attempts at political censorship and favoritism had to prove themselves. While in other historical circumstances, there would not have been much evidence of a failed thesis, the correspondence shows how vulnerable, unsettled, and open academic autonomy was in the context of post-Stalinist attempts at democratization. The case thus complements the history told in Chapter 3 that focuses on the historical actors at the center of the stage. In contrast to much of the literature on academia during the Thaw, Strnad's case shows that, despite increased party influence, universities were not willing to give up their academic ethos and maintained the basic mechanism of academic inclusion and exclusion

---

[3] Regarding PhD examination rules, which purportedly even applied to West Germany, see Bleek and Mertens (1994).

that takes place at the bottom floor of academic reproduction: the committee granting doctoral degrees.[4]

In this context, as we will see, questions of character are a main channel through which the political and the academic interact. Strnad represents the case of someone who, as a person, draws from a symbiotic relationship with the generation of his parents, and their sufferance as communists during National Socialism. As a member of a family with a party history going back to prewar times, Strnad's character was afflicted by the trauma of political ostracism that his father suffered during the war and was radicalized during the first cleansing wave after the war. This is expressed in a strong radicalism of his political attitude, a radicalism that is typical of the young and which makes them instrumental for the consolidation of authoritarian regimes. As a scholar at the margin, he perceived the academic change as part of a political mission, fighting a deep false consciousness of bourgeois intellectualism. In the person of Strnad, the radicalism of advancing science joins the radicalism that is typical for political upheaval. Ultimately, however, he would be perceived as an arrogant loner. The case of Strnad provides insight into the contingent, episodic, and personality-driven nature of changes in the SED's attitude toward the intelligentsia.

The Thesis

In 1953, the year Stalin died, Ernst Strnad began writing a doctoral thesis entitled *The Reactionary Ideological Foundation of Modern Bourgeois Economic Statistics*. After his odyssey as a communist minority among the German minority in the Czech then German then Czech Sudetenland, in 1946, he enrolled at Humboldt University Berlin to study economics. He thus belonged to the first cohort of postwar students that witnessed, first, the difficult denazification and, second, the transition to a socialist university described in Chapter 2. Strnad witnessed the forced exclusion of business economists considered bourgeois, such as Konrad Mellerowicz, and of social democrats such as Bruno Gleitze, as well as the suspicion by political economist Robert Naumann, returning from Soviet exile, about

---

[4] For a quantitative treatment of academic reproduction in socialist Hungary, in particular the role of party institutions in doctoral committees, see Péteri (1996).

economic historian Jürgen Kuczynski, returning from Western exile. These confrontations often led to tensions among students. Strnad thus studied during the years when questions of ideology and loyalty were debated and fought for on a daily academic basis. He learned that dominance in science is fought for with political means. He also might have been inspired by Ulbricht's speech, given in 1950 at the 3rd Party Congress, that called for a radical critique of the bourgeois elements in East Germany's intelligentsia. Universities, so Ulbricht claimed, "have neither really started the scientific discussion of the unscientific views of reactionary university teachers, nor the implacable fight against reactionary influences, against cosmopolitanism and objectivism."[5]

Strnad's thesis aimed to contribute to the establishment of a truly socialist methodology of Marxist-Leninist political economy. Statistics plays a twofold role in this tradition. On the one hand, it promises to liberate the socialist mind from ideological distortions of reality, as Lenin, among others, hoped. On the other hand, it is subject to ideological manipulation, as many classical political economists thought. Debating the political status of statistics is balancing these two roles. Does the kind of statistical methods make the difference? Does statistical sophistication increase its truthfulness or does it render it more amenable to manipulation? Which elements of statistics are common with that of the class enemy (and the previous regime) and which not? To put the same question in institutional terms: how much influence of the party apparatus is necessary such that the discipline of statistics serves the socialist cause? Or to put it in terms of the scientific ethos of the scientist: how important is political loyalty for a career as a statistician under socialism? And how should a socialist statistician relate to the works of the class enemy? In short: how to be a socialist statistician?[6]

Reading Marx provides few answers to these questions. On the one hand, Marx was critical of the law-like character that British political

---

[5] Cited in Feige (1995: 1074).

[6] The literature on statistics in socialism mainly discusses the accurateness and the specific practice of statistics, but there is very little on its role as a methodology in the social sciences; see, in particular, Steiner (2006), Von de Lippe (1996), and Praschek (2000). Regarding the Soviet Union, see Sheynin (1998) and Blum and Mespoulet (2003); for the case of Hungary's Thaw, see for example Péteri (1996, 1997). A recent article by Mespoulet (2022) comes closest to the present discussion on the socialist epistemology of statistics.

economists argued for, which suggested some kind of empiricism. On the other hand, Marx himself added his (historical) reinterpretation of the laws of political economy and gave little indication what kind of empirical methods he would favor. In the wake of World War II, when statistical methods boomed in Western social science departments, Marx was a poor guide for those who wished to follow up on his call for a truly empirical science (let alone for organizing disciplinary relationships in the social sciences). There was but one French statistician that Marx read, Adolph Quételet, whose notion of "social physics" became a standard in Marxist writings. Quételet considered statistical regularities as a kind of natural law, hiding, according to Marx, the imperialist agenda underlying these laws. Bourgeois statisticians after Marx, according to Strnad, developed more refined forms of the same reactionary epistemology of statistics. This is the starting point of his thesis.[7]

Lenin added his share to the polemics against bourgeois science and the belief that class conflict is fought by epistemological means. He was more proactive than Marx in using statistics as a liberation from bourgeois distortions of truth and a means to install a matter-of-fact attitude in Soviet science. As Lenin's famous dictum for a socialist statistics reads: "In capitalist society, statistics was the exclusive reserve of 'people of the state' or narrow-minded specialists; we have to bring it to the masses, popularize it so that workers can gradually learn to understand themselves and see how and how much they have to work, how and how much they can rest."[8] But Strnad does not analyze or generalize the actual statistical methods by and under Lenin, such as those favored by the Soviet Central Statistics Administration.[9] Instead, he draws heavily on Lenin's critique of bourgeois science being

---

[7] About Marx and Quételet, see Hacking (1990). For an attempt to make sense of Marx's use of quantitative methods, see Rubin (1968).

[8] Cited in Mespoulet (2022: 51). On Lenin and statistics, see also Kotz and Seneta (1990).

[9] The Soviet debates on socialist statistical methods during the 1930s is fully analyzed by Mespoulet (2022). Sample methods, for example, were based on types rather than being random, and notions of probability in general were treated carefully because of the potential conflict with the presupposition of classes. The mean and the law of large numbers, to give another example, was considered fatalism as it undermined the avant-gardist role of the party. An aspect that was central for the Soviet discussion that is not mentioned by Strnad was the reduction of statistics to accounting.

reactionary, as put forward in his classic *Materialism and Empirio-criticism* (1947 [1909]). Even if the constructive agenda of a socialist statistics, meaning that statistical education helps to counter ideological reasoning, had already been on the agenda in both the Soviet Union and the young GDR, Strnad's thesis provides merely a conceptual critique of statistics with little about the actual techniques that are and should be used.[10]

Who then were the "bourgeois" statisticians to which Strnad referred? With limited access to the emerging literature in Western econometrics, his references are mostly recognized German authors. That is, he refers to those who had been accepted both during the preceding National Socialist regime as well as during the Weimar Republic, such as the "reactionary (Ernst) Wagemann, the forger of Marx (Rudolf) Meerwarth, the inconsistent (Paul) Flaskämper."[11] Moreover, his main references are less the current research of these scholars, but *textbooks* – which lag behind the state of the art, particularly during times of political change. But this lack of knowledge of the international literature might be explained by the fact that his actual targets were the *remnants* of bourgeois sentiments still existing in the GDR among the older generation of statisticians. His thesis was a call for more political radicalism in academia, voiced by a young scholar addressing the older generation that, suspiciously for Strnad, set up their careers in politically adverse times.

His main target was the aged Felix Burkhart (1888–1973) at Leipzig University, who was already an established statistician before the war, and a pioneer of mathematical statistics in East Germany.[12] Between 1920 and 1938, he worked at the Saxon State Statistical Office in Dresden, receiving a doctorate in 1923 from the University of Frankfurt/Main. He published on infant mortality and the cost-of-living index. His career during Nazism continued. In 1934, he took over the editorship of the *Deutsches Statistisches Zentralblatt*, and from 1935 he was co-editor of the *Archiv für mathematische Wirtschafts- und Sozialforschung*. In 1938, he was

---

[10] See for example Gottfried Handel (1956), "Historischer Materialismus und empirische Sozialforschung: Gründliches Studium der Wirklichkeit hilft Dogmatismus zu überwinden, näher an die Gegenwart," *Neues Deutschland*, 153, June 28: 6. Another entrance point for discussing a Marxist epistemology of science could have been Rosental (1956) that he could read in Russian original.

[11] SAPMO-BArch, DY 30 83342: 400.

[12] On Burkhardt, see Wirzberger (1968) and Fair-Schulz (2009).

appointed associate professor of actuarial mathematics at the University of Leipzig, and in 1943 became full professor. In this period, he was also an early member of the Econometric Society. In 1945, as a member of the NSDAP since 1933, he was dismissed from university. His appeal was rejected by the mayor of Leipzig. With the support of many academics, it took until 1950 for him to return to university as professor of a chair of actuarial mathematics, economic mathematics, and mathematical statistics, and later director of the Institute of Statistics in Leipzig. On his initiative, business mathematics became a study degree at the mathematics institute. He left a strong impression as an old and accomplished scholar, and initiated an entire generation of East German statisticians. Strnad knew Burkhart as a lecturer at Humboldt University before his professorship in Leipzig, thus from a time when he was not yet reestablished.

Next to Burkhart, Strnad, as we will see, also counted Friedrich Behrens and Jürgen Kuczynski among those who did not sufficiently break with the bourgeois regime of knowledge. And since these latter scholars, after the Soviet break with Stalin, were indeed under attack by the party, Strnad's thesis received more attention than would have been the case under other circumstances. In this sense, the topicality of his thesis was less an update of Marx's critique of Quételet through tackling what was happening in the West than a follow-up on the political call to purify academia in the GDR that he experienced during his student years. His thesis can be viewed as a contribution to the transition of the intellectual culture in the GDR that sought to build up socialist academic institutions. Surveying the contents of his thesis in the next section helps us to identify the potential topics of the political debate about statistics, as well as to make us aware of how unpremeditated were early debates on the Marxist-Leninist foundation of individual scientific disciplines.

The Argument

In what he calls his "defense speech," Strnad summarized his doctoral thesis in seventeen pages.[13] He begins by tackling various "bourgeois" definitions of statistics, which, according to him, "hide the historical

---

[13] SAPMO-BArch, DY 30 83342: 400–416. For reasons explained later, the thesis itself is not accessible.

and, in particular, the class character of statistical research."[14] The argument behind this idea is that statistics is not a method or discipline independent of individual sciences but an *aspect* of them: the "factual" aspect. Statistical laws are not the laws of statistics but the laws of an individual discipline in statistical form. Economic statistics, criminal statistics, and population statistics belong to different disciplines. As soon as statistical laws are considered to be formulations of the laws of the individual disciplines, they no longer hide their historical and social character. Economic laws, for example, are historical laws of development, as described by Marx, and thus refer directly to the class struggle.[15] To support his argument, Strnad cites a range of bourgeois definitions of statistics from various sources. Among these, he quotes Hans Gebelein's "applied mathematics" (1943), Otto Donner's "universal method" (1937), Jean Marchal's "inductive method" (1950), Johannes Müller's science of "quantities" (1927), Marcel Nicolas' "empirical concepts" (1952), and Ernst Wagemann's science of "empirical number" (reference unknown). These definitions, according to Strnad, suggest that statistics is a neutral method that is independent of its objects of application, and thus, in economics, independent of the underlying class character.

It is difficult to think of the class interest shared by these disparate scholars. Hans Gebelein was a mathematical engineer at the National Socialist Aeronautical Research Institute, Otto Donner was a statistician in Göring's planning office, Jean Marchal was a French political economist, Johannes Müller was an interwar clerk at the statistical office of Thuringia, Marcel Nicolas was the author of a recent West German textbook, and Ernst Wagemann was the best-known German statistician and founder of business cycle research before and during the war. Some of them cooperated with the National Socialist regime, some did not; some aimed at innovative research, some not at all. To today's reader, the notion of "bourgeois statisticians" appears to be a straw man. Considering, however, that fascism was, in the GDR, the

---

[14] SAPMO-BArch, DY 30 83342: 416.
[15] The following argument by Lenin could have been an inspiration for Strnad's definition of statistics as a nonseparate science: "The central administration of statistics must not be an 'academic' and 'independent' body, which it currently is, for 9/10ths following old bourgeois habits, but one for constructing socialism, for verifying and controlling the accounts of what the socialist state needs to know now, today" (cited in Mespoulet 2022: 49).

continuation of monopoly capitalism, this difference might not have mattered much to Strnad.

Strnad strengthens his argument by claiming that bourgeois statistics is free from factual reasoning because it is *unfalsifiable* and thus against Lenin's dictum: "Experience generates a thought, it is spun off and compared and modified again with experience" (Lenin 1947 [1909]: 152). "If one refers with acuteness to unspecific facts," wrote Strnad, "one can prove every hypothesis."[16] Ignoring an entire tradition discussing the nature of abstraction in economics since John Stuart Mill, Strnad quotes from a German translation of a British introduction to statistics by Leonard Tippett that political economists "were often criticized for their negligence of statistics and facts."[17]

As a rite in Stalinist intellectualism, Strnad applies Lenin's critique of "reactionary" bourgeois science, as developed in *Materialism and Empirio-criticism*, to statistics (1947 [1909]). "The method of modern bourgeois economic statistics is based on a reactionary philosophy: subjective idealism, agnosticism, indeterminism, empiricism, formalism, and the like."[18] Regarding "subjective idealism," he refers to Charlotte Lorenz, mathematical statistician at Humboldt University during the National Socialist period, who argued that "as soon as the economy loses its free trade character, the establishment of (statistical) laws loses its significance."[19] The historical dependence on laws, however, does not limit their objective content. Regarding what he calls "agnosticism," that is, the overemphasis on the limits of knowledge, he refers to Jan Tinbergen, who argues that one cannot prove a theory by using statistics. Although this was a truly standard topic in the philosophy of statistical causality at the time, Strnad cites a Slavic dissertation that cites Tinbergen rather than Tinbergen himself. Regarding "indeterminism," he refers to the overly emphasized role of chance in Wagemann's "statistical law of chance." "In this way, one hides that there are also causes behind seemingly random events, which still can be explained."[20] Regarding "empiricism," he refers to those who

---

[16] SAPMO-BArch, DY 30 83342: 410.
[17] Ibid.: 411; See Tippett (1952 [1931]: 206).
[18] SAPMO-BArch, DY 30 83342: 412.
[19] Reference unknown; see SAPMO-BArch, DY 30 83342: 412.
[20] SAPMO-BArch, DY 30 83342: 412; regarding the cited law, see Wagemann (1950 [1935]). The use of probability measures was also heavily critiqued in the Soviet Union, as surveyed by Mespoulet (2022).

observe without generalizing their observations, which he exemplifies using an American textbook by Albert Waugh (Waugh 1952 [1938]). Regarding "formalism," he admits that some mathematics can be useful for economic theory (as Marx's reproduction schemes show) and for empirical research (as means, averages, and probabilities are calculated rather than observed). However, more advanced mathematics, he argues, would be an overuse.

Strnad calls the statistics developed in the Econometric Society, founded in 1930, the "extreme (*überspitzte*) application of mathematics at the basis of vulgar economic theory." Mathematics makes econometrics appear politically neutral, a claim that Strnad attributes to Erich Schneider, a leading West German Keynesian economist and head of the Kiel Institute for the World Economy.[21] He equally cites the then recent contributions of the American Paul Samuelson, for hiding class notions behind the appearance of a natural science as Samuelson used the notion of equilibrium in analogy with the law of physics. As examples of statisticians critical of the approach of the Econometric Society, he refers to a rather unknown economist at Columbia University, Theodore Wilbur Anderson, and Mussolini's famous statistician, Corrado Gini. From today's perspective, it might be surprising that he did not refer to more prominent critiques featured in major American economic journals, such as the institutionalists at the National Bureau of Economic Research, but these discussions might not have been readily available to a young doctoral student in East Germany.[22]

Strnad goes on to discuss concrete examples of statistical laws that prove the bourgeois bias of econometrics – in particular, Vilfredo Pareto's so-called law of distribution. This law states that a larger percentage of income in an economy is owned by a smaller percentage

[21] Strnad cites the September 11, 1955 edition of the weekly press journal *Der Volkswirt*. But in this edition, there is no article by Schneider. Strnad stated that the approach of the Econometric Society became important in West Germany since the 17th meeting of the Society in 1955 that took place at the institute in Kiel (see "Report of the Kiel Meeting, September 1–3, 1955," *Econometrica*, 24 (3): 299–337). It is unlikely that Strnad had been present at this meeting, though he could have been.

[22] The 1947 debate between the institutionalist Wesley Mitchell and Tjalling Koopmans is known as the "measurement without theory" debate. The same critique of bourgeois statistics justifying the "unshakable" nature of capitalism can be found in the Soviet literature of the early 1930, such as Iastremskii and Khotimskii (see Mespoulet 2022: 51).

of the people in that economy, implying a single-peaked income distribution. Strnad falsifies this law using West German income data from 1950. Without "smoothing" the data and using a more "detailed breakdown," he argues, "you can even get multiple peaks."[23] The class case to be made is obvious: a single-peaked distribution presumes the existence of a preponderant middle class, while a double-peaked distribution appeals to the class difference between the lower and upper classes. He attacks Felix Burkhart at Leipzig University, a member of the Econometric Society, for defending Pareto's law of distribution as well as the entire econometric approach.

Beyond these epistemological arguments, Strnad also criticizes the concrete practices of bourgeois statisticians, such as the arbitrary selection of facts. At this point, he attacks directly one of his famous teachers, Jürgen Kuczynski, who, in a study using West German statistics, showed that the cost of living in the GDR had fallen since 1937; thus, there was less shortage before the war than ten years after the war (reference unknown). Strnad comments on this study by critiquing Kuczynski's statistical reasoning: while prices of basic dietary products such as bread, beef, and potatoes have indeed increased, their share compared to secondary foods such as fruits, tea, and coffee has decreased, and prices of the latter have equally decreased. Another critique of the same kind is that the samples of the official statistics are not representative, since middle-class families are given more weight than working-class families due to their higher income. Also, he identifies contradictions between the official statistics and the data published by the Emnid Institute in Bielefeld. "Clearly, someone is cheating. It is, of course, the official statistics."[24]

This concludes the summary of the thesis that Ernst Strnad finished in late summer 1955. He had written the thesis at his own initiative without the supervision of a university professor in his free time while being employed as a lector of foreign languages in the publishing house *Die Wirtschaft*. He now had to try his luck in contacting several statistics professors around the GDR, most of whom he critiqued in his thesis. Writing unsolicited dissertations and approaching referees

---

[23] SAPMO-BArch, DY 30 83342: 414.

[24] Ibid.: 415. Strnad's critique is consistent with, and possible informed by, the Soviet discussion of sample methods reflecting the class composition of society. The same applies to the debate on national accounting and "socialist indices"; see Mespoulet (2022).

with a full draft to set up an examination committee was uncommon before and after 1955. But considering the fact that this happened at a time of a changing scientific regime, this practice was up for reevaluation. Would his political agenda be sufficient for overcoming academic custom?

Rejection

According to the East German dissertation regulations, which were, at this point, the same as the preceding regimes, Strnad needed positive dissertation reports (*Gutachten*) from two university professors. This was the requirement for setting up a doctoral defense and oral examination in the department of the professor who wrote the first report. The first professor he contacted was the then still celebrity and national prizewinner Friedrich Behrens, director of the Central Statistical Office and vice-head of the Central Economics Institute at the Academy of Sciences. Without reading or discussing his draft, Behrens gave Strnad a position at the Central Statistical Office as personal associate (*persönlicher Referent*) in the fall of 1955.

Strnad had high hopes that Behrens would write him a positive report, and, without informing Behrens, looked immediately for another professor at another university to write the second report. In October 1955, he contacted Gotthart Forbrig, associate professor of statistics, and Herbert Luck, professor of political economy, both at the University of Rostock. Though Forbrig showed general interest, he and Luck were surprised by what was going on and wrote to Behrens to inquire about Strnad. After Behrens read the thesis, he reported to Luck in January 1956 that he had rejected Strnad's thesis. Behrens judged the text good enough for a diploma thesis (the equivalent of a master's thesis) but not for a dissertation. Strnad, Behrens said, should confine himself to carefully analyzing specific statistical problems rather than discussing them in abstract general terms. Although he told Strnad that he should fully rewrite the thesis, Behrens knew that he would instead seek potential referees elsewhere, notably Felix Burkhardt in Leipzig.

But Burkhardt, too, was unwilling to write a report. In a document without an addressee entitled "Experience of a Doctoral Candidate," dated April 20, 1956, Strnad reported that Burkhardt, not a party member, refused the thesis "because a critique of West German statistics damages the unity of Germany."[25] Indeed, the official position of the GDR regarding the unity of Germany was still an open question. In 1952, Stalin still wished for a unified and neutral Germany and the Soviet Council of Ministers did not accept the sovereignty of the GDR until September 1955. Strnad and Burkhart might have had different opinions on that question, bolstering Strnad's claim that political factors were standing in the way of scholarly recognition. He then contacted the next person on the list of the most central statistical economists, his former professor at Humboldt University, Jürgen Kuczynski. Strnad did not receive a positive response from Kuczynski either. Although he found nobody willing to write the first report, he received encouragement from others who signaled that they were willing to write a second report once Strnad secured a positive first report. Along with Forbrig, he received encouraging remarks from Rudolf Agricola, one of Behrens' colleagues at the Academy of Sciences, and from Hermann Scheler, a philosopher at Humboldt University. But without the first report, a second report would never be written.

Since Behrens had refused to write the first report, there was little basis for Strnad's further employment as his assistant. The reasons why Strnad left the Central Statistical Office, whether voluntarily or not, would be the subject of further debate. The fact was that by July 1956, Strnad was without employment and without the prospect of defending his thesis. But by then the political climate had changed in ways favorable to Strnad.

Concentration Camp Bonus

This first half of 1956, when Strnad was searching for a first referee, was the beginning of the Thaw following the break with Stalin at the 20th Party Congress in February 1956. The hopes for a new, more democratic form of socialism, were soon disappointed by Walter Ulbricht, who in March 1956, played the question of Stalinism down by, first, reducing Stalinism to a cult of personality and, second, denying that there ever was such a cult in the GDR. The entire intelligentsia was soon under the party's radar. In the official party

[25] SAPMO-BArch, DY 30 83342: 359.

publication *Neues Deutschland* of July 31, 1956, which reported on the party's response to the Soviet turn, Behrens, Kuczynski, and others were called *dogmatic* for clinging to ideas preventing the GDR's progress.[26] Having received negative academic judgments from exactly those professors, Strnad's perception of the rejection of his thesis and his loss of employment changed. It not only changed his own perception but also that of his father, Josef Strnad, a member of the KPČ since its very first hour in 1921. The very day the article about Behrens and others appeared in *Neues Deutschland*, Josef Strnad wrote to none other than First Secretary Walter Ulbricht:

I write to you, Comrade Ulbricht, in the hope of getting your advice and your help in a matter in which I see no other possibility. It is about Comrade Ernst Strnad, my son . . . He worked for some time in publishing houses . . . and for a short time with Professor Behrens at the Central Statistical Office. At present, he is without work . . . You are surely aware of the criticisms recently put forward against Professor Behrens (partly in *Neues Deutschland*). Indeed, there was also a dispute between Comrade Behrens and my son about West German statistics with the result that Behrens refused to continue to employ my son with allegations of "not greeting properly" and "crooked sitting!" Apart from the fact that such allegations seem ridiculous to me, being a party member for thirty-five years and having spent six years in concentration camps, I have the feeling that my son's life continues to be made difficult. In his efforts to find a new job, he was told . . . that he could not be hired because of his "mentality." Professor Behrens seems to be part of this, as I know that he has called for caution regarding my son. Personally, I believe that the caution which Professor Behrens advises should apply primarily to himself.[27]

Josef Strnad continued by explaining his son's difficulties in finding a referee for his thesis. Despite preliminary positive reactions to the thesis, he claimed that Kuczynski declined to write a report because "he does not write first reports for students that are not his own," and Burkhart declined to even read the thesis because a critique of West German statisticians was detrimental to the political goal of uniting Germany. He then closed his letter by asking Ulbricht "to help my son find employment," and "that he . . . be allowed to defend his dissertation." As personal reference, he listed Florian Schenk of the Federal Board of the Free German Trade Union Federation. Schenk, like Strnad, was one of the German-speaking "veteran" communists of Czechoslovakia who had been expelled from their homes after World War II, and whose East German career climaxed in the GDR's Patriotic Order of Merit in 1955. The reference to Florian Schenk shows that Josef Strnad must have been connected to the highest circles of Czech communists of the early days.

From today's perspective, one would expect Ulbricht's office to forward the letter to either the university or to the related ministry, the State Secretariat for Higher Education, which would have been capable of evaluating the academic dissertation procedure. But in this particular situation, Ulbricht's office forwarded the letter to the deputy head of the CC Department for Science and Propaganda, Otto Reinhold.[28] The political reason was that by July 1956, as we saw in Chapter 3, Friedrich Behrens was under observation by the party and the Stasi. After Ulbricht put him on the spot in the *Neues Deutschland*, he became suspicious for being too sympathetic to the Yugoslavian decentral way of running the economy. Without the suspicions about Behrens' loyalty, the case of Strnad might not have been taken up and documented at all.[29]

Once in charge of the affair, the CC Department for Science and Propaganda asked for reactions from both Behrens and Kuczynski. In addition to his scholarly judgment, Behrens was asked to comment on the allegation of having dismissed him for "not greeting properly" and "crooked sitting."[30] Kuczynski was also asked to comment on the allegation of not writing first reports for students who were not his own, as if this practice were subject to the party's approval. Behrens

---

[28] It is unclear if Ulbricht himself read Strnad's letter. Otto Reinhold, born in 1925, studied economics at Humboldt and at Jena between 1946 and 1950; thus he could have known Strnad from classes. In 1954/1955, he became professor of political economy at the party academy, and then deputy head of the CC Department of Science and Propaganda. Later he became head of the Academy for Social Sciences; see Herbst and Müller-Enbergs et al. (2010).

[29] Most of the documentation used to reconstruct the debate about Strnad's thesis can be found in one folder that gathers documents related to Behrens (SAPMO-BArch DY 30 83342). Thus, the account in this chapter is made possible because of the witch hunt against Behrens described in Chapter 3.

[30] September 3, 1956, SAPMO-BArch, DY 30 83342: 386.

replied that Strnad had left his position as his personal assistant *on his own initiative*. He also reported repeated disputes with other comrades over Strnad's "excessive arrogance," which led to discussions with the party-group. And he repeated his academic advice that Strnad should focus on specific statistical problems rather than discussing them abstractly. Kuczynski's reply reads very differently, with a sense of annoyance for having to report on academic affairs to the party apparatus:

Comrade E. Strnad is an arrogant and naughty liar. I looked at his so-called dissertation about two years ago. To my question of what, according to him, is the new scientific contribution of his thesis, he had no answer. About 14 days ago, the Institute for Social Sciences at the Central Committee sent again a revised version of the dissertation. I read the work again and wrote to the institute what I thought about it.[31]

The CC Institute for Social Sciences was in fact the next office that Strnad had approached – a party institution that just recently had received the right to issue doctoral degrees. Werner Mussler, vice-head of the Department for Political Economy, informed the Department for Science and Propaganda about their experience.[32] Although they hesitated to accept Strnad as a candidate, they did so because he "came from a family with an important party tradition."[33] One of the junior staff of the institute knew Strnad from university and reported that he thought of Strnad as "arrogant" and a "loner" (*Einzelgänger*). As a student candidate to become a member of the party, he failed the "party exam" (*Parteiprüfung*) because he was not sufficiently engaged in party activities. Mussler also knew of Heinz Puhlmann, chief editor at the editing house *Die Wirtschaft*, where Strnad worked between 1953 and 1955. Puhlmann also confirmed Strnad's negative personal qualities, but approved of his abilities as translator. It was only while at the publishing house that Strnad passed the party exam. Mussler continues:

In his personal behavior at the department, he [Strnad] defended his affair with an obstinacy that could almost be described as obtrusive. In a conversation with me, he burst into tears when he told me of the unsuccessful attempts

[31] Kuczynski to Reinhold, September 6, 1956, SAPMO-BArch, DY 30 83342: 388.
[32] Mussler to Fischer, September 28, 1956, SAPMO-BArch, DY 30 83342: 389–390.
[33] Ibid.

to find acceptance of his thesis elsewhere. We had three preliminary reports prepared to decide whether to open a doctoral procedure (two internally and one by Kuczynski). All three were negative. Therefore, we asked him to rewrite his thesis and to seek a position as "unofficial aspirant."[34]

The same day that the Department for Science and Propaganda received these reports, they wrote to Josef Strnad, answering his letter to Ulbricht. After "thorough investigations," the letter reads, the department concluded that Strnad's difficulties in defending his thesis were due to the fact that he did not follow academic custom: "It has always been common practice for a doctoral candidate to consult with a professor about the topic and ask for supervision as a so-called 'doctoral supervisor' *before* beginning the research. Your son did not do so ... which makes the whole thing much more difficult, but should not make it impossible."[35] In the same vein, the letter also referred to alleged positive scientific value as proven by the preliminary reports. Behrens, Kuczynski, and two readers of the CC Institute for Social Sciences were negative, for scientific reasons only. The department encouraged his son to learn his lesson and revise the manuscript. A few days later, Josef Strnad was invited to the Department for Science and Propaganda to talk things over in a personal meeting, an *Aussprache*.[36] He responded that he was helping with the potato harvest and would call them later.[37] There is no evidence that he ever called or that such a meeting took place.

In September 1956, the Council of Ministers issued new doctoral examination regulations.[38] In substance, these regulations did not differ from the preceding ones; however, the novelty was that a central institution, the State Secretariat for Higher Education, rather than the individual universities, was the legal body in charge of doctoral degrees. Another novelty was that party and state schools were allowed to issue doctoral degrees, such as the Institute for Social Sciences of the CC that Strnad contacted. Even if this latter change

---

[34] Ibid.
[35] Diehl to Strnad, September 28, 1956, SAPMO-BArch, DY 30 83342: 392.
[36] Letter to Josef Strnad, October 2, 1956, SAPMO-BArch, DY 30 83342: 393.
[37] Josef Strnad, October 7, 1956, SAPMO-BArch, DY 30 83342: 394.
[38] "Verordnung über die Verleihung akademischer Grade," as discussed in Bleek and Mertens (1994: 29–31). Western universities refused to apply the rules because of the inclusion of party institutions.

increased the political influence of the party on doctoral degrees, the former also limited this influence since universities were bound by the State Secretariat for Higher Education rather than the CC Department for Science and Propaganda that Strnad had mobilized. Strnad might not have known of these changes, but any further attempt to mobilize political help from the political class would challenge the autonomy of the institution in charge, the State Secretariat for Higher Education.

Freeriding on the Revisionism Campaign

During the months that followed in the fall of 1956, Ulbricht felt close to being ousted. The events caused by Khrushchev's speech heated up. Strikes in Poland, tanks in Budapest, a show trial against the Harich group in Berlin calling for free elections, the show debate against Behrens and Benary calling for the "withering of the state," and a party trial against Behrens for searching data at the Kiel Institute for the World Economy showing the high reparation payments to the Soviet Union. Then, at the 30th Plenum of the CC, at the end of January 1957, Ulbricht cited and critiqued Behrens and Benary along with the Petöfi Club in Hungary, Kardelj's ideas in Yugoslavia, and the Harich group (Ulbricht 1957). The critique of bourgeois ideology and the battle against the "revisionist" forces within the party were reduced to one and the same thing – just as Strnad had it in his thesis.

Once Ulbricht's speech became public, Strnad saw an opportunity to push his agenda further. The speech must have heightened his sense of political ego to such an extent that immediately after, on February 10, 1957, he wrote directly to Ulbricht. What might have otherwise appeared as mere narcissism demanded attention, at times, when questions of personal loyalty overshadowed questions of academic custom. Strnad argued that the rejection of his dissertation not only concerned him personally but had greater significance because statistics professors in the GDR were unwilling to battle against bourgeois ideologies, as Ulbricht had fiercely called for. These statisticians, he argued, were subject to a "cult of personality" of bourgeois scientists. They followed the authority of the bourgeois Felix Burkhardt, who rejected Strnad's thesis for the wrong political reasons:

I think it is well known how much this professor remained a man of the old school. He suppresses public criticism of his West German "colleagues" on the pretext that this would harm the "unity." That's why he never had even a look at my thesis. But the verdict of the entire profession seems to stand and fall with the judgment of Burkhardt.[39]

In the appendix, Strnad included the positive evaluations of Forbrig, Agricola, and Scheler, adding two new approvals by Siegbert Kahn, the head of the German Economic Institute (DWI), and by Masslov, the author of a Soviet statistics textbook (reference unknown), who affirmed "undoubtable scholarly [*wissenschaftlich*] value" of his thesis.[40]

In order to increase party support for his dissertation, Strnad wrote not only to Ulbricht but also to another prominent Old Communist, Hermann Matern, deputy president of the *Volkskammer*. Matern had written an article in *Die Einheit* in which he evoked Lenin's epistemological work when attacking the Petőfi Club and other revisionists (Matern 1957). Having spotted potential sympathies, Strnad wrote him a pleading letter that included his thesis summary:

I wrote about this topic although certain older professors do not want to engage in an argument about bourgeois opinions, much less a criticism, or even a discussion. It was suggested to me that I should by no means accuse West German statisticians of being "inconsistent," let alone other allegations regarding their "presuppositions" and "intentions."[41]

In both letters to Ulbricht and Matern, Strnad played on the suspicion that was common among those communists who lived through the oppressive years before 1945, be it in Nazi Germany, in Western exile, or in Stalin's Soviet Union. The multitude of experiences and compromises that survival in these regimes required resulted in a struggle over a multitude of visions of socialism in the new GDR, which was characteristic of the period of the Thaw. In Strnad's case, what reinforced his suspicion about impure socialist motivations must have been the intergenerational trauma from the concentration camp memories of his father. These memories indeed remained with him for the rest of his life (Strnad and Strnad 1990).

---

[39] SAPMO-BArch, DY 30 83342: 397.   [40] Ibid.: 397.
[41] Strnad to Matern, March 12, 1957, SAPMO-BArch, DY 30 83342: 399.

Success

The two letters to Ulbricht and Matern seemed to be successful. Although no direct response from Ulbricht is documented, after a few weeks, the Department for Science and Propaganda reported to Ulbricht that they had contacted the Higher School of Economics in Berlin-Karlshorst: "We have managed that the faculty in charge takes over the case and that he will probably be able to defend his doctoral thesis and graduate there. Strnad was informed by telephone."[42] Party pressure did it. On March 20, 1957, "after proper examination of the general documents and preliminary report," as Alfred Lemmnitz, rector of the Higher School for Economics would report, the doctoral committee of the economics faculty accepted Strnad as a candidate.[43] Strnad had the right to suggest referees and proposed the university reader (*Dozent*) in philosophy Herrmann Scheler from Humboldt University, and Schultze from the University of Halle (first name unknown). The committee accepted these propositions.

Apart from this arrangement, however, the party continued its own investigation of Strnad. Matern had forwarded Strnad's letter to Kurt Hager, the long arm of Ulbricht and CC secretary in charge of sciences, who asked the statistician Koslow, a visiting professor at the Higher School of Economics, to write an expert report. Having only read the summary, Koslow took a position regarding Strnad's notion of statistics not being a separate science:

In our opinion, this point of view is wrong. It contradicts facts and practice. Statistics has existed as an independent science for a century and has undergone a wide development in the countries of the socialist camp. The majority of scholars consider statistics to be an independent material science, which has its own object and its own research method.[44]

Also, Strnad's criticism of bourgeois statistics did not convince Koslow because "false statements on individual statistical questions are not proof of the inadequacy and inaccuracy of bourgeois statistics as a whole."[45] Koslow suggested that Strnad should rather show how the history of the discipline of bourgeois statistics was intertwined with the history of capitalism in general. This was the only time when someone from the

---

[42] March 15, 1957, SAPMO-BArch, DY 30 83342: 430.   [43] Ibid.
[44] Koslow, April 18, 1957, SAPMO-BArch, DY 30 83342: 423–424.
[45] Ibid.: 424.

academic sphere communicated a scholarly judgment regarding the content of the thesis to the party apparatus. Though Koslow was critical, it appeared that the thesis seemed at least worth a discussion.

In addition to Koslow, Hager also asked the head of the Department for Science and Propaganda, Karl Kampfert, for an evaluation of the case.[46] After having collected personal information about Strnad, Kampfert submitted his report on April 16, 1957. He began by referring to Josef Strnad's standing in the party, including his time in the concentration camp, and continued about Ernst Strnad:

> For about a year and a half, the comrade has been trying hard to find a place to defend his dissertation. He contacted all our leading statisticians and institutes and they completely disavowed him. He blames the persistence of bourgeois ideology in the minds of our economists. However, in our opinion, this is not the main cause [of his difficulties], as this applies only to a small part of our professors (such as Professor Burkhardt in Leipzig) ... The main reason is the strong individualism of comrade Ernst Strnad, which is associated with his excessive arrogance and which led him to an inappropriate self-overestimation of his scientific ability and the scholarly (*wissenschaftlich*) value of his research.[47]

Kampfert then referred to the negative letter written by Mussler from the CC Institute for Social Sciences calling Strnad a "loner" and "arrogant." He added his comments on the scholarly value of the thesis summary:

> The presumptuous character typical for Comrade Ernst Strnad also characterizes his thesis summary sent to Comrade Hermann Matern. The arguments put forward correctly state that the bourgeois definitions of statistics conceal the class character of statistical research ... but the justification for these theses seems to be somewhat obvious and written from the point of view of the superior Marxist scientist, as it were. The arguments in defense of his theses, if there are any at all, are not profound enough ... Comrade Strnad does not give any theoretical analysis of the opinions of bourgeois statisticians, even when he attacks a specific approach, such as econometrics. He merely describes them by some examples as false and superficial without analyzing or theoretically refuting the ideas at stake.[48]

---

[46] Considering how central Kampfert was for the campaign against Behrens and Benary, it is possible that it was him who collected the material about Strnad as found in the party archive today.

[47] SAPMO-BArch, DY 30 83342: 419.   [48] Ibid.: 420.

Though negative in its tone, Kampfert's letter concluded that "it has now been made possible . . . that his dissertation is accepted for defense at the Higher School of Economics in Berlin-Karlshorst."[49]

On May 16, 1957, the committee at the Higher School of Economics received Schultze's report. Schultze suggested *accepting* the thesis with the mention of *rite*, the lowest possible grade to pass. It seemed that Strnad had made it! However, after circulating the report among the members of the general faculty committee (*Fakultätsrat*), the committee decided that Schultze should write a more extensive report, because he merely listed an abundance of typos, stylistic errors, and exaggerations, and said little about scholarly quality. On June 19, Scheler, the second referee, informed the dean that he could not write a report, as he was not a statistician.

Having learned about Scheler's refusal, Strnad tried to obtain a report from one of the most Soviet-loyal hardliners in political economy, Robert Naumann from Humboldt University. Naumann became a professor without a doctoral degree and was one of the early GDR academics who made a career because of loyalty rather than merit. But Naumann also understood that statistical expertise was required and recommended Janakieff of the Higher School of Economics, who, in turn, recommended Koslow, who had already been shown to be critical. Strnad must have been informed about the search falling back on Koslow and did not know what to do other than contacting the party apparatus *again*. He wrote another letter to Strohbusch (unidentified party official) on July 30, 1957, politicizing his academic affair once again via personal appeal:

Despite all the requests of our party to tackle bourgeois ideology, my criticism is not accepted at any institute . . . (and this is so) because Behrens and Burkhart reject it . . . The former said we would not at all 'keep up with' bourgeois statistics while the latter refuses criticism for being politically unsound . . . They send me to other professors, who in turn refer me to others . . . Since, among others, the oldest Marxist professor has explained to me that my standpoint is on the correct line, I ask the party for support for admission to the defense, if not in Karlshorst, then in Halle.[50]

And, once again, the party apparatus responded positively. Strohbusch sent an internal note to the CC Department for Science and Propaganda,

[49] Ibid.   [50] SAPMO-BArch, DY 30 83342: 426.

asking them to help Strnad. "May you please call Comrade Strnad for an *Aussprache* one of these days. I think we should see how we can help this Comrade."[51]

Failure

By June 1957, the revisionism campaign at the Academy of Sciences stabilized. Behrens and Benary's texts were published with several counter-statements by, among others, Kampfert and Scheler.[52] As we have seen, Benary left academia, and Behrens lost his job as director of the Central Statistical Office and was demoted to a mere researcher. The official party punishment against Behrens was given because he used data that he received from Fritz Baade, president of the Kiel Institute for the World Economy, to show that the reparation payments to the Soviet Union were higher than officially reported. Behrens received a "rebuke" (*Rüge*) because of "lacked vigilance . . . that Baade used them [these statistics] for campaigning against the Soviet Union," according to the verdict.[53] This was the party's position regarding the political status of statistics, and Strnad's thesis would certainly not help in strengthening it. In any event, the end of the Behrens affair consolidated the relationship between the party and academia to such an extent that the party was no longer interested in using Strnad for its own interests. He now could be presented as an individualist and arrogant opportunist.

On the one hand, the Department for Science and Propaganda resisted Strohbusch's demand. They responded that the case involving Ernst Strnad "was closed with the statement of Comrade Kampfert of April 16, 1957," and finally drew a line regarding responsibility: "It should be clear to Comrade Strnad that it is . . . the university senate or a committee appointed by the senate who decides alone about his acceptance as a doctoral candidate."[54] On the other hand, the committee at the Higher School of Economics acted more autonomously and refused Strnad's demand to exclude Koslow as a referee. Thus, even if the first referee, Schultze, had submitted a more extensive and positive report by September 9, which would have forced the university

---

[51] Strohbusch to Hörnig, August 2, 1957, SAPMO-BArch, DY 30 83342: 425.
[52] See all articles in *Wirtschaftswissenschaft*, 3. Sonderheft (1957).
[53] Secretariat minutes, SAPMO-BArch, DY 30 J IV 2-2-549, 12–14.
[54] SAPMO-BArch, DY 30 83342: 426.

to find a third referee, considering Koslow's negative report, in early November, Strnad simply gave up.

The candidate wrote to the rector of the university that he rejects all officials at the university that are involved in his doctoral procedure as "biased." On November 8, 1957, Mr. Strnad withdrew his doctoral application ... We understand that he is preparing a Russian translation with the intention of submitting the thesis elsewhere.[55]

Anticipating Strnad's further attempts to graduate at other universities, the committee sent a letter to the State Secretariat for Higher Education, which is a state rather than a party institution. This switch of agency was significant, and from our point of view, outstanding all along. The committee recommended that Strnad not be allowed to receive a doctoral degree from *any* other university in the GDR: "Mr. E. Strnad has withdrawn his doctoral application at the Higher School of Economics. The State Secretariat for Higher Education is asked to prevent Mr. Strnad from other attempts at receiving a doctoral degree elsewhere with the same thesis."[56]

Also in November 1956, Lemmnitz wrote to the Department of Science and Propaganda, copying the report he wrote to the State Secretariat for Higher Education cited above. It was only now that Lemmnitz finally drew the line between academic and political concerns, as one would have expected from the start. In his letter, Lemmnitz made it clear that Strnad acted improperly in involving the party, and that the party was not in charge of the affair. Lemmnitz asked the party to *cooperate* with the universities and not demand again that Strnad be granted a doctoral degree:

Strnad is a member of the Socialist Unity Party of Germany and has been felt authorized to call upon the support of his case at our university by comrades of the Politburo, in particular Comrade Matern. The department is asked to support the request of our university and stop Comrade Strnad's future attempts to submit the same work at other universities in the GDR (which we expect), since he apparently fears that he will not be able to obtain a doctoral degree from our university.[57]

Such was the documentation of the case involving Strnad. In contrast to the Behrens–Benary case as well as countless other cases, academia (barely) managed to defend its terrain. Strnad did *not* receive his desired academic title despite the party's support as described in this

[55] Ibid.   [56] Ibid.: 429.   [57] Ibid.: 428.

chapter. His thesis does not appear in any library. All we have is the seventeen-page summary discussed in the first section.[58]

Strnad kept on working as a translator of economic and military books until the end of the GDR.[59] In 1968, he wrote another doctoral thesis, which was, this time, indeed accepted at the Wilhelm-Pieck University of Rostock. He wrote on "the Cuban public budget before and after the revolution" (Strnad 1968). The thesis appears in the library catalogue of the university, but there is no documentation as to how he received the degree. After retiring, he studied the economy of the Etruscan people, gave several lectures at Humboldt University on this topic, and self-published his research (Strnad 1990). Jointly with his twin brother Walter, he also investigated the war crimes committed against socialists in the concentration camps of the National Socialist regime, based on the memoirs of his father, which were also self-published (Strnad and Strnad 1990: 70).

* * *

The case of Strnad can be read as an example of successful academic resistance to the political attempt to intervene in its sphere and its customs. Even if party careers seemed to be a necessary condition for career advancement, they were not, as the case of Strnad shows, a sufficient condition. Inversely, it also can be read as an example of the extent to which the party was willing and active in injecting an ad hominem logic into the academic sphere and also the extent to which parts of academia were sensitive to this logic.

When thinking of the underlying issue of the epistemology of political economy, Strnad's case shows that the older generation of GDR statisticians was largely unwilling to question the standards of statistical reasoning in Marxist-Leninist terms. Some elements of "bourgeois" social sciences would remain as the scientific basis of political economy. Indeed, beyond the conceptual sophistry of the political

---

[58] In 1957, without referring to Strnad, Forbrig at the Higher School of Economics argued in a very similar fashion as Strnad, showing that his argument was not beside the point at all. He "warned of too much autonomy of statistics … and demanded a close connection between statistics and political economy" (cited in Strohe 1996). This can also be related to the Soviet notion to subsume statistics under accounting.

[59] As, for example, a translation of the memoirs of a Russian secret agent; Philby (1983).

economy of socialism, the social sciences in the GDR were increasingly open to descriptive statistics, though always stalled by the secrecy surrounding data.[60] However, in terms of methodological innovation in the social sciences, the GDR experienced less change than did Western academia. There never was any serious confrontation or understanding of what happened in the Econometric Society. The case of Strnad, without anticipating any of these future changes, can be read as a missed opportunity to discuss the nature of socialist statistics and its relationship with Western innovations. The overly politicized situation of post-Stalinism did not allow for such a debate. While in other cases, such as the Behrens affair, the agent that inhibited scientific change was the party, in this case, agency also fell back on the established class of scholars. Perhaps the stubborn support of the party apparatus for Strnad actually contributed to *not* engaging fully in the development of econometric methods.

The revisionism campaign was only the beginning of East Germany's history of negotiating the balance between the party and academia. University reforms would continue until the end of the GDR, giving opportunity for many other cases of tensions between these two spheres. For, after all, even if academics wished to credibly legitimize the scientific character of party decisions, they had to do so by holding up the standards of knowledge that were not solely born out of the womb of the revolution.

---

[60] See Steiner, "Probleme mit der DDR-Statistik." Later advances in statistics became manifest through its acceptance in other social sciences, such as sociology, demography, and also socialist business economics.

PART III

Reforming Reforms towards Bailout

5 | *Ulbricht's Modernist Reforms*

It's got to look democratic, but we must have everything in our control. (Walter Ulbricht, May 1945)[1]

The building of the wall has been called the "stealthy second" foundation of the GDR.[2] Young professionals, such as economists heading for a career as a professor, did not think of it much differently from their party: an unfortunate but necessary means of protection against capitalism. The wall was deemed necessary for the so-called *Störfreimachung*, the 'making free from disturbances' from the West. The regime pointed to the economic dependency on the crisis-ridden swings of capitalist countries – an argument that goes back to Stalin, who cut off the Soviet Union from international trade. In addition to the increasing number of highly educated workers that moved to West Germany, both the Berlin crisis in 1959 and West Germany's threat to cancel the inner German Trade Treaty showed how vulnerable East Germany's industry was to political pressure. Since 1955, West Germany had applied the so-called Hallstein Doctrine to cease diplomatic relations with states that recognized the GDR. The protagonists of this book might have agreed with the term officially used for the wall since 1962, the "antifascist rampart." According to their generational instinct, they saw an opportunity to finally build a socialist society on its own foundation. The wall made it possible for the laws of socialism to become effective, even in a global context of continued class struggle. With higher responsibility regarding the regime's success, notably in economic terms, economists could expect to be in the spotlight of the policies to come.

---

[1] Cited by the later historian Wolfgang Leonhard, one of the members of the so-called Ulbricht group, which in 1945 was sent from the Soviet Union to East Germany to revive communism (1958: 303).
[2] According to the historian Staritz (in Steiner 2004: 123). For the long-dated plans of Ulbricht to build the wall and his attempts to convince the Soviet Union, see the classic study by Hope Harrison (2003).

The building of the wall also improved the security of individual career prospects. Those young assistant economists who survived the campaign of the 1950s, nearing thirty years of age, were at the tipping point of their careers, with clear prospects of being promoted to professorial status.[3] In addition to those who left the country, many of the Old Communists retired in the 1960s and 1970s, giving up their place to the young. It should be noted that this did not apply to the higher-ranking party positions, notably those in the Politburo, which were held until the end of the state by Old Communists.[4] The hope generation's gratitude for having received an education, reinforced by their rejection of those who did not show the same gratitude, turned into an obligation to give back to the state, which meant becoming ambitious members of society seeking a career. As for the three remaining protagonists to be dealt with in the remainder of this book, Erwin Rohde became a professor in 1962, Dieter Klein became a professor in 1964, and Harry Maier became a professor in 1968. All of their careers would prosper during the late Ulbricht and early Honecker period. Under the influence of this generation, sealed off from the West, the GDR would develop its own distinct intellectual culture.

The two decades of the 1960s and 1970s to be surveyed in this chapter and Chapter 6 were the main period of the professional activity of the hope generation. Their professional ambition became

---

[3] "The wall provided the security of planning one's career and private life for all those who accepted the conditions of the GDR" (Middell 2012: 274). The mid-ranking positions that the hope generation would obtain would block the younger generation from taking on these posts until their retirement in the early 1990s. "Considering the many open posts after the expansion of the educational system and the wave of those who flew to the West, the high career expectations were by no means unrealistic. Only the subsequent cohorts, those born after 1950, faced the tendency of closure of the higher posts, once their precedents, those born between 1930 and 1950, divided the cake among themselves" (Middell 2012: 345). At Humboldt University, for example, in the early 1980s, more than three-quarters of the close to thirty professors were born around 1930 (see the list in Düppe 2017). See also the striking evidence of Fulbrook's "1929 anomaly" showing that a significantly high share of all the entries in a "Who's Who" of the GDR were born between 1925 and 1935 (Fulbrook in Schüle 2006: 113–130).

[4] Politburo members in the early 1970s that were still Old Communists included Erich Mielke (b. 1907), Erich Mückenberger (b. 1910), Kurt Hager (b. 1912), Erich Honecker (b. 1912), Willi Stoph (b. 1914), and Hermann Axen (b. 1916). Only Günter Mittag (b. 1926) was of the Hitler Youth generation.

manifest in a commitment to an ongoing attempt to improve and reform socialism. The hopes that had been projected onto the young adults were internalized and institutionalized as a will to reform. The core virtue of these reforms was the practical relevance of economic knowledge obtained in a continuous process of criticism and self-criticism. Science, and economic science in particular, thus represented one big "construction area of reforms" (Middell 2012: 291 ff.). But considering that the "leading role of the party" was both the *force* and the *limit* of change, as we will see, the reformist spirit was in fact a structural element of the very legitimacy of the state. Torn between modernization and party conservatism, the state was legitimized by what it could become rather than what it actually was.[5]

The remarkable trait of the hope generation's professional attitude was thus the ability to forget and to repeat the cycle of frustrated and renewed hopes, or, in other words, to accept the contradiction between the ideals of socialism and the reality of the GDR. As Dieter Klein frankly put it: "For someone like me, who grew up under state socialist conditions, it was simply normal to be able to deal with contradictions. One could agree and at the same time not agree" (Klein interview 2021). This applies not only to the renewal of the reforms, but also to the contradictions that existed between the reforms, which were in fact expressions of power interests of internal party struggles. Yet, instead of seeing the power interests of the party being in contrast to those of the people, as a class as it were, the dominant narrative remained that of the continuous development of socialism, stylized as a law of the development of socialism. Their flaunted reformist spirit, as this chapter and Chapter 6 show, had the ideological function of placating and conciliating the lagging behind of official goals and thus *reproducing* hopes for a better future.

I illustrate this reformist spirit during the last ten years under Ulbricht and the first ten years under Honecker through the example of Erwin Rohde, a public finance economist at Humboldt University. In contrast to the other protagonists of this book, Rohde can be considered representative of East German economists. He was party-loyal, ready to look inwards into his own field of specialization without asking the big questions, involved in the reforms of the institutions

---

[5] For the tension between conservatism and modernization, see Land and Possekel (1994: 14).

of economic science, ready to change the outlook of his research according to the official party line, and, most importantly, aware and accepting of the increasing contradictions between ideals and reality that were increasingly covered up by a veil of secrecy. Even if Rohde contributed little to the few actual debates that existed in East German economics during this period, he is a telling case because he stood at the crossroads of the central pillars of the regime of economic knowledge.[6] In his research, he was close to the Ministry of Finance; as dean and vice-rector during the third university reform, he played a central role in the faculty reorganization; and as the head of the group of "international finance," he would educate those who were employed in one of the most well-kept secrets under Honecker, the area of commercial coordination (KoKo).

Combining the epistemic virtues of an East German economist, his resulting intellectual profile is rather conformist, bureaucratic, and mediocre. This mediocrity has been acknowledged by many academics as well as by the party. As Rohde said of himself in hindsight: "We, like everyone in the GDR . . . were intellectually rather mediocre. We did more or less well, but we have not brought forth really great people who had big visions about finance" (Rohde 2009). We will see that this mediocrity was structurally conditioned by East Germany's academic world at large. In other words, a representative of East Germany's regime of economic knowledge, Rohde helps explain the role of economists in maintaining the *stability* of East German society during these two long decades.

Erwin Rohde until 1962

Before becoming a professor in 1962, Rohde had been an assistant at the university since 1950. At the beginning of his career, in his mid-twenties, he was practically running the department of finance alone since the leading chair, Martin Schmidt, held a position in the Ministry of Finance. He was proud of what he had established and soon received recognition: "Within a few years, the institute had developed into an important institution in our republic," he would later say of his achievements (NR 5: 1). His relationship with the Ministry of Finance developed when, in 1954 and 1955, he became member of a research collective at the ministry that aimed to create a new system for the state

[6] For a survey of the theoretical debates in the late Ulbricht and early Honecker period, see Krause (1998b: 157–190, 205–235).

budget. Public accounting became Rohde's field of expertise, a field that had little political risk, particularly in the way he practiced it, as part of the public administration and thus as an approach to economic planning that gives much flexibility to politics.[7] In 1956, the ministry gave him the task of helping install the new system of "public budget abatement" (*Haushaltsausgleich*). In the GDR, as in the Soviet Union, the budget of a lower municipal unit was integrated into that of a higher unit. The local budget of a city, for example, was integrated into that of a district, which was integrated into that of a province, and so forth, rather than being relatively independent as in most Western countries. In the early 1960s during Ulbricht's NES, however, Rohde would work in partially undoing this change.[8]

In addition to his work at the ministry, Rohde had a high teaching burden. He thus would not submit his doctoral thesis on the budget abatement until 1957, seven years after his undergraduate diploma. During the period of the Thaw, Rohde stayed away from controversial positions. As we saw in Chapter 3, he even contributed at the demand of Naumann to the bashing of revisionism against Kohlmey (Rohde et al. 1958). Later, Rohde would take positions close to that of Kohlmey's ideas regarding a stronger and more independent role of a central bank. But Rohde also recalled, after retirement, that his first significant publication, a manual on the state budget written with Fengler (1959), was criticized by Naumann as "economistic" and "legally conservative," since the authors gave too much emphasis to rules of administration in contrast to political will.[9] At the same time, Rohde was still celebrating Lenin as a "treasure" (*Fundgrube*) of

---

[7] For more on financial planning in the GDR, see Wagener et al. (2021: chapter 4.2). On public accounting and its relationship to statistics in the Soviet context, see Mespoulet (2022).

[8] About his early work, see the list of references in NR 1 and NR 5. He published several articles in the journal *Deutsche Finanzwirtschaft* on public finance of municipalities, contrasted with the imperialist public finance in West Germany that secured the power of monopolies. Rohde also wrote more political contributions on the existence of the middle class in West Germany, on the difficult financial situation of students in West Germany, and on the National Socialist past of the president of the West German central bank (*Bundesbank*), Karl Blessing. He also edited the publications of administrative regulations in public finance (*Loseblattsammlung*).

[9] This critique was informed by the results of the Babelsberg conference that abandoned administrative law, thus limiting the rule of law and the accountability of the state.

modern socialist finance (1960). For Lenin's notion of rational planning, national accounting being a sophisticated form of administrative bookkeeping was indeed central.[10]

After his doctoral thesis, Rohde became first a member and then the head of another research collective at the Ministry of Finance on regional financial planning and the simplification of the tax system. Having shown himself to be a party-loyal economist, in 1959 and 1960 he even became the head of a research group summoned by the Economic Commission of the Politburo run by Erich Apel. The leading clique of the political class thus knew his name. This research was subject to security clearance and possibly involved knowledge of the plans that Ulbricht would carry out in 1961. The regional consequences the construction of the wall would have on the financial system was certainly something Ulbricht wished to inquire into before realizing his year-long plan of building the wall.[11]

Rohde's policy research held him back from writing his habilitation. Knowing, however, that his engagement with the leading class would be rewarded, in 1960 he applied for special treatment, a "simplified" habilitation of a set of eight articles submitted in a cumulative fashion rather than a book – a then unusual procedure.[12] A year and a half later, he received his habilitation degree from Higher School of Economics, which allowed him to become a professor and director of the Institute of Finance in May 1962. By then, he had already received several prizes and acknowledgments in the sophisticated system of symbolic recognition.[13] With the new course that Ulbricht would announce after the building of the wall, he would have to undo, in parts, elements of the centralized public finance system that he himself had installed.

---

[10] See the discussion in Mespoulet (2022), and in Kotz and Seneta (1990).

[11] "This working group, which included leading practitioners, professors and lecturers in my field from all universities and colleges, had to make scientifically well-founded proposals to the party leadership for the complete redesign of systems and methods in a sub-field of finance that cannot be described here" (NR 5, 5). I have not found documentation of this working group.

[12] See his letter to Franz Dahlem at the State Secretariat for Higher Education (October 11, 1960, NR 5).

[13] See NR 1 and NR 6 for a full list of his prizes. In 1960, he received a medal as activist of the Seven-Year-Plan; in 1971, he received the Patriotic Order in Bronze (*vaterländischer Verdienstorden*); in 1982, he received the military Order for Folk and Fatherland in Gold (*Kampforden für Verdienste um Volk und Vaterland*); in addition, he received the Arthur Becker medal of the FDJ and the Fritz-Heckert medal of the labor union.

The New Economic System

After East Germany's economy was politically secured, socialism was to be made attractive through a "modernization" of the ailing economy in a fashion that would have been ideologically illicit some years before. In summer 1963, Ulbricht announced the New Economic System of Planning and Management (*neues ökonomisches System der Planung und Leitung der Volkswirtschaft*, NES).[14] NES was meant to secure the party regime through sustained economic growth as had been promised since the foundation of the GDR and notably since the introduction of Ulbricht's slogan of 1957 to "take over without catching up" (*Überholen ohne Einzuholen*). The name "New Economic System" alluded to Lenin's New Economic Policy of the 1920s, a program that had been undone by Stalin. In the Soviet Union, discussions about a similar reform were under way due to an article written by Evseï Libermann in 1962, but the actual reform that paralleled Ulbricht's NES, the so-called Kosygin reforms, were introduced later.[15] Indeed, NES represented a certain degree of autonomy and independence from the Soviet Union that Ulbricht ventured in his late period. The NES allowed economic policy to be seen as a way to manage a *specific* national system rather than a socialist society that was on the same track toward communism all over the globe.

Ulbricht presented NES as a response to the so-called scientific-technical revolution. The reform can indeed be understood as the East German variant of the faith in scientific and technological progress that had spread across the globe in the 1960s. The importance of technology for the economy required specialized knowledge on the local level and more complex coordination due to a higher degree of the division of labor and a greater importance for innovation. Even if the whole economy was affected, technology-driven production profited the most from Ulbricht's NES, including mechanical engineering, chemistry, and optics, but also the health system. Science had become a driving force of the progress of society, and economic science was in the midst of it. As a regime of economic democratization, NES

---

[14] See Ulbricht's 1963 speech (1965). The most complete in-depth study on NES is Steiner (1999); see also the more succinct account in Steiner (2004). One of the English sources is Kopstein (1997: 41–72).

[15] The classic study on the Soviet reform of the 1960s is still the book by Ellman (1973).

also created a general atmosphere of cultural liberalization and prom-ised a more "democratic centralism."

With lower pressure of delimitation from the West, NES introduced an astonishing degree of decentralization, measures that Ulbricht would have rejected as revisionist only a few years earlier. The transi-tion to the "intensive advanced reproduction" (*intensiv erweiterte Reproduktion*), as it was called in GDR jargon, and the complex problems associated with this transition, could not be dealt with cen-trally. The NES reformed the industry-based price system and created performance-based incentives for firms and for individual workers, as well as for innovations. Put succinctly, NES was an imitation of the market economy without the actual risks taken with private property by capital holders. Emphasis was put on the independence of lower control units, notably state-owned firms as well as the unions of state-owned firms. They were given more responsibility in deciding on the use of their funds, while planning was reduced to mid-term benchmark goals in so-called perspective plans rather than spelled out in detail. So-called economic "levers" (*Hebel*), not to say incentives, were supposed to create harmony between the interests of the firms and that of society. Thus, the price system became key for planning, allowing firms to make profits or "bonus funds" (*Prämienfonds*) that could be reinvested at the will of firm managers. These funds created the security for plan fulfillment in the next period, which was the actual incentive for performing well on the firm level. Although Ulbricht had to expli-citly distance himself from the ideas of market socialism, notably the "regulatory" function of markets, NES was nevertheless compatible with some elements of this current of thought.[16]

Ulbricht's focus was on the "intensification" of production. Incentives for performance at the level of the firm and also at the level of workers' wages were meant to increase efficiency and innovation. The goal was, just as Behrens and Benary argued years earlier in the context of the Yugoslavian reform, to better use the "creative (*schöpferisch*) activity of

---

[16] Krause surveyed the so-called plan–market debate during the mid-1960s delimiting the regulatory function of markets in the planned economy (1998b: 297). End-states of the economy must be subject to the plan and cannot be the result of the market mechanism. The most complete source about the ideas of market socialism in several socialist countries is the recent collection of essays edited by Kovács (2022). See also the original study by Bockman on market socialism in Hungary (2011).

the workers." Thus, NES again opened up the discussion about the meaning of planning. By reducing the bureaucracy of central planning, accurate profit accounting should guide the management of firms. The NES broke with the primacy of "material balances" to count in monetary terms. Individual firms were to be led by their own "material interests" in which the overall plan was to harmonize with the "social interest," something that is impossible in capitalism. Planning is not only "command" (*Weisung*) but "management" (*Leitung*) using economic "levers". This was discussed as the paradigmatic shift from "administrative control" toward "parametric planning."

After the 7th Party Congress in 1967, NES was redubbed "the economic system of socialism," that is, not only a political reform, but a placeholder for a new stage of development of the socialist society. It correlated with the stage of "developed socialism," as Ulbricht had called it. The NES thus put discussion on the transition to communism on the shelf, as it focused on the inner consistency of socialism as a distinct economic system. Socialism was not only a stage in history but a system of its own. By making this claim, Ulbricht stylized what was one among several possible economic policies as a manifestation of the course of history itself. But saying so also meant that the economy had taken an independent and complex shape that required the *expertise* of a systems science, which was to be called economic cybernetics.

Reforming Economic Knowledge

While workers were rather skeptical of Ulbricht's NES, economists were enthused. The reform created an optimistic atmosphere of a new departure, an *Aufbruch*, one that resembled the period after the foundation of the country in 1949 and the period of the Thaw. During NES, economic knowledge in East Germany witnessed its most productive and transformative period, as it became more pluralistic and even internationally oriented. Economists gained prominence and were more heard in political committees and councils. Many easily recognized the fingerprints of Behrens and Benary's ideas of decentralization.[17] Yet the campaign

---

[17] In 1961, Behrens had published a book that cautiously updated his ideas of the mid-1950s and anticipated much of NES (Behrens 1961; see also Caldwell 2000, 2003). He argued that the increasing complexity due to the technical revolution rendered firms necessary and thus the coordination between firms by the "law of value." That is, commodity production demands "socialist property rights,"

against them had left its mark, which might explain why the reform did not come from academic economists. Erich Apel, who replaced the Soviet-loyal Karl Mewis as the head of the State Planning Commission, and Günter Mittag were the figureheads of the reform. Academic economists were only in the background, such as Walter Halbritter, Herbert Wolf, Otto Reinhold, and Wolfgang Berger, a former student of Behrens. Berger and Reinhold wrote a central manifesto of NES titled *On the Scientific Foundations of the New Economic System of Planning and Management* (1966). The Economic Research Institute of the State Planning Commission under the lead of Herbert Wolf also gained prominence during NES, which is notable, as it was a state rather than a party institution (*Ökonomische Forschungsinstitut der Staatlichen Plankommission*).

But Ulbricht also wished to back up his new course with new experts coming from a party institute. Thus, in 1965, the Central Institute for Socialist Economic Governance was founded (*Zentralinstitut für sozialistische Wirtschaftsführung beim ZK der SED*). Helmut Koziolek was its founding director, and he remained in this post until the end of the GDR. He became something of a public intellectual of NES. In contrast to the Party Academy and the Academy for Social Sciences, the institute was not subject to the CC Secretary for Science and Culture under the head of Kurt Hager but was subject directly to the CC Economic Secretary and thus Günter Mittag. The institute became something like East Germany's "business school" (Wagener et al. 2021), offering classes and workshops for future or existing managers to increase their technical expertise. The institute also studied economic planning methods in general, which brought it into competition with other party schools.

Koziolek was also one of the economists in charge of the new textbook of political economy that was to stylize Ulbricht's NES as the standard of economic knowledge.[18] The novelty of the book was that it was not a mere translation of a Soviet textbook, but was specific

which are different from the rights of capitalist property since the state integrates market values back into a scheme of use values. The plan resolves, he loftily argued, the contradiction between necessity and freedom. At a conference in 1962 at the Academy of Sciences that discussed Behrens's ideas, the fear associated with his ideas were still strongly felt, according to Steiner (1999: 68–69).

[18] Officially, Günter Mittag was in charge, next to other authors that included Walter Halbritter, Wolfgang Berger, Werner Kalweit, Otto Reinhold, and Herbert Wolf; see Autorenkollektiv (1969).

to East Germany, as it was titled *Political Economy and Its Application in the GDR.* The book was to replace the textbook translated from Russian that was once initiated by Stalin even before the war and published by the Soviet Academy of Sciences in 1955. Combining the ideas of NES with the classics of Marxism-Leninism, Ulbricht could have put into stone his politics of "developed socialism." In 1969, the book was published and approved by many members of the Politburo, including, at first, Honecker.[19]

There were other significant changes for the discipline of economics. The emphasis on technology and efficiency and the notion of socialism as a system required a new technical language in economics in addition to Marxist nineteenth-century political economy: the language of "economic cybernetics."[20] Cybernetics, as I discuss later, was primarily a philosophical discourse compatible with that of Marx; only secondly was it a set of techniques, using operations research as a decision guide, forecasting techniques as a planning tool, data sciences, and so forth.[21] Cybernetics offered a new language to speak of decentralized planning in a "modern" fashion without using the language of the market. With its emphasis on independent firm decisions, NES also meant a renewal of management as a discipline, that is, socialist business economics.[22] In addition to the technical knowledge of new socialist managers, NES revived sociology, notably industrial sociology and the sociology of labor, a field also called the "socialist management of man" (*sozialistische Menschenführung*).[23] Lastly, NES also required the organization

---

[19] See the mention of Honecker in Autorenkollektiv (1969: 20); for Stalin's political economy, see Düppe and Joly-Simard (2020).

[20] On East German cybernetics, thus far, see the participant account of a collection of essays edited by Dittmann and Seising (2007), Caldwell (2003: 141–184), and Segal (2001). Already by 1961, cybernetics was officially accepted by way of being discussed in the party journal *Einheit* (Klaus 1958, 1964), and regular conferences took place beginning in 1962 at the Central Economics Institute at the Academy of Sciences. The cybernetics movement in East Germany was paralleled, without being preceded, by the same movement in the Soviet Union. Khrushchev supported automation in 1961, but the methods of linear programming by Kantorovich were not fully accepted before 1965, when he received the Lenin prize jointly with Nemchinow. The most detailed and extensive source on the Soviet use of cybernetics for planning is still Ellman (1973).

[21] Forecasting techniques in particular were pioneered by Haustein (1969)

[22] On socialist business economics in East Germany, see the complete account in Wagener et al. (2021: chapter 4.3).

[23] At Humboldt University, in 1961, there was a working group called "Sociology and Society." In 1963, Kurt Braunreuther ran a working group for sociology at

and management of science itself, which resulted in the foundation of the Institute for Theory, History, and Organization of Science in 1970 at the Academy of Sciences (ITW).[24]

This liberalization of economic knowledge resulted in a seemingly pluralistic culture of economic knowledge. Pragmatism superseded dogmatic or theoretical criteria of method choice. Though it appeared that NES opened up economic knowledge toward a sphere that is shared with Western countries, this transformation of knowledge had to be framed in a way limited to socialism and supplementing the Old Communists' discourse of class struggle. Thus, the new forms of economic knowledge were tagged with a title obscuring the Western origin: Marxist-Leninist Organization Studies (MLO). In the late 1960s, entire faculties for MLO were founded at several universities all over the country. Ulbricht even planned a new Academy of Marxist-Leninist Organization Sciences that opened in 1969 in Berlin Wuhlheide. The academy was a research center that offered advanced learning classes, hosted the computer center, and was also an exhibition location that was to "make visible the plan-based access to the future" as technological progress was propagated.[25]

Cybernetic Reform

Georg Klaus was the pioneer of cybernetics in East Germany. He combined all the virtues necessary for placing the discourse of cybernetics at the center of power: he had been put in prison by National Socialists for two years, spent four years in the concentration camp in Dachau, and was trained as a Marxist-Leninist philosopher *and* in the natural sciences. As the director of the philosophy institute at the Academy of Sciences since

the economic institutes at the Academy of Sciences, a group that later moved to the philosophy institute. In 1964, the Politburo asked to form a scientific council for sociology under the auspices of the sociology department at the Academy for Social Sciences. The largest institute for sociology was the institute for youth research in Leipzig founded in 1966. For an institutional account of sociology in East Germany, see Meyer (1995).

[24] On the history of the ITW, and its head Günter Kröber, see Laitko (2018). The ITW would become important for the career of Harry Maier, the subject of Chapter 7.

[25] On the academy, see Sukrow (2019). Critics bemoaned the absence of the human moral aspect of technological development and its danger of feeding into convergence theories.

1959, Klaus stood for the compatibility of cybernetics and Marx's philosophy, arguing that cybernetics is the material manifestation of Marxist dialectics in a time of technological revolution. As the mathematics of Marxist-Leninist dialectics, cybernetics was the modern language potentially of all sciences. The concept of dynamic, self-organizing, self-regulating systems could be integrated as a guiding methodology into a range of disciplines (such as biology, mathematics, philosophy, psychology, semiotics, and economics); hence, it had the potential for changing the role of Marxism-Leninism in the political economy of socialism. It would be less of a philosophy or a set of ideas from which to derive practical implications for fields that Marx had not written about but more of a flexible language that could be associated with the technical elements of cybernetics. Klaus presented cybernetic self-regulation as a means to realize the socialist epistemic virtue of self-criticism, that is, as a "means to see our own stupidities in a greater perspective" (cited in Dittmann and Seising 2007: 24).

Apart from philosophy, economic cybernetics was linked with the notion of "optimal planning." The central ingredient came to be known as operations research, in particular linear (and nonlinear) programming techniques. These techniques nourished faith in the feasibility of the computational determination of interindustrial prices, the use of bonuses relative to production costs, and of course the idea of matching firm interests with the interests of the society. The self-regulation of such a system of parametric planning was in stark contrast to the hierarchical structure of bureaucratic planning. As a foundation, input–output analysis was a first step to creating an empirical basis for optimal planning on the intraindustrial level. In 1962, Kuczynski and Koziolek promoted input–output analysis, so-called *Verflechtungsbilanzierung*, calling it the "General Staff map in our struggle for the fastest possible, correctly proportioned construction of socialism."[26] Operations research promised to realize the notion of science being a productive force, as Günter Mittag emphasized in 1967: "Operations research is an excellent method for the complex examination of the activities of the firms, Kombinate, cooperation associations and entire branches of industry, which helps to convert

---

[26] Jürgen Kuczynski and Helmut Koziolek (1962). "Verflechtungsbilanz: Generalstabskarte der Wirtschaft," *Neues Deutschland*, November 17: 4.

the productive force of science into economically effective results" (cited in Dittmann and Seising 2007: 29).[27]

Such was the idea. When looking closely at what effect the cybernetics hype had on economic knowledge production beyond new jargon and considerable institutional changes, we find little. Cybernetics in fact did not change the nature of economic discourse, as it was still conceptually grounded in ideas rather than becoming a technical discipline driven by methods or models. Being educated in the sphere of Old Communists, most economists did not acquire, in their early thirties, the techniques of programming the optimal production plan. One example of how economists incorporated cybernetics is Kohlmey's article published in 1968 titled "Planning as Regulating and Steering" (*Planen als Regeln und Steuern*).[28] For Kohlmey, the cybernetics hype was a chance to plead for more worker autonomy and decentralization in a new language without using the actual techniques. As Behrens had already done, Kohlmey argued that an administrative command economy is necessary only in the first stage of socialism. In an age of technology, however, the command economy creates contradictions between the plan and the forces of production. Since labor intensity cannot be measured directly but only through its effects in the system, the harmony between plan and forces of production require a bottom-up "steering" of the economy. Only a self-regulating system via feedback circles could achieve this goal. Planning would need to take place in monetary rather than natural terms, putting the State Bank rather than the State Planning Commission at the center. Citing Stalin to back up this claim, he contrasted such a system with that of capitalism that is driven by profit maximization. The absolute distinction between socialism and capitalism thus holds. His text, however, gives no hints as to the technical implementation of this vision.

The economics of decentralized planning dates back to the late 1920s and was known under the term market socialism. Oskar

---

[27] Since 1964, a conference series on mathematics and cybernetics in economics had been organized. In mathematics, Manfred Peschel was central to bringing algorithmic methods forward; see Dittmann and Seising (2007: 43–75).

[28] See also Caldwell (2003: chapter 4). As Caldwell argued, "for the half decade from 1963 to 1968, it remained possible to introduce some revisionist ideas back into official political discussion, and this happened through the language of cybernetics" (2003: 148).

Lange developed this idea in neoclassical terms, first at the University of Chicago and from 1945 in Poland. He defended the notion of the "formal equivalence" of capitalism and socialism, saying that both systems face the same problem – efficiency – but look to solve this problem through different institutions. Lange conceived of the neoclassical framework as an institution-free language that could be used in both capitalism and socialism. In 1959, Lange published a textbook that combined Marx's political economy of capitalism with a "modern" neoclassical political economy of socialism. In addition to the "causal" reasoning as known in Marx, neoclassical modeling techniques added "functional" and "stochastic" reasoning. In the course of the reforms of the 1960s, it became possible to translate Lange's work into German even though there was no economist equivalent to Lange in East Germany.[29] The protagonist of Chapter 6, Harry Maier, edited the translation jointly with Peter Hess.

In his introduction, Maier tried to establish legitimacy for neoclassical economics in East Germany's profession. He began by reminding the reader of the virtue of criticism by saying that a "fruitful discussion inevitably also requires dissenting voices, sometimes also passionately" (Maier in Lange 1969: 6). Regarding the bourgeois origin of the "auxiliary" methods used by Lange, he writes:

> The bourgeoisie has a practical interest in the development of auxiliary disciplines of political economy such as econometrics, operational research, linear, non-linear and dynamic optimization, economic cybernetics, game theory and others … These auxiliary disciplines are of great importance for the determination of the optimal strategy of the capitalist producer … (and for) the instruments that are necessary for the … imperialist state to reproduce the processes of late capitalism. (Ibid.: 8)

These auxiliary disciplines became prominent in bourgeois economics, as Maier argued, because they helped to avoid the true questions of political

---

[29] Apart from the textbook, more of Lange's works were translated into German in the late 1960s (Lange 1968a, 1968b). There were other "progressive" editions such as Ottomar Kratsch's edition of Grigori Feldman's growth theory, or Gunther Kohlmey and Johannes Behr's edition of Pierro Sraffa. But in the GDR, there was no Ota Šik such as in Czechoslovakia, no Włodzimierz Brus or Oskar Lange or Michał Kalecki as in Poland, no János Kornai as in Hungary, who developed "rational" theories of national planning that are not directly derived from Marxian discourse; see Krause (1998b: 145–146), and the collections of essays by Kovács (2022) and Wagener et al. (2021).

economy, that is, questions on the power relations in capitalism. However, the exact relationship between bourgeois economics and economic policy is highly complex and country-specific to the extent that the same auxiliary methods can be used for different purposes in a socialist context. Considering the importance of technology in developed socialism, these auxiliary disciplines are "a spontaneous part of the socio-economic development of the forces of production," and therefore have to be a subject of the discipline of political economy. But Maier also criticized Lange's view of bourgeois economics as ideologically neutral, exemplified by his naïve view of welfare economics.

A vital question of the legitimacy of a neoclassical framework was the "law" character of its basic tenets, above all Pareto efficiency, with respect to the laws of development in Marxism-Leninism. Regarding these "structural, functional, as well as stochastic laws," Maier wrote: "Even if it seems to us that Oskar Lange expands the concept of the law too much, his analysis undoubtedly helps to overcome a certain narrowness in the consideration of processes of economic laws" (1969: 10). Maier defends the central concept in Lange's analysis, economic rationality, as an *addition* to the theory of value. Economic rationality can be a "categorical nucleus to develop the inner logic of the economic system of socialism" (ibid.: 11). But economic rationality should not be limited to the individual. The question of the integration of economic systems (not to say markets) and of the historical progress of a society (not to say growth) as well as the progress of humanity as such is not sufficiently discussed by Lange. Maier alluded to his own research in growth theory, which does address just these questions.[30] Because bourgeois economic science is incapable of discussing the rationality of goals, it cannot discuss the social and global logic of capitalism and

---

[30] Regarding growth theory, see Maier et al. (1968), and the short comments in Krause (1998b: 301). This work is strongly influenced by what was known in the West as the Harrod–Domar model, and to a lesser extent optimal growth theory, that is, the Ramsey model. However, these origins were quoted only indirectly via the interpretations of Eastern scholars, notably Grigory Feldman, János Kornai, and Michał Kalecki. The authors do not attempt to make an explicit contribution to this literature, as they needed to legitimatize the economics of this model within the Marxist discourse and that of Ulbricht's NES, and to delineate it from its bourgeois elements – hiding the crisis character of growth and not aiming at the actual wellbeing of the people (ibid.: 26 ff., and for a critique of the Harrod-Domar model, 114 ff.). Growth theory was subordinated to Marxist reproduction theory, and thus decoupled from its Western debate, see Krause (1998b: 312).

is thus ahistorical. Maier might have hoped for a discursive shift in the political economy of socialism, a hope that was soon crushed, as we will see. In East Germany, market socialism, let alone its neoclassical framework, was never officially accepted even under the conditions of NES.

Erwin Rohde exemplifies better what Ulbricht's NES actually meant for the majority of economists. Without the technical knowledge of economic cybernetics, he integrated the new jargon as an interpretative framework of his own specialty: public finance.[31] He partook in several committees that were formative for research in public finance. He was head of the scientific council at the Ministry of Finance and head of the working group of university finance departments across the country as well as a member of the Council for Economic Sciences at the Ministry for Higher Education. The NES increased the importance of public finance as an "economic lever," but also challenged its established cameralistic habitus. If firms were to generate their own funds and decide about their own investments, the size of the investment has to come with a cost: the interest rate. Rohde argued for a distinct socialist nature of the interest rate linked to technological progress that differs from the historical situation that gave rise to the capitalist interest rate. The interest rate as an economic lever increases profitability on a firm level and allows tuning in the interest of the overall society. But we do not find anything more than the mere programmatic notion of this harmony and how to measure or anticipate the uncertain effects of technological change – a key question of the theory of optimal planning. For Rohde, it is as if the mere idea would fulfill its promise.

Rohde also contributed an argument about how the general accounting system needs to adapt to the full production cycle, which in the case of a technology-based society is much longer than one year. The one-year cycle goes back to an agriculture-based economy when, during the nineteenth century, the bourgeoisie claimed more transparency over payments to the aristocracy. In an advanced technological society, however, these cycles can be much longer and are largely independent of the

---

[31] Related to public finance, see on monetary theory during NES, Krause (1998b: 297–299). In spite of the supposedly increased importance of monetary terms for NES, Krause observed a lack of theory in monetary discussions. Finance, after all, remained administration, as the example of Rohde shows well.

Figure 5.1 Erwin Rohde, ca. 1985.
Rohde (1985).

cycle of the seasons. In this historical situation, the one-year budget can turn into a means for the bourgeoisie to exploit workers since wage negotiations are based on annual measures without consideration of the long-term benefits of technologies. In a similar fashion, Rohde wrote on the management of cities and municipalities as key units of the "socialist human community."[32] Municipalities, he argued, should have more self-responsibility in using their funds. Cultural institutions such as theaters and museums should function like firms. A kindergarten has local knowledge of the needs of a small community and needs to plan on its own initiative. For this reason, cities and communities need "perspective plans" for the full production cycle of their products (say four years in the case of a kindergarten). Rohde argued for the transition from what he called "gross financing" to "performance financing" (*Bruttofinanzierung* versus *Leistungsfinanzierung*), that is, the change from ex ante to ex post payments according to the actual expenses and income. The centralization he himself undertook some years before, he now partially was to

---

[32] See Rohde et al. (1966), and Rohde and Siebenhaar (1972) that became the standard textbook.

undo: local budgets regained the autonomy they once had. Instead of actually showing how this framework can be technically implemented, he rather interpreted the new concepts in a way that made them consistent with the conceived dogma. Considering that individual workers and managers had to be willing to work according to the new rules, NES needed to be propagated in the public. Rohde gave several public radio talks to explain NES in general and the reform of the public finance system in particular.[33] Such radio talks could certainly count as a form of public discourse on economic matters, an opportunity that NES created. But the public presence of economists had more of a function of public education and of the ex post justification of party decisions.

The reform of economic knowledge under the conditions of NES led the Western sociologist Peter Christian Ludz, in 1972, to the diagnosis that a new elite was to arise in socialism that would replace the authoritarian logic of Old Communists by a regime of technocratic control. Ludz identified the young generation of new professors as the "technocratic counter-elite" against the "strategic clique" of Old Communists. This elite would replace reliance on party loyalty with rational organizational principles. The new socialist technocracy, according to Ludz, even had the potential to free East Germany from the historical narrative of socialism as a response to fascism. The propaganda of the last years of Ulbricht might have created the impression of such change, but before the reform could be fully applied, certainly when Ludz published his diagnosis, in 1972, this path of change had already been given up, as we will see at the end of this chapter.

Reforming University

Declaring the scientific-technical revolution, Ulbricht's NES put a heavy burden on the education system as a pillar of the future society.

---

[33] See NR 19, 24, 27, 29. In 1968, he explained NES in the *Berliner Rundfunk*, speaking about the relation of cost accounting, profitability, and planning by means of economic levers. Rohde travelled regularly to West Germany to report the party's standpoints of East German public finance. In 1966, Rohde presented the NES approach to public finance to the West German Society for Business Economics (*Deutscher Betriebswirtschafter Tag*), speaking in particular about the role of the interest rate. He did the same at the Sorbonne in Paris as well as in India, to mention but two examples (see NR 42).

A university independent of Western influences should produce a new type of scientist adapted to the requirements of the "developed socialist society." Thus, soon after NES was announced, the CC decided on a reform of higher education, which was called the "third" university reform in continuity with the first reform of denazification in 1945 and the second Marxist-Leninist reform in 1950. The third university reform was East Germany's version of the worldwide growth of the education and knowledge sector as well as the general belief in science. Much of this reform also took place in the West, notably the increased specialization and differentiation of disciplines. But it took a very different form in the East, with a particular emphasis on the instrumental character of knowledge as a productive force that would even undermine the traditional disciplinary milieus. The reform lasted almost a decade.[34] It began in 1963, following a party resolution at the 6th Party Congress on a Unified Socialist Education System evoking a "great learning process of all people." The corresponding law was not published until 1965:

The realization of the historical task of the program of socialism decided by the VI Congress of the Socialist Unity Party of Germany, the mastery of the technical revolution and the development of the socialist community, requires in the interests of both society and each individual a higher quality of education: the Unified Socialist Education System ... The full love and care of the workers-and-peasants state is given to the young generation that brings about great achievements in production, in political and cultural life ... (The system) serves the growth and becoming of more educated, that is, more socialist-conscious, highly qualified, healthy, mentally and physically efficient, cultured people that are ready and prepared to fulfill the historical tasks of our time.[35]

Much in the spirit of NES, universities were supposed to be run like a business and officially gained the status of a firm (*Betrieb*) with explicit business rules.[36] Like firms, application-oriented disciplines should compete over funds from industry. For others, a bonus system could

---

[34] The third university reform is well studied for the example of Humboldt University, but there is little on a national level (see Middell 2012: 310 ff. and Schulz 2010).

[35] "Gesetz über das einheitliche sozialistische Bildungssystem," February 25, 1965, *Gesetzesblätter der DDR*, I, Nr. 6: 86; see also Middell (2012: 296).

[36] See Humboldt University Archive (UA), 1653 (further references to the university archive, if not otherwise indicated, refer to the section of the archive of

create incentives for higher performance in research and teaching. The economic orientation and plan fulfillment were controlled by so-called Social Councils on the faculty and university level. Social Councils represented a fifth dimension of bureaucracy, next to the self-administration of the university, the party, the labor union, and the students' representation. They included party functionaries and business representatives who exercised control over research and teaching activities. Also, each working group had so-called praxis partners that included representatives of other institutions and government or party agencies for which the university provided services. These partners had the right to consult, vote, and control. They provided topics for diploma theses and dissertations, could organize special seminars, and were in charge of internships and job posts. Research and teaching activities depended on the goodwill of these partners. While some professors had good relationships with their praxis partners, others felt a clash with their academic ethos:

One has to accept a reasonable dialectical interaction between theory and practice, without which the task of university education gets lost. If you do not pay attention to the inner dynamic of the development of theory, it is impossible to develop innovations that could be useful in practice. (Radtke interview)

Even if the praxis partners were supposed to enhance utilitarian aspects of science, they ended up exerting ideological control insofar as that which counts as practical progress is defined by party resolutions. In Kolloch's frank words: "The decisive problem of the relationship with the praxis partners was that their opinion was after all to be respected, and that they judged the results of research. Worse, the praxis partners were no more than the long arm of the party" (2001b: 294).

But the most radical consequence that set East Germany's universities apart from those in the West was the reorganization of disciplines. So-called sections were to be created that were intended to replace the former faculty structure. The core of these sections was supposed to be a complex assemblage of various former disciplines, such that academia was organized according to social problems rather than intellectual specialization. Sections reported directly to the rector

the economics faculty to be found under "Wirtschaftswissenschaften." The number indicates the folder.

and were not composed of institutes but of working groups. Students were assigned to sections, which simplified cost accounting at the section level. Decisions on scientific staff and doctoral students were also made at the section level so that the individual institutes and thus professors no longer had any decision-making power over the next generation of scientists.

The reform also reinforced the institutional separation of research and teaching: universities, comparable to liberal art colleges, would focus on teaching, and the institutes of the Academy of Sciences would focus on research. As a result, universities became more school-like. The curricula were unified for the entire GDR, replacing the traditional lecture calendar. Each discipline had a Council for Research at the Academy of Sciences and an Advisory Board at the Ministry for Higher Education that designed the curriculum. The academy reform separated university from academy careers and cancelled the double positions that had been common. With more focus on teaching, universities were given more responsibility for the "educational" aspect of knowledge production (*Erziehung*). Universities were to create a socialist personality, a "new socialist man." In 1963, Ulbricht had already integrated his "ten commandments for the new socialist man" in the official party program.[37]

In the Academy of Sciences, instead, the priority of the "practical," that is, of economic interests, resulted in tensions with industry, specifically in chemistry and physics, which were central to the technological development envisaged by NES. In 1968, the reform of the Academy of Sciences put into question the professional autonomy that remained part of the institutional ethos of the Academy of Sciences. The economization of academic research was difficult to realize. There were difficulties finding a vice-president for planning and economics since this function was supposed to have more powers than the traditional president. Contracts with industry were supposed to finance research, which was difficult to apply as this required

---

[37] The ten commandments included, among others: 'you should always stand up for the international solidarity of the working class; you should help eliminate the exploitation of man by man; in building socialism, you should act in a spirit of mutual help and comradely cooperation; you should protect and increase public property; you should always strive to improve your performance, be economical and consolidate socialist work discipline; you should raise your children in the spirit of peace and socialism; you should live cleanly and decently and respect your family' (SED party program 1963).

contract lawyers in all departments. Scientific administration became increasingly unattractive. "Contract-related research is interpreted as the 'dictation of industry' vis-à-vis science," one informant reported.[38] The Law of the Unified Socialist Education System of 1965 only indicated the guidelines for the reform. In 1966, the State Secretariat for Higher Education published the "Principles for the Further Development of Teaching and Research at the Universities of the GDR," which required the creation of sections but did not specify the exact rules for doing so.[39] The implementation of the reform would initially involve the universities from below, which dragged on for a long time. The traditional disciplinary structure at universities, with their perceived individual interests, brought the reform to a standstill in 1968. It took seven years from the first announcement of the reform until the concrete order of the ministry to form committees that realized the section structure. This, in turn, diminished the acceptability of the reform. Ultimately, the section structure complemented rather than replaced the old faculty structure. As Honecker would require further reforms, the university landscape transformed in the early 1970s into a huge reform construction site.

These problems with the implementation of the reform can be best illustrated by the example of Humboldt University, in which Erwin Rohde also played a role. In 1963, at the beginning of the reform, the university was still feeling the shock of the so-called Havemann affair.[40] In view of the increasing pressure on science as a productive force, the chemist Robert Havemann dared to speak out, in several speeches, about the relationship between philosophy and the natural sciences by questioning the relevance of Marxism-Leninism to the development of natural science. Anyone who remembered Stalin's interference in scientific debates could easily recognize how obvious such an argument was. But not Ulbricht's party clique, who felt threatened by the presence of apolitical top performers in science. In spite of his prominence as an anti-fascist fighter, in 1964, Havemann was put under house arrest and expelled from the party. The decision had consequences for the entire

---

[38] "Problems of the implementation of the academy reform," October 25, 1968, individual information 1155/68, MfS, ZAIG 1600. On the academy reform, see Nötzold in Kocka et al. (2003).
[39] See Middell (2012: 297) and Schulz (2010: 130).
[40] See Middell (2012: 300–310). On Havemann see Florath (2004), and Hoffmann in Macrakis and Hoffmann (1999: 269–285).

party apparatus at Humboldt University. A few days later, Werner Tzschoppe, the party secretary of the university, had to resign because of a "lack of vigilance." Even the party-loyal Robert Naumann was affected, despite being vice-rector for social sciences, an elected member of the CC, and since 1960 even a member of the Politburo's ideological commission. In March 1964, he resigned "at his own request" as vice-rector and shortly after retired and disappeared from the stage of political economy.[41] The Havemann affair increased the pressure on the university, with the third university reform becoming an act of party faith.

The replacement of the central positions gave occasion to realize the spirit of the university reform. It was the hour of economists in the university administration. Heinz Sanke, director of the Institute for Politics and Economic Geography, became the new rector of the university, implementing a more central and firm-like organization. Robert Naumann was replaced as vice-rector for social sciences by Hans Arnold, director of the Institute for Industrial Economics, and, since 1960, dean of the Faculty of Economics. As a member of the economic advisory board of the State Planning Commission, Arnold was also closely related with the leading figures of NES.[42] All cooperation with industry was to be coordinated through him as vice-rector. Heinz Mohrmann, also an economist, became vice-rector for young scientists, and Erwin Rohde, in turn, replaced Hans Arnold as dean of the economics faculty. Sanke, Arnold, and Mohrmann, three economists with energetic confidence, were at the head of the university and were well versed in and willing to enforce the spirit of the Unified Socialist Education System.[43]

The third university reform not only put in question the organization inside the university but also between the universities. The Higher School of Economics, which at first specialized only in economic planning, had developed into an economic university of high esteem. Facing the utilitarian imperative of the university reform, two institutions in the same city with the same purpose were considered unnecessary. Thus, at a meeting of the deans of all economic faculties,

---

[41] Naumann's position in the political economy of socialism was taken over by Wilhelm Schmidt, who would not make any remarkable contribution to the field.
[42] See Middell (2012: 305).
[43] See Sanke's first speech as president in UA Rektorat 1 AE: 116–135.

the relocation of the economics faculty at Humboldt University to the Higher School of Economics was discussed, which would have meant closing the economics faculty at Humboldt University altogether. In comparison to other institutions, Humboldt University was treated as a stepchild: it did not spring from the womb of the revolution and was loaded with the impeding weight of tradition.

As Rohde, dean between 1964 and 1968, recalled, a decisive move that secured the university's continued existence was the foundation of a new curriculum in military finance.[44] The qualifications of financial administrators of the rather isolated army would be improved by a civilian educational institution. Military finance was a secret area and so required institutional isolation from the rest of the faculty. Having already provided advanced learning classes for military staff, Rohde created a full-time curriculum. Everyday academic life changed as soldiers in uniform appeared in the faculty's hallways. Since military finance was already being offered at Humboldt, and only Halle, Leipzig, and the Higher School of Economics offered specialization in finance, it was agreed that the faculty would specialize in training public servants in finance. In 1969, the entire public finance department of the Higher School of Economics, about thirty faculty members in total, moved to Humboldt University.[45] Political economist Hans Wagner, director (dean) of the section (faculty) since 1969, recalled the rescue of the faculty differently: "It was Johann Lorenz Schmidt who saved us. He went to the rector, the world-famous mathematician [Kurt Erich] Schröder, who in turn went to Ulbricht and was received immediately. When Schröder got back, the phone call came: The matter is settled, we're staying."[46]

At the university level, Sanke's economic management failed, as university structures were too rigid for an economic mobilization. Regarding the acquisition of research contracts with industry, firms were not willing to pre-finance research and paid only after the research had been completed. For some time, the wage payments at Humboldt

---

[44] See UA 1651, on military finance, see also the account by Keil (2015).
[45] Karlheinz Tannert, Heinrich Bader, Klaus Kolloch, Erhard Knauthe, and Günther Radtke came as professors. At the same time, Horst Oertel, Hans Wagner, Gerd Gebhardt, Heinz Körth, Georg Wintgen, Alexander Schink, and Siegfried Apelt were promoted to the status of professor. The reform thus meant a generational change in the faculty.
[46] Interview with Hans Wagner, *SED-Reformdiskurs*, TB Wagner.

University were uncertain, which led to the partial withdrawal from industry-dependent research funding.[47] Also, the discussion about how to form the new "sections" created confusion: which disciplines should join up, and which should remain independent? Should sociology, for example, be in the economics, the philosophy, or the MLO section? Ultimately, the unrest was resolved by a compromise in which sections were incorporated into the existing faculty structure without replacing it, as the Ministry (former State Secretariat) for Higher Education decided (*Ministerium für Hoch- und Fachschulwesen*). The reform could thus not be implemented from the "bottom up." The formation of the section was carried out by a working group appointed by the ministry in 1967. Sanke was replaced as rector by the Americanist Karl-Heinz Wirzberger.

As a "quota economist" in the university management, Erwin Rohde, in 1968, was asked to become vice-rector, which was a thankless task in several respects. As a full-time job, it prevented him from research activities. A letter from the Council of Ministers (*Ministerrat*), that is, someone from the Ministry of Finance, to Rector Wirzberger asked *not* to call on Rohde to become vice-rector because of his importance to research for the ministry.[48] In 1971, Rector Karl-Heinz Wirzberger became an elected member of the *Volkskammer* and then a member of the UNESCO-Commission of the GDR. It is likely that this put more of a burden on Rohde's post. Rohde administered the introduction of the sections, and kept the student unrest looming in 1968 under control. Rohde's detailed activities as a vice-rector are not documented, yet they possibly were mostly of an administrative and less of a political nature. He stood for stability rather than for change.

On the university level, the former ten faculties were transformed into thirty sections, with new divisions in particular in the natural sciences. In the social science, there remained a section for Marxism-Leninism, for economic cybernetics and organizational research, for economics, for philosophy, and for history.[49] In the natural sciences, the breakdown was more detailed, and in addition to the chemistry and physics section, a "food technology" section and "horticulture" section were founded. Since traditional communication channels were interrupted, the introduction of cross-sectional sections, such as an

---

[47] See Middell (2012: 298).   [48] See NR 8.   [49] See Middell (2012: 323).

electronics section, was soon discussed to better coordinate the shared research interests between sections, which in fact was their initial purpose that apparently failed to materialize. Also, the separation of the natural sciences could not prevent them from again coordinating their activities as before. Though the section structure of the university gave the university a new look that was clearly separate from Western universities, it was simply "old wine in new bottles," as many commented.

In the course of the formation of the section structure, the economics faculty remained prominent enough to constitute its own section. In the economics section, the working areas (*Arbeitsbereiche*) replacing the former institutes consisted of a director, two to four professors, and a dozen assistants.[50] More than thirty core professors experienced few faculty changes until 1990, with few professors replacing those born around the 1930s.

After the Reform Is before the Reform

Ulbricht's late reforms had multiple endings. Some place the beginning of the end in 1964, when in Moscow Brezhnev took over from Khrushchev. Even if the Kosygin reforms that resembled NES were still to come, this meant an end to the greater social liberty, and conservatives in the CC enjoyed tailwind against Ulbricht's reform. This became visible at the 11th CC Plenum in 1965, the so-called eradication plenum (*Kahlschlag*). Some in the plenum thought that Ulbricht's liberalization of cultural life as a result of the democratization of the economy had gone too far. Honecker, then secretary for security issues (*Sekretär für Sicherheitsfragen*), gave a speech calling the work of several artists "nihilistic," "skeptical," and "pornographic." In the same vein, he thought of "beat music" as a means of the Western enemy to undermine the class consciousness of East Germany's youth. Many films and books were censored – a foretaste of Honecker's petit-bourgeois cultural

---

[50] Political economy, socialist business economics (*sozialistische Betriebswirtschaft*), finance, economic law, economic history, statistics, economic education, military finance, demography, and later also "economics" (*Volkswirtschaft*), that is, planning. There was a stable number of around 2,000 students in the economics section; half of these were "direct" students, who were all guaranteed a stipend, and the other half were distance-learning and advanced training students.

policy of a morally clean society. Artists, in turn, criticized the "econo-mistic" emphasis of the party, thus Ulbricht's NES.

In addition, while the 1960s witnessed an important growth rate, NES did not deliver on its promise to actually "take over" the West. The decentralization of the economy was limited by any conflict that was perceived with "the leading role of the party," as Steiner argued in his in-depth study.[51] This meant, above all, that top-down bureau-cratic planning, as a main tool of party governance, continued to dominate the economy. To mention just a few problems, innovations on a firm level did not really "pay off" as additional funds, since the prices for the related products were still bureaucratically defined; the principle of public ownership and the legal framework of the economy was not touched at all, and thus was always limited by the last word of the party; Brezhnev's turn toward the military also had consequences in East Germany; the Soviet trade plan of 1965 made East Germany dependent on Russian supplies, which limited the range of planning within the GDR; and the production of Western-like technologies required imports that increased the national debt, a problem that worsened during the 1970s.

But the most significant international event that marked a turning point in Ulbricht's reform spirit was the Prague Spring. In Czechoslovakia, economic democratization had led to thorough political democratization, which included Dubček's demands for free speech, free press, and free movement. Brezhnev felt threatened. When Soviet tanks rolled into the streets of Prague, the meaning of the concept of "class conflict" again gained war-like urgency. Even if Ulbricht was one of Dubček's strongest critics, conservative forces against Ulbricht's "modernization" course revived. For many young students in their early twenties and thir-ties, this was the first time they had witnessed open violence. They witnessed, just like the hope generation during the Thaw, how the Soviet invasion increased pressure on party loyalty and the moni-toring activities of student reactions. While this shock put only some, such as Rudolph Bahro, on a dissident track, the majority

---

[51] See Steiner (1999) as well as Steiner (2004): "The intention to secure power limited the degree of independence that could be allowed in the economy" (2004: 132).

went into "internal emigration."[52] For the hope generation, however, who still remembered Soviet tanks rolling into Berlin, the
Prague Spring came as no surprise (Klein interview 2021).
It was against this background that support for the new forms of
economic knowledge scrambled. In an immediate response to the
events in Prague, Günter Mittag attacked Kohlmey's article on cybernetics discussed at the 9th meeting of the CC in 1968. Mittag appealed
to the old pillars of the supremacy of the party. "Mastering the
economy," he said, "is class struggle," while Kohlmey undermined
the leading role of the party.[53] Also, Kurt Hager, in a speech at the
10th meeting of the CC in 1969, began backpedaling on the support
for cybernetics. He argued that, in contrast to what Klaus had established, cybernetics is in fact *not* compatible with the leading role of
political economy. Cybernetics abstracts from what is essential to it:
class conflict. Cybernetics simplifies society because it "abstracts from
the material, social, and class nature of the systems under investigation" (in Dittmann and Seising 2007: 13). Two years later, after
Honecker took power, Hager was yet more explicit, arguing that
cybernetics "undermines (*aushöhlen*) in a positivist fashion the class
character of socialism" (Hager 1971: 1214). From then on, cybernetics
was no longer an option for the careerists in the economics profession,
and it was easily put aside by those who used it as mere jargon. The
Academy of MLO, completed in 1969, would be discontinued by
Honecker in 1973. Technical knowledge moved into the second rank
of the many forms of economic knowledge. Cybernetics continued its
existence as a field of specialization mostly in the natural sciences as
well as under the label of systems analysis, as Chapter 7 describes in
detail.[54] Harry Maier, the protagonist of Chapter 7, felt the changing

---

[52] As Land and Possekel argued, the movement in the 1980s was nourished by and
associated with those memories (1998).

[53] "Meisterung der Ökonomie ist für uns Klassenkampf," *Neues Deutschland*,
October 27, 1968: 4–5. Regarding Kohlmey's article, see Caldwell (2003).
Caldwell's interpretation falls back into the interpretative framework of the
Hayek–Lange debate on centralization and decentralization.

[54] The cybernetics hype in the West ended around the same time, a time when
computing techniques became more integrated in the cultures of individual
disciplines. Chapter 8 treats the difficulty of technical social sciences as a means
of bridge building between East and West during the Honecker regime using the
example of Harry Maier. While the era of détente was indeed favorable for the
further production of technical economic knowledge in the Soviet and the

attitude about cybernetics immediately. His edition of Oskar Lange fell into disgrace for being not critical enough of Lange's thoughts. Maier later reported that even a profession ban was in the air, as confirmed by his wife, who led the institute's party-group at the time.[55] Udo Ludwig, who edited the mathematical chapters of the edition, recalled the difficult discussions in the party-group. However, these discussions were put off the Politburo's agenda during the power struggle between Ulbricht and Honecker.

In 1969, the new textbook *Political Economy of Socialism and Its Application in the GDR* was published (Autorenkollektiv 1969). Immediately after its publication, scholars at the Party Academy criticized the book, even if the Party Academy took part in the discussion during its revisions. They argued that references to Lenin and other Soviet literature were missing and that the use of mathematics was exaggerated, even if the support of formal methods was entirely informal, without one formula in the book. The book was an expression of an exaggerated search for novelty (*Neuheitssucht*) and did not serve the current needs of the party.[56] These criticisms might have been informed by the Soviet-loyal forces around Honecker, as once Honecker came to power, the one million copies of the book disappeared from the bookshelves and were no longer used for teaching.

In preparation for the 8th Party Congress, which he no longer witnessed as first secretary, Ulbricht set up, next to several others, a working group run by Wolfgang Berger. The group consisted of around fifteen people and was formed to inquire into what needed to be done for productivity in East Germany to catch up in the coming decade with West Germany. Dieter Klein, who is central to Chapter 8, was called into this committee.[57] After a year of work in the rooms of the Academy for Social Sciences, the group concluded that this progress was not possible despite a positive growth rate and a steady increase in quality of life. Instead, a cultural democracy with an

Western regime, this was not the case in the GDR, which, under Honecker's reign, continued the Old Communists' logic of class conflict.

[55] See MfS 58363-92, as well as N-2693-19; see also Nick (2011: 26).

[56] See Wagener et al. (2021: chapter 3.1).

[57] See his account in Klein (2014). The report of 1970 can be found in *SED-Reformdiskurs*, TB Klein (Band) 1, "Probleme der Klassenauseinandersetzung zwischen Sozialismus und Kapitalismus in Deutschland bis 1980."

emphasis on personal development beyond the global economic competition might be a strength of East German society. Class struggle, the report says, will increasingly take place on the level of the experienced "meaning of life" that results from the social and economic system. As Klein later witnessed:

We considered how the likely absence of a GDR victory in the global competition for the highest labor productivity could be reinterpreted as a positive result. Perhaps capitalism could be relegated to a lower place, if not in labor productivity, then in humanistic terms of personal development, individuality and attractive lifestyles. The GDR could strive for ... social security, education and culture for everyone in a humanistic spirit, so that consumption would recede into the background of what is desired in the East and ultimately in the West ... We painted the future socialist cultural society in bright colors and wrote an optimistic paper with the recommendation to the Party Congress to shift the fight between the systems to the field of human dignity and personality development. (Klein 2014: 93)

Giving up the idea of superior economic growth was still heresy in the late 1960s, as it could have led to a changing conception of class conflict with wide-ranging consequences for Marxism-Leninism in general. The result of the study was sent to Ulbricht some months before the 14th CC Meeting, when Ulbricht was forced to resign. The study thus got lost in the power struggle between Ulbricht and Honecker. For Klein, as for many other economists who had put hopes in Ulbricht's NES, the impression of a missed opportunity remained, just as in the wake of the 20th Party Congress in 1955.

6 | *Honecker's Bourgeois Reforms*

After a blackout in the State Council Building, Honecker meets Mielke: "Man, I was locked in an elevator for two hours" Mielke says. Honecker replied: "That's nothing; I stood on an escalator for two hours."

At the 8th Party Congress in 1971, followed by a forceful power struggle and with Soviet support, Erich Honecker became general secretary. To stabilize his power, Honecker wished to achieve immediate economic success without the use of indirect levers in a complicated system, which as he knew was hampered by bureaucracy. In an attempt to buy the favor of the population, Honecker dismissed Ulbricht's NES, recentralized economic planning, and focused on individual consumer industries such as housing at the cost of industrial development. He again spoke of the "developed socialist society" rather than the "developed social system of socialism" where cultural norms and moderate mass consumption created a general petit-bourgeois atmosphere. This is what he meant by the so-called Unity of Economic and Social Policy. It should be noted that by doing so, Honecker further nourished West-envy in a fashion not so different from Ulbricht.[1]

Apart from the consumer orientation, a truly important success of the early Honecker period was the international recognition of the GDR by the United Nations in 1974. The renewed importance of international policy became manifest in the foundation of a new research institute in 1971, the Institute for International Politics and Economy (*Institut für Internationale Politik und Wirtschaft*, IPW).[2]

---

[1] The details of the Honecker regime are covered by Malycha (2014); two of the English accounts focusing on economic policy are Zatlin (2007) and Steiner (2004).

[2] The IPW was founded in the image of the Institute for the World Economy and International Relations in Moscow (*Institut mirovoj ekonomiki i meždunarodnich otnošenii*). It combined the former German Institute for Contemporary History (*Deutsche Institut für Zeitgeschichte*) and the DWI, and

International recognition, however, did not translate into the opening of the academic sphere to the West. Honecker's consumer-oriented policy required increasing imports from the West that made it more and more difficult to finance the travels of scientists to Western countries due to the shortage of foreign currency. For the same reason, there was a limited supply of foreign literature in the libraries. Middell spoke of "the elimination of international standards for performance evaluation" of science and of a "decoupling from the international scientific dialogue" during the Honecker era (2012: 335). International recognition, for Honecker, was an occasion for *demarcation* rather than *cooperation* without giving up the logic of the two camps as the single most important source of the legitimacy of the state.

After a short period of revived hopes, it soon became obvious that what was spent at one point was missing at another. Honecker's wasteful economic policy and the increased political tutelage and surveillance increased the existing contradiction between pragmatic prudence and ideological loyalty, a contradiction that could only be resolved by evoking repeated reform efforts that were neutralized through a huge bureaucracy while moving strategically relevant but ideologically less acceptable activities into secrecy. It is for this reason that the 1970s and 1980s, in spite of the reformist spirit, appear in Niethammer's words like the "blank space of the experiential history" of the GDR (1994: 109) or, in Middell's words, a "grey continuum, . . . (in which) the scientific landscape dawned inactively towards its own erosion" (2012: 331).

Given Honecker's focus on consumption, higher education lost relevance in comparison with Ulbricht's NES. Universities and academies were no longer seen as central players of social progress. The ideal figure of economic progress was, rather than the scientific expert, the skilled worker (*Facharbeiter*). While university education was associated with slow, long-term investment processes, the training of the skilled worker was faster. This change reinforced the epistemic virtue of practical relevance *and* the importance of ideological education. Under Honecker, the contradiction between the two functions of universities in fact increased. The repeated references to the unity of

soon had a respectable size of around 500 employees. This was the beginning of what could be called political science in East Germany, which had previously been refused as an imperialist discipline. For political science in the Soviet context, see Miller in Düppe and Boldyrev (2019).

(ideological) education and (professional) training shows the extent to which they in fact differed.

Economists' social profile therefore waned under Honecker and enthusiasm about new forms of economic knowledge vanished. Cybernetics, as already mentioned, was no longer a unifying model of economic knowledge but mainly a specialty in the engineering sciences. With the centralization of the economy, bureaucrats in the party and ministries regained power over economic experts. Economics lost its aura of modernism. The result was that the pluralism that emerged from the liberalization of the late Ulbricht years transformed into a fundamental nontransparency of fields of specialization related by an increasingly empty ideological framework. The recentralization of the economy also applied to universities and the organization of economic science. Under the control of the CC, in 1972, *Scientific Councils* were founded for all social sciences which rendered research yet more rigid. Every lecture was planned by a national curriculum committee (*Beirat für Wirtschaftswissenschaften beim Ministerium für Hoch-, und Fachschulwesen*). All subdisciplines in economics had their own national "working group" that met once a year to discuss the national curriculum.

In this context of the Honecker era, the structure of the professional lives of the hope generation settled. A last hiring wave of the late 1960s secured their professional career. For many economists, the 1970s meant a *turn inwards* into their own "collective" defined (and redefined) by specific responsibilities and to some extent as bearers of vital secrets. The hope generation was ready to live the contradictions of Honecker's regime, mindful of the fact that this was the world they themselves had created:

The socialist intelligentsia now settled in that space, which it had itself brought about. A massive wave of hiring of professors between 1968 and 1972 related to the new university structures pushed that change further. The character of the traditional *Ordinarius* was not only institutionally, but also habitually marginalized.[3]

---

[3] Middell continues, however: "which did not exclude that individual representatives of the new Intelligentsia could fill this gap and develop their own enthusiasm about bourgeois professorial behaviour, which as an exceptional phenomenon could even find approval" (Middell 2012: 345). In other words, some scientists were able to create "free spaces" (*Freiräume*) for themselves. Such freedom, however, could only be taken within one's own specialization and only under the facade of the benefit for the party and a constant willingness to

Considering the stability of the early Honecker period, it is thus appropriate to survey the life of university economists in a sociological rather than a chronological fashion. Erwin Rohde serves as a representative example of economists in Honecker's regime.

Democracy as Bureaucracy

The amount of bureaucratic labor was a dominant factor in a professor's life under Honecker. It centered on the continued reflection of the relevance and ideological coherence of one's work in light of the reform ideas of higher bureaucratic units. At each level of the university – university, faculty, section, and working group – there were five different bodies, each with a committee, official representatives, and specialized committees for responding to societal questions, teaching, and research. In addition to the traditional university self-management, the preceding chapters have already shown the central influence of the party representation in party-groups, from the university level (*Kreisleitung*) to the department level (*Abteilungsparteiorganisation*).[4] The party system – this is how it governed – mirrored and was infused in all levels of society. There was also the labor union of university workers, which had an uneasy relationship with the party representatives – officially, separate workers' representation is unnecessary in a society ruled by the working class. Union posts were often held as ersatz proof of societal engagement by those who held no party membership, mostly middle-ranking faculty. In each committee, there were also representatives of the FDJ organization of students as well as the mentioned "praxis partners," representatives from ministries and industry that had been integrated in the university system since the third university reform.

Holding one or several posts required carrying out the tasks assigned from above, but also implied degrees of freedom in interpreting higher-level signals, in controlling lower levels, and in reporting back to higher orders. The university and academy archives are flooded with all sorts of reports and plans such as achievement reports (*Leistungsberichte*), account reports (*Rechenschaftsberichte*), planning drafts (*Planentwürfe*),

---

compromise. Dieter Klein and Harry Maier, who we deal with in Chapters 7 and 8, are two examples.

[4] At the university level, there was a distinction between the Scientific and the Societal Council.

perspective plans (*Perspektivpläne*), functional plans (*Funktionspläne*), structural plans (*Strukturpläne*), forecasting plans (*Prognosepläne*), and working programs (*Arbeitsprogramme*) that defined the role of every single employee in addition to several guidelines for writing such documents.[5] These reports were written at short intervals, synchronized by the rhythm of Party Congresses. After a Party Congress, a week was dedicated to reading and evaluating how the new decisions would affect the university or academy level right down to each individual department. Also, statistics about the efficacy of these evaluations were created.[6]

The reports and plans reveal a highly repetitive structure. First, the author would show commitment to the collective of socialist states, swear to the state's fraternal relationship with the Soviet Union, and summon the latest party resolutions and their slogans (*Losungen*). Then, one had to "derive the topic of the report from the party documents ... The more critical the proposition made in a document, the more glamorous had to be its political framing" (Kolloch 2001b: 294). Having justified the contribution to party resolutions, one would end with the obligatory self-criticism that showed what still needed to be done to achieve this goal. This interpretive labor was completed at all levels and ranged from a commitment to general slogans such as "intensification" to a commitment to greater cleanliness in the classroom. Obviously, all of this was written in a language of heavy jargon that would have been incomprehensible to anyone in Western Germany.

It was by way of this interpretive labor that most economists in the GDR were subjected *to* the plan rather than subjects designing the plan. The frequent accounts of one's own activities resulted in a high awareness of the teleological structure of society and one's position in it. That was the basis of the planned economy as a democratic institution. Democracy in the GDR meant participating in its social creation by means of, firstly, translating abstract ideas into concrete measures and, secondly, providing feedback on the extent to which these goals were realized. The continuum of meaning between general national goals and every individual professional act carried out made the planned society, as one might view its ideal, a plan-based rather than a representative

---

[5] UA 1651, UA 2864.
[6] UA 071. Next to the sequence of Party Congresses, committees were also created for many special occasions such as anniversaries of the state, anniversaries of the party, Marx's birthday, the Lenin year, the liberation from fascism, and so forth.

democracy. "Join in to work, join in to plan, join in to govern!" (*arbeite mit, plane mit, regiere mit!*), as one article of the GDR constitution said. Central administration was a form of democracy.

The main task given to university professors was the *teaching* of new "cadre" (*Kader*). Applying the ideal of the *Facharbeiter*, the curriculum was designed to meet the task profile (*Anforderungsprofil*) of practicing economists. Vocational training would be sufficient for getting access to university, and distant learning allowed studying alongside work. Insofar as the planned economy was a matter of bureaucracy, economic knowledge in higher education was more oriented toward institutional rules of conduct than a set of theories or methods. Apart from the intellectualism assigned to the corpus of Marxism-Leninism, in today's terms, economic knowledge resembled more public administration than an autonomous corpus of theories, techniques, and models. Compared to Western universities, the school-like character of teaching economics was striking. The section decided which students to accept with praxis partners on the committee. Students were grouped together in "seminar groups" of about twenty students and a tutor. The curriculum was designed to meet the needs of the future workplace with three major internships during the studies. Before entering the university, there was a preliminary internship of four weeks (*Vorpraktikum*). In one of the plans of 1976, one could read how, "during the preliminary internship, all opportunities to develop a professional pride among the young women and men should be used."[7] In the third year, students took a professional internship of three months (*Berufspraktikum*), and in the fourth year a diploma internship of another three months (*Diplompraktikum*). Students thus had a clear idea of what their later jobs would look like and would judge their classes in light of this prospect. The diploma thesis was awarded in relation to their future placement and also defended in the presence of a praxis partner. The school-like character of university education was often a topic of discussion. To "fight mediocrity," as the ministry called for, talented students were to take a research-oriented degree (*Forschungsstudium*) that was more academically oriented and entailed individual student plans.[8]

[7] UA 2896.
[8] See Middell (2012: 339). Graduates of finance at Humboldt University would be employed in district and county financial departments, the Ministry of Finance, the State Bank of the GDR, the Industry and Trade Bank, the Bank for

The lower the importance of scholarly qualification, the more important became the "educational" aspect of teaching (*Erziehungsanteil*), which one might translate as the socialist version of the old Humboldtian virtue of *Bildung*. Teaching was expected to help students acquire not only the technical expertise needed for the job, but also increase class consciousness, contribute to character building, and foster belief in the state of the GDR. One guideline required that students "acknowledge the leading role of the working class and its party" and that they develop "hate against the capitalist exploitative order."[9] Students were expected to take over social functions that included summer jobs in construction and the obligatory two-week labor of first-year students at the university for cleaning and kitchen tasks. The official curriculum in 1986, provided by the Ministry for Higher Education, said that students were supposed to "develop the political-ideological mindset and moral character of a socialist personality that includes bonds with the working class, political-ideological persuasiveness, readiness to take on the responsibilities of a leader, discipline, honesty, modesty, purposefulness, creativity, availability, and readiness for continued education" (Böhme 1986: 5).

As Rohde explained in front of incoming first-year students in 1977:

Whoever believes to be able to work as an economist without an active commitment to our social order in word and deed will fail in his profession if not already during his studies . . . We want to train you as excellent specialists (*Fachleute*) in the field of finance who are capable of leading collectives with a high social commitment, who make high demands on themselves and thus on other workers, who self-confident and at the same time modest. This type of student of economics also includes that you gradually adopt such a relationship to the German Socialist Unity Party that the desire grows in you to become a member of the party, and if the opportunity presents itself, to also apply for admission. Actually, let me say this from my own experience: all students of economics should be potential candidates for membership in the SED. (NR 15: 12–13)

Nevertheless, there were repeated debates between those seeing little connection between political devotion and scientific fitness and those who, like Rohde, thought of personality as a condition for the social

Agriculture, the German Foreign Trade Bank, the State Audit Commission (Finanzrevision), local banks, and insurance offices (see UA 1651).
[9] UA 1658. On education in economics, see also UA 1660, 1974.

meaningfulness of formal knowledge. The latter warned not to overdo the achievement-oriented elements of teaching and warned of the dangerous and imperialist deideologization of economics in the West. Attempts were made to quantify the personality development of students to increase the "spiritual-cultural efficacy" of education. In the end, however, one ended up summoning "the unity of teaching and education" in the same fashion as one summoned the unity of the productive and the ideological function of political economy – and given how often it was summoned, it is apparent that little was actually achieved.[10]

Research played the least important role in the professional lives of university economists. The GDR was not a place in which an individual research culture in economics could flourish, not with a state wary of public intellectuals' uncontrolled interventions in democratic discourse. Research was part of the planned economy, contract based, carried out mostly in teams, and often published anonymously as an "author collective." The contracts entailed details of questions, methods, and "often an expectation of the results," as Kolloch, dean of research at Humboldt University, pointed out (2009). Contracts were grouped according to the commissioning institution. The most important projects were commissioned by the CC; however, this research was carried out almost exclusively by the party institutions, such as the Party Academy or the Institute for Marxism-Leninism. In addition, the ministries commissioned research topics, as well as the university, which meant more individual freedom but also more political control. Apart from research contracts with praxis partners in industry, the production of *textbooks* was also central to professorial labor.

Since research was subject to a plan, little valorized under Honecker, contracted with praxis partners, and preferably carried out in the Academies of Sciences, dissertations and habilitations were for many economists the highlight of their individual research activity. Knowledge of the financial system, for example, was limited to the official notion that money has no economic function other than as an accounting device. Questions about the nature of money in socialism are replaced by the knowledge of rules of conduct in a monetary bureaucracy, reducing the ethos of a financial economist to that of an instructor in public administration. This is one of the reasons why

[10] See UA 1721, 1722.

there were few "big debates" in GDR economics. One debate noted by
Krause that took place during the Honecker period was between
orthodox paper money and fiat money theorists, the latter, as was
argued, being in conflict with Marx's notion that prices reflect value.
In any event, the benchmark of such theoretical questions was ideological coherence and furthermore had no consequence whatsoever for
the bureaucracy of monetary policies.[11]

International contacts were possible but highly regulated. To travel
to the West, one had to pass travel cadre controls that excluded those
considered politically less reliable as well as those who had family in
West Germany. Next to contacts with the USSR and other socialist
"brother countries," contact existed with countries under the influence
of both regimes (Middle East and Africa) as well as with Western
Europe, Japan, and, lowest in the hierarchy, North America. The most
regular opportunities for Western travels were international conferences where national delegates represented the Eastern bloc. Political
interests, however, overshadowed scientific exchange. A detailed plan
had to be submitted to the International Relations Office, which
decided on the disposal of the persistently scarce foreign currency.
Approval would come with a travel directive that entailed an official
agenda and included a list of the contacts to be made and those to be
avoided. The directive prescribed how Western German colleagues
were to be dealt with – with reserve, distance, and without making
any agreements and refusing their criticism. A general directive
included demands such as to "explain the political situation of the
GDR in conversations, conference breaks, receptions, etc., and force-
fully represent the standpoint of Marxism-Leninism."[12] Conferences
were generally visited by a delegation of GDR scholars jointly with
scholars from other socialist countries. Critical interventions had to be

---

[11] The debate took place, among others, between Alfrd Lemmnitz and Waldfried
Schliesser, who were in favor of paper money, and Wili Ehlert, Klaus Kolloch,
Karl-Heinz Tannert, and Hans Wagner, who were in favor of fiat money. The
debate is covered in Krause (1998a: 218–230; 1998b: 310–312). As noted by
Wagener et al. (2021) the central textbook for "economics," that is, planning,
did not even entail a chapter on money until the very end of the GDR. For a
more sociological account of money in the Honecker period, see Zatlin (2007),
who points to the discord between ideological framing, political measures, and
economic reality in a regime that denounced and simultaneously promoted
Western consumerism.
[12] UA 2874.

coordinated with other members of the delegation. One decided jointly, for example, to protest the elections of offices of international organizations. Following the trip, a detailed travel report had to be filed that summarized all conversations, activities, contacts made, and cases of ideological confrontation.

Erwin Rohde had long been a travel cadre and often visited Western countries.[13] At a meeting at a public finance conference in Hamburg in 1978, he and his delegate faced confrontations with James Buchanan and public choice theorists. Obliged to criticize Western approaches, public choice theory was downplayed as responding to a problem that only existed in capitalism. Buchanan, in turn, fiercely attacked Soviet politics. Knauthe, a member of the delegation, reported that their own arguments were more telling and added:

In summary one can say that public choise-theory [*sic*], coming from the USA, will continue to find support in capitalist countries. Considering the lack of an overarching and convincing market theory of bourgeois economic science, the analytical and formal aspects of public choice theory can function as a valve for critical assessments of this or that governmental decision.[14]

Whatever misunderstandings underlay such random encounters, they were reinforced by language barriers. Hardly any of the East German economists had sufficient command of the English language to engage in a real debate.

In sum, considering the institutional life-world of an ordinary East German economist, their bureaucratic labor was much less a matter of democratic participation in economic planning than a matter of political control. Bureaucracy was a means for both mobilizing and neutralizing the intellectual labor of reform efforts.[15] The omnipresent

---

[13] Rather than economics conferences, he was mostly invited by business economics and management conferences. See, for example, in 1969, a talk in Heidelberg at the Management Institute about the increasing concentration of capital in Western economies (NR 32, NR 41). These were in fact contributions to the political economy of capitalism from the point of view of finance.

[14] UA 2874.

[15] In terms of Krause: "For many years they (GDR economists) lived with the notion that their ideas, conceptions and proposals were providing a scientific foundation for SED policies. Ultimately, this notion proved to be self-deceptive ... They increasingly became convinced that economics in the GDR had no major impact on economic policy or the development of the economic system" (1998b: 266).

imperative of reform and of adapting to a dynamically changing society resulted, paradoxically, in "institutional inertia" (Wagener 1998). It was in this sense that the economists of the hope generation stabilized Honecker's regime during the long 1970s without necessarily being in favor of it.

Secrecy

Honecker's regime cannot be understood without recognizing the increasing degree of secrecy and its resulting culture of mistrust and suspicion. Once established as a state in the United Nations, the pressure to hide state violence by using subtler measures of exerting political pressure was higher than before. The international image of a state supported by its own population had to be maintained. But since Honecker's economic and political strategy increasingly contradicted the public image of the regime, the importance of the secret apparatus increased equally. Notably, Honecker needed to paper over the fact that consumer wealth came at the cost of an eroding economic structure. Erwin Rohde played a role in this, exemplifying well the party-loyal economist in Honecker's reign of secrecy.[16]

After five years as vice-rector of the university, in 1974, Rohde returned to the section of economics. The integration of the entire finance department of the Higher School of Economics allowed for a higher degree of specialization. In response to the increasing importance of trade with the capitalist West, deputy chairman of the Council of Ministers, Gerhard Weiss, a doctoral graduate from the economics section, asked Rohde to create a separate program in international finance.[17] In 1972, the working area for international finance opened with the task of investigating bank exchanges and currencies in capitalism concerning their possible use in the interests of the GDR. This was capitalist finance beyond socialist foundations and was thus difficult to justify ideologically. On the one hand, the political goal of this

---

[16] Another example of the increased importance of the Stasi during Honecker was the foundation of the Institute for Secret Security (*Geheimnisschutz*) in 1976 at Higher School of Economics (see Alisch 2010).

[17] See the lecture manuscript in NR 14. For the development of Western trade, see Judt (2013).

specialization was similar to that of the political economy of capitalism, as it aimed to explain how Western financial markets exploit the workers' class and increase the risk of overproduction and crises in capitalism. On the other hand, his lecture also responded to the increasing importance of these markets for socialist countries and thus the importance of knowing how they worked. Responding to a basic fear since the time of Stalin that foreign economic relations would create a dependency on capitalism, knowledge of Western finance, as Rohde argued, was important to avoid the disadvantages of economic relations with the capitalist West. But once this danger was avoided, through the "exploitation of the contradictions of imperialism between different imperialist states (we can) achieve advantages for our national economy," he argued (NR 14: 2). International finance can also add to "the struggle for the politics of peaceful coexistence" and the extension of this peaceful coexistence through foreign trade, he added in line with Honecker.

The students following this program would later work in firms (*Kombinate*) that traded with Western countries, in banks, in the Ministry of Finance, and in the Ministry of Foreign Trade, but some of them also worked in the area of commercial coordination (KoKo), which was one of the best-guarded secrets of the Honecker period. KoKo had been founded in 1966 in the late Ulbricht period. Administratively, it was part of the Ministry for Foreign Trade, but it was a separate bureaucratic unit. The area was in charge of more than a hundred firms that were granted special rights compared to the Publicly Owned Enterprises. In contrast to the rigid bureaucracy usually imposed on Western transactions, KoKo firms were largely free in making contracts and in negotiating terms of trade without the approval of another bureaucratic unit and with special arrangements regarding tariffs and even customs control. KoKo firms were not subject to a plan and were not controlled by the Financial State Audit Commission (*Staatlichen Finanzrevision*). In addition, KoKo firms could freely dispose of their profits, only paying a fixed amount, a fee, to the state budget. The revenues of KoKo firms could be freely invested in other trades and even in Western financial markets, thereby generating further income; about a quarter of all KoKo capital was invested in Western financial markets. KoKo firms held bank accounts in Western countries to allow for transactions with Western firms, could take credit from Western banks, and also held anonymous accounts in Switzerland. Since firms could freely negotiate the terms of trade, they could build up trust in business relations independent of the political Cold War situation. The KoKo imperium was, as Egon Krenz called it, a "capitalist island in socialism" (in Judt 2013: 25). Obviously, as these privileges were in contrast to the morals of the socialist plan, they were unknown to the public and kept under secrecy. Alexander Schalck-Golodkowski, the head of KoKo, was unknown to most GDR citizens. He reported directly to Honecker, Mittag, and Mielke, the three figureheads of the late GDR.

The initial occasion for the foundation of KoKo under Ulbricht was to respond to the uneven supplies of raw material from the Soviet Union and the limited access to convertible currency as a result of the West German Hallstein Doctrine. But with the political obstacles largely being lifted after the recognition of the GDR by the United Nations in 1973, KoKo nevertheless gained importance for covering up Honecker's wasteful economy that increasingly relied on Western imports. KoKo firms became a crucial factor in generating Western currency and balancing the increasing Western debt. In 1984, the share of the entire foreign exchange that was run by KoKo was at its peak of 44 percent (Steiner 2004: 201). In other words, KoKo was to finance the wasteful consumerist policy, that is, create ideological coherence in a fashion contrary to its ideology. To put it differently, Honecker made socialism attractive to his population by providing gifts financed by capitalist means.

KoKo initially developed from the so-called _Intershops_, a network of "currency shops" close to the borders, where Western visitors could buy Western products at a cheaper price. _Intershops_ were the beginning of a consumerist culture coined by West-envy, most notably among the members of the Politburo themselves. KoKo furnished the Politburo members, living closed off in a forest colony in Wandlitz in the outskirts of Berlin, with Western supplies, mostly electronic and fashion products but also pornographic material for Honecker that was forbidden in the GDR. But most KoKo firms traded the same products as other foreign trade firms. The firm with the highest trade volume was called _Intrac_, which developed complex business models, most notably in the international oil market. They bought crude oil from BP, the USSR, and Iraq and delivered processed oil to West Berlin, covering a quarter of West Berlin's oil consumption. Considering its limited refinery capacities, they also led crude oil refining in West Germany and then sold the refined oil back to West Berlin. In 1974, refinery capacities increased the importance of the oil trade, and imports of crude oil from the USSR and Iraq doubled during the 1970s. Schalck-Golodkowski managed to attract Western firms, such as Salamander shoes or Triumph underwear, to build up production units in East Germany. These required higher production standards than usual in the East but paid lower salaries. Thus, Western firms profited from subsidies of cheap labor behind the Iron Curtain. They also profited from a different legal setting, such as blood imports as well as medical tests run on East German patients without applying Western ethical standards. KoKo firms were also known for rent-seeking behavior such as three-way deals with oil based on offshore companies. Another semi-legal trade was that of art and antiques (*Kunst und Antiquitäten GmbH K&A*).

KoKo firms also ran secret political business. First, there was the international arms trade run by the firm *IMES*. They sold weapons, mainly Kalashnikovs, to other countries, trade that did not match the image of a peaceful GDR. The firms *CAMET* and *Delta Export und Import GmbH* acquired spying technology for the Stasi, notably for the HV A, circumventing the embargo regulations of the West. There were also firms located in the West that were property of the party, such as the *SIMPEX GmbH*. Old members of the KPD living in West Germany were owners of these firms. Other important political business was with political prisoners in the GDR ransomed by West Germany. These trades required coordination with the Stasi, which selected the prisoners to be liberated. The KoKo firm *Intrac* took into possession the goods received in exchange, such as oil, silver, copper, or mercury. Between 1962 and 1990, 3.4 billion DM were generated by such ransom transactions. The Stasi was thus an integrated part of KoKo, but it had less ideological control than it had over other institutions such as firms, universities, and academies.[18] KoKo firms could act as they wished, informing the Stasi about possible economic advan-

---

[18] The KoKo working group for the Ministry of Foreign Trade was in charge of the embargo business for the Stasi. They procured communications and computing technology for the operational needs of the Stasi and its head intelligence office. Their staff consisted exclusively of officers on special employment; see Buthmann (2003: 40).

tages regarding economic espionage. KoKo was a nebulous, secrecy-shrouded economic imperium that exemplified well the double life of the GDR created under Honecker.

KoKo and Schalck-Golodkowski became vital for preventing the bail-out of the GDR during the credit crisis in the early 1980s.[19] As a reaction to the riots in Poland, in 1982, Western banks stopped giving credit to the GDR. One strategy was to negotiate longer payment terms with the Soviet Union. Another was to force exports at the expense of internal consumption; while shirts and towels, for example, were delivered to West Germany, they were missing on Eastern shelves. In ideological terms, this was exactly the type of economic dependence on capitalism that had always been feared. But the most spectacular deal was the bank credit negotiated in 1983 with the anticommunist minister-president of Bavaria, Franz-Josef Strauss. This credit again opened up the door to other credit from Western banks. Strauss knew that a bailout of the GDR would not lead to a reunification of the two parts of Germany. The deal could thus strengthen East Germany's relationship with West Germany at the cost of its relationship with the Soviet Union.

The dependency, economically as well as politically, of the Honecker regime on Western finance was obvious to everyone who knew of this deal, certainly many KoKo employees. In total, there were around 3,000 employees in KoKo firms, and they clearly had to acquire different skills from the managers of ordinary state-owned firms. While many might have been trained on the job, some might have come from the general training of foreign trade economics at Higher School of Economics. But the one degree that was in fact explicitly designed to acquire skills for Western financial markets was that of international finance run by Erwin Rohde at Humboldt University. Rohde's agenda in international finance fits well that of KoKo, as is apparent in his 1981 textbook, entitled *Banks, Stock Markets, and Currencies in Current Capitalism.*[20] Rohde argued, just like Schalck-Golodkowski, for the exploitation of international credit market developments for the growth of GDR's economy. Having control over the social effects of the credit economy, socialist countries could profit from their relationship with capitalism. Knowledge of the financial

---

[19] The credit crisis is fully analyzed in Judt (2013).
[20] For a sketch of the lecture on "finance and credit in imperialism" of 1975 that would result in his later textbook, see NR, 14, 71.

system helped in using capitalism for socialist goals, which was in fact identical with the justification of the many KoKo activities mentioned earlier.[21] While in political economy, such an argument would have been easily dismissed as the support of, say, convergence theory, the institutional situation surrounding KoKo created freedom from the pressure of legitimacy. Rohde's agenda, if put under the standards of the political economy of socialism, would have resulted in a barrage of control activities.

What then did Rohde know of the final destination of some of his students and the potential purpose behind the specialization in international finance? There is no doubt that Rohde did not know of all the KoKo deals mentioned here. However, it is very unlikely that he did not know at all of KoKo activities in one way or another. In fact, the education in international finance was not subject to the ordinary rules at the faculty. The Ministry for Higher Education did not play a role in setting up the curriculum as it did with all other degrees but, just like KoKo, it was subject to the Ministry of Foreign Trade and furthermore to Günter Mittag. About thirty students were admitted each year, who, just like the teachers, were personally selected. The specialized classes, including English, came at the cost of advanced classes in Marxism-Leninism, which was not considered practically relevant for their later service to the state. Given the privileges and special status of the students in international finance, everyone certainly had notions about what was going on. But nobody would inquire, not even Rohde:

I've personally never felt that something special was going on (in relation to Schalck-Golodkowski) ... When I proposed the concept of the curriculum to the Ministry of Finance – the responsible person was Herta König – she mentioned in her confirmation letter that we are not supposed to do research. Only later I understood that they did not want us to talk about their business. When there was the campaign to bring our graduates more into the combines (*Kombinate*), I went to the graduates in commercial coordination, but they said we should talk later. I only realized later how all that is related to one another. (Rohde 2009)

---

[21] That is, Rohde had to struggle against the market skeptics in the East and was easily identified as a socialist dogmatic in the West. It was clearly impossible that Rohde could have made a contribution to the Western literature on finance, which at this point was discussing Mandelbrot's mathematics rather than the nature of money in a collectivist state.

In the archives of the Stasi that remained after the turmoil of 1989, there are only a few minor records of Rohde unrelated to KoKo. Other records – those from HV A, for example – no longer exist. In 1968, Rohde was confirmed as a person entrusted with secret information (*Geheimnisträger*) still related to his work in military finance.[22] In the department that was in charge of universities, HA (*Hauptabteilung*) XX, there is no information about Rohde, which is not surprising since the area was subject to the Ministry for Foreign Trade and not the Ministry for Higher Education.

Rohde lived in Berlin Hohenschönhausen, in Manetstr. 34, in a picturesque and quiet area with two small lakes for bathing and idyllic walks. One of his close neighbors some houses down the street was Alexander Schalck-Golodkowski, living in Manetstr. 6. Their neighbourship was not an accident. After the war, the district was first used by the Soviet secret police, responsible for the many cleansing actions, as a closed off safe place. In the 1950s, it was then gradually bought up by the Stasi transforming the area as an open residential enclave with control over the accommodation of its officers and informants.[23] Offering an anonymous and decent lifestyle, the Stasi created a peculiar cohesion between life and work, including a party-group of the housewives of Stasi employees and a kindergarten. To be accommodated in this area, Rohde must have had good contacts to the Stasi, if not a formal connection. The area is also known for some material privileges. Most notably, Schalck-Golodkowski's house was a West German construction known for its art and weapon collection shown at several informal receptions of the state prominence. The travel cadre files notes that Rohde, too, like many of the Old Communists, aspired to a petit-bourgeois lifestyle, including nice furniture, a little personal luxury, and a house bar with international spirits.[24] Schalck-Golodkowski's access to Western products that he delivered to the Politburo probably did not remain unknown to his neighbors. Indeed, according to the KoKo historian Mathias Judt, Rohde received foreign currency now and then for his travels to the West from Schalck-Golodkowski. Even if

---

[22] There is only one travel cadre investigation dating from earlier in 1968 (MfS HA/AKG RK, 521–540).

[23] The history and sociology of the Stasi domestic district is described in Schulze (2003).

[24] MfS HA/AKG RK, 521–540.

Figure 6.1 Manetstrasse 36 in Hohenschönhausen.
Possibly resembling Rohde's house, number 34 next door (currently rebuild).
Photo taken by author, 2022.

Rohde was most likely not involved in any concrete decision making at KoKo, it is also very unlikely that he knew only little about Schalck-Golodkowski's secret realm. In any event, considering that the HV A files were destroyed and most of what is left about KoKo is known from the reports prepared for the party leadership, it is not surprising that Rohde does not appear in the documents.

The link between Rohde and KoKo is likely but not apparent. This half knowledge, and in particular the acceptance of this half knowledge, is specific to the functioning of the Honecker regime. Accepting this half knowledge without inquiring further – as Rohde did regarding KoKo and Rohde's colleagues regarding Rohde – increased the degree of personal speculation that was in fact essential for the stability of the

Honecker regime: mistrust would both increase acceptance of internal control and grant credibility to the political narrative of threats from abroad – two political sentiments at the heart of GDR's society under Honecker.

* * *

The hope generation was willing to bear the contradictions inherent in Honecker's GDR, and thus they were critical to the stability of the regime until the late 1980s. They were able to split their minds to the extent that perceptions of the shortcomings of the regime were excused by the historically early state of socialism, projected into ideas for further reforms. Thus, the gap between reality and the ideal in fact nourished their ideological convictions. This capacity was made possible by a strong turn inward into one's own collective, in which the big questions would simply never be discussed. This capacity ultimately had its origin in the belief in the moral superiority of Old Communists. Indeed, the culture of worshiping the heroic deeds of communists during Nazism was increasingly fostered, censored, and controlled during the Honecker era, as Epstein showed among others in her classic study.[25]

Another way of making the same point is to highlight the astonishingly few "dissidents" during this period. The few examples of critical voices come from the older generation, underlining the fact that Old Communists are not to be identified with Stalinists. Behrens was one of them, and Havemann was another. During the Honecker period, Kuczynski can be added to this list. In 1977, he wrote a book entitled *Dialogue with My Great-Grandson*, a critical essay on the regime. His main topic was, unsurprisingly, Stalinism. He criticized the control of the media in the GDR, the bureaucratic apparatus, and the dominance of the state in society, just as Behrens did in 1957. But Kuczynski also excused these shortcomings as part of the world class struggle, which shows how his way of thinking was deeply embedded in the kind of thinking he criticized. The book, written in 1977, was published only in a censored version in 1983.[26] For some, this book recreated hopes

---

[25] See Epstein (2003: chapter 7). About a historical critique of Honecker's biography, see the excellent work by Sabrow (2013).

[26] On Kuczynski, see Fair-Schulz (2009: chapter 4). As mentioned in Chapter 3, Behrens came into conflict with the party when he gave an unauthorized speech

for reforms while others were disappointed that he did not go far enough in his critiques. The former tended to be those of the hope generation, the latter those of the perestroika generation.

For the hope generation, being in the midst of their professional careers, the consequences of open criticism were more severe, which partially explains their absence. The most public and shocking intervention was the expatriation of the popular songwriter Wolf Biermann in 1976. As a consequence, those showing solidarity equally were subject to state oppression. Among intellectuals, an open critique was expressed by Rudolph Bahro drawing on Marx to criticize the GDR by claiming that alienation of the working class continued on a new level in state socialism. Also, Bahro suggested a form of socialism without focus on economic growth. He came to be considered a traitor and dissident once he had published his book in 1977 secretly in West Germany, titled *The Alternative in Eastern Europe*, along with an interview in the news magazine *Der Spiegel*. After imprisonment and protests, he left for West Germany in 1979.[27]

Among economists, there was one remarkable and exceptional case of Hermann von Berg (1933–2019), a secret agent who turned against the East German state. Berg had been active in secret negotiations with, and also against, Western politicians, notably Willy Brandt. In 1972, he received a cover-up position as professor of economics at Humboldt University. In 1978, he transmitted a critical article, again to the West German magazine *Der Spiegel*, entitled *Manifest of the Alliance of German Democratic Communists*, which he probably wrote himself. After a period of imprisonment, another illegal Western book publication criticizing the GDR and the Stasi in 1985 led to his dismissal in 1986. After pleas from Western politicians, he left for West Germany.[28] Although all of his colleagues at Humboldt University knew of Berg's special status, there was little questioning of what was going on. To recall what Behrens' daughter said when summarizing the lesson of the revisionism debate: "Never wear your heart on your sleeve!"[29]

---

in Frankfurt in West Germany, using Marx to critique the "class" interest of the regime. This led to his forced retirement (see Behrens 1968: 288–299).

[27] See the book by Bahro (1978) as well as Herzberg and Seifert (2005).

[28] On Berg, see Wielgohs in Müller-Enbergs (2010).

[29] Hannamaria Loschinski. Interview with author.

There were countless other affairs that led to party exclusions and thus the end of the career of many intellectuals.[30] But overall, the repressive measures described in Chapter 3 had lasting effects on what appeared as the consensus of the hope generation's economists: that the party, all in all, was right. "Resigning from the party would have meant the same to me as resigning from mankind," Kuczynski wrote in 1973.[31] Most of those of the hope generation that followed Kuczynski as a role model might have agreed.

---

[30] Two other examples that deserve mention were the philosophers Peter Ruben and Bernd Gehrke at the Economics Institute at the Academy of Sciences (see Müller-Enbergs et al. 2010). On dissidents in general, see for example Kuhrt et al. (1999).

[31] Cited in Keßler (2005: 42).

PART IV

Letting Go

7 | *Diverting West during the Détente*

The very confidential and personal atmosphere, and the generous scientific working conditions at IIASA, which are also characteristic of other scientific institutions in the non-socialist area, can be an immediate means of *political diversion*. They promote a growing lack of criticism towards previously existing enemy images and class convictions. In return, working conditions in the GDR and the connection between ideology and science are increasingly viewed critically.[1]

In October 1972, shortly before East Germany was recognized as a state by the United Nations, GDR officials signed the Charter of the International Institute for Applied Systems Analysis (IIASA). This membership was a real success for the policy of détente, or Brezhnev's "peace program," as it was called in the East. The early 1970s saw a true symmetric effort of better diplomatic relations between the superpowers in East and West, of disarmament of nuclear weapons, and of "peaceful coexistence" as was one of the slogans of détente. An attempt to build political bridges, IIASA sprang from the idea that the modern social sciences are alike on both sides of the Iron Curtain and thus could further the cause of détente. The institute was a unique research center that was to bring together researchers from the East and the West to address, as equal partners, "global" problems like acid rain and "universal" problems like transportation or an aging society. The institute's founders believed that society could be modernized through a more scientific and rational policy.[2] In contrast to the scientific competition that had dominated the preceding decades, the IIASA Charter expressed the hope that "science and technology, if wisely directed, can benefit all mankind . . . [and] that

---

[1] Wolfgang Schirmer, "Erarbeitung einer politisch-operativen Bestandsanalyse der Wissenschaftsbeziehungen der AdW der DDR zum IIASA," August 20, 1988, MfS HA XVIII 2036: 20, emphasis added.

[2] Of course, what was understood as political, social, science, and progress was negotiated rather than presumed, as Rindzevičiūtė showed in her book-length study on IIASA (2016).

international cooperation between national institutions promotes cooperation between nations and so the economic and social progress of people."[3] Previously called "economic cybernetics" in the East and, among other things, "decision sciences" in the West, this current of knowledge was tagged with the more generic term "systems analysis."[4]

For East Germany, membership in IIASA was a true novelty in international relations. The nonrecognition policy and the exclusive mandate claimed by West Germany was a major obstacle in the negotiations about IIASA between the Soviet Union and the United States. It was only after West German chancellor Willy Brandt opened up to the East, and only under the condition that IIASA members were nongovernmental institutions, that the IIASA Charter could be signed by both German states.[5] Two months later, in December 1972, the GDR and the Federal Republic of Germany (FRG) accepted each other as equal members in the United Nations. Participating in an international scientific organization on a par with West Germany and the Cold War superpowers was a matter of national pride. IIASA membership offered an occasion, comparable to sports competitions, for "socialist science propaganda and the display of the performance capacity (*Leistungsfähigkeit*) of science in the GDR," as Karl Bichtler, the head of East Germany's Committee for Applied Systems Analysis, wrote.[6]

But IIASA was also a real challenge. By the early 1970s, East German academia was populated by a reclusive generation, many of

---

[3] IIASA Charter (Laxenburg: IIASA, 1972, www.iiasa.ac.at/web/home/about/leadership/iiasacharter/charter.pdf, accessed May 10, 2020). The literature on IIASA consists of extensive studies on the political negotiations of its foundation, such as McDonald (1998) and Riska-Campbell (2011). There are also several participant accounts from the Western perspective, for example Levien (2000). For further historical studies, see Schrickel (2018) and Duller (2016). The most extensive research on the Eastern perspective on IIASA is the book by Rindzevičiūtė (2016). However, it entails no reference to East Germany.

[4] For the importance of systems analysis in the West, see Erickson et al. (2013) and Heyck (2015). For the importance of economic cybernetics in the East, see Gerovitch (2002) and Düppe and Boldyrev (2019). Comparing the military context of RAND and the global problem-solving context of IIASA, Duller argued for an intellectual mutation of systems analysis in IIASA (2016: 173).

[5] The twelve founding members were Bulgaria, Canada, Czechoslovakia, the Federal Republic of Germany, France, the German Democratic Republic, Italy, Japan, Poland, the Soviet Union, the United Kingdom, and the United States of America, to which was added Austria (1973), Hungary (1974), Sweden and Finland (both 1976), and the Netherlands (1977). East Germany was not invited to the first meeting of founding members in Sussex (McDonald 1998).

[6] Report Bichtler, in DY 30 84541: 9.

whom had known nothing apart from East German academia. Spiritually and physically separated, the socialist intelligentsia had developed its own culture largely independent of the Western sphere. As noted in the preceding chapters, the third university reform reinforced by Honecker resulted in a turn inward in East German academia, to the extent that Middell observed the "elimination of the international criteria for evaluating scientific performance" (2012: 335). In addition, individual initiative in science was hamstrung by the requirements of the Five-Year Plans, as mandated by the third university reform and the academy reform of the late 1960s. Research was oriented toward the needs of the party bureaucracy and collective industry, an epistemic virtue worshiped as "practical relevance." And the administration of science was dominated by the formal and hierarchical party roles professors usually held. After two decades of repeated battles over how to found knowledge on the doctrine of Marxism-Leninism, East Germany's institutions of science were intimately linked to the notion of class consciousness. Whereas "bourgeois" Western science was but the ideology of monopolistic power, only socialism creates the conditions of true scientific progress. This belief was policed both by the party-groups that were part of the academic system and by the Stasi. In the case of IIASA, two Stasi departments were in charge: Department 5 of HA XVIII, which over-saw the Academy of Sciences, and Department K of the infamous HV A (*Hauptverwaltung Aufklärung*), which concerned itself with the "use of legal relationships" with nonsocialist countries. While the documents of the former department are one of the sources I have used for this chapter, the files of HV A were largely destroyed during the turmoil of 1989 – the significance of which the reader will come to understand by the end of this chapter.

The clash of cultures was considerable. While in East Germany, being a social scientist meant being a partisan scholar, residence at IIASA meant living out the global politics of "peaceful coexistence," which was a rich and indeed a festive experience. Geographically, IIASA was in the West, in a picturesque castle outside of Vienna; it offered a sense of adventure and privilege to the otherwise isolated Eastern scientists.[7] Unlike in the East, all Western literature was freely

---

[7] East Germany imposed upper limits of foreign income of IIASA salaries which partially compensated for the membership fees paid in foreign currency. This led to financial differences between Eastern and Western scholars (see Rindzevičiūtė 2016: 104). Yet, IIASA visitors could go shopping in the United Nations Center

available. The use of funds at IIASA was decided not by party bureaucrats but autonomously by research areas. And there was space for speculative research, beyond the immediate pressure of "practical relevance," as in the methodology area founded by George Dantzig.[8] Political discomfort was, as far as possible, formally excluded, as classified research and the use of confidential data were not allowed at IIASA (which is one of the reasons it never acquired the same mystical aura as the RAND Corporation). As noted by several visitors, scholars could talk freely about politics in a nonjudgmental fashion. For a long-term visit, one had to be selected by the research director, and so intelligence services could not infiltrate nonscientific agents.

More importantly, the "carefully assembled internal culture of informality," as Rindzevičiūtė observed, rendered IIASA highly inclusive (2016: 125). While curiosity about other scholars was naturally great, the first research directors, Howard Raiffa and Roger Levien, created an atmosphere that was welcoming for all. To be at IIASA was to be part of a family. Mutual respect, tolerance, and team collaboration created a relaxed atmosphere unknown in East German academia. Highlights were the international dinner parties and the frequent celebrations of all sorts of national holidays. The IIASA experience was festive, which was a natural way to create bridges, if not friendships, between people. As an early long-term visitor from East Germany, the engineer Lutz Blencke, reported:

The institute organizes a large number of events to pass one's leisure time and maintain personal contacts between employees. This includes institute-wide events such as dance evenings, balls, picnic excursions, children's afternoons, trips abroad at greatly reduced prices, ski excursions, visits to

without paying customs, needed no visa for Austria, and were pampered regarding all practical issues from housing to kindergarten by the local staff (see report, November 17, 1979, DY 30 84541). As Rindzevičiūtė argued for Soviet scholars: "Used to passing through innumerable bureaucratic hurdles and formalities, they experienced these free, spontaneous travels not only as a gust of personal freedom, but also as confirmation of their special status within the tightly controlled system" (2016: 106).

[8] In 1975, IIASA's reputation was heightened through the joined Nobel Memorial Prize for Tjalling Koopmans and Leonid Kantorovich, both IIASA visitors in Dantzig's group. Koopmans donated part of his prize to IIASA.

the theater, women's meetings. . . . If you include personal invitations and return invitations, this makes for a program that cannot be managed in terms of time or finances.[9]

This informality was in stark contrast to the formal behavioral rules imposed on East German scholars by their travel directives. To give but one example, a directive for a conference delegation in 1975 reads as follows:

The conference takes place under the conditions of dense influence of the capitalist world. The members of the GDR delegation have a high level of political and professional responsibility with regard to their appearance, attitude, and discipline. . . . All members of the GDR delegation are obliged to represent the politics of the party and the government consistently, object-ively, and in a well-founded manner.[10]

For East German scholars, this political restraint applied not only to general political discussions but also to their actual research. As we read in another travel directive: "When reporting on your own research strategies, the information should be limited to the technical aspects without giving any insight into the research strategy of the current Five-Year Plan."[11] IIASA visitors were asked to represent East Germany's research priorities, to adopt predefined attitudes about specific topics and methodologies, and to promote national achieve-ments. All of this activity was monitored carefully by the Stasi, which required personal reports about each scholar's own activity and that of other East German visitors. Despite ongoing rumors about spying at IIASA, such internal surveillance seemed to be the Stasi's main role in the first year of IIASA.[12]

How then did East German scholars manage this paradoxical situ-ation, placed as they were between norms of cooperative research and

---

[9] Blencke report 1979, DY 30 84541: 19–20. For more on informality and festivity, including Soviet drinking habits and other strategies of establishing political inclusivity, see Rindzevičiūtė (2016: 102 ff.).

[10] "Reisedirektive . . . ," 1975, MfS HA XVIII, 38388: 4. This was standard procedure for any travels to the West, but not for anyone from the West.

[11] Travel directive, September 1, 1981, Knop and Wölfling, 9th global modelling forum, September 14–18, 1981, MfS HA XVIII 20020: 7.

[12] See the early meeting reports to the Stasi entailing commented lists of mostly East German scholars; "Treffbericht zur IIASA Reise 25.-29.8.1975," "Einschätzung des IMS Horn zur der KP," "Treffbericht, 26.9.75," MfS HA XVIII 38388.

the requirements of partisan scholarship? Did it force them into the role of the misfit at IIASA, or did it reinforce a sense of being compromised by their own institutions back home?[13] Each visitor had to deal with the tension in his or her own way. But there is one well-documented case that helps us spell out the clash of cultures: that of Harry Maier, one of the few East German social scientists who visited IIASA for two years (1978–1980) and who then, in 1986, used a conference visit to escape from East Germany. Without being representative, Maier's case reveals East Germany's disposition toward scientific cooperation with the West. The documents pertaining to Maier help reconstruct East Germany's ambivalent and complex role at IIASA and offer a window on the social self-perceptions of GDR's scientific elite. Interweaving individual, institutional, national, and global history, Maier's case shows the extent to which East Germany's contribution to the venture was caught up in the image of the Western scholar as a class enemy.

The Two Cultures

East Germany was slow in claiming its place at IIASA. The first person to represent the country at the meetings of IIASA's National Member Organizations, who was at the same time the head of the Committee for Applied Systems Analysis at the Academy of Sciences, was the best-known economist within the party apparatus, Helmut Koziolek, director of the CC Institute of Socialist Governance. He was replaced in 1975 by the younger economist Karl Bichtler from the Central Economics Institute at the Academy of Sciences, the same Bichtler who was central during the revisionism campaign against Behrens and Benary covered in Chapter 3.[14] The first conference visitors were either young scholars, mostly from the engineering sciences, or established scientists in higher positions who could show off East Germany's

---

[13] Such as reported by Klaus Fuchs-Kittowski, reading a belated passport as an intended act to undermine his travel (personal conversation).

[14] For Koziolek, see his contribution to the IIASA opening conference (1976), his report of the council meeting, November 1974 (DY 30 54540), and Müller-Enbergs et al. (2010). For Bichtler, see his personal files in MfS AIM 3238-71; his committee meetings reports are all available (DY30 27231; DY 30 54540; DY 30 84541).

expertise.[15] But they had little influence on IIASA's research agenda. East German scientists played only minor roles in the first flagship programs of IIASA, such as the energy project run by the nuclear physicist Wolf Häfele and the famous first computer network between East and West, the IIASANET, established in 1977.[16]

Two to three long-term visitors from East Germany were expected to be at IIASA at any given time. However, the Committee for Applied Systems Analysis, as Bichtler complained, could never "assure the permanent and proportionate presence of the GDR at IIASA even approximately."[17] One reason was that systems analysis, the focus of the institute, had never been developed into a paradigm for all disciplines in East Germany, as it had in the Soviet Union and the United States. More than in other socialist countries, systems analysis in East Germany was dominated by the official discourse of political economy. There were the remnants of "economic cybernetics" that flourished for a short time during Walter Ulbricht's NES, but since Erich Honecker wished to differentiate himself from Ulbricht's regime, enthusiasm vanished in the early 1970s. The constant fear of disclosing confidential data, and the

---

[15] This included economist Werner Kalweit, vice-president of the Academy of Sciences, psychologist Friedhart Klix, biochemist Samuel Mitja Rapoport, chemist Eberhard Leibnitz, economist Hans Mottek, then head of the commission for environmental research at the Academy of Sciences, the mathematician Manfred Peschel, and Erich Rübensam, president of the Academy of Agriculture. There were also visitors from the economic research institute of the State Planning Commission, such as Gerhard Köhler and Klaus Steinitz; but there was nobody from the party schools. One of the young visiting scholars was Klaus Fuchs-Kittowski. For him, IIASA opened a door of collaboration with, and travels to, Johns Hopkins University (see his travel report in DY 30 54540). Between 1975 and 1980 a total of 236 short-term visitors participated at conferences, mostly not from the social sciences (see the overview in DY 30 84541). Joint presence at IIASA hardly ever resulted in collaboration between the disciplines in East Germany.

[16] In 1981, Häfele became head of the atomic research center in Jülich. For his project, see Schrickel (2014); IIASANET was designed by Alexander Butrimenko, Gennadji Dubrov, and Vinton Cerf, and connected with data centers in Moscow that were part of "Akademset"; see Rindzevičiūtė (2016: 117 f.) and Dittmann (2009).

[17] Bichtler, "Stand und Probleme ... " ca. 1980 (DY 30 84541: 16). The first long-term stays were that of Konrad Grote (1975) who was later a protagonist in Macrakis (2008), Claus Riedel in the energy project (1976–1977), and the young engineer Lutz Blencke (1977–1978, see his report in DY 30 84541). Riedel used his IIASA visit to remain in the West, but no further documentation of his case was found.

difficulty of integrating IIASA activity into the fixed Five-Year Plan, did not help the search for qualified candidates. There simply were not enough scholars who met the double criteria of sufficient quality and political reliability, as Bichtler repeatedly complained:

The GDR has an insufficient cadre of candidates [*Kader*] with sufficient qualifications in the field of applied systems analysis. As a result, the associated organizations [*Basisorganisationen*] of the committee have faced extraordinary problems in finding scientists who are adequately qualified to work at IIASA and at the same time meet the specific political and executive requirements associated with working at IIASA.[18]

Nevertheless, although East Germany could never send a large number of visitors to the institute, IIASA membership, according to Bichtler, brought the country new expertise, such as the increased mathematization of the social sciences, and new technologies. New board computers in Berlin's S-Bahn trains, for example, optimized energy use.[19]

The first substantial contribution from an East German social scientist came from Hans Knop, vice-rector of the Higher School of Economics.[20] Knop visited IIASA between October 1974 and February 1976. He was the head of the research group "Management of Large Organizations" in the research area Management and Technology. He also had contributed to the celebrated global modeling conference series hosted by IIASA that took up the Club of Rome reports.[21] For his work at IIASA, Knop received East Germany's Order of Merit in 1977. After his return, it would be two more years before another economist, Harry Maier, was chosen for a long-term stay at the institute in 1978. He would remain at IIASA until 1980.

By the early 1970s, Maier was one of the promising economists of his generation. After his dissertation on the bourgeois character of

---

[18] "Stand und Probleme der Mitarbeit der DDR im IIASA," ca. 1980, DY 30 84541: 15–16.

[19] Ibid. The research on computer-controlled urban transportation was carried out by Horst Strobel from the Higher School of Transportation in Dresden, who was member of the Council of IIASA's research area "Human Settlement and Services."

[20] See the documents of Knop's travel permission (MfS AP 24942-92: 51–54), and his HV A registration (see MfS HA XVIII 36675).

[21] This work was joint with Manfred Wölfling from Maier's group in the Academy of Sciences; for more on global modeling see Rindzevičiūtė (2016); see also the travel directive and the travel reports on the 9th global modeling forum, 1981, in MfS HA XVIII 20020: 7–8; 10–14.

West Germany's Christian socialism, he moved into the political economy of socialism and wrote his habilitation on the question of meas-
uring labor intensity jointly with the later head of the Committee for
Applied Systems Analysis, Karl Bichtler.[22] Developing a measure for
reducing abstract to simple labor led Maier to the economics of education.[23] The topic of education was very much in the spirit of Ulbricht's
NES and the third university reform, and Maier came to be known as
the pioneer and authority of this field in East Germany. The topic of
education, in turn, led him to growth theory, which, after discussions
at the institute about its bourgeois character, was called the theory of
intensive advanced reproduction (Maier et al. 1968). In 1968, he
became a professor of economics at the Academy of Sciences and head
of the research group "Factors and Criteria of Economic Growth." He
was familiar with the prominent Western models of economic growth,
notably the Harrod–Domar model and in parts the Ramsey model,
though filtered through the reception of Janos Kornai and Michał
Kalecki. As compared to the Western literature, his work remained
largely conceptual and only to some extent technical. Nevertheless, he
was celebrated for his "constant search for and use of modern research
methods."[24] Maier was one of the few who managed to bridge the gap
between the literary discourse of Marxism-Leninism and the formal
discourse of Western social science, a gap that was perhaps the greatest
obstacle to East–West knowledge transfer in the social sciences.

Maier's openness to technical economics and Western thought
became apparent in 1968, when he edited Oskar Lange's *Political
Economy*, known for its neoclassical market socialism (Lange 1969).
This, however, as we have seen, won him no praise but, instead, fierce
critique from the party. Nevertheless, in 1973, he became member of
the national council of economic research. Known for being "energetic
and goal-directed toward completely fulfilling the plan," as one of his
recommendation letters said, Maier received several national awards,

---

[22] For his PhD thesis, see N 2693-1 and Maier (1965). For his habilitation with
Bichtler in 1967, see N 2693-1 and the article by Maier and Bichtler (1967).
Bichtler's support, as head of the committee for applied systems analysis, might
have been instrumental for initiating Maier to IIASA.

[23] See Maier (1964, 1967), and Maier, Wahse, and Ludwig (1972). Still in the early
1990s in West Germany, it was him who wrote the textbook on the economic of
education with a known publisher (1994).

[24] MfS 58363-92: 59.

such as the Friedrich-Engels Prize of the Academy of Sciences in 1975.[25] Once Fred Oelßner retired, Maier hoped to become the head of the academy's economics institute, but the party instead chose the scientifically inexperienced and politically more orthodox Wolfgang Heinrichs. As joint editors of a two-volume book on economic growth, Heinrichs and Maier received the Banner of Labor in 1977 (Maier and Heinrichs 1976). Such a career went hand in hand with important party functions. Between 1963 and 1964, he was a member of the party leadership at the academy's economics institute, and secretary of the party-group between 1967 and 1969, and until 1978 a member of the party committee of the Academy of Sciences (*Parteikreisleitung*). Maier's career trajectory also suggests cooperation with the Stasi. Recruited in 1954, he indeed had a longstanding record of "operative cooperation," as the activities of informants were called.[26] Like those of many others of his generation, Maier's career was made possible by the high demand for politically devoted *and* intellectually engaged political economists during the tumultuous Ulbricht era that allowed for a mixture of party-loyal mediocrity and intellectual creativity at the edge of "bourgeois" individualism. Intellectually curious and open to economic methods used in the West, Maier was the ideal candidate for IIASA. His selection in 1978 as the head of the IIASA research group on innovation in the research area Management and Technology was a real triumph for him and for the Academy of Sciences.[27]

Once settled in Laxenburg, Maier quickly made friends, for example with Clopper Almon from the University of Maryland, with the West German economists Lothar Hübl from Hannover and Erhard Ulrich from the Institute for Occupational Research, and in particular with Häfele, who, like Maier, was an outspoken scholar and a bon vivant. But he also kept in touch with the party as the party-group organizer at

---

[25] Lebenslauf Maier, 1982, MfS U 25-89: 373.
[26] See MfS U 25-89. His early reports are not available.
[27] As Bichtler wrote in the protocol of the committee meeting of 1979: "From our point of view, the changes that have resulted from the meeting of the advisory committee on the research area Management and Technology are remarkable, because there is now a good opportunity to influence the goal and content of research in a field by leading a research task, which is of great interest to the GDR" (March 16, 1979, in DY 30 84541: 4).

the GDR embassy in Vienna, and he was registered as a Stasi informant.[28] His research team had members from all around the world. They studied the influence of technology on economic growth in different cultural settings, inspired by the ideas of Joseph Schumpeter and Nikolai Kondratiev, considering specific national policies and focusing in particular on microelectronic technology and energy.[29] Heinz-Dieter Haustein from the Higher School of Economics joined the team in August 1979. Haustein, too, stayed for two years, and jointly with Maier was highly productive in terms of research output. Though much of this research was informed by formal techniques, Maier contributed mainly to qualitative institutional analysis. In his work with Haustein, he also presented a formal model of the optimal investment rate in innovation considering a given rate of increasing labor productivity (Haustein and Maier 1985). They matched the model with empirical data from different nations, and applied it conceptually to the development of the lighting industry. Discussing the role of education, automation, and employment structure, they derived normative conclusions for industrial policies on a national and global level. Compared to what East German economists had written in their own journals, this work was indeed refreshing since it did not unfold from the mantra of Marxism-Leninism alone. Back home, however, their work was hardly noticed.[30] At the end of his time at IIASA, Maier presented his research on innovation at the 1980 World Congress of the International Economic Association in Mexico, where he was proud to be one of the five section organizers (Maier 1983).

At IIASA, in addition to experiencing a Western lifestyle, Maier got to know what it was like to do research free from the constraints of the party bureaucracy. This experience, rather than encouraging him to remain at IIASA, inspired him to make a difference back home, as his wife recalled. Having demonstrated East Germany's scientific force to

[28] He was registered with section HA XX, AKG headed by Comrade Lieutenant Colonel Buhl; see MfS U 25-89. Unfortunately, the detailed report Maier must have written about his stay is not available in the archives. But we do have his wife as a witness, as she was with him for the entire period.

[29] Publications of this period include Haustein and Maier (1979) and Haustein, Maier, and Robinson (1980). For innovation research in the GDR, see also Wagener et al. (2021: chapter 4).

[30] As witnessed by Udo Ludwig, personal conversation. See also Haustein's short memoir, "Erlebnis Wissenschaft: Wirtschaftswissenschaft in Ost und West aus der Erfahrung eines Ökonomen," unpublished manuscript, August 2011, http://peter. fleissner.org/Transform/HausteinErlebnisWissen_3.pdf, accessed May 29, 2020.

Figure 7.1 Harry Maier (right) with Erhard Ulrich (left) from the West German Institute for Occupational Research at IIASA, ca 1979–1980.
Photo courtesy Siegrid Maier.

the international community, upon his return, at first it seemed that he would have the chance to do so. He received orders to draw up a plan for his own institute "for the study of scientific-technical innovation processes and the use of applied systems analysis," which was to become the main source for future IIASA scholars. But this was not to happen. Two years after his return, in September 1982, Maier wrote to the president of the Academy of Sciences, Werner Scheler:

Please excuse me if I turn to you with a personal problem. ... You have known me for several years and know that I am not one of those people who quickly resign or give up easily. However, the unpleasant, nerve-wracking and unproductive things that happened to me in the two years after my return from IIASA in Laxenburg, Vienna, exceeded what I thought was possible. It is in stark contrast to what I have experienced in more than two decades of work at the academy. Allow me to explain my problem to you in more detail.[31]

---

[31] Maier to Scheler, September 28, 1982, MfS HA XVIII 16682: 221–226.

Reverse Culture Shock

To understand what happened to Maier after his return from IIASA, his experience must be put in the context of global and national politics. A series of events – the Soviet invasion of Afghanistan in December 1979, the boycott of the 1980 Summer Olympics in Moscow, and the election of Ronald Reagan in November 1980 – brought the policy of détente to an end. In that climate, longstanding speculations about intelligence service activities at IIASA intensified and spread.[32] East German officials were perceptive as to the new post-détente conditions. Werner Scheler, the president of the Academy of Sciences, expressed skepticism about the value of IIASA. As early as January 1981, he wrote to Kurt Hager, chief ideologue of the party's inner circle:

A number of problems arising from this membership cause me to ask you to what extent it is still necessary and sensible to maintain membership in IIASA. I would like to expressly state that such a need cannot be justified from a scientific and economic point of view. Effort and benefits are in no reasonable relation to each other. However, it must be borne in mind that membership was a matter of political rather than scientific and economic reasons.[33]

Scheler wished to withdraw from IIASA also because he had in mind a different distribution of the highly sought *valuta* (foreign currency) assigned to the Academy of Sciences. He proposed that the significant fees reserved for IIASA could better be used for financing politically more acceptable knowledge transfers with the West, such as other kinds of travels there, as well as for "the purchase of fine chemicals, bio-materials, appliances, and other research materials from nonsocialist areas." Hager agreed. He wrote to Oskar Fischer, minister of foreign affairs. Fischer also agreed and asked that the withdrawal be coordinated with the Soviet Union.[34]

---

[32] In April 1981, an Austrian newspaper reported that Gvishiani, president of IIASA, was the head of the European section of the KGB (*Die Presse*, April 14, 1981). Later, a former IIASA public relations agent wrote a spy novel, in which IIASA staff member are the source of inspiration (Posey 1998).

[33] Scheler to Hager, January 9, 1981 (DY30 27231: 1).

[34] Fischer to Hager, February 6, 1981 (DY30 27231: 5); Erich Mielke and Johannes Hörnig were included in this exchange.

But the United States beat them to it. In the fall of 1981, as part of the sanctions against the Soviet Union, the United States announced that it would cancel its IIASA membership in 1983 and subsequently suspend payments to the organization. The United Kingdom, under Margaret Thatcher, followed suit. The reason given was that a Norwegian intelligence officer caught a Soviet official red-handed stealing US documents from IIASA, though it is unclear that there were confidential documents at IIASA in the first place. As a consequence, the Reagan administration deemed that IIASA was illegitimately transferring technology from West to East.[35] Indeed, while negotiations about the founding of IIASA might have been motivated by a fear that the Soviet Union was ahead in technology development, very soon the reverse became clear. The more IIASA developed, the more apparent it became that the East lagged behind the West, with respect to computing technology in particular.[36]

With the institute on the brink of collapse, IIASA representatives, along with several US senators and scientists, tried to keep it going. But this had no effect on GDR officials. In August 1982, the CC Secretariat decided "to seize the favorable opportunity of the exit of the United States and Great Britain" and end GDR membership in IIASA. The Secretariat's decision repeated Scheler's assessment that "membership in IIASA was accepted for political reasons during the détente process" and that "efforts are not in proportion to benefits."[37] Evidently, a sentence was missing between the two reasons that every Secretariat member agreed on: without the policy of détente, IIASA served no political purpose.

Even if withdrawal had been decided on, however, it was not to happen. The United States resumed its membership, with membership fees now being paid not by the National Academy of Sciences but by a nongovernmental institute, the American Academy of Arts and Sciences. The United States also began to put more pressure on IIASA's research

---

[35] See the 1982 US "Report of a Study Mission to Western Europe, November 4–13, 1981 to the Committee on Foreign Affairs, U.S. House of Representatives," *IIASA in Relations between the United States and Western Europe*, US Government Printing Office: 17. See also Bichtler's reports in DY30 27231, Rindzevičiūtė (2016: 123), and McDonald (1998: 70).

[36] For the early fears, see Gerovitch (2009); for East Germany, see Naumann (2018), and Solomon (2003).

[37] Vorlage für das Sekretariat des Zentralkomitees der SED, zugestimmt August 10, 1982, MfS HA XVIII 21110: 48.

agenda. The Soviets too recommitted, matching the significantly reduced amount of US funding.[38] Though Scheler repeatedly pushed for withdrawal, in November 1984, the CC Secretariat decided that East Germany too would remain a member of IIASA.[39] As a consequence, Bichtler was replaced as the IIASA representative by a scientist of greater political and scientific stature, the chemist Wolfgang Schirmer. In addition, general bureaucratic control over East German involvement in IIASA increased.[40] Apart from the scientific council and the newly founded executive office at the Academy of Sciences, an interministry Council for Applied Systems Analysis was created, whose members were to monitor the "practical relevance" of IIASA research. There was thus greater political control over IIASA, which apparently was considered too independent.

Scheler's skepticism might not have been known, but it must have been felt in the negotiations between Werner Kalweit, the vice-president of the Academy of Sciences, Heinrichs, the head of the Central Economics Institute, and Maier over his conception of the new IIASA-oriented Institute for Systems Analysis planned for the Academy of Sciences.[41] In addition, there might have been personal differences between Heinrichs and Maier, two different types of intellectual characters. Before Maier's return from IIASA, Heinrichs had replaced Maier with Klaus Steinitz as deputy chair of the institute and head of the research group on growth, which increased tensions between Maier and Heinrichs and ended the friendship between Maier and Steinitz.[42] When Maier's conception of the new institute

---

[38] Also in the Soviet Union, a high-level decision to withdraw had been made, but Gvishiani brought together party secretaries to ultimately convince Yuri Andropov, then head of the KGB, and in 1982 successor to Leonid Brezhnev, of the importance of IIASA (McDonald 1998: 71).

[39] See secretariat protocol, November 16, 1984 (DY 30 59383); for Scheler, see letter to Hager, October 27, 1983 (DY 3027231: 27).

[40] Schirmer was a chemist, head of the *Leuna-Werke*, head of a research group at the Academy of Sciences, professor at Humboldt University, and candidate of the CC – no comparison to the smaller authority of Bichtler; see Müller-Enbergs (2010); about the statute of the new committee, see "Ordnung ... ," October 1, 1985, MfS HA XVIII 17656; regarding the composition of the committee, see Schirmer to Scheler, January 21, 1985, MfS HA XVIII 18295: 53.

[41] See "Aktennotiz über ein Kadergespräch," March 9, 1981, MfS HA XVIII 16682.

[42] Personal conversation, Steinitz.

was discussed in the academy's social science colloquium, his ambitious vision was deemed "soaring and unrealistic" and perceived as an expression of his individualist intellectualism.[43] Thus, for the 1981–1985 Five-Year Plan, Maier would be demoted from running his own institute to running a research area no longer located at the economics institute but instead at the Institute for Theory, History, and Organization of Science (ITW). Only two of his many assistants opted to join him, while the rest of the economics institute lost touch with Maier. He had to rebuild his research team from scratch. For Maier this was a great loss, as he had considered the economics institute his academic home.[44]

In 1982, Maier thus became deputy chair of the ITW and head of the research group "Analysis and Forecast of Scientific and Technical Innovation Processes," which numbered, in the end, thirty-two scientists, seven of whom were professors. The group was part of the interdisciplinary research program "Scientific-Technical Revolution, Social Progress, and Intellectual Debate," which Maier jointly ran with Günter Kröber, the head of the ITW.[45] Despite the disappointment, Maier was very engaged in the research area and the whole program. He helped involve natural scientists in the social sciences, a novelty in the Academy of Sciences. In collaboration with IIASA, he organized a series of international conferences in East Germany at which younger scholars could connect with international researchers, mostly West Germans. This increasingly raised the suspicions of the Stasi, as Maier would later

---

[43] See MfS AP 58098-92: 37.

[44] "At the time, I was very reluctant to accept this suggestion. The proposal to found an institute for applied systems analysis at the Academy of Sciences and to lead it was not at all attractive to me, as was apparently assumed. For one, I still was attached to my old institute, which I had been a member of for twenty-four years and where I was able to develop into a scientist under the guidance of my scientific teachers AM [academician] Fred Oelßner and AM Gunther Kohlmey. Also, from 1967, when I succeeded AM Gunter Kohlmey as head of the department of the political economy of socialism, I initiated, designed and directed a large part of the institute's work in the field of socialist reproduction theory. This has resulted in a large number of studies and publications ... which have decisively determined the profile of the institute and brought it prestige at home and abroad" (Maier to Scheler, September 28, 1982, MfS HA XVIII 16682: 222). For the history of ITW, see Laitko (2018).

[45] *Analyse und Prognose wissenschaftlicher Neuerungsprozesse*, being part of the *interdisziplinäre Forschungsprogramm wissenschaftlich-technische Revolution, sozialer Fortschritt und geistige Auseinandersetzung* (see N 2693-17; MfS HA XVIII 16682: 115). For Günter Kröber, see Müller-Enbergs et al. (2010).

come to understand.[46] Knowing of the crisis at IIASA, in the summer of 1982 he planned to travel to the institute to prepare a book that, he hoped, would help refute the hypothesis of West–East technology transfer. However, he was denied permission to travel, which brought him to write the letter to Scheler quoted earlier. "On all travels that I have been able to carry out in more than two decades, as well as during my two-year stay at IIASA, there was not the slightest incident or doubt about my party-loyal appearance."[47] The letter worked. He was allowed to travel and the book was published (Haustein and Maier 1985). But his suspicions that higher powers in the academy's bureaucracy were working against him might have intensified.

While Kröber approved of Maier's research, he would also note that Maier "hardly got involved as a deputy director of the institute (ITW). The rest of the institute only interested him to the extent that the work and results of other areas were of interest to his own work."[48] Thus, when it came to the new Five-Year Plan for the period 1986–1990, Kröber became the sole head of the interdisciplinary research program, and Maier's research area was discontinued. He protested and succeeded in getting his program reintegrated, but at the cost of his influence on its overall agenda. The string of national awards that he had received before his visit at IIASA came to an end. While in the early 1980s many might have expected that Maier would soon be elected a member of the Academy of Sciences, the highest honor for a scientist in East Germany, by the mid-1980s this was no longer the case.

The tensions between Maier and the Academy of Sciences reached their peak after he returned from an IIASA trip in November 1985. At customs, Maier declared a "personal computer" and noted that he was carrying "conference material." Along with the personal computer,

---

[46] The Western scholars at these conferences were, among others, physicists Wolfgang Weidlich and Alfred Kleinknecht, and economists Wilhelm Krelle, Holger Rogner, and Walter Goldberg from Göteberg, another important Western friend of Maier. Conference themes were "flexible automation" in 1982, "energy system strategies" in 1983, and the large and successful conference on Kondratiev's long waves in 1985 that was under the control of the Stasi; see the proceedings Vaska (1987), and Maier's CV in N 2693-4. The 1985 conference was cancelled at the last minute by the Stasi, but since people were already on their way, it took place anyway (letter September 14, 1986, in N-2693-14).

[47] Maier to Scheler, September 28, 1982, MfS HA XVIII 16682: 225.

[48] Kröber, April 3, 1986, "Zur Einschätzung der möglichen Motive ... ," MfS AP 58098-92: 38.

however, he was bringing in additional items, such as a printer, a data recorder, floppy disks, and tape cassettes, and the "conference material" included the _Frankfurter Allgemeine Zeitung_, the _Herald Tribune_, and the _Times_, the importation of which was forbidden. He was held at the airport for over ten hours of questioning.[49] As the minutes of the interrogation state, he excused himself by declaring that he had purchased the computer with money saved up from his daily allowances, in addition to financial help from a Western colleague to whom he "offered" an edition of the Marx-Engels collection. He also brushed off the newspapers, claiming they were for work and that he would have access to them anyway. Maier was annoyed, as the minutes suggest: "During the entire procedure, Maier appeared arrogant and conceited toward the customs officer. Throughout the exchange, he threatened the controller with an official complaint and the personal consequences such a complaint would produce. He was asked several times to contribute to the factual clarification of the procedure."[50] Even though Maier eventually signed the protocol stating that he regretted not enumerating in greater detail the items he was bringing into East Germany, he added, "I would like to express my lack of comprehension for the problems I had here today."[51]

A few weeks later, on January 13, 1986, Maier was called to a discussion (_Aussprache_) with Kröber, the ITW party secretary, and the academy's Vice-President Kalweit. The discussion was to determine whether a disciplinary procedure would ensue. Maier had to respond once more to the customs charges, as well address the fact that he had not immediately informed Kalweit or Kröber of these charges after his return. "Prof. Kalweit demonstrated to Prof. Maier that his actions and behaviors are clearly to be seen as a disregard for valid legal norms, political misconduct, and serious breach of discipline that are in gross contradiction of his special duties as travel cadre."[52] Maier emphasized his good intentions, focused on advancing his research, and explained that he had not informed Kröber of the planned purchase before his travel because he did not yet know if his savings would be sufficient to buy the computer in the first place. On his return, he informed Wolfgang Schirmer and Hermann Herold, respectively the head and the secretary of the Committee for Applied Systems Analysis,

---

[49] See Maier's CV in N 2693-4. [50] MfS U 25-89: 23. [51] MfS U 25-89: 26.
[52] "Notiz über eine Aussprache," MfS AP 58098-92: 14.

of the events; he could not inform Kröber because he was absent, and others, such as Kalweit, were not in charge of travels to IIASA.

In the subsequent discussion of his statement [*Stellungnahme*], Professor Maier was emphatically criticized. ... As a result of the discussion, Professor Maier took a self-critical position on his behavior and promised that he would consistently comply with legal standards and his obligations as a travel cadre in the future. Taking into account his understanding and conclusions at the end of the debate, no disciplinary procedure was carried out. ... A reprimand [*Missbilligung*] was issued to Comrade Professor Harry Maier for disregarding legal norms and violating his duties.[53]

The disciplinary procedure would have involved a travel ban, which was unacceptable to Maier. It was then, after his next conference visit at IIASA, on March 27, that Maier decided to take a plane to Cologne rather than back to Berlin. It was a simple but symbolic act: Maier was viewed as a "traitor to the republic" in one part of Germany, and as a "political refugee" in the other. He was hosted and supported by his IIASA friend Wolf Häfele in Jülich.

Puzzlement

That night Maier called his wife, Siegrid Maier, who was also employed by the academy's economics institute. His wife, in turn, reported the next day to Kröber. According to Kröber, "the reason given was that he (Maier) had not gotten over the discussion with comrade Vice-President Kalweit (about his offenses against customs regulations after his last trip to IIASA). ... Comrade Siegrid Maier affirmed that she had not noticed any signs of an intended escape from the republic (*Republikflucht*) before his departure. She gave the impression of being stunned and horrified."[54] Maier's escape came as a shock to everyone, including the Stasi, which immediately opened an operation (*operativer Vorgang*) on him nicknamed "OV Rechenberg." His wife's phone was tapped ("A measures"), his letters were read

---

[53] Ibid.: 14–15.

[54] Kröber, in DY30 27231: 35–36; see also MfS U 25-89: 4–5: "According to Maier's wife, in the almost daily phone calls with her after his decision not to return to the GDR, he repeatedly mentioned that he found the discussion with Vice-President Kalweit to be degrading and humiliating, and that he was fed up with the gauntlet he had experienced at the Academy of Sciences." See also MfS AP 58098-92: 36.

("M measures"), and his office was searched and sealed, all under the presumption that there was more going on than what he reported to his wife on the phone.[55] The stakes were high, given that Maier himself knew the Stasi well and was involved in the internal preparations for the 11th Party Congress. Thus, in the Stasi's view the most plausible initial explanation was that the West German Federal Intelligence Service (*Bundesnachrichtendienst*, BND) had detained Maier and that he could be convinced to return to the East:

It must be assumed that this is a targeted enemy measure to disrupt the preparations for the 11th Party Congress. The operational approach was directed toward using all options to bring Maier back to the GDR. The wife was informed in several conversations that Maier could return to the GDR without having to expect sanctions. The efforts have so far been unsuccessful.[56]

Both Maier and his wife knew that major punishment awaited him upon his return, despite what she was instructed to tell him over the phone. On Sunday, March 30, Maier confirmed in a fourth telephone conversation that he would not be returning.

A few days later, Maier's official explanation for his actions came in a formal letter to Scheler resigning from the Academy of Sciences. He felt obliged to explain himself to the academy, if to no one else. Referring to the disappointment regarding the plans for his own institute for systems analysis, as well as to the humiliation of the discussion with Kalweit in January, he added:

I am in a phase of my life in which, based on my previous work, I believe that I can again make a contribution to the research on scientific and technical innovations and their socioeconomic effects. To do this, however, I need working conditions that I believe are no longer available to me at the Academy of Sciences. With such considerations in mind, I decided to take this difficult step to end my employment at the GDR Academy of Sciences. The motives of my scientific work have remained unchanged. My loyalty to the GDR, as one of the two German states, remains unbroken. Also, in my new field of activity, I will try to advocate for a coalition of reason and international understanding [*Verständigung*].[57]

---

[55] See the arrest warrant (MfS U 25-89: 19). Maier had no knowledge of so-called operative actions.

[56] MfS U 25-89: 19; "She influenced her husband in a way that was explained to her and tried to convince him to return" (ibid.).

[57] Maier to Scheler, MfS U 25-89: 67–68.

Maier's explanation that he left because of some trifling harassment at customs seemed inadequate. Hence, not only did the Stasi speculate about deeper reasons behind the escape; so too did his closest collaborators at IIASA. An unattributed comment to the Stasi, most likely written by Haustein, reported: "American and German nationals were actively gathering around Maier ... seeking contacts and starting targeted recruitment campaigns."[58] The problems Maier had had with customs made him vulnerable to attempts by Western intelligence agents to "blackmail" him. The closing remark of this comment shows how intensive the perceived political pressure to distance oneself from Maier in fact was:

He [Maier] is brutal and disregarding, but at the same time cleverly calculating; he has deceived those around him about his real attitude. ... I am a scientist with all my heart, but at the same time I know very well that all of our scientific work is built on sand if, at any point, the enemy acts against us. ... Our ideological unity is the greatest force that no power of darkness can resist.[59]

In the economics department at Humboldt University, one informant reported on the perplexity and the general uncertainty in the entire field of economics, and the fear of future travel restrictions after Maier's escape. Disbelief in the reason Maier gave made them speculate: "The suspicion was expressed that Maier could either have worked for Western intelligence or that the MfS (Ministry for State Security) had 'deposed' him."[60] Another informant who knew Maier personally reported: "Personally, I fear that he fell victim to political blackmail. ... Harry Maier was very talkative, not to say gossipy and equally vain. ... Maybe the fact that he spoke so freely was held up to him ... with the certainty that he had committed a criminal offense and that in such a context he decided to take this step."[61]

---

[58] "Information zur Republikflucht des Maier, Harry," May 12, 1986, MfS HA XVIII 18669: 79.
[59] Ibid.
[60] "Information HA II on a discussion on 15 April 1986," IM at Humboldt University, April 20, 1986, MfS HA XVIII 16682: 54.
[61] "Position ... ," former student colleague at Humboldt University, MfS HA XVIII 16682: 147–148.

The Committee

To clarify matters, the Academy of Sciences formed a committee that submitted a report to the Stasi about two weeks after Maier's flight. Kröber wrote the two central documents, about the damage caused by and the motives for Maier's escape, reports that perhaps tell us more about his perception of what the Stasi and the party expected to read than what he actually thought of Maier's defection.[62] The damage, according to Kröber, was primarily political: the reputational blow sustained when a highly trusted scientist turned his back on the East German state. As if in an act of self-shaming, Kröber listed Maier's accomplishments over several pages, including his party involvement since 1954, his career as an economist, and the prizes he had received. By April 9, the anticipated political disgrace had come via a report in a Western newspaper: the *Frankfurter Allgemeine Zeitung* reported a "sensation before the Party Congress. . . . Leading GDR economist remains in the West. . . . The motives are not yet known. . . . But for the SED, Harry Maier's escape is bitter and embarrassing in any case."[63] But that was about it – at first. Some notes in the daily press, forgotten the day after. For most economists in West Germany who read the article, it would likely have been the first time they had heard the name Harry Maier.[64]

The scientific damage sustained involved calling off many of Maier's planned publications, in particular those for the forthcoming Party Congress.[65] Also, his scientific positions at the Academy of Sciences,

---

[62] MfS AP 58098-92. Members were Claus Grote, executive director of the Academy of Sciences, Achim Sydow, deputy director of the social sciences, Jahn, head of the Department of Analysis and Control (AKG), Heene, head of the Party District Control Commission, Kursawe, intelligence delegate of the president of the Academy of Sciences, and Hermann Herold, head of the Scientific Bureau for Applied Systems Analysis.

[63] Hans Herbert Götz, "Das Sein verstimmt das Bewusstsein," *Frankfurter Allgemein Zeitung*, November 4, 1987: 14.

[64] A month after his escape, in May 1986, in an interview, Maier blamed the defeatism of Honecker's regime. "The GDR is plagued with the Ringelnatz syndrome" – Ringelnatz being a satirist from Saxony: "If I were so rich and powerful that I could change everything, I would leave everything as it is" (*FAZ*, May 9, 1986). The Stasi took this as sign that Maier has ceased being a Marxist-Leninist (see MfS HA II 46832).

[65] For the proceedings of the Weimar conference in 1985, co-edited with Haustein (Haustein and Maier 1985), the Stasi decided that Maier's text should be published since it helped to discredit him. "It is expected that the existing

at IIASA, and in governmental programs had to be filled. Some of these could be simply eliminated because there was no second Harry Maier: "The structure and content of his research area at the ITW were largely tailored to his person and his conceptual ideas."[66] The same applied to his IIASA position. This shows the extent to which institutions were built around Maier as a person rather than him adapting himself to existing institutions, a typical feature of what was considered bourgeois intellectualism.

The informational damage was relatively slight. Yes, Maier had had security clearance since 1977 and was privy to secret documents of the academy and of several ministries, such as the Ministry for Science and Technology, the Ministry for Higher Education, and the State Planning Commission. However, he seemed to have little interest even in viewing the documents he had clearance to see. Some of the confidential documents, notably minutes of meetings he had attended, were found unopened in his office. The informational damage was, rather, in his soft knowledge about all sorts of informal practices in East Germany's central institutions: "The possible informational damage must therefore be measured according to the level of knowledge of confidential processes. It is difficult to assess it in detail. ... Maier's pronounced sociability brought him a large circle of friends and therefore lots of information about the economic and scientific development of the GDR."[67]

This soft knowledge found its way into a book that Maier wrote immediately after his escape, titled *Innovation or Stagnation: Conditions of Economic Reform in Socialist Countries* (1987). He combined his insider knowledge as an economic researcher in industry and the State Planning Commission with personal anecdotes and his own theorizing about the party, industry, and the academy, seeking to understand what had to be done to link up East Germany's economy with that of the West. Why had the technological gap between East and West widened since the early 1970s? The major mistake, he argued, was Honecker's "uninhibited wave of centralization of decision-making processes after the 9th Party Congress" (ibid.: 21).

contradiction between theoretical knowledge and personal action will not serve his international reputation as a 'serious scientist'" (MfS HA II 49500).

[66] MfS HA XVIII 20960: 19.

[67] MfS AP 58098-92: 37. For a list of all confidential documents, see MfS HA XVIII 16682: 121–122. No confidential documents were missing.

The "decreasing rationality of economic activity ... due to the ano-
nymity of the risk" inhibited innovation. The double bureaucracy of
party and ministries had led to collective irresponsibility. Publically
owned firms (*Kombinate*) are "industrial dinosaurs" (ibid.: 21),
lacking the training of managers as in West Germany. He showed
how the official party intelligentsia in the Academy for Social
Sciences and the Institute for Marxism-Leninism had diverged from
Marx. The alternative he proposed was a controlled market using the
profit motive as an engine for innovation, which he considered possible
within existing socialism. Summing up his own experience, he wrote:

The main reason for the insufficient relevance of innovation to research and
development in the socialist countries lies in the current forms of organization and planning of science and technology, which in turn are fairly accurate
reflections of the current planning and decision-making mechanism of the
economic process in the socialist countries ... There is a mechanistic egalitarian education concept, which is based on the idea that every student of
average talent is allowed to study basically everything. (Ibid.: 123, 149)[68]

This clearly could be read as an internalization of the elitism at IIASA.
Accordingly, the Stasi's evaluation asserted that the book proved that
Maier had moved away from Marxism.[69]

Kröber's second report, speculating about the motives behind
Maier's treason, amounts to an official rewriting of his past in the light
of his escape.[70] Maier's own account of his reasons had to be supplemented with deeper reasons, since Maier directly blamed Kröber for
the bureaucratic harassment he had endured. Kröber again listed
Maier's career achievements, showing how much he owed to the state
and how his escape revealed a profound lack of gratitude – gratitude
being the key civic virtue of this generation of GDR citizens. And hand

[68] Egalitarianism in education was a widely discussed topic at the time in East
Germany, associated with the sociologist Manfred Lötsch.

[69] The book received positive reviews in West Germany. "So far, no one has
described the difference in the atmosphere of discussion in the Soviet Union and
in the GDR so precisely" (Hans Herbert Götz, "Das Sein verstimmt das
Bewusstsein," *FAZ*, November 4, 1987); Adolf Wagner, "Textbook for
Gorbachev," *Die Zeit*, October 30, 1987; Wolfgang Stinglwagner, *Deutschland
Archiv*, 11 (88); see also N 2693-7. For the Stasi's reaction, see "Stellungnahme
zu '*Innovation oder Stagnation*'," MfS HA XVIII 25675; and MfS HA
XVIII 20960.

[70] Kröber, April 3, 1986, "Zur Einschätzung der möglichen Motive und
Hintergründe der Republikflucht von Harry Maier," MfS AP 58098-92: 36–40.

in hand with gratitude should come the capacity to accept criticism; the lack of it was the ultimate vice of those who opposed the party line. "Maier generally only accepted his own conceptual ideas, and was unable to tolerate other opinions, especially those that were critical of him."[71] Thus Kröber tried to wipe his own slate clean with respect to the party authorities by pointing the finger at Maier's anticollectivist personality:

All of the events mentioned were not of the type and weight that would explain or even justify an escape from the Republic. The fact of betrayal can only be explained if it is viewed against the background of Maier's personality, the dominant features of which were immense self-esteem, excessive vanity, boundless arrogance and pronounced subjectivism.[72]

Personality is of course not a given in socialism but the result of ideological education (*Erziehung*), and so Kröber's arguments could have been used against him as a supervisor. Therefore he added: "Educational measures, which began to be taken, apparently came too late to change something in his solidified personality structure."[73] All of this shows, as the final report stated, that "the explanation in his letter to the president of the Academy of Sciences therefore lacks any foundation and is a further indication of his arrogance to claim special rights."[74]

The committee's report had to be evaluated and approved by Department 5 of HA XVIII.[75] In the words of the Stasi officer, Kröber's analysis boiled down to the simple statement that "the main motive for his betrayal was that he increasingly turned away from Marxism-Leninism as the driving force of his actions."[76] By April 7, Maier was expelled from the party; by April 24, the Academy of Sciences publicly announced his treason; by May 16, he was convicted; and by October 8, "OV Rechenberg" was closed without result. Gone is gone.

---

[71] Ibid.: 38.   [72] Ibid.: 39.   [73] Ibid.: 42.   [74] Ibid.: 39.
[75] "The MfS forces employed in the working group, officers in special duty and reliable, knowledgeable IMs, ensured from the outset an objective and politically clear examination of the acts of treason and their effects. The assessment can be approved" ("Stellungnahme zur Einschätzung der Akademie," April 21, 1986, MfS HA XVIII 16682).
[76] Ibid.: 34.

IIASA as Political-Ideological Diversion

Though Maier was the only social scientist, many other scientists from the Academy of Sciences used travel to the West, and to IIASA in particular, as a chance to escape.[77] Numbers increased, such that the Stasi noted a certain "pull effect." To prevent this, the political requirements for traveling increased to the extent that after Maier's defection there was no other long-term visitor from East Germany at IIASA. There was no one left who could pass both the IIASA director's test of scientific quality and the Stasi's test of political trustworthiness, a fact that clearly speaks to the clash of the two intellectual cultures exemplified in this chapter.

It was only after Maier's escape that the Stasi formulated an actual strategy for IIASA. Numerous Stasi documents illustrate the confrontation between the two intellectual cultures. To begin with, the party-group of the Academy of Sciences analyzed the defections and insisted, regarding IIASA, that the "specifics of this institute, its working and living conditions, and the current objectives of research must be considered more thoroughly."[78] Comparing the motives in cases of defection, the report presented as a "subjective circumstance" Maier's "egocentric personality development, vanity, limitless arrogance, tremendous self-promotion, pronounced subjectivism, and excessive material interests."[79] But now emphasis was also given to the "objective circumstance" of the atmosphere at IIASA, which caused a "moral softening" (*Aufweichung*) of the personality of IIASA visitors. The Stasi suspected systematic attempts by other intelligence agencies to use, or even create, this aspect of the IIASA experience. This strategy

---

[77] Engineer Manfred Grauer used an IIASA visit in December 1986 to stay in West Germany (see MfS HA SAA AU 9398/87). On other travels, in 1984 and 1985, around 15 members of the Academy of Sciences escaped, another 15 in 1986, 22 in 1987, 49 in 1988, and 108 in 1989, until they stopped counting. For a full list, see MfS HA XVIII 18295: 63–82, as well as MfS HA XX AKG 2721.

[78] MfS HA XVIII 22725: 7, 8.

[79] Report party-group, MfS HA XVIII, 21111: 102. Regarding "material interest," there is only one report that testifies of personal enrichment, saying that Haustein and Maier "received NSW salaries from the institute in Laxenburg; Professor Haustein and Maier received the equivalent of State Secretaries or Ambassadors in non-socialist foreign states (NSW) . . . Contrary to the GDR rule, where NSW salaries exceeding 1500 of the respective NSW currency are to be paid to the GDR embassy, they kept all the money for themselves and used it up" (MfS U 25-89: 85–86).

was tagged with a technical Stasi term: "political-ideological diversion." In other words, going to IIASA was put in the same subversive category as listening to heavy metal music:[80]

The atmosphere at IIASA and the generous scientific working conditions had a definite influence on these acts of treason. Characterized as confidential and very personal ... this atmosphere works as a means of *political-ideological diversion*. It promotes a growing lack of criticism toward previously existing enemy images and class positions, and on the other hand encourages critical attitudes toward the GDR.[81]

In the wake of the academy's party-group meeting and report, it was up to Department 5 of HA XVIII to take a position regarding new "tasks that arise in the context of the development of the situation of international class struggle for the management of the GDR Academy of Sciences."[82] They demanded more careful consideration of subject-ive circumstances when selecting travel cadres to the West, including their career ambitions and their chances for individual development. They also acknowledged that the informal working atmosphere did have unwanted effects:

The political-ideological and moral state of the international travel cadres as well as their image of the enemy has considerable weaknesses ... The ability to recognize classes is partially only theoretically developed ... There is often insufficient clarity in conveying a practical image of the enemy ... As a result, changes in personality take place that result in the fact that the travel and foreign cadres do not, or no longer, meet the travel requirements ... Insufficient political and ideological work is also evident in the cases where

[80] On the notion of political ideological diversion, see Engelmann (2011: 67).
[81] Report party-group, MfS HA XVIII, 21111: 103, emphasis added. Of course, no intention of Western intelligence could ever be proven. Nine former East German scientists are listed for contact, but no action, with western intelligence ("Übersicht über ehemalige DDR-Bürger ... ," September 30, 1987, MfS HA XVIII 22725). The funding regime of East German scholars in West Germany, and in particular the treaty for scientific cooperation between the Federal Ministry for Science and Technology and the Council of Ministers of the GDR of September 1987, was read as an intention of political-ideological diversion, saying that the really important institutions, such as the Max Planck Institute, were excluded from the cooperation. At the same time, the AKG complained that department 5 of HAXVIII too easily blamed Western intelligence for their own faults ("Stellungnahme HA XVIII," AKG, MfS HA XVIII 22725: 84–87).
[82] "Stellungnahme," February 13, 1987, MfS HA XVIII 22725: 18.

the policy of dialogue, developed in the interest of peacekeeping, causes illusory ideas that stand in the way of the necessary vigilance, nurtured by "intelligence-specific ideologies" such as the unlimited exchange of information, convergence theory, and the consideration of the representative of the capitalist-imperialist system as a "colleague." In this context, it should be noted that a significant proportion of the travel cadres to nonsocialist countries have been in contact with certain partners from nonsocialist countries for many years, some of them regularly, such that their relationship has developed the character of friendships.[83]

Dialogue, yes; but friendship, no. And it is in this context that even the Stasi had to acknowledge *expressis verbis* what everyone already knew but was not supposed say aloud for the sake of scientific propaganda: that East Germany's technological development was lagging behind the West.

From findings on acts of treason, it becomes clear that disappointment and resignation among international travel cadres result from the insight and experiences that, despite the largely equal level of knowledge and basic research ... in both systems, the implementation of this knowledge in new products and technologies/processes in imperialism is generally done faster.[84]

The topic then came up at a strategy conference (*Linientagung*) of higher Stasi officials in March 1987, in a talk on the causes of treason by members of the scientific community. The main cause was now narrowed exclusively to the strategic actions of the class enemy. The assumption was that Western intelligence services aimed to collect information about East Germany's science and steal their knowledge through "skimming" (*Abschöpfung*) in the course of exchanges of scientists and through instigating the defection of East Germany's scientists.

Comrade General, Comrade Officers ... Today we can clearly say that these provocations to commit acts of treason are based, above all, on the immense intensification of the activities of our enemies within the framework of their long-term programs, which is still characterized by political-economic and military confrontation. ... Demagogic promises, lucrative job and salary offers, as well as the promotion of the material conditions belonging to the imperialist lifestyle are attempts to persuade our scientists to commit

---

[83] Ibid.: 19.   [84] Ibid.: 19.

treason. ... These actions are carried out by the BND (Federal Intelligence Service) and the BAfV (Federal Office for the Protection of the Constitution) with the political aim of provoking a so-called intelligence crisis in the GDR.[85]

The Stasi officers overseeing the Academy of Sciences could not imagine anything other than that cooperation with Western scientists was corrupting the minds of socialist scholars. Western science being a form of false consciousness, East Germany's contribution to IIASA was thus being structurally undermined. And so tensions between the Academy of Sciences (Schirmer and Scheler in particular) and IIASA (directors Thomas Lee and, later, Robert H. Pry) continued until the end of the East German state.[86]

Integration in West Germany

What – many back in the East might have asked themselves – could Maier possibly do in West Germany? As a scientist he would just be one among many others, and as a Marxist he would be on the margins for having betrayed the GDR, some thought. Maier's ideas about West Germany were better informed than those of most of his countrymen, but still, without an offer in hand, a position as professor of economics was not a certainty for him. In West Germany, there was no link between systems analysis and the political left – and, at this point,

[85] "Diskussionsbeitrag Linientagung," anonymous, March 20, 1987, MfS HA XVIII1: 23–25.

[86] A frequent issue were membership fees that should preferably be paid in East German currency, for example by financing contractual research for IIASA in East Germany, so-called network contributions. Another issue was that IIASA's research agenda should fit the national interests of East Germany, hidden as a demand for practical relevance. Yet another issue was that US funding was increasingly substituted by corporate funding. Lee and Pry both recruited from General Electric, and did everything to rebut the allegation of West–East technology transfer. This made Schirmer call IIASA an exploitation of "cheap labor" of socialist countries (in MfS HA XVIII 21110); for these discussions, see Schirmer's report, "zur Effektivität der Mitarbeit der DDR am IIASA," 1987, MfS HA XVIII 15324; and "zum Stand und zu den Aufgaben der Erhöhung des Nutzeffektes der Mitarbeit der DDR am IIASA in Laxenburg," March 15, 1988, MfS HA XVIII 17656: 69; see also the political-operative strategy of Leutnant Johannes Neuss, head of HA XVIII (MfS HA XVIII 18553: 60 ff.). Neuss referred to an "Operation Matrix" directed against Häfele; see also the reports of later informal collaborators at IIASA, IMS "Henry Kraatz," IMS "Mathias Kessel," IMS "Anton" (ibid.).

not even with economics proper. Maier's intimate knowledge of the East German bureaucracy, which he fled from, made him an ideal candidate for the so-called East Research Centers.[87] But given their reputation for being critical of socialist regimes, that was out of question for him. He wished to find a position as an economist. The first information the Stasi kept track of regarding Maier are indeed pieces of evidence showing that he had difficulties finding a job. He tried without success in Kiel and in Cologne, and there were rumors that he even hoped to become director of a Max Planck Institute.[88] But these reports might tell us more about the Stasi than about Maier. For in fact it took only two months, until June 1986, for Maier to become a scientific collaborator at the Ifo Institute for Economic Research in Munich.[89]

Maier nevertheless sought support and understanding from other East German expats in the so-called working circle of former GDR scientists that was founded in May 1987.[90] A loose discussion group of about five former East German scientists, the circle was founded out of "solidarity with colleagues who are new to West Germany and who have a hard time gaining a foothold here, and in turn, also with those who have difficulties over there because of a professional ban."[91] Being attached to Marxism to different degrees, they knew that the aging

---

[87] Such as the Institute for Society and Science at the University of Erlangen, which the Stasi considered anti-socialist propaganda; see MfS XVIII 23244.

[88] "Aktennotiz," April 14, 1986, MfS HA XVIII 16682: 50–51; see also the report of May 2, 1986, ibid.: 75. As Maier continued working with Häfele, Schirmer complained in a personal talk with IIASA director Lee that this would count as an illegitimate knowledge transfer from East to West; see "Grundsätzliche Fragen unseres Verhältnisses zum IIASA," January 1987, MfS HA XVIII 21110-21: 441.

[89] See his application to the director Karl Heinrich Oppenländer (May 26, 1986, N 2693-13).

[90] *Arbeitskreis ehemaliger DDR Wissenschaftler*. Other members were Wolfgang Seiffert, former professor of foreign law at the Academy of Political and Legal Sciences in Potsdam-Babelsberg and former consultant of Honecker, Franz Löser, philosopher from Humboldt University, Hermann von Berg, economic historian at Humboldt University (with a long Stasi history), and Edda Hanisch. The Stasi considered the circle enemies of the state. Visitors to West Germany were warned about them, and friends back in the East were observed as if they were in touch with members of the circle. For Seiffert, there was IM "Klee" and IM "Steffenhagen," for Maier, there was IM "Modelle" and IM "Seemann" to understand his connections back to East Germany, including his family; see MfS HA XVIII 20960.

[91] Interview with Seiffert, *Deutschlandfunk*, May 11, 1987, cited in MfS HA XVIII 20960: 11.

Honecker government would soon be replaced and that pressure from the Soviet Union would lead to political and economic reform. They thought of themselves as a mouthpiece for their Eastern colleagues:

We want to openly express, what many think and want in the GDR, but cannot say without further upheaval: the appeal to the democratic renewal of the GDR. .... There is a real need among our colleagues from the GDR that we, who have the opportunity to express ourselves freely and know their problems, make this clear.[92]

Now that he was free to express himself, Maier's writings could be used to test the hypothesis that self-censorship was a motivation for his escape – or, as the Stasi argued, that he had turned away from Marxism. However, comparing his writings before and after his defection, there is little in the latter that could not be inferred from his earlier writings. Apart from the book, already mentioned, on market reforms in East Germany, the highlight of his public intervention in political discussions was a series of newspaper articles in which he commented on perestroika, the fall of the East German regime, and German reunification. Between 1986 and 1992, he regularly published long commentaries in *Die Zeit*.[93] They exemplify well how his generation's mindset had transformed from reforming to rescuing the GDR, followed by the critique of the new regime, a transition that resembles the transformation of the socialist party itself that we describe in detail in Chapter 8.

The series begins with five long articles in November and December 1986 on the conditions for the success of Gorbachev's reforms. In 1987, he commented that the struggle for power was a matter of party "radicals" against scientific "technocrats," the main obstacle in the GDR being the economic "emperor" Günter Mittag. In March and May 1989, he explained how the reforms in the Soviet Union could translate to East Germany, arguing – typically for his generation – that the economic relationship between the East and the West would determine what was possible in the political superstructure. And this, said Maier, depends on the development of technology-intensive production, such as microelectronic technology. However, he went on, there currently were no incentives to innovate, because risk was shared. And

---

[92] Ibid.: 3.
[93] *Die Zeit*, 1986, issues 46–50; 1987 issues 37 and 38; 1988 issue 23; 1989 issues 11, 12, 21, 44, and 47; 1990 issues 16 and 39; 1991 issue 8.

as if commenting on his own career, he added: "This [lack of innovation] only strengthened a process that has deep roots, namely, the decades-long isolation of GDR science from the West. Since GDR researchers were prevented from taking part in the discussions of the international scientific community, they could not take up and respond to the impulses from there."[94] Starting in November 1989 and continuing until 1992, Maier directed his voice against Western reformers who sought to dismantle East Germany's economy. He still asked how one could balance out the economic differences between East and West, but now he blamed the mistakes made by the Bundesbank in April 1990. He argued for an economic "shift" instead of a "conversion" (*Wechsel statt Wandel*) and critiqued the notion that East Germany's was an "ailing economy."

But the greatest difficulty of Maier's integration into West Germany might have been the slow and frustrating process of family reunification. Ten times, beginning in the summer of 1986, Siegrid Maier submitted applications to emigrate. They were not processed because officially her husband could still return to the East. She continued working at the academy's economics institute, in constant fear that the Stasi was using her close friends to spy on her. In August 1987, worried about his wife's health, Maier mobilized resources at all political levels, writing to several provincial ministers, to Chancellor Helmut Kohl, to President Richard von Weizsäcker, and to Honecker.[95] In those letters he revealed another reason for his escape that he had not previously disclosed, perhaps in order to protect his family. In his letter to Weizsäcker, he wrote:

I still would work in the GDR today if agents of the Ministry for State Security, Department for Information (HV A), had not forced me to do something, which I despise at heart and contradicts entirely what I always stood up for: the honest and trusting collaboration of scientists from East and West.[96]

In the letter to Honecker, copied in the letter to Weizsäcker, he elaborated on the agency of the Department for Information HV A:

---

[94] *Die Zeit* 1989, issue 11.
[95] All letters can be found in N 2693-17. See also the written account of Siegrid Maier in N 2693-14. Weizsäcker had invited Maier to the Bergedorfer circle in preparation of Honecker's visit in September 1987.
[96] Maier to Weizsäcker, August 11, 1987, in N 2693-17.

When I acquired a personal computer (Commodore 64) that was urgently needed for research at the end of October 1985 in Vienna by saving my daily allowances, I was subjected to a ten-hour, nonstop, and degrading interrogation at Schönefeld Airfield. This interrogation was continued in a stricter form with the vice-president of the GDR's Academy of Sciences, Professor Werner Kalweit. ... A few days later, agents from the Ministry for State Security, Department for Information, appeared, offering to save me from such inconvenience in the future if I were ready to take on tasks for their institution during my travels. At the same time, the MfS attempted to set up a special working group at the Institute for Theory, Organization, and History of Science ... to use scientific contacts with Western scientists for the purposes of this ministry.[97]

Maier thus called out the Stasi's "attempt at blackmail," to use his "friendly-collegial relationships to scientists from Western countries" for the purpose of spying, which he felt was "in contradiction of the conscience and ethos of a scientist."[98] He felt forced to leave East Germany. Thus, it is possible that Maier's unfortunate experiences preceding his escape, such as the discontinuation of his research area, the Stasi's supervision of the 1985 conference, the interrogation at the airport, and the discussion with Kalweit, were more than personal interference and bad luck with bureaucracy but in fact were orchestrated by the Stasi – say, in an operation of "psychological manipulation" (*Zersetzung*) to counteract the political-ideological diversion of IIASA. However, since the documents of HV A were destroyed, we cannot know for sure. The fact is that what is left in the records of HA XVIII, which was in charge of the Academy of Sciences, shows *no* trace of the agency of HV A.[99] The letter to Honecker is available only in

---

[97] Maier to Honecker, August 11, 1987, in N 2693-17.

[98] Ibid. The same justification already circulated a year earlier in West Germany: first, in his application to Karl Heinrich Oppenländer at the Ifo Institute (May 26, 1986, N 2693-13), then in an official plea against a refusal of the status of refugee category C (political refugee from the Soviet Zone) in July 1986 (N 2693-14), and was alluded to in an article in *Die Zeit*, November 7, 1986 (*Den Erpressern aus dem Weg gegangen*). Maier noted that by summer 1986 everyone in East Germany would know of this reason, for which, however, I have seen no evidence.

[99] There is but one note in the investigative documents of the Stasi that show that after the transferal from HA XX, AKG to the district section Berlin in May 1984, he was taken over, in December 1985, by HV A, sector K (*Koordinierungsstelle*). See MfS U 25-89: 19: Speaking of his ignorance of secret operations, "according to Comrade OSL (Hans) Buhl, HA XX, and

Maier's personal papers, access to which is controlled by his wife. In other words, in the case of Maier the special legal status of the Stasi archive creates a bias in favor of the Stasi. Worse, it favors a narrative that was staged by the Stasi insofar as it results from its "principle of conspiracy" of mutual ignorance between the departments: HA XVIII made up ideological reasons for an escape, of which HV A knows that it was caused by the Stasi itself. The order of the narrative in this chapter reflects this bias.

The letter to Honecker, lost in the tumult of the dismantling of the Stasi, did not make a difference for Maier's family (nor did the intervention of the famous lawyer Wolfgang Vogl). Only after President Weizsäcker made a personal plea to Honecker, in June 1988, could Maier's wife and son leave the country. They joined him in Flensburg, where Maier had taken a position as a professor and founding dean of the economics faculty of the new university.

* * *

The archival material documenting the case of Maier is rich but may nonetheless be incomplete, as the contradictory information in his personal papers and the Stasi archive suggests. However, the aim of this narrative has not been to present a final judgment on the motives for Maier's escape. What stands out regarding his career is that, in contrast to what was claimed by the party apparatus, he might not have experienced any inner intellectual change, remaining true to the idea of a more democratic socialism from start to finish. Inspired by the post-Stalinist enlivening of the Thaw, he pursued innovation in the economics of education during the era of Ulbricht's NES, sought to contribute critically to Honecker's regime with an economics of growth, and got further inspiration for how to reform socialism through systems analysis from IIASA, as well as struggling for the realization of his ideas during the Cold War flare-up of the early 1980s. And even after he defected to West Germany, he tried to influence the path of perestroika. The intellectual development of Maier

---

Comrade Oberst Lange, department XV Berlin, this applies also to the period when Maier was taken over by the HV A." The lack of communication between HV A and HA XVIII, in spite the huge amount of labor caused by this lack, is consistent with the so-called principle of conspiracy that different departments at the Stasi did not know of each other's work.

was the result of the different institutional contexts that he passed through, rather than any inner change that occurred in him when exposed to Western science. His class consciousness might have matured, but it was never corrupted.

Thus, the lesson of the material presented here has not so much to do with Maier himself. Instead, I have presented his case as a way to illuminate the underlying institutional structures of East German academia. East Germany's membership in IIASA, in the early 1970s, was welcomed as an occasion to display the achievements of the German socialist state. Science propaganda appeared to be a shared motivation for both East German scholars and the party apparatus surrounding them – that is, the party-groups and the Stasi's Department 5 of HA XVIII that watched over the intelligentsia. The fact that the scientific ethos evoked by IIASA's agenda of peaceful coexistence contradicted the interests of the controlling party apparatus came to be understood only through a learning process. At the end of the 1980s, the academy's party-group and the Stasi could not help but classify scientific cooperation with the West as political-ideological diversion. This classification might have opened other channels of knowledge transfer. However, these were transfers that did not nurture the "bridge-building" policy of détente and the idea of peaceful coexistence.

The East German party regime sought international recognition, but it was recognition as an opposed regime – as a class enemy. Therefore, the fact that the party apparatus itself, with the help of the Stasi, undermined the knowledge transfer it officially promoted – by injecting suspicion into friendly relationships, by actively boycotting collaboration, and by suppressing communication within Stasi departments themselves – had to be kept secret. The contribution of East Germany to IIASA's attempt to build bridges between East and West through science was structurally undermined.

8 | *Saving Socialism from the GDR*

If the Party falls out with the trade unions, the fault lies with the Party, and this spells certain doom for the Soviet power. (Lenin, 1921)[1]

To think of Berlin in the fall of 1989 is to think of those cheering at, and on, the wall. For many of the older generation who spent their entire professional life in the GDR, these events caused mixed feelings. "We were pondering joy, hope, but also fear," the first freely elected dean of the economics section at Humboldt University, Klaus Kolloch, recalled (2001a: 296).

The joy was that the state was willing to accept, finally, far-reaching reforms *without* using force. To a large extent, 1989 represented a peaceful change without the violence many recalled all too well from 1953, 1956, 1961, and 1968, and from June 1989 in Beijing. Many of the older generation shared an enthusiasm for the political change out of a feeling of *pride* that their state proved itself more adaptive and open than ever before. The hope was that with the overdue resignation of the Old Communists a new generation would take over their own reformist spirit and continue building up a better and more democratic socialism. "The revolution was peaceful, since a consensus prevailed up to the top that the old generation came to an end. Nobody wanted the demonstrations to be beaten down because the system was so ready to reform itself," Johannes Gurtz, the last nominated dean of the economics section at Humboldt University, recalled in a personal conversation. But then there was also the fear caused by the uncertainty of what would follow, the fear that without the protection of the

---

[1] Speech at the Second All-Russia Congress of Miners, 1921, cited by Hans Wagner in November 1989 for "describing the gist of our current situation" (Lenin Werke, Band 32: 43, in *SED-Reformdiskurs*, TB FMS, 4).

wall their lifework will stand in a very different light once in open confrontation with the class enemy in West Germany. In a matter of months, after the fall of the wall, this joy, hope, and fear turned into deception as the integration of their state into the class enemy's system became inevitable. As with all professions that were considered close to the party regime, so was the economics profession dismantled in a way that their lifework became an object of history.

This chapter tells this episode of East Germany's last reform, later known as "the turning point" (*die Wende*), through the example of Dieter Klein, political economist of capitalism and vice-rector for social sciences at Humboldt University.[2] By the end of the 1980s, Klein had built up a profile as a progressive economist and science manager, who then, without ever breaking the belief in the possibility of reforming the party and thus the state, found himself in the midst of the events that caused the party state to fall. In his writings, he had broken with Lenin's theory of imperialism by granting capitalism the possibility to be peaceful, and supported as vice-rector younger intellectuals in proposing a new democratic socialism. In December 1989, he then ended up in the committee that, after Honecker's old regime fell apart, was to

---

[2] The literature on East Germany's *Wende* is huge. The political day-to-day events are easily accessible, for example, via the governmental page "Chronik 1989/ 1990 – Der Weg zur Deutschen Einheit"; the page "Chronik der Mauer" (published jointly by Leibniz Center for Contemporary History Potsdam, the Federal Agency for Civic Education, Deutschlandradio and the Berlin Wall Foundation); as well the public broadcast page "Chronik der Wende." For historical reconstructions see the book by Kowalczuk (2009) and with more light on the civil movement Links et al. (2004) and Kuhrt et al. (1999). For an excellent English reconstruction, see Dale (2006), as well as the comparative in-depth study by Pfaff (2006). This chapter profited strongly from the project "The SED Reform Discourse of the 1980s" (*Der SED-Reformdiskurs der achtziger Jahre*, in the following *SED-Reformdiskurs*) by Lutz Kirschner, Erhard Crome, and Rainer Land, funded by the German Research Foundation and collected, among others, at the Archive Democratic Socialism of the Rosa-Luxemburg Stiftung. The project analyzed the so-called gray literature, unpublished papers, privately circulated discussion papers, and internal publications, including interviews with several central party reformers of the late 1980s. This is also the only chapter in which the main protagonist, Dieter Klein, could personally recount his memories in personal conversations with the author in November and December 2021. The chapter largely follows the narrative that unfolded through Klein's own perception of the late 1980s, and puts it in dialogue with archival material, other witnesses, and the themes of the preceding chapters.

rescue the socialist party with a new program. Some months later the population voted off the leading role of the party and followed the call for reunification of West Germany's chancellor, Helmut Kohl. Klein then found himself in the role of the opposition in a political system that was no longer his own but that of West Germany.

Placed between the forces that pulled the strings in this revolutionary change, Dieter Klein is a telling example for the intellectual history underlying East Germany's perestroika movement: which ideas prepared its ground, which carried it, which resisted its degeneration, and which ideas were left after it failed. In a time of political upheaval and chaos, Klein's ideas about socialism and capitalism between 1985 and 1992 show an astonishing consistency. They thus serve as a mirror of the changing forces in East Germany's society in the advent of its decay. The notion of class conflict, on which the "leading role of the party" was based, and which the preceding chapters have shown to be a key element for the legitimacy of the state, is equally crucial for understanding the internal logic of the *Wende*.

Klein assumed the role of something of a public intellectual in the last period of the GDR. Acting within the power structures, he tried to influence them through the dissemination of ideas. In contrast to experts or scientists, intellectuals interpret the basic values of society, confront them with reality, keep them in the open as a future task, and thus protect them from being controlled by a minority. Klein shared the basic values of socialism, tried to prevent them from becoming stunted as a dogma, and defended them against attacks.[3] During perestroika, he incorporated the ideal of what economists of his generation aspired to but often lacked the courage for. The perestroika era promised to undo what went wrong several times before – during the Thaw, and during Ulbricht's and then during Honecker's reforms. Klein's case shows the extent to which the ideas that grew out of his

---

[3] As a type of scholar in political economy, Klein was not exceptional. There were others of the same generation that shared his intellectual spirit, but were less active in science management and less central to the transformation of the party. One could mention his colleague at Humboldt University, Hans Wagner (1929–2012), Harry Nick (1932–2014) at the Academy for Social Sciences, and the philosopher Peter Wolfgang Heise (1925–1987), who were scholars that all inspired Dieter Klein (interview in *SED-Reformdiskurs*, TB Klein, 1). Among other important *Wende* intellectuals of his generation, Uwe-Jens Heuer and Rolf Reißig play a role in this chapter.

generational experiences paved the way for the revolutionary changes in 1989, but then turned out to be out of touch with the inner dynamic of the historical events brought about by the party-critical civil movement (*Bürgerbewegung*), and then by the popular movement in Westrush (*Massenbewegung*). Since the hopes to reform socialism, as I argued in Part III, were a structural element of the stability of the state run by Old Communists, the young had difficulties trusting the will to reform of their parents. Therefore, Klein, who appears to build a bridge between his and the perestroika generation, at the same time tells us about the clash between them. As Niethammer put it:

When this generation [the hope generation], by then ready for retirement, finally deposed the "old comrades" in the face of the many drop outs of the young, they proved to be completely incapable of politics and were washed away together with their young opponents and the culture-oriented civil movements by the desire of their purported (party) base to join West Germany. (1994: 108)

Dieter Klein, Political Economist of Capitalism

Up until the mid-1980s, Dieter Klein incorporated the core epistemic virtues of an economist in the GDR that were nourished by the key events that the preceding chapters have identified. Inspired by scholars like Jürgen Kuczynski and Johann Lorenz Schmidt, both returning from Western exile, he wrote his dissertation and habilitation in the political economy of capitalism and remained in this field until the end of his career. He focused mainly on the Western European political system as the manifestation of what was called "state monopoly capitalism." The field of the political economy of capitalism was the closest to the official ideology of Marxism-Leninism, and was central to the state propaganda that had to frame the twentieth-century Cold War in Marx's nineteenth-century terms of class struggle. But at the same time, it was rather inconsequential for the actual policies within the state and thus allowed for a considerable degree of intellectual autonomy. As a career choice, the field was less risky than the political economy of socialism that addressed directly the rationality of the latest party decisions. Scholars in the political economy of capitalism were habitually more conservative but also more cohesive given their natural affinity to Marx. They were at the heart of expertise in

Marxism-Leninism, and crucial for bringing about a socialist intelligentsia among the young.[4]

The intellectual challenge of the field was twofold. First, one had to reconcile Marx's conjecture that capitalism will, at some point, run out of steam with the reality that this did not seem to be the case. Instead of an ever-increasing crisis, for example, real wages increased and work became more human, which could not all be explained away by false consciousness and Western propaganda. Second, one had to guard the conceptual boundary between capitalism and socialism even if capitalism used means that resemble those in socialism, and even if socialism used means that resemble those in capitalism. This second challenge has been subject to what in the West and the East came to be known as "convergence theory," which is based on the notion that the two systems are not that fundamentally different. Convergence theory diverted from the premise of class conflict between the systems, a premise that was also shared in much of Klein's later work that developed the notion of peaceful coexistence. However, convergence theory remained a taboo for him as it was for all East German political economists.

Klein's intellectual profile was formed through the key episodes that have been identified in the preceding chapters. Socialized during Stalinism, and coming of age during the Thaw, he balanced out his desire for an undogmatic socialism and the struggle for political stability. "I have never denied the dogmatic traits that I kept with me for a long time," he commented in retrospect about his time as young scientist (interview 2021). He knew in concrete terms what it meant to defend the stability of the state in ideological terms. In the wake of the 20th Party Congress, Klein was FDJ secretary of the university, and thus involved in fighting the resistance in veterinary medicine that demanded free elections. His way of dealing with these critiques reflects a key virtue of his generation that I noted at several points of the preceding chapters: exercising control by creating dialogue:

That was a very complex situation. On the one hand, there has been a highly problematic development in Hungary where about three thousand

---

[4] There is very little historical literature on the political economy of capitalism, as most accounts focus on the political economy of socialism. But there are important studies on some of its innovative elements, such as convergence theory and its connection with perestroika (Zweynert 2019). For the last textbook edition for this central class in economics, see Klein et al. (1986), as well as the documentation in *SED-Reformdiskurs*, TB Klein, 2.

communists were executed. It had something of a rebellion against Stalinism, but also of backwardness, if not to say counterrevolution. Also at the university the situation was very complex. There were democratic movements, yes, ... but also slogans like ... "away with Marxism-Leninism," "away with Russian lessons," "use rifles, and turn them against the FDJ functionaries if necessary." Some of these slogans were highly suspicious to me, so I went to the seminars and objected ... We sensed that students wanted answers, and at some point offered so-called forums: an answer to every question. Franz Dahlem and Wolfgang Harich sat at the first forum. Even if not all questions were answered – times were not like that – we showed that one could not simply keep quiet. Problems had to be debated. (Klein interview 2021)

Knowing what it meant to defend the ideals of the party, he also knew what it meant to be pilloried by the party. In his dissertation on "the integration of financial capital in Western Europe," defended in 1961, he criticized the first attempts at European integration as a case of monopolistic state capitalism. But the fact that he granted some perspective on the further existence of this union was reason enough to call the thesis revisionist. Once the accusation appeared in the university newspaper, some comrades at the university would no longer talk to him. Klein knew how to play both roles: the party warrior and the reformist free thinker. Both were part and parcel of his professional ethos.

In the wake of the Havemann affair, in 1965, Klein replaced Robert Naumann as professor and director of the Institute for Political Economy. In his early time as professor, he was exceptionally prolific, publishing more than the average of his colleagues. His long list of publications address problems such as the global organization of international capital and the essence of the East–West conflict as the "contradiction between productive forces and relations of production" (1967). He also interprets the nature of economic planning in West Germany, the changing conditions in capitalism after the oil crisis, and local problems such as the Ruhr crisis.[5] With an interest in the reformist strategies of capitalism, Klein also wrote a Marxist critique of the field of "futurology" that prospered in the West in the 1960s (Klein 1972). This broader social angle in interpreting capitalism was necessary since the focus on economic problems increasingly ran into a dead end. He also traveled frequently to the West, linking

---

[5] See a list of his publications in *SED-Reformdiskurs, Teilbestand* (in the following TB) Klein, 1.

up with the Western left. In West Germany, he had a good relationship with the Institute for Marxist Studies and Research (*Institut für Marxistische Studien und Forschungen*) in Frankfurt, founded in 1968 and partially financed by the GDR.[6]

One of the books that gives a taste of this research program is a book co-authored with Hannes Wunderlich, published in 1963, entitled *Monopolies, Integration, Aggression: The EEC, An Unholy Alliance of Imperialists against Peace, Democracy and Socialism*. Departing from the idea that the increasing power of monopolies in the West is the greatest danger for the working class, he interprets the European Economic Community (EEC) as a bulwark of this power, closely related with "U.S. imperialism" and NATO. He identifies a network of key actors, their fascist background, and their relationship with big industries and firms, showing the "neocolonial" character of the political institutions of the EEC. Debunking the growing support for the European integration in the West, he thus unravels the exploitative character of Western state monopoly capitalism. The European integration is seen as a symptom of the increased contradictions of capitalism that fosters the militarization of the West.

In his role as the head of the Institute of Political Economy, Robert Naumann's emphasis on the dominance of political economy was a negative example for him. Embracing the spirit of the third university reform, he allowed for disciplinary differentiation along "real problems" rather than disciplinary hierarchies. He thus supported the creation of a separate working group in sociology, which later resulted in an independent institute for sociology, as well as the independence of demography, run by the Iranian Parviz Khalatbari, as its own teaching and research unit. Sociology and demography were previously part of, and dominated by, political economy. Sociology was considered a bourgeois, and demography a biologistic, theory of society. Klein's appreciation of peaceful disciplinary pluralism was his way of realizing the virtue of open debate and creativity in a knowledge-based socialism.[7]

[6] Jörg Huffschmid, who belonged to the reformist wing of the (West) German Communist Party (DKP), was interested in Klein's work. Klein recalled tensions with the left wing of the DKP because of his less radical position regarding possible reforms in capitalism (interview 2021).

[7] Other disciplinary differentiations at this time included environmental economics by Günter Streibel (1975) and the economics of the world economy by Karl-Heinz Domdey (in UA 1651).

Klein's sense of moderating disciplinary relations between the social sciences was recognized when, in 1978, the university authorities put further confidence in his loyalty and competence by granting him the position of vice-rector for social sciences (*Prorektor für Gesellschaftswissenschaften*). This position, as we will see, would be critical in creating the infrastructure for the East Germany's perestroika discourse. In 1979, he received, jointly with Harry Maier, the National Prize of the GDR, which was a great recognition of his research also for the university more generally. Some five years later, in 1983, Klein also became a member of Berlin's SED district group (*Bezirksleitung*).

Making Peace with Class Conflict

The contribution that put Dieter Klein in the spotlight of the last years of the GDR was his book on peace, titled *The Chances of a Peaceable Capitalism* (1988b). The book was written in 1985 but, for reasons described later, only published in 1988.

Peace research was certainly an outgrowth of the détente policies of peaceful coexistence, and in the West also an outgrowth of the student movement. For Dieter Klein, as a political economist of capitalism, the question of peace confronted him with the postulates of Lenin's theory of imperialism.[8] In this theory, Lenin had developed Marx's notion of the aggressiveness of capital, including the thesis that war is a necessary consequence of the expansive nature of capital. The mere question of whether capitalism is capable of peace, and thus capable of maintaining a peaceful relationship with socialist countries, was a heresy against orthodox Marxism-Leninism. It required a revision of the important image of the enemy, an image that has been evoked over and over again as a pretext for violence against their own population.

---

[8] Peace research in East Germany emerged with the same wave as did political science, both a result of the policy of peaceful coexistence. Max Schmidt (1932–2018) was an important figure as the founder and head of the Scientific Council for Peace Research at the Academy of Sciences and deputy chairman of the National Committee for Political Sciences founded in 1974. Another important reference was Rolf Reißig's peace research at the Academy for Social Sciences.

For once the peacefulness of capitalism is accepted, the historical determinism of the transition from capitalism to socialism needs to be reinterpreted, as does the historical superiority of socialism. This was not only a theoretical issue, but also put into question the historical premise of the East German state: that only socialism secures peace, that supporting peace is to support socialism, and that fighting for peace is fighting against capitalism. In short, the applicability of the logic of class conflict to the historical situation of the Cold War was at stake, an application which, as we saw in the preceding chapters, was vital for the justification strategies of power in East Germany.

The gist of Klein's book was the argument that even if capitalist societies are currently not peaceful, there is no reason that this must be the case. Capitalism is not in and of itself belligerent. The current global situation of capitalism, Klein argued, even requires peace as a means of expansion: "Today, the development of the new type of productive force requires global economic relations that are peace-oriented ... particularly in developing countries. This can only be realized if all states of both systems coexist peacefully and cooperatively."[9] Since the book put much of the orthodoxy in question, the critical response from the party came as no surprise. Academic resistance came from Kurt Tiedtke, then director of the Party School. Klein speculates that it was Tiedtke who wrote a critical report that prevented the publisher, *Dietz Verlag*, from printing the book in 1985. The ideas also evoked resistance directly from the Politburo, something that could have resulted in immediate career termination some years before. Hermann Axen, head of the Politburo's foreign policy section, consulted with political economists about their conception of the current state of capitalism. Before Klein could even write his statement, at one point in 1987, he was called to Axen's office. Klein's recollection of this conversation demonstrates a direct confrontation with the discursive logic of Old Communists:

I came a little early because I was nervous. It was the first time that I met Axen, and this for receiving criticism, so I knew it would be tough. He asked me if I was aware that we both had the same teacher of Marxism-Leninism, Johann Lorenz Schmidt. He then told me that in the French internment camp he had been given the task of protecting Schmidt who gave illegal lessons on Marx in small groups of seven prisoners. Had he been caught would have

[9] See Klein's summary of the book in *SED-Reformdiskurs*, TB Klein, 2.

meant his death sentence. So Axen had appropriated Marxism under camp conditions when life and death was at stake. When he criticized me, it was completely clear to me that, considering his biography, he could not argue differently [than critiquing my position that capitalism could be peaceful] . . . After our conversation, I wrote down my position and sent it to him. I once again wanted to make clear how I see it: that a reform-open form of capitalism that is permanently peaceful is possible. And I stuck to this position.[10]

Apparently, Klein was impressed by Axen's biographical argument, but, forty years after this argument was first put forward, he stood up for his intellectual autonomy and did not change his position.

Klein also used his position as a vice-rector to advance his research in a way that would make Humboldt University a center of peace research. In contrast to Western institutions, peace research in East Germany could not tackle head-on military-related questions of disarmament, information that was limited to the strategic political and military class. As an alternative, Klein set up the Central Circle for Peace Research (*Zentraler Arbeitskreis Friedensforschung*) in an interdisciplinary fashion inquiring into the socio-historical conditions of peace. He mobilized historians to analyze historical conflict situations, regional and literary studies to analyze differences in cultural perceptions, and theologians that were commonly an eyesore for social scientists. Klein did not consider a Marxist theory of peace superior, but compatible, with other notions, notably a Christian notion of peace.[11] He himself played the role of an economist reflecting on the economic conditions of peace, and that of a moderator bringing disciplinary studies together. After all, peace research was done in more than a dozen disciplines, which was the trademark of Humboldt's research group. The results were published in a university-based publication series, the *Humboldt Journal of Peace Research*. There was also a large audience outside the university as well as abroad, which shaped Klein's profile as a public figure. He presented his peace research in front of different audiences, at the State Planning Commission, the Academy of the Arts, and several ministries, and also at schools, in firms, and at embassies. Aiming at a dialogue between Marxist and

---

[10] Interview in *SED-Reformdiskurs*, TB Klein, 1.
[11] See the interview with Klein dating April 1987 on peace research at Humboldt University in *SED-Reformdiskurs*, TB Klein, 1.

non-Marxist peace research, Klein also received invitations from West Germany. He did not have a permanent visa and thus had to apply for every single trip. In 1986, he used one of his trips to give a second, unauthorized, talk at a conference with Philip Potter, the president of the World Council of Churches. As a result, he was denied travel for a year and a half.

One of the central peace research centers in West Germany, the Institute for Peace Research and Security Policy (*Institut für Friedensforschung und Sicherheitspolitik*) at the University of Hamburg, tried to set up a cooperative arrangement with Humboldt University. In early 1987, Egon Bahr, the director of the institute and the leading figure of East–West rapprochement, had a personal meeting with Klein and proposed a joint lecture series that should take place in both Hamburg and Berlin. Apparently under observation, only moments later, Klein was called to Kurt Hager's office. The lecture series, according to Hager, would require an official cultural agreement with West Germany, which did not exist. After this exchange, Klein was called for a second time to meet with Axen, Bahr's political interlocutor, who warned him that it was not Humboldt University that was in charge of foreign policy. The lecture series was to be cancelled. Nevertheless, Klein found an agreeable compromise. Instead of opening the lecture series with a public press conference of Bahr in Berlin and Klein in Hamburg, the two would speak last, and the individual talks were announced in sets of three. It worked out that way. The "lecture series" was held between 1987 and 1989.[12]

Peace research being a revision of orthodox political economy, Klein had the chance to *make official* this diversion when, in 1987, he was put in charge of coordinating the revisions of the official textbook for the political economy of capitalism. The last edition of 1986, to which he had already contributed, was to be updated for 1990 in the light of the perestroika reforms.[13] While still putting emphasis on the general

---

[12] Ibid. Klein's lecture in Hamburg is published in Klein (1990).

[13] Alfred Lemmnitz was the preceding coordinator. Other authors included Günter Höll from Higher School of Economics, Hannelore Riedel from Halle, Peter Hoffmann from the University of Commerce in Leipzig, and Hans Wagner from Humboldt University. Klein wrote the chapter on "Contemporary Capitalism: An Introduction in the Methodological Foundations of Its Characteristics," and "The Global Problems of Mankind and the Competition between Socialism and

critique of capitalism in terms of the concentration of power and its exploitative character, they also wished to elaborate capitalism's potential development. By doing so, his intention was to revive the discussion about a better socialism:

An important basic theme was always: We don't think socialism is good as it is, but because otherwise we get caught up in capitalism, which is even more terrible and which is getting into ever deeper crisis, we cannot give up socialism. It was important to break through this idea by saying: We may not find capitalism good, but at least consider it capable of reform.[14]

One way to discuss the peaceful character of capitalism was the inclusion of so-called theories of modernity in the textbook. While short-term interests of firms were still explained in orthodox Marxist terms, the "strategic" interests of reproducing the conditions of capitalism require different terms. If capitalism advances not only by deepening its own crisis, but also by becoming more "modern," socialism was not the only modern society, and capitalism and socialism could thus be understood in the same conceptual terms. The question was thus whether or not Marxism-Leninism was supplemented with a more general cultural theory, or whether political economy, with its primacy of economic forces, remained the master discourse under these historical conditions. While the older scholars clung to the old paradigm, the younger scholars were willing to go beyond Marx with Marx, as the Western left would put it. Klein seemed to take a position in the middle ground, and as the coordinator he had to justify the new approach as an advance *within* Marxism-Leninism. The draft of the textbook was ready in summer of 1989, but it was never published, let alone used in teaching.

In 1988, the political situation changed favorably for Klein's peace research. The SED came to an agreement with the West German SPD, which was titled "The Dispute of Ideologies and Common Security."[15]

Capitalism" (unpublished manuscripts in *SED-Reformdiskurs*, TB Klein, 3; see also the interview with Hans Wagner, ibid., TB Wagner).

[14] Interview in *SED-Reformdiskurs*, TB Klein, 1.

[15] See the documentation in Hahn (2003). Regarding the reactions on the SED-SPD paper, see MfS, ZAIG 7222: 8–15. The document undercut the incompatibility resolution (*Unvereinbarkeitsbeschluss*) of the SPD against any communist parties dating from 1971. It was thus celebrated as a further success of Honecker's international policy to gain acceptance of the GDR as a state on an equal level with West Germany, as Honecker had already stated when visiting

The agreement came to redefine the relationship between the left in the East and West in that it required mutual acceptance and thus made an end to the prevalent logic of class struggle. The parties acknowledged shared global problems such as war, environment, and poverty, the solution to which is in the interest of both systems:

Neither side may deny the other's right to exist. Our hope cannot be that one system will abolish the other. Aim is to ensure that both systems are capable of reform and that the competition between the systems strengthens the will to reform on both sides. Both sides must try to prevent the other from perceiving them as if they were seeking expansion.[16]

The declaration was coordinated with the director of the CC Academy for Social Sciences, Otto Reinhold and Rolf Reißig, director of the Institute for Scientific Communism and head of another peace research group.[17] In August 1987, the agreement was approved and presented at two press conferences, one in Bonn by Erhard Eppler and Thomas Meyer and another in Berlin by Reißig and Reinhold. The agreement undermined much of the ideological coherence of the overall party line since all party teachings could be openly criticized with reference to this agreement. This caused great confusion in all party schools. In fact, even if the declaration was approved by the Politburo, after publication Honecker distanced himself from it. But the mere presence of this debate legitimatized Klein's point of view to such extent that in 1988 his book on peace could be published.

Managing Perestroika Research

Klein's career as vice-rector for social sciences at Humboldt University lasted from 1978 to 1990. He saw himself in contrast to previous vice-rectors who considered themselves the guardians of Marxism-Leninism. Instead, he wished to create opportunities for new discussion to emerge and for individuals to express themselves (*Freiräume*). "This

Helmut Kohl in September 1987. The party put emphasis on the sections that demanded noninterference in inner affairs that appeared to undermine the Western critique of human rights.

[16] *Neues Deutschland*, "Der Streit der Ideologien und die gemeinsame Sicherheit," August 28, 1987: 3.

[17] See Mertens (2004: 215 ff.) on the role of Reinhold and Reißig at the Academy for Social Sciences. Reißig's contribution to the GDR's perestroika discourse is fully documented in *SED-Reformdiskurs*, TB Reißig and Berg.

resulted in an ongoing interaction of scientific and political negotiations for small changes," he commented later.[18] But his openness for dialogue, as we will see, resulted not only from a desire for change but also from a more fundamental desire for stability insofar as it was obvious that Gorbachev's reforms necessitated a more radical response than the stubborn Politburo thought. Supporting open debates about social change was a way to warrant stability.

One upfront way to create free spaces was to work against political attempts to control hiring decisions. In 1988, for example, the literary studies department wished to appoint Frank Hörnigk as professor against the will of the party. Hörnigk wrote a habilitation ("dissertation B") on Heiner Müller, an East German author and playwright who would become a central figure for the civil movement against the party regime. The Stasi tried to intervene in this decision by collecting compromising material about Hörnigk, in particular contacts to the West. According to Kowalczuk, part of this material had been collected from Dieter Klein and reported to Smettan without Klein's knowing (2012: 525). As Klein recalled, a Stasi collaborator came to see him in his office trying to convince him that he should oppose Hörnigk's appointment as professor, a fact that Klein had communicated to Hörnigk in order to warn him that he was being watched by the Stasi.[19] Archival material and memory do not contradict each other, and both could have taken place as such. In the end, Hörnigk received the position as professor.

Aside from peace research, another platform supported by Klein as vice-rector since the mid-1980s concerned a taboo of another kind: homosexuality. Since peace is not only peace among nations, but also peace within a society, it requires tolerance regarding those who think and feel differently, a virtue that he considered socialist.[20] Supporting research on homosexuals was an outright attack on the petit-bourgeois character of the Old Communists' notion of a socialist society. Homosexuals were viewed by the Stasi as a security issue for being

---

[18] Interview in *SED-Reformdiskurs*, TB Klein, 1.   [19] Ibid.

[20] Reiner Werner was the professor in charge of the group, as well as Christine Karohl as scientific collaborator of Klein. Education studies were implied, as were medical doctors and the forensic department that challenged the Stasi's approach to homosexuals. See the interview with Klein in Grumbach (1989) and the extensive materials in *SED-Reformdiskurs*, TB Klein, 3. On homosexuality in the GDR, see also Marbach and Weiß (2017).

susceptible to Western blackmail. In addition, homosexuals suffered from the same general discrimination as they did in the West. Yet they were not on the political agenda, and there was no ready-made response to their interests. As vice-rector, Klein again played the role of a moderator between the disciplines and a bolster against political attacks:

The ways one could be critical in these days were many. I mean, the most common way, of course, was to join the church opposition and attack the system head-on. But here, we initiated a very consciously calculated approach that demonstrated that one cannot go on like this, and also fostered the idea that this kind of studies must and can be applied also to other affected groups ... It wasn't exactly the great discourse that would have fundamentally called the system into question. But it started at a point where people who act differently, who are different, who present themselves differently, so far fell out of society.[21]

One of the public events that the group organized took place in the professors' cafeteria, which was significant for many as it represented an occasion for coming out. "It was unbelievable for the days back as some indeed got up and said: Yes, I am one of them and I want to express this publicly for the first time."[22] Their research resulted in a study with concrete proposals of jurisdiction that was sent to several political bodies including the CC. Their intervention was successful in that it gave voice to those opposing the closing down of clubs, such as the Sunday Club in Berlin.

After the publication of his book on peace, Klein took the discussion on this topic a step further. He tried to involve openly the growing civil movement that called for thoroughgoing democratic reforms and gathered mainly under the protection of the church. In February 1988, at the 7th ecumenical symposium of the section of theology at Humboldt University, members of the church movement were invited too. Next to Klein and Reißig for East German peace research, Eppler from the West German SPD spoke, as well as Frei Betto, one of the most important liberation theologians in Latin America. Though firmly in the spirit of the SPD-SED agreement, the event took place shortly after the Liebknecht–Luxemburg demonstration in January 1988, at which more than hundred members of the church movement

---

[21] Interview in *SED-Reformdiskurs*, TB Klein, 1.   [22] Ibid.

were arrested and intimidated for demanding freedom of speech. At this point, the party apparatus, with the help of the Stasi, still kept control over the church movement.[23] As the symposium would provide a platform for those considered enemies of the state, the party secretary of Humboldt University, Harry Smettan, tried to prevent the event from taking place. Smettan was a party-loyal, power-conscious, and intellectually rigid functionary, a type of person who was critical for maintaining and reinforcing party discipline at a local level until the last minute. Among students, he was known as a "brutal political police officer." Klein, the "tactical compromiser," as Hans Wagner called him, was one of the few that were in the position of negotiating with Smettan.[24] He recalled his tactics that made the event possible:

The church public was invited, and it was clear that many representatives of the opposition groups would take part. The SED district secretary (Smettan) recommended that the symposium be canceled. I refused, and explained – which was actually correct – that it might not make sense to leave people standing in front of closed doors and thus making them organize a demonstration in front of the university. Somehow this argument got caught, and we held the symposium ... It was a very dramatic story, since we knew that every word was recorded. Smettan had sent his then newly appointed secretary for agitation and propaganda to the event, who had to report to the district leader hourly ... He was not quite sure what to report, and (my colleague) Christine Karohl assisted him by telling what to leave out.[25]

The reason for Klein's cooperation with those outspoken critics of the regime are complex. In his own view, he presented himself as being open to dialogue in line with the virtue of scientific debate. Accordingly, his talk was titled "dialogue as an opportunity for one's own theory development," showing that the party can benefit from the engagement with opposing views (1988a). This surely could have been a way to legitimize these views insofar as he sympathized with them. But integrating their more critical claims into the discussion also had the effect that, first, his own ideas would appear more moderate and thus more legitimate, and second, would equally conciliate the oppositional character of the critiques, thus preventing their radicalization.

---

[23] For this demonstration, and the role of the Stasi in its response, see Dale (2006: 6–56), and Kowalczuk (2009: 262–286).

[24] For Smettan, see Kowalczuk (2012: 508); for Wagner, see the interview in *SED-Reformdiskurs*, TB Wagner.

[25] Interview in *SED-Reformdiskurs*, TB Klein, 1.

This latter strategy was consistent with that of the MfS, which tried to infiltrate their informants into the civil movement to influence it in a way that would prevent them from acting against the state. In fact, as we have seen at several points in the preceding chapters, the virtue of an open debate can mean both a form of democratic inclusion but also a form of political control, while the latter often came in disguise of the former. But more on this later.

One of the leading figures of the church movement and a critical figure in the events of the fall 1989, Friedrich Schorlemmer, was present at the symposium. As Schorlemmer recalled, Klein "was visibly under pressure und tried to use new tones in old SED-jargon" (1992: 81). Schorlemmer then posed the following question to Klein: "What chances do you see for people who use other methods on the street to be invited to a discussion (like here) and not brought in for interrogation?" (ibid.) Though Klein agreed that this would be desirable, he and Schorlemmer never cooperated with each other, as they later bemoaned.[26] "Just as the civil movement did not come to me, I did not go to them. Later I agreed with Friedrich Schorlemmer that this was a fundamental mistake on both sides. That did not even have to do with caution, as I was not that careful at all ... It just was not my sphere. I lived in a world that I had become familiar with and tried to transform from within."[27] Those who, like Klein, believed until late on that political change has to come from within the party were separated from those who, after decades of failed attempts, had lost trust in the possibility of reforming the party. They did not perceive each other to be in the same sphere even if they shared the same ideas. SED reformers and the civil movement were separated by mutual distrust that built up since decades. The power structure of the party institutions was more solid than the ideas that crossed the limits of these structures.

As vice-rector, Klein was responsible for moderating discussions about the research orientation of the upcoming planning period up until 1994. In May 1988, he gave a talk asking that future research should *explicitly* focus on those contradictions that were never truly resolved.[28] In the name of self-criticism, he asked his colleagues to

---

[26] See Schorlemmer (1992: 79–85).
[27] Interview in *SED-Reformdiskurs*, TB Klein, 1.
[28] See *Referat*, held on May 12, 1988, in *SED-Reformdiskurs*, TB Klein, 3. He opened the talk by quoting Honecker, who asked the social sciences to be "creative in posing a solving new questions."

name the actual problems rather than jumping to ready-made solutions. There should be clarity regarding which of the theoretical notions no longer fit the current situation and should be given up. "Smoothed perspectives, narrow-minded procedures, repetition of what is considered certain but in reality already overcome with scientific certainty must be eliminated," he said.[29] This demand certainly created an opportunity for those who practiced self-censorship to stop doing so. But the call for being undogmatic was in fact not new, echoing the rhetoric of the mid-1950s, such that many still feared that following Klein's call would result in political control and confrontation. The reaction of the CC Department for Science was as expected, and asked for modification of the speech. But after negotiations in person, the talk was authorized, which for Klein showed that "right up to the top, they knew that one had to do it differently" (Klein interview 2021). It confirmed his belief that the party was capable of change.

Some months later, in August 1988, Klein gave another talk as vice-rector in preparation for the so-called red week, a week of compulsory political discussion for all students at the beginning of each academic year.[30] Both teachers and students came to hear Klein speaking about the Soviet reform, and the biggest hall of the university was packed. As with many other party members, Klein followed Gorbachev's turn with curiosity. He showed sympathy with the notion of individual creativity, and argued for "extending and rethinking the conditions for a significantly more achievement orientation, for the development of individuality, creativity, and self-responsibility of socialist personalities."[31] This would be one of the key elements of his contribution to the *Wende* discourse in the year to come. Free personal development was indeed the bottom line of the civil movement's call to end state-run oppression through a culture of fear and control. For Klein, however, the call for free personal development was not anti-socialist (let alone pro-capitalist) at all, as Western observers might have read it. For Klein, personal development was of course related to the Marxist notion of lived labor and the spontaneous development of productive

---

[29] Ibid.
[30] "On the social and economic strategy of the SED" (*Zur Gesellschafts- und ökonomischen Strategie der SED*), held on August 31, 1988, SED-*Reformdiskurs*, TB Klein, 2.
[31] Ibid.: 57.

forces: "Wealth, for Marx, is always the wealth of the personality, the unfolding of the needs within the totality of an individual" (Klein interview 2021). Note also that the same notion of creativity and innovation was already implied by Behrens and Benary in 1956 when opposing the Soviet and the Yugoslavian model, as well as being implicit in Ulbricht's NES. At the same time, Klein also warned in his speech that once the state loses too much control, one might also loose socialism. Yes, political democratization is necessary for sustained economic growth, but what "democratization" would concretely mean in institutional terms, in particular with respect to the leading role of the party, was an open question.

Having openly defended such opinion, Klein became the inspiration for a small group of young party intellectuals at Humboldt University that developed a new paradigm of socialism: the research group of the theory of modern socialism.

Modernizing Socialism

Klein's most important contribution as vice-rector to the perestroika discourse in East Germany was his role as the political and intellectual patron of a research group on the theory of modern socialism. The project was the response of a small group of young party intellectuals at Humboldt University to the perestroika movement in Poland and the Soviet Union. What began as a small informal network, during the fall of 1989, became one of the party's progressive reform discourses.[32] By calling out for a "modern" socialism, the then current form of socialism was not considered to be sufficiently modern. Even if the project was in continuity with previous reforms of "modernization," it went much further and even largely overlapped with what the civil

---

[32] This was not the only group within the party that was inspired by perestroika, of course, but one that was particularly outspoken in its novel conception of socialism. Another intellectual circle, for example, was the group around Peter Weiß in Jena (see *SED-Reformdiskurs*, TB Jenaer Peter-Weiss-Rezeption). At the Higher School of Economics, in 1988, a group was formed around Christa Luft, Eugen Faude, Waldfried Schliesser, Ekkehard Sachse, Hans-Joachim Dubrowsky, and Hans Knop that developed a reformist project using long-term data collection; at the Academy of Sciences' Economics Institute, Norbert Peche, Klaus Steinitz, and Dieter Walter had outlined a reform program (see Krause 1998b: 317). In preparation of the official Party Congress, of course, many new proposals for reform were discussed in party-groups all over the country.

movement demanded – except the knowledge that without the party there would be nothing to hold the GDR together. As a political economist of capitalism rather than socialism, Klein did not directly contribute to this research program. However, his peace research was immediate inspiration for the members of the group, and he provided conceptual advice and played a critical role as vice-rector for social sciences in creating its infrastructure by rendering the project official. His protection as patron allowed the group to propagate ideas that might have been (self-)censored in other institutions.

The project was initiated by Michael Brie, a lecturer (*Dozent*) for historical materialism at the section for Marxist-Leninist philosophy. Born in 1954, he was seven years old when the wall was built and in his early thirties when perestroika began. The two other initiators belonged equally to the generation of those "born into" the GDR: Dieter Segert, born in 1952, lecturer for scientific communism, and Rainer Land, born in 1952, lecturer in political economy in the economics section.[33] All three were active party members, Brie and Segert with a higher degree of loyalty and attachment.[34] The age difference between Klein, as a patron with official functions at the university and in the party, and the young researchers seemed complementary. While the young had the courage to take radical positions, Klein had the means to create safety and an audience.

In a talk at a conference in Plovdiv in autumn 1987, Brie had presented the ideas that would later frame the project. He called for a new paradigm of socialism that was appropriate for the global historical situation. The works of Marx and Lenin would be only one among several foundations

---

[33] Other members were Hans-Peter Krüger, Harald Bluhm, Wilfried Ettl, Jürgen Jünger, and Rosemarie Will, among others. The group is subject of appraisal, for example, in Süß (1999: 478–488) and Sturm (2000: 21–49), as well as critically in Kowalczuk (2012: 531–532). Some members of the group participated in a study group called "philosophical and methodological problems of political economy" run by Hans Wagner since 1977, a political economist and colleague of Klein at Humboldt University (see interview in *SED-Reformdiskurs*, TB Wagner). Wagner was known for his work on value theory with Peter Ruben using the work of Pierro Sraffa (Ruben and Wagner 1980). Another important influence on the group was the political scientist Uwe-Jens Heuer (ibid., TB Heuer).

[34] Land was secretary of the Teachers' Party Organization, and Segert was party secretary of the party-group of the philosophy section. Segert accepted this job after Klein's advice that the position would allow him to protect the research project (see interview in *SED-Reformdiskurs*, TB Segert).

of this new and higher form of socialism. Next to Soviet perestroika thinkers, Brie was one of the few in East German philosophy who was influenced by the French philosophy including the works of Jean-François Lyotard and Louis Althusser, who were unfamiliar to the older generation. He put the new paradigm in social-philosophical terms with a specific emphasis on the "plurality of subjects of power and property."[35] He contrasted the "new socialist man" of Ulbricht's Ten Commandments with a more postmodern, nonmonolithic subject in a public sphere of democratic socialism:

At the center of the new paradigm of the theory of socialism . . . must be a new understanding of the relationships between the social subjects of socialism: a conception that emphasizes the diversity of subjects of property, power and consciousness on the basis of shared economic, social, political, and spiritual living conditions. From this shared basis unfolds, rather than the bourgeois pluralism of estranged and hostile subjects in relation of private property and exploitation, the associative unity of developing diversity. This unity does not come about through standardization and compulsory equalization. It is a special relation of the manifold, its associative development.[36]

This early citation shows two important characteristics of the research group: firstly, the idea of a "third way" between state-bureaucratic socialism and capitalism, and secondly, its philosophical character – trusting the social force of aloof ideas. When the reform discourse later boiled down to the question of one-party system versus free elections of parliamentary democracy, the third way, let alone the "associative development of the unity of diverse subjects," would appear abstract to many.[37]

---

[35]   The Soviet thinkers that inspired Brie, and with which the group was partially in contact, were Antolii P. Butenko, Viktor L. Sheinis, Evgeny A. Ambarzumov, and Igor Kljamkin. Other members of the group were inspired by Western philosophy. Hans-Peter Krüger confronted Habermas with the dominant views on Marxism (Habermas 1989; Krüger 1989). Rainer Land was inspired by Schumpeter; Niklas Luhmann was discussed by all three of them (see interview Land, *SED-Reformdiskurs*, TB Land). These discussions led away from an economic- to a culture-centered notion of socialism that was vital for perestroika at large. Krüger recalled that he did not have the courage to discuss Foucault in his publications, as he anticipated that the notion of "discipline" would be censored (see interview in *SED-Reformdiskurs*, TB Krüger).

[36]   "Zu einigen Problemen der Entstehung eines neuen Paradigmas in der Sozialismustheorie," 1987, unpublished, in *SED-Reformdiskurs*, TB FMS, 1: 6.

[37]   This leads Kowalczuk to the conclusion that this group of "SED reformers were not interested in creating a public sphere. They did not merely avoid any association with such a possibility, but actively opposed it, in accordance with

In January 1988, the group began drafting a formal description of the project, in which they called for the development of a new, consistent, and comprehensive concept of socialism that was appropriate in the new context of global interdependency, breaking with the introverted small-country attitude of the GDR. Issues such as world peace as put forward by Klein, the overall importance of technology as already put forward by the late Ulbricht, and also global justice and notably shared ecological problems as put forward by the young civil movement, were not the same problems as those of the Soviet Union of the 1930s or the GDR of the 1950s. The political institutions of socialism were lagging behind and prevented the development of the individual productive forces.[38] Modernization had to "catch up," they wrote echoing Ulbricht's rhetoric.

In July 1988, the draft of the project was sent out to around sixty potentially sympathetic scholars, including an invitation for an opening consultation, which took place in November 1988 and led to the first publication of the proceedings in spring 1989.[39] In their lectures, Brie, Land, and Segert demanded the application of the performance principle in the economy, a public intellectual sphere, including a free press, as well as the rule of law as the normative basis for a new socialism. Their notion of democracy, economically speaking, was heavily influenced by Ulbricht's late NES, that is, decentralized planning that ensured the personal development of individuals – indicative planning, autonomous firms, participation of workers, shortening of working hours, and public control of firms in order to protect consumer interests but also the environment. Politically, it referred to individual rights, including the right to labor, rights that could be enforced against media and firms; it required transparency of political decisions and access to information; it meant peaceful

their elitist self-image as the avant-garde. The SED reformers were engaged on a purely theoretical level ... Their language only operated within the official frame of reference, while their provocation toward the regime consisted in subverting that language – something that nobody noticed outside of themselves and the party purists" (cited in Fair-Schulz 2009: 48).

[38] "Entwurf, Vorbereitungskonzeption des Projekts Grundlagen der Sozialismustheorie ... ," January 1988, in *SED-Reformdiskurs*, TB FMS, 1.

[39] *SED-Reformdiskurs*, "Philosophische Grundlagen der Erarbeitung einer Konzeption des modernen Sozialismus: Materialien der Eröffnungsberatung November 1988," Humboldt-Universität zu Berlin 1989, *SED-Reformdiskurs*, TB FMS, 1.

cooperation in the international community; but above all, it meant an open public dialogue of all interest groups led by the party. They envisioned a political society in which citizens had more rights than they had in the West, such that there would be "less" state than there was in Western state monopoly capitalism. In this fashion, the group revived Behrens and Benary's discussion about Marx's idea of the withering away of the state, and gave it a new touch by fostering ecological questions in particular – environmental issues fueled the discontent of the civil movement, and were ignored by the older generation for which industrialization was equal to progress. Regarding the question of power of oppositional parties and the electoral system, they remained consciously vague. Democratization, for them, meant a different relationship between party and people. Their project thus remained in the tradition of reform proposals possibly to be considered at the coming Party Congress without changing the structure of society. Like Klein, Brie knew of the underlying dilemma between stability and change mutually depending on each other:

> For the GDR, perhaps even more than for other socialist countries, on the one hand processes of change are necessary to preserve and expand the mentioned historical achievements; but on the other hand, political stability and social security are in turn prerequisites for successful change.[40]

The project was planned for the period between 1989 and 1995. Klein knew that it needed to be placed within the official planning system for institutional support. A critical study in potential conflict with the party had to be presented as an evolutionary opportunity rather than as a diverging alternative to the status quo, that is, only *within* the party discourse. "It was clear that this work had to be made official, and the first step was that I, as vice-rector, said: I take responsibility for the project."[41] As a research project placed within the research plan at the low university level, it could have been easily dismissed as factionist activity, while as a project placed within the CC there would be too much control. Klein, jointly with Brie, managed to integrate it into the mid-level research plan of the Ministry for Higher Education.[42] The research project was approved *within* the existing political structure,

[40] Ibid.: 6–7.   [41] Interview in *SED-Reformdiskurs*, TB Klein, 1.
[42] The central plan of the social sciences was assessed by the CC Department for Science and Education, but the Ministry for Higher Education was in charge of some parts of this plan that did not have to be approved by the Politburo. Klein

and within this structure, critical thinking was not only legitimate but in fact desirable. Thus, it would be largely free of political control, notably the control of Harry Smettan and the Stasi informants at the university.

Officialized by the ministry, and being close in content to the ideas of the rising civil movement, the members of the project were in the position of being "operationally relevant" for the Stasi. In addition to the need of informants that kept an ear on the rising civil movement, the Stasi's interest was also to place individuals that possibly could influence the movement in a way that prevents greater danger. But also for the members of the group, cooperation with the Stasi was interesting as they would not only be officialized from the point of view of the party, but also free in their activities as they were approved by the Stasi control apparatus. According to Kowalczuk's research on the Stasi activities at Humboldt University, many members of the research group were part of a so-called operative group that dates back even to 1982:

As early as 1982, the university management and the SED district leadership had developed an active counter-strategy to combat the opposition and the churches ... An "operative group" had been set up with the vice-rector for Social Sciences, Dieter Klein, ... This group, which worked until the end of 1989, was one of those "social forces" that the SED and the Ministry of State Security purposefully sent to "anti-state" church events, firstly to fill and secure the events with their own comrades, secondly to be informed precisely about what was going on in the discussion and thirdly to have well-versed comrades with counterarguments in such discussions in order to unsettle pastors, theologians, parishioners and above all members of the opposition, at best to influence them politically and ideologically so that they move away from their "anti-state activity." This operative group at the university included a whole range of those who also worked on the research project 'modern socialism,' including Dieter Segert, Michael Brie, Rainer Land, ... and Dieter Klein as the main person responsible.[43]

---

was in good contact with his former colleague at Humboldt, the historian Gerhard Engel, who was in charge of the social sciences at the ministry.

[43] In Kowalczuk (2012: 531–532). As source, Kowalczuk cites MfS, Ast Berlin Abt. XX 3608: 93, and 3609. See also Wolle writing of the modern socialism research group as "Stasi confidents," without providing evidence (1998: 340).

When asked about this group in 2021, neither Klein nor Brie knew of it. Klein seemed to feel rather immune to the Stasi, as he had direct contact to the party – he was member of the Berlin district party leadership:

We clearly thought that one should talk to the church people, even if they hold oppositional views. But if you mean that there was an operative group directed by the State Security, I must say that this was not the case. Of course, the university's state security officer(s) came to see me and wanted to hear my views on the political situation in the university. There were also questions about what I think about our influence on the church people. But that is different from intruding into the church movement in a targeted or directed manner through the State Security. (Klein interview 2021)

In a personal note by Michael Brie, he too denied that he had contacts with the church movement that were intentionally orchestrated by the Stasi. He would have known, since he was a collaborator for the HV A in the context of the support of anti-colonial and anti-apartheid movements abroad. Holding this important position at the Stasi, according to him, he "deliberately had no contact with the civil rights movement so as not to end up in the wrong position, even if such people were in my environment" (Brie, personal communication). So he too did not know of this group mentioned by Kowalczuk. According to Land, Segert sometimes went to church events out of curiosity, while he himself avoided doing so out of political loyalty to the party.[44]

When reading the Stasi files that Kowalczuk presented as sources, there is indeed proof of the intention of the Stasi to use Klein's peace research group for infiltration in the church movement. As a document of March 1986 says:

With the support of the party, we are making increased efforts to reach out to hostile people in peace circles. Initial attempts have been made in cooperation with the SED district leadership of the Humboldt University (Smettan). Last year, seven people from Humboldt University were named for political work.[45]

However, further documents do not support the interpretation drawn by Kowalczuk. There was not an "operative group" set up by the Stasi

---

[44] See interview, Land, *SED-Reformdiskurs*, TB Land. Unrelated to the speculations about Berlin's group, Jürgen Jünger recalled that in the mid-1980s in Leipzig, he was forced to report to the Stasi about meetings between Marxists and Christians. He intentionally did not go to some of the meetings in order to avoid reporting on them (interview in *SED-Reformdiskurs*, TB Jünger).

[45] MfS, BV Berlin, Abt. XX 3609: 50.

but two academic "working groups," one on "women for peace" and another one on "church issues." The latter was an academic initiative of the Ministry for Higher Education and the State Secretariat of Church Questions, headed by Klein and coordinated by his scientific secretary, Christine Karohl. This group consisted of around twenty young party members from various disciplines including philosophy, economics, law, history, and the literature department. All three key members of the research group, Segert, Brie, and Land, are indeed listed as members of this group. The purpose of the group, according to the Stasi, resembles Kowalczuk's description, though in a less systematic fashion: "The aim of the assignments (*Einsätze*) is to recognize certain strategic intentions of the church in a timely fashion and to react accordingly in a centrally coordinated manner ... Their appearance should be offensive, and they should debate on ideology without camouflage."[46] There is no evidence, however, that the group was intentionally put together by the Stasi. First, the group received instructions from, and had to report to, the State Secretariat and the party secretary of the university rather than the Stasi. The group members were reviewed by the Stasi regarding their political trustworthiness, but there is no reason to believe that they were recruited as official informants. When visiting church events, they may have acted out of their own academic interest in an open debate between Christians and Marxists. Their individual reports to the party organs might have been of interest to the Stasi without the participants knowing of the Stasi's collective management of them as a group. Indeed, the direct link between the Stasi and the group might not have been the group members themselves, but informants that the Stasi placed within their research group. Evidence for this is the report written by informant "IMS Thomas."[47]

Whatever form the cooperation with the Stasi took for each individual, it certainly had several shades. The ambiguity shows the extent to which the group behind the theory of modern socialism placed itself in the midst of the forces pulling the strings of the *Wende*. For those who experienced the change as a question of being for or against the party regime, the group at Humboldt University counted as a subtle attempt

---

[46] Mfs BV Berlin, Abt XX 3608: 93–99.
[47] See the report of a meeting June 22, 1989, see MfS AIM 2533/91, 74-83, in *SED-Reformdiskurs*, TB FMS, 1.

to rescue the party regime. For others, it counted as another lost chance
to save socialism from the regime of Old Communists.

Factionalism

By the early summer of 1989, the political situation changed. When
Hungary began dismantling its border to Austria in May 1989, when
the demonstrations in Beijing were run down in June 1989, and when
inside the GDR the legitimacy of the local elections were openly put
into question, the atmosphere in the East German civil rights movement heated up. Yet thus far, the movement counted no more than a
couple of thousand people gathering in small groups, mostly in
churches, and there was no sign that the old Honecker regime would
change course. The fears of a violent confrontation were great among
the members of the group. In this situation, it became increasingly clear
that the desired reform would not come from the increased pressure of
social scientists on the Politburo, but from a new *faction* in the party.
Yet for the SED, as with the Socialist Unity Party, factionalism was the
sin of all sins.[48]

This change of strategy happened on the occasion of the most
extensive text of the research group, a study written in July that went
through several modifications in the coming months, and was later
known as the restructure-paper (*Umbaupapier*).[49] It was written at the
demand of Klein in May 1989, who wished to have a substantial
contribution to the forthcoming student discussions in the red week
of fall 1989. The text took a clear position in favor of Gorbachev's

---

[48] Lenin himself prohibited political factions, or independent platforms, in 1921 in
response to critiques against his centralism and the demand for more workers'
influence that was expressed in the sailors' uprising in Kronstadt. The
prohibition derives from the fact that the party not only represents a particular
(class) interest, but all workers in the workers' state.

[49] The original title was "Reflections on the Problems and Perspectives of the Social
and Economic Change of Socialism and the Further Development of Socio-
Strategic Concepts of the GDR and other Socialist States of the Comecon." The
text was at first a university publication of the section Marxist-Leninist
philosophy at Humboldt University (see *SED-Reformdiskurs*, TB
Forschungsprojekt Moderner Sozialismus (in the following FMS), first version
Band 1, second version Band 4). In November, a revised version was published
by the editing house *Dietz*, titled *Study on Social Strategy* (Brie et al. 1989), and
then entered in another publication in February 1990, edited by Rainer Land
(1990) titled the *Re-structure Paper*.

reforms, and thus against Honecker's line. In addition to the ideas mentioned earlier, the study was more concrete in proposing new economic and social policies, focusing on the possibility of personal development in an economically dynamic and just system, including workers' councils at the firm, municipal, and state levels. Changes in the political system toward greater plurality were justified by the necessity of economic innovation, the restoration of trust in the party, and thus ultimately the prevention of a violent confrontation with the civil movement. The study also discussed practical questions of transition, but all in all remained an academic reflection on long-term political strategies and an intellectual exercise in social theory.

Klein wished to print and circulate 200 copies of the study, which had to be approved by the party secretary, Harry Smettan, who had been critical of the study. Smettan missed the sense of class problems in their description of the global situation, and noted regarding their discussion of democracy: "This sounds as if we now had no democracy."[50] Thus, he allowed only fifty copies to be printed. It was on the occasion of this confrontation with Smettan that Klein changed from his diplomatic strategy of appeasing power (i.e., to present reform ideas as an improvement of the status quo) to a strategy based on the confrontation of power (i.e., to create a *faction*). In a note Klein left in the archives, he recalled the swing in strategy. "July 27. Hard argument with Smettan! Accuses me of building a platform. I think now is the time to jointly reject firmly. Discuss with Micha [Brie]. Wera [Thiel] also says, 'Now, we have to act ... Tactical acting no longer makes sense, we have to go into offense.'"[51]

The historical events accelerated to such an extent that a faction became evermore necessary. In August, more than 20,000 East German citizens managed to illegally flee the country via the Hungarian border, and on September 11, Hungary officially declared its border open. Everyone who wished to do so could leave, which transformed the civil movement slowly into a mass movement of the people. At the same time, the so-called New Forum as well as Democracy Now were founded, the mouthpiece of the civil movement,

---

[50] In *SED-Reformdiskurs*, TB FMS, 1.

[51] *SED-Reformdiskurs*, TB FMS, 1. Later at a public discussion of the study in September, however, Klein still strategically began by saying that the only aim of the study is the "solidification of socialism in the GDR on the basis of the party program in force" (ibid.).

at first as illegal political groups. The New Forum was founded, among others, by "dissidents" such as Rolf Henrich who left the party to join the illegal opposition. Democracy Now gave out flyers on September 12, saying that "socialism must find its proper democratic form, if not it is historically lost" (in Schüddekopf 1990: 32). The first sentence of the founding declaration of the New Forum refers to the gap between party and people: "In our country, communication between the state and society is apparently disturbed."[52] Both statements reflect the perception of the research group at Humboldt University. By forming a new faction in the party, they tried to maintain communication with the civil movement, which, as a socialist party and thus avant-garde, they were supposed to consciously guide and unify. But how to gain their trust?

The new faction was to be formed by means of another article written by the group that was to be distributed widely in both the party and the civil movement. They wrote a short and programmatic piece called "the position paper" (*Thesenpapier*).[53] Speaking, in Gorbachev's perestroika language, of the "shared house" of Europe, and the "global problems" in the interest of all mankind, the paper covered Brie's ideas about the public sphere, including freedom of the press, Segert's ideas of different forms of democratic representation of interests, and Will's ideas of the rule of law and the separation of power between party and state.[54] Aiming mainly at more democracy within the party, without calling for general elections, the authors asked for a "great collocation (*Aussprache*)" as also demanded by the civil movement. The factionalism came in the form of a demand for a "cadre change," thus implicitly, a demand that Honecker was to step down. The urgency of the reform was clearly felt:

[52] "Gründungsaufruf des Neuen Forum," September 10, 1989; in "Chronik der Mauer."
[53] "Zur gegenwärtigen Lage in der DDR und Konsequenzen für die Gestaltung der Politik der SED," *SED-Reformdiskurs*, TB FMS, 1 and 2 for several drafts. The paper had already circulated in September, but is dated October 8. The main authors were André Brie, Michael Brie, and Wilfried Ettl. The final draft can also be found at www.ddr89.de/texte/SED1.html, accessed January 21, 2022. For further discussion of the article see Süß (1999: 483).
[54] See Will (1989), also demanding investigation committees at parliament, and a constitutional court.

The GDR is economically, socially, politically and ideologically in a latent crisis ... Mass dissatisfaction and frustration that have emerged in these years have taken on a dangerous momentum of their own. It is predictable that in the next two to three years, after the accumulation of unsolved problems in several social areas, there will be a crisis of the entire reproductive mechanism. Only if the party takes the lead in renewing (society), which can no longer be postponed, the socialist character of our collective development, and that which has been achieved, will be preserved and expanded.[55]

A crucial point of the paper was the treatment of the legal status of the opposition, thus the leading role of the party. There was no consensus in the group. Klein recalls that he was more conservative on that question than the young members, and saw less potential for an official role of a political opposition. But also Brie knew that the opposition, after decades of oppression, was incapable of governing.[56] Their ultimate position was controversial for compromising both the party and the civil movement. They argued that the opposition should be legalized and included in public discussion, which might have gained applause from some parts of the civil movement, but they also wished to prevent the opposition from seizing power, which might have caused critical voices from other parts of the civil movement:

It must be examined how oppositional forces are given a limited legal space in the public sphere, since their repressive suppression is impossible and could also fundamentally discredit the process of change. At the same time, this limitation must be secured with utmost responsibility, so that the content of opposition is reduced to the choice of different variants of socialism. Opposition to socialism is not to be permitted. Constitutional procedures, subject to judicial review, are needed in this respect.[57]

[55] Ibid.
[56] At the end of September, in a university discussion, Klein still emphasized that any reform of socialism required the leading role of the party and the dominance of socialist property in a planned economy, and that by assuming leadership in reform discussions, anyone who does not agree on these principles would be weakened. All that was needed was to accept different opinions *within* the party, as was required ever since the foundation of the party in its statutes (*SED-Reformdiskurs*, TB FMS, 1, "Notizen zur Diskussion ... "). Regarding Brie's position, see the interview (ibid., TB Brie). He was critical about the opposition also because he did not want to appear as dissident and thus loose credibility.
[57] Position paper, cited in note 55. Stefan Wolle, who took part in the dismantling of the Stasi, commented critically about this paper: "The supposedly ingenious conspirators were constantly running after events. Only when Erich Honecker, afflicted with an old-fashioned stubbornness, had long since become a

Justifying this position later, Brie spoke of a "trap" he felt he was in: he knew that without the party the GDR could not persist in a vacuum of power, yet it appeared impossible to regain trust that the party was really capable of change. What thus appeared as a false compromise regarding the leading role of the party to some, was for him simply the correct understanding of the historical situation, certainly in hindsight.[58]

The choice of who to send the paper to was heavily discussed among the members of the group, agreeing that it should not be sent to the Politburo. They produced in-house prints, and in order to protect themselves, titled them "internal discussion paper" and added a note saying "further dissemination requires the instructions of the vice-rector." The paper was, however, send out widely to other social scientists as well as to artists, in an effort to mobilize a critical mass of party members. It was discussed within the university, and party-loyal functionaries were also invited to express their criticism, which created legitimacy for the discussion.[59]

In addition, the group distributed the article among their Stasi contacts. On October 3, Rainer Land cautiously delivered the paper in person to the home address of former HV A head Markus Wolf, who since 1986 had become ever more critical of the regime and more and more sympathetic to the civil movement. Wolf, however, already knew about the paper as it had circulated within the HV A, though maybe not in other departments of the Stasi. Hartmann recalled later:

The head of my department at the HV A, who was of a high rank, a colonel, gave me a conceptual paper of the research project with the advice to read it; I would recognize how consistent our positions, he meant his and mine, were with those in the paper. I should also show this paper to other comrades without producing other copies.[60]

laughingstock, did they decide to overthrow him. When the socialist reform ideas had already landed on the garbage heap of failed ideologies, a pitiful and half-hearted socialism paper, which Stasi confidants at Humboldt University had prepared, saw the light of day ... yet these heresies of yesterday no longer interested anyone inside the GDR" (1998: 340).

[58] See interview, in *SED-Reformdiskurs*, TB Brie.
[59] See *SED-Reformdiskurs*, TB FMS, 4. For Klein's talk, see his notes in "Studie Sozialismustheorie und Diskussion am 26.9.1989," Manuskript und Computerabschrift, unveröffentlicht, *SED-Reformdiskurs*, TB FMS, 1.
[60] Interview Hartmann, *SED-Reformdiskurs*, TB FMS, 2. Regarding the Stasi's role in fall 1989 more generally, see Münkel (2014) and Süß (1999), in

Wolf replied to Land, noting the defensive quality of their proposals: "The most important task for all of us is now to avert the dangers you describe so well."[61] Though Wolf was certainly not representative of the mindset of the Stasi in 1989, the quote shows that there were other parts of this ministry that were sympathetic to critiques of the old regime. In professional interrogations with Stasi officers at HV A in 1989, according to Hartmann, 70 percent were critical of the Politburo. Brie, who had also passed on his texts to the Stasi, even hoped that via the Stasi reports to the party, some CC members could have been drawn into their project. Most Stasi employees certainly remained orthodox until the end, as police were not supposed to pursue any political agenda. But Brie would later defend this approach by arguing that it might have added to preventing the "Chinese solutions," and thus helped to keeping the protests peaceful:

What is completely underestimated is that, with the exception of Romania, no blood was spilled in the countries of east-central Europe. This was a great achievement. It was possible because the party and the security apparatus did not give the order to shoot, or this order was not carried out. The discourses in the party and security organs were essential for this … I deliberately passed on the materials (which the Ministry had anyways) to secure the project and to draw attention to the group's point of view … In view of the uncertainty in the apparatus, it was not naïve to assume, in retrospect, that such discourses would remain completely without influence. (Brie, personal communication)

Since all Stasi activities were later strongly associated with the lack of legitimacy of the regime, Brie's and other's cooperation with them put the group in a rather murky light. Kowalczuk even speculated that the research group was in fact staged by, and under protection of, the Stasi – even if he adds that "this could so far not been verified" (2012: 532). This author has not found evidence that would verify this claim.

particular the discussion about the "Chinese solution" in Süß (1999: 177). Next to painstakingly recording the rising civil movement, the Stasi proposed, first, "de-escalation" through dialogue, "conspirational disruption" (*konspirative Zersetzung*), that is, manipulation through informants, and the identification and possible imprisonment of key actors. Informants within the civil movement were thus in high demand. These strategies had been deeply anchored in Stasi culture since the mid-1950s, as described in Chapter 3. In October, however, even the Stasi proposed to legalize groups such as the New Forum in order to stabilize the situation, as documented by Münkel (2014: 18).

[61] Wolf to Land, October 3, 1989, in *SED-Reformdiskurs*, TB FMS, 1.

On October 3, the position paper was ultimately sent to several CC members, including Helmut Koziolek and Otto Reinhold, as well as party district secretaries, as Brie recalled:

We thought about which Central Committee members could be won over [and] . . . would accept this as a platform of their own and thus bring about a split in the party leadership at the Central Committee – since nothing was to be expected from the Politburo. Such a split in the higher party ranks would have been the prerequisite for the formation of a faction, otherwise we could expect nothing but exclusion from the party. But we did not even find one Central Committee member who would have been willing to send the paper to other CC members with a note saying: an interesting opinion, please take note of it.[62]

Without signs that the CC members could be mobilized, less and less could be expected from the existing party leadership. And this became particularly apparent to the entire nation during the festivities of the 40th anniversary of the GDR on October 6 and 7. Honecker simply ignored the fact that anything different was going on, still trying to control the demonstrations by arrests and intimidation, maintaining the illegality of the New Forum and other platforms as enemies of the state. Gorbachev was an official guest at the celebrations, and openly opposed Honecker's backwardness. "There are dangers lurking only for those who do not respond to life," he said in an interview with Western television. The civil movement fired up. After the demonstrations in Leipzig had already grown in September, they exploded in size in October in Dresden and Berlin. One turning point was the demonstration on October 9 in Leipzig, which many feared would be suppressed by police or even military force. But all remained peaceful.[63] In the weeks that followed, the demonstrations grew from 70,000 to 500,000. On October 17, Honecker ultimately had to resign, and was replaced by the younger but still conservative Egon Krenz. At Humboldt University, the party organization of the university was occupied, and Harry Smettan had to leave his post on October 26.

---

[62] See the interview with Brie in *SED-Reformdiskurs*, TB Brie.
[63] This demonstration is discussed in detail in Dale (2006: 6–34). According to Jünger, speaking for Leipzig, the internal party discourse akin to the civil movement granted legitimacy, created trust, and encouraged the civil movement: "Knowing that one will encounter solidarity was important for gaining courage to go out onto the streets" (interview Jünger, *SED-Reformdiskurs*, TB Jünger).

Having failed to mobilize the CC members for their democratic reform of socialism, the group discussed to what extent they should now get directly involved with the civil movement. Rainer Land was much in favor, but Michael Brie was rather skeptical. However, they did get involved notably through a text titled "Immediate Measures to Initiate a Fundamental Democratic Renewal of Socialism in the GDR," dated October 11.[64] The overlap with the civil movement's demands were striking, including a change of leadership, freedom to travel, a free press, and the rule of law as a control of state power. They then warned of a "reunification campaign." The text was sent to opposition parties and representatives of the civil movement. They presented the text at several press conferences and at the Academy of Arts, gave radio interviews, and on October 15, shortly before Honecker resigned, spoke at the concert "Rock against Violence" in the main church of the movement, the *Erlöserkirche*.[65] Now they actually took part in (creating) the public debate they had always missed. Though they joined in the call to legalize the New Forum, the delicate question of power was treated again in a rather hesitant and philosophical fashion. What was in-between bourgeois parliamentarism and one-party bureaucratic centralism? What would be a party-based socialism without the party intruding into the state? They appeared to dodge the question:

The leading role [of the party] can only consist of introducing strategically well-founded and convincing positions into the public discussion … Therefore, a process of de-nationalization of the party, the separation of the party from the state apparatus, is necessary, such that, on the one hand, the party can again fulfill its real function in society, that is, to lead the dialogue about strategies for the development of socialism. On the other hand, a democratic reorganization of the processes of governmental decision and legal execution becomes possible, through which other political forces can be integrated.[66]

---

[64] "Sofortmaßnahmen zur Einleitung einer grundlegenden demokratischen Erneuerung des Sozialismus in der DDR," October 11, 1989, *SED-Reformdiskurs*, TB FMS, 2. For the different positions regarding the civil movement, see the interview with Will (ibid., TB Will).

[65] For the many interventions of the members of the project in the public discussion, see *SED-Reformdiskurs*, TB FMS, 2. See also the video of the discussion at the Academy of Arts in the same folder.

[66] "Sofortmaßnahmen … ," *SED-Reformdiskurs*, TB FMS, 2: 68.

Treating the question of the role of the party at a rock concert in such a haphazard way might explain why there was so little resonance for their ideas within the civil movement. It might have been too late to actually influence the inner dynamic of the events, which was hardly possible with a project that had been officially commissioned by the ministry, and which was based on new concepts in postmodern social philosophy.[67]

But during the last weeks of October, all political groups, whatever strategies they pursued, joined together in an united call to bring Krenz down. They thus opted for "real" change rather than the consolidation of power with possible minor changes. On November 4, a demonstration mobilized well-known artists, notably Stefan Heym, and those from the church, notably Friedrich Schorlemmer, in calling jointly for a democratic socialism. For many this demonstration was a key event of the peaceful revolution when the opposition parties, inner-party reformers, and the civil rights movement joined together in their mutual democratic respect and in their call against Krenz (in Sabrow 2010: 8). The members of the group helped in organizing another demonstration against Krenz, which took place on November 8 in front of the CC. Brie was one of the speakers at this demonstration, and called for an immediate Extraordinary Party Congress, a new formation of the party, and a "coalition of all parties and political forces": "Share power and responsibility with us!" he planned to say. "Over decades, the party leadership has formed a secret faction against its own party," should have been another line. But emotions ran too high for his overly intellectual speech. He was shouted down and had to interrupt his talk.[68] On November 9, the *Berliner Zeitung* published this demand in an article authored by prominent party intellectuals, including Klein, Rolf Reißig, Wolfram Krause, and Heinz Albrecht, party secretary of Berlin.[69]

---

[67] According to Kowalczuk's critical research on the group, the fact that still at this point in October, the leading role of the party was not put into question, shows that their ultimate objective was to rescue the party regime (2012: 531; 2009: 311–317).

[68] For the planned speech, see *SED-Reformdiskurs*, TB FMS, 6.

[69] "Was wir vom außerordentlichen Parteitag der SED erwarten: Gedanken von Wissenschaftlern zur Überlebensfrage der DDR," *Berliner Zeitung*, November 9, 1989: 11.

Chaos and Joy

On the night of November 9, almost as a bureaucratic slip, the borders to West Germany were opened, and the civil movement turned into a mass celebration. To everyone inside but also outside the country, it became clear that everything was possible, and thus everything was at stake. The threat that the movement would be appeased by minor changes was gone, but the urgency of providing a concrete alternative increased. In a university newspaper article titled "Between Opportunity and Ruin," Klein wrote on November 16: "This is a dramatic day when hundred years reduce to hours . . . Anyone who has the freedom to travel will travel back only if there is also freedom at home. Now we have decided that there finally will be a unity of socialism and democracy in the GDR. Or there will be no socialism."[70]

Establishing freedom at home meant first of all bringing about the fall of Krenz, and Klein played an active role in it. On November 13, Klein's friend and Krenz's opponent, Hans Modrow, became chairman of the Council of Ministers – Klein and Modrow had known each other since the late 1950s when Klein was FDJ secretary at Humboldt University and Modrow FDJ secretary of Berlin. Some days after Modrow took office, he published a governmental declaration, which Klein among others helped to compose.[71] In this declaration, Modrow commited himself to the demands of the civil movement and distanced himself from the former understanding of the state, calling for a "re-imagined, creative political alliance" of several parties that is liable toward its citizens. But he did not embrace parliamentarism. "The change in the GDR is irreversible," he admitted, but still proposed a renewal of socialism, a reform of the political system, and an integration of the GDR into the European Union.

In an attempt to secure his position, Krenz tried to get the reformist wing of the party on his side (as Klein had earlier, when integrating critical voices). The day after the celebrations at the wall began, on November 10, Krenz proclaimed at the party rally in *Lustgarten* that

---

[70] In *SED-Reformdiskurs*, TB Klein, 4.
[71] Other authors included Karl-Heinz Arnold and Wolfram Krause. See Klein's draft in *SED-Reformdiskurs*, TB Klein, 4. Klein also sent the members of the research group for a personal consultation with Modrow's secretary to Dresden, a conversation that was disappointing for Land, who subsequently became critical of Modrow (interview Land, *SED-Reformdiskurs*, TB Land).

"we are serious about the politics of renewal, and that we reach out our hands to everyone who wants to join us."[72] Krenz might have had Klein in mind, who also spoke at the demonstration demanding an Extraordinary Party Congress. Krenz understood that he was increasingly marginalized, and tried to get in touch with the members of the group. On November 26, Klein sent Krenz a letter in the name of Brie and Segert informing Krenz that they did not wish to meet him and asking him to allow an Extraordinary Party Congress, and thus indirectly to step down.[73] As Klein recalled:

There was a short interim phase in which functionaries at upper levels said: Yes, many things are not going well, now give us ideas. Schabowski had given the impetus to summon scientists who were known for their criticism ... Everyone brought their articles, and thus a text listing requests came into being. Schabowski also wished a conceptually oriented presentation for Krenz, which was worked out especially by me. However, I was concerned if it would be a good idea to give the text to Krenz, with which he then could present himself as a reformer ... I thus reached Modrow in Berlin just before the CC conference ... "No way!," he said to me, "don't give the report to Krenz, give it to me, and I'll launch an attack on Krenz at the CC meeting. Krenz does not mean it that way anyway ... We would only help him present himself, falsely, as someone who is up to date." So the presentation did not go to Krenz, and Modrow ... processed it in his contribution to the discussion.[74]

These maneuvers might have contributed to the fact that on December 3, in the last meeting of the CC, Krenz, the Politburo, and the entire CC stepped down. Since the leading role of the party had been voted off GDR's constitution on December 1, Hans Modrow, as chairmen of the Council of Ministers, would now be head of state. In the same meeting, it was decided to hold an Extraordinary Party Congress, and Klein became one of the twenty-six members of the committee to prepare it. This position showed the degree to which Klein had gained prominence within the remaining party in the preceding months and years. After all, the factionalism appeared to be successful. However, now

---

[72] Chronik der Mauer, www.chronik-der-mauer.de/chronik/#anchoryear1989, accessed July 6, 2021. Klein's speech at Lustgarten is printed in *Humboldt-Universität*, 11, November 16, 1989: 2; also in *SED-Reformdiskurs* TB Klein, 4.
[73] For the letter, see *SED-Reformdiskurs*, TB FMS, 6.
[74] Interview in *SED-Reformdiskurs*, TB Klein, 1.

that the party was constitutionally decoupled from the state, more than a party reform, but the existence of the state was at stake.

The other groups of the civil movement perceived the same threat. After decades of policies that nourished West-envy, the mass celebrations of the open borders came with an immediate consumer rush. Soon the New Forum published a call saying: "You are the heroes of a political revolution, do not let yourself be pacified by traveling and debt-increasing consumption injections!" (in Sabrow 2010: 11). The consumer rush, among other factors, might explain why, some days after the opening of the wall, at the Monday demonstration on November 13, the first marginal voices for a reunification of Germany were expressed. In response, and in anticipation of further events, the many political groups pushing for change – inner-party reformists, oppositional parties, church and civil rights groups – came together in writing and signing a joint petition titled "For Our Country." Along with Günter Krusche, general superintendent of the Protestant Church in Berlin-Brandenburg, and Konrad Weiß, a spokesman for Democracy Now, Klein wrote one of the drafts. On November 28, the writer Stefan Heym presented the petition to the press. The petition text reads as follows:

Our country is in a deep crisis. We cannot and do not want to live as we did up to now ... Structures shaped by Stalinism had permeated all areas of life. In a nonviolent way, through mass demonstrations, the people have forced the process of revolutionary renewal, which is taking place at breathtaking speed. There is little time left for us to influence the various options out of the crisis. *Either* we can insist on the independence of the GDR and try with all our resources ... to develop a solidary society in our country, in which peace and social justice, freedom of the individual, freedom of movement, and the preservation of the environment are guaranteed. *Or* we have to tolerate that a sellout of our material and moral values begins, caused by strong economic constraints ... , to which influential circles ... in the FRG link their aid for the GDR. And sooner or later, the German Democratic Republic will be taken over by the Federal Republic. Let us go the first way ... We can still reflect on the anti-fascist and humanist ideals from which we once started. We call on all citizens who share our hope and concern to join this appeal by signing it.[75]

[75] First published in *Sächsische Zeitung*, November 29, 1989: 281, Bezirksleitung Dresden der SED. For more documentation including Klein's contribution, see the interview in Borchert et al. (1994), and *SED-Reformdiskurs*, TB Klein, 4.

This was the first and only big public signature petition in East Germany's history, and it was a huge success. By mid-January, 1,167,048 citizens had signed the petition, which amounted to nearly 7 percent of the entire population. But the same day that the petition was launched, in Bonn, West Germany's Chancellor Helmut Kohl surprised the parliament and the international scene with a so-called ten-point plan that listed German reunification as a goal, even if it did not yet come with a concrete schedule.

In the weeks following the fall of the wall, the skepticism that the socialist party could rescue the GDR was nourished by the revelations about the corruption surrounding the old Politburo. Everybody was shocked by the privileges that came to be known about the Politburo members living outside of Berlin in a residential forest district, the *Waldsiedlung* in Wandlitz. In particular, the extravagant consumer lifestyle based on imported Western products, such as Margot Honecker's party-financed jewelry, revealed the Politburo's hypocrisy. In this context, Alexander Schalck-Golodkowski's reign and the area of commercial coordination was also revealed. Secret weapon store-houses were opened, as reported by *Der Spiegel*, debunking the idea of the GDR as a peaceful state. On November 18, the People's Chamber set up a committee to investigate cases of abuses of office, personal enrichment, and corruption. The same day that Krenz resigned, on December 3, Schalck-Golodkowski no longer felt secure and fled to West Germany.[76]

The more shocking the news about the Politburo's corruption, the more confident were those who supported Modrow that they were on the right path. Since the most serious problems of the GDR were associated with the old Politburo clique, the forthcoming democratic reform that replaced them would prevent the same from happening in the future, or so they thought. For many in the West, however, the revelations proved the illegitimacy of the party state itself. This differ-ence in perception became apparent when, on November 29, represen-tatives of the West German SPD came to discuss the current situation with Modrow and others, Klein included. They proposed cooperation on the condition that they would confront their past and get their

---

[76] See his own account in Schalck-Golodkowski (2000).

"skeletons out of their closet." "But we had already dealt with our 'skeletons'," Klein recalled their response. "They were pretty baffled, said they would get in touch with us, but never showed up again."[77]

Saving Socialism from the GDR

Without the protection of the wall, and the old Politburo including the CC having gone, East Germany's institutions crumbled into an anarchic state. The police began acting anxiously, not knowing who to support, Stasi staff ceased functioning and turned toward self-defense, soldiers no longer wanted to obey orders, payments from the state were due, and party members resigned en masse. The committee that prepared the Extraordinary Party Congress faced a daring task. New elections were supposed to take place within six months, and the party had little time to regain a new profile while managing at the same time the collapse of its own structures. It was clear to Modrow that the existence of the party and thus the state itself was at stake:

Everything went haywire. The working committee was seen as a substitute government. Nobody knew what to do and was waiting for instructions. People from the administration of the State Security in Erfurt called because they feared that their headquarters will be stormed, asked whether they should defend themselves and use violence. Institutions had to be dissolved, entire delegations from the party apparatus appeared and somehow wanted to negotiate about their future.[78]

Even if the committee considered itself independent from the CC, it met, and basically lived, in the CC building. They were thus located at the same place where days before the old regime had been in place, which caused great confusion. Days after Krenz stepped down, a demonstration took place that tried to force him to admit the election fraud:

The demonstration came towards the Central Committee building ... , and someone from the committee now had to deal with it. Someone said: you do it. I went downstairs and found a crowd whistling and drumming ... It was extremely difficult to explain plausibly that Krenz was not there and that we are not the same as the old CC.[79]

---

[77] Interview in *SED-Reformdiskurs*, TB Klein, 1.　　[78] Ibid.　　[79] Ibid.

While the state structure fell apart, the groups constituting the civil rights movement including the New Forum, Democracy Now, the opposition parties and the green party, formed the so-called central round table. It was formed at the initiative of church representatives, and met for the first time on December 7. Its main task was to manage the dismantling of the Ministry for State Security, which began in early December by occupying Stasi offices, and second, to draft a new constitution to be voted on at a later point. The round table could have assumed the role of a managing government but did not. Of course, it was out of question that the SED would partake in this round table.

The Extraordinary Party Congress took place at the same time, December 8 and 9, and a week later on December 16 and 17. In his opening speech, Herbert Kroker made clear that in view of the entanglement of state and party, the congress was about the future existence of their country. In line with Modrow, he demanded the integration of the GDR into the European community and argued against its integration into the FRG. The practical task of the congress was to guarantee that the party remained operational. The main committees had to be reelected, as many of the high functionaries were dismissed.[80] Brie was elected as a board member. One topic vividly debated was the question of what to do with the substantial finances of the party, an issue that gained prominence due to the revelations about Schalck-Golodkowski.[81] One of the members of the group, Krüger began withdrawing from the party when his proposal to share finances with the opposition was not considered. Also, Segert was disappointed as none of the topics he submitted for discussion, regarding workers' councils in firms, for example, were discussed.[82] An important question was the identity of the party whether to found a new socialist party or a reconstitution of the SED. In accordance with Klein but against the opinion of Brie, it was decided to "modernize" the existing party, though the party was

---

[80] Gregor Gysi was elected the new head of the party. For the full documentation of the Party Congress, see Hornbogen et al. (1999).

[81] The assets of the party included party buildings, publishing houses, recreational facilities, foreign assets to support socialist parties and movements abroad, and around 160 party-owned firms.

[82] Interview in SED-Reformdiskurs, TB Segert.

Figure 8.1 Dieter Klein making final changes to his programmatic speech at the Extraordinary Party Congress, December 16, 1989, Dynamo sports hall, Berlin.
Copyright Ulrich Burchert.

renamed SED-PDS (Socialist Unity Party-Party of Democratic Socialism). All in all, the congress was characterized by a struggle over the self-identity of the party between its previous role in power that everyone was ready to compromise, and the role as a parliamentary opposition, an idea that was not yet ready to come to the party's mind. There must be something in-between, everyone hoped.

Klein's speech was to frame the discussion about the new program of the party. Largely inspired by the research on the theory of modern socialism, it was titled "The Refoundation (*Neuformierung*) of a Modern Socialist Party and Its Contribution to a New Socialist Society."[83] The speech was the peak of the political influence of the ideas of the group. The main argument was to propose democratic socialism as a "third way" between capitalism and bureaucratic socialism. Even if democracy had always been a core value of Marx, and even if the GDR had carried this title in its very name, the state never lived up to this ideal. Democracy, according to Klein, stands for the socialist values of individual freedom, equality of conditions, solidarity, sustainability, and peace. "We want neither the reformist adjustment in capitalism, nor the simple smashing of modern economic systems, parliamentary democracy and the public. We are fighting for a way that will lead us beyond capitalism, and not back into bureaucratic socialism" (Klein in Hornbogen et al. 1999: 228).

Regarding economic policy, there was little new in Klein's speech. He asked for opening up to the world market, but also the protection of workers from monopoly power. In the spirit of Ulbricht's NES, which heavily influenced the very idea of modern socialism, the use of technologies should set the workers' creative powers free and allow for environmentally friendly management. "Planning," says Klein, is planning "that starts from below," by which he meant a democratization of the economy within an open public sphere. As with most preceding proposals relating to decentralization, this too was more political-philosophical than technical in nature.

More importantly for his speech, the specter of the old regime had to be broken. The central argument for Klein was the turn away from

---

[83] The speech was published in *Neues Deutschland* under the title "Ready-Made Solutions – That Would Be the Beginning of the Old Structures" ("Fertige Lösungen: das wäre wieder der Anfang von alten Strukturen"), *Neues Deutschland*, December 18, 1989: 10–11. See also Klein in Hornbogen et al. (1999). Apart from the modern socialism project, the Academy for Social Sciences also provided input in this text. Humboldt's research group also published their ideas about the new formation of a party separately in *Neues Deutschland*, titled "For a Socialist Party in the GDR: A Contribution to the Program Discussion" ("Für eine sozialistische Partei in der DDR: Ein Angebot für die Diskussion zum Programm"), December 12, 1989: 3–4; see also *SED-Reformdiskurs*, TB FMS, 6.

"Stalinism" as the vice of bureaucratic socialism. Stalinism, so Klein, together with the "criminal practice of the GDR leadership ... tore the greatest idea in the history of human civilization into dirt" (ibid.: 226). Marxism-Leninism was misused as the "confirmation propaganda for a dead-end policy."[84] Before Klein, Michael Schumann had given a speech officially breaking with Stalinism, which was hypocritical for many such as Brie, since Schumann was known as a rather orthodox party member. The shared rejection of Stalinism being the negative criterion of the new democratic socialism turned the congress into an undoing of mistakes that had officially been corrected already thirty-five years before in the wake of the 20th Party Congress. Implicitly, Klein thus admitted that East Germany's intellectual history was a series of failed attempts to escape the specter of Stalinism. In December 1989, they finally made it. Klein's speech could indeed be read as stealthy thoughts held back for many years, and thus caught by the logic of those who oppressed these ideas. Also, this last reform, as with all preceding reforms, was to undo the failures of the preceding reforms, which explains the déjà vu and mistrust among the civil movement.[85] As Sabrow put it, the idea of the third way "belonged to a past world of the meaning of the political (*Sinnwelt des Politischen*)" (2010: 10).

Intellectually, since Stalinism stands for the misuse of Marx, democratic socialism made it possible to appropriate Marx anew as well as the many Marxist traditions vilified by the Stalinist orthodoxy. "Did the narrowing down (of Marxist thought)," Klein asked, "carried out under Stalin to a few traditions, actually to one, not contribute to the formation of an ideological conception that was called Marxism-Leninism, in the name of which bureaucratic socialism and its monopoly of power was justified?" (Klein in Hornbogen et al. 1999: 228).

---

[84] Note, however, that Klein, as for example the younger Hans-Jürgen Krüger did, does not associate Stalinism with fascism, which would have deprived any legitimacy of the work of the Old Communists (see interview in *SED-Reformdiskurs*, TB Krüger).

[85] Dieter Segert is most explicit in saying that the failed reforms during the Thaw, and those of Ulbricht's 1960s, were the main inspiration for his contributions to the theory of modern socialism. The Honecker regime got stuck in the 1930s, he argued, and thus in a world of persecution and war; see his interview in *SED-Reformdiskurs*, TB Segert. Regarding 1989 as a belated 1968, see also Miethe in Schüle et al. (2006).

Following a communist instinct to search for justification from preceding authorities, he quoted Rosa Luxemburg:

Without general elections, without unrestricted freedom of the press and assembly, without a free struggle of opinion, life dies out in every public institution, becomes a mere semblance of life, in which only the bureaucracy remains as the active element. Public life gradually falls asleep, a few dozen party leaders of inexhaustible energy and boundless experience direct and rule. Among them, in reality only a dozen outstanding heads do the leading and an elite of the working class is invited from time to time to meetings where they are to applaud the speeches of the leaders, and to approve proposed resolutions unanimously – at bottom, then, a clique affair – a dictatorship, to be sure, not the dictatorship of the proletariat but only the dictatorship of a handful of politicians, that is a dictatorship in the bourgeois sense. (Luxemburg 1961: 24)

Recognizing the plurality of socialist traditions was natural to Klein, who had always believed in an culture of open debate that he and many of his generation aspired to but never genuinely achieved. In this fashion, he would also put into question the party's monopoly on the understanding of history, such as the unfortunate split between social democrats and communists going back to the late Weimar Republic:

We do not forget radical left-wing sectarianism, which damaged the formation of a unified anti-fascist front. We do not forget the struggle of upright social democrats against fascism, nor their resistance to Stalinism, and we acknowledge the successes of their reform policy for more democracy in the present. (Klein in Hornbogen et al. 1999: 228)

The party should thus refrain from demarcation from other left movements and look for points of contact. In the same vein, Klein spoke out against the "decoupling of world processes" and the "small-country strategy" of the GDR, turning against the provincialism and inward orientation of East Germany's society. Against the petit-bourgeois spirit of Old Communists, he also picked up the issues occupied by the Western left, being "against right-wing forces, against nationalism, against xenophobia." In the same way, the party would not only speak for "workers" as the oppressed class, but also for women.

After all the criticism of the Old Communists' worldview, however, Klein also expressed the sentiment that has always held back his generation from making a clear break with the party regime: the gratitude for what the founding generation had done. "How shall we deal with that which we have achieved in the GDR?" he asked. "Considering the forty years of GDR history, according to me, we might have reason to doubts its model of society. But we have no reason to consider the work of the post-war generation as failed" (Klein in Hornbogen et al. 1999: 231). Honoring the work of the founding generation, as we have argued in this book, also means to excuse their shortcomings. Klein indeed refers back to the historical script of Old Communists that there was no Marshall Plan for East Germany, that the arms race left no space for economic development, and that East Germany had to pay more reparations than West Germany. He then praised the moderate economic success of the 1960s, the cultural atmosphere of the GDR, and "the solidarity of the majority of the population with peace-oriented politics." He thus associated the peace as propagated by the party for decades with what would come to be known as the peaceful revolution of 1989.

With regard to the decisive question of power and the leading role of the party in the new democratic socialism, Klein said the following:

A new political system in which the people really rule, not simply a copy of bourgeois parliamentarism ... but a political system that is based on the personal and political rights of every person and on public property, must enable the articulation of diverse interests, involving parties, interest groups, citizens' initiatives at the many round tables ... And this has to happen very quickly. (Klein in Hornbogen et al. 1999: 237)

Democracy should be based on human rights, public discourse, a press free from both the state and from media monopolies, and the separation of legislative, governmental, and judicial powers. Nevertheless, in a socialist society, the socialist party cannot be a mere element of a parliamentary bourgeois system, but must moderate the articulation of interest groups, and must continue to secure the prevalence of public property. Just as the party statues had said since its foundation, democracy refers to a friendly dialogue moderated by the party, but not the bourgeois competition for power between parties. Though breaking with state socialism, Klein's attachment to the party still required its privilege as the guard of socialism.

All in all, the response of the congress delegates to Klein's speech was cautious. It was the peak of the influence of his and the group's ideas of modernizing socialism, but at the same time the end of this very influence:

There were Party Congress delegates who stood for an intellectual departure, but they were probably in the minority ... Most of them were very happy that a founding consensus of a programmatic nature had been promoted, otherwise a new formation [of the party] would not have been possible. But we also felt something like a lack of intelligence, a distance to an intellectual way of dealing with the upheaval ... And I did not get the feeling from this larger part of the Party Congress delegates that the program was well received.[86]

Nor did the future voter necessarily welcome the results of the Party Congress. They appeared to listen to other voices. Two days after the congress ended, on December 19, Helmut Kohl visited Dresden and gave a speech at the symbolic site of the *Frauenkirche*. To many outside observers it appeared that he was better equipped to communicate with his "fellow countrymen," as he began his speech. Even if there was no agreement among the audience regarding reunification, the speech was a surprising success in making it appear to the world that this was the wish of the people. The international community would soon support Kohl, who relied on and nourished the rising West-rush. The civil rights movement representing those who wanted change were washed away by a people's movement of those who just wanted to get away, as Sabrow put it (2010).

* * *

Twenty years after the *Wende*, Klein would say that "it was one of the most chaotic, but also one of the most beautiful times" (2009). In a later interview, he associates the beauty of these days with the main theme of this book. It was a time that allowed living out the sentiment in which this generation felt most home, hope:

For the whole year of 1989, even to the kind of people like me, it was clear that state socialism was not working and that the GDR was heading towards the end. But that does not mean that there was no hope to be able to influence the events and also save something. Until March 1990, a majority

---

[86] Interview in *SED-Reformdiskurs*, TB Klein, 1.

of the people in the GDR wanted a GDR on par with the Federal Republic . . .
I also hoped that, even though I didn't believe it anymore . . . This was related
to having grown into (social) structures, with decades of life experience.
(Klein interview 2021)

Located between the party apparatus and the civil movement, Klein's
contribution to the intellectual history of the *Wende* mirrors its inner
dynamics. Supporting many ideas of the civil movement within the
institutional structures of the party, the project of modern socialism
describes the shift from reforming the party state to letting it go. While
at the beginning of the perestroika period, both the party system and
the civil movement were driven by similar ideas, the distance between
the two increased as it became clear that the Politburo was not capable
of political negotiations while clinging onto power. While the
factionalism of the group might have contributed to the prevention
of the Chinese solution, the mistrust of the civil movement in an inner-
party reform ultimately opened the space for more forceful institutions
outside its own population to influence political events. The civil
movement had nothing inside the GDR to hold on to when the masses
turned toward the West.

The question of the leading role of the party was certainly a
decisive ideological turning point. On the one hand, the superiority
of the party was implicitly put into question by Klein's notion of
capitalism being peaceful, which he put forward since the early
1980s. For once the Old Communists' logic of class conflict is given
up, the dominant strategy of legitimizing the state falls apart. On the
other hand, we have seen that neither Klein nor the project members
were willing to fully give up this leading role, afraid of the vacuum of
power this would open up. A population that had been politically
patronized over decades was not capable of political agency from one
day to the next. "It was not unreasonable to think that if socialism in
Germany were begin to slide, then it would possibly disappear and we
would have a capitalist system everywhere in Germany. That is what
happened after all. My interest was to keep socialism stable so that it
could change" (Klein interview 2021). The door to a "third way"
thus never really opened up.

As I argued in Part III, the will to reform was a structural element of
the stability of the GDR. Also, Klein remained true to this reformist
hope until the very end of the state. The two basic sentiments of his

early career – the gratitude toward the Old Communists and the faith in the superiority of socialism – never lost their hold on him. The role of Klein during perestroika is thus an example, rather than an exception, of the ethos of East German economists and intellectuals in general, between the stability and renewal of the party regime, that is, between loyalty and pragmatism. He thus reveals a fundamental pattern of his generation caught by the back and forth between attachment and detachment of the party, echoing a childlike and symbiotic relationship with Old Communists.

Conclusion
Retiring with the State

In the wake of the fall of Honecker's regime, not only the party, but also most other institutions that had been subject to the party, were now free to reform themselves. And so was the entire economics profession. The common expectation among East German economists, in spring 1990, was a reform from within of their profession as of their state (*Selbstreform*), rather than their end.

In the first faculty meetings at Humboldt University, in January 1990, there was agreement that the local strength, compared to West German departments, lay in the faculty's diversity, which should remain the focus in future. Despite its specialization in public finance, the faculty hosted business administration, demography, ecological economics, economic history, computer science, and economic pedagogy. The new profile of the faculty also put emphasis on the location of Berlin as an intermediary between East and West. They wanted to meet the "tasks of Berlin as a central European hub for economic integration in the European community." (Schmerbach and Günter 2010: 402) Free elections took place, and Johannes Gurtz was replaced as dean by Klaus Kolloch.

Also at the Higher School of Economics, the fall of the old Politburo was seen as a chance of renewal.[1] Some wished to provide input into the debates about economic reform at the New Forum, something that the CC Academy for Social Sciences, for example, refused to do. In January 1990, those close to the old Politburo were voted off, most notably Christa Luft, who was replaced by Rudolf Streich as head of the school. Also in January, the institute for security protection (*Geheimnisschutz*) that had collaborated with the Stasi was closed at the school's initiative. After further personal cleansing, and the

---

[1] See "Bericht zur Entwicklung der politisch-operativen Lage an der Hochschule für Ökonomie," November 6, 1989; MfS HA XVIII 8618; cited in Alisch (2010: 74).

application of early retirement rules, in spring 1990, 120 of around
180 professors had left, a number that showed the closeness of the
school to the old party regime. In this process, those who had been
oppressed professionally in the preceding years were in part promoted
through a committee of "rehabilitation." However for some, these
changes were not radical enough. In summer 1990, some complained
that former "Stasi employees, Stalinist leaders, and party officials"
kept on working in disguise, preventing "democratically minded and
technically competent" colleagues from taking over.[2]

At the Academy of Sciences, there were efforts for self-reform at a
round table that met for the first time as late as February 1990.[3] As
they knew of the Western model of provincial rather than national
academies, they emphasized the national unity of the Academy of
Sciences. The easiest part was to cancel reference to the party in the
statutes, even if some natural scientists, notably the biochemist Samuel
Mitja Rapoport, were against this. The party organizations, as everywhere, were abandoned. Elections took place in May, and Horst
Klinkmann replaced Werner Scheler as president. But apart from these
formal procedures, there was little that had been done. Would it be
enough to remove references to the party, and go on with science
as usual?

Dieter Klein also prepared academically for new times. As a platform for the continuation of the research on modern socialism, and still
in his function as a vice-rector, in February 1990 he founded the
Institute for Interdisciplinary Civilization Research, which hosted all
sorts of social and natural scientists.[4] Klein knew of the difficult
conditions for the continued existence of the institute. The media and
newspapers were quick to taghim as one of those who belonged to the
old regime. In public perception there was little space between
"oppressive regime" and "liberated people."[5] He thus tried to create
a politically sustainable profile for the institute by inviting prominent

---

[2] Cited in Alisch (2010: 163).
[3] The long end of the Academy of Sciences is analyzed in detail by Mayntz (1994).
[4] See the conception of the institute in *SED-Reformdiskurs*, TB Klein, 4.
[5] This became obvious to him when, in February 1990, he was to give a talk still as
vice-rector prior to the first university elections in the Senate Hall of the
University at a conference called *Quo vadis Germania?* "It was very debated if
people like me were allowed to appear at all – there were efforts to prevent this"
(interview in *SED-Reformdiskurs*, TB Klein, 1, and his talk in 4).

speakers such as Jürgen Habermas and Cornelius Castoriadis, "partly to expose us to their criticism, partly to gain their support."[6] Their research program developed the idea of a "double transformation" of the West and the East, in contrast to grafting the Western onto the Eastern model of society. The modernization of socialist societies would be an occasion, he argued, for a modernization of capitalism – combining, as it were, the historical lessons of the political economy of capitalism and socialism in a post-socialist era.[7] Most of the former members of the project on modern socialism, such as Brie, Segert, Ettl, and Jünger, took part. Under the new historical conditions, however, they understood that their political self-identity was less coherent than before, when they shared a common point of critique: the old regime of Honecker and then Krenz. Rosemarie Will tended toward social democracy, Rainer Land had already found his own Independent Socialist Party, critiquing Modrow as just another Krenz, and Brie left the board of the party once his proposal of self-dissolution of the party was rejected. Segert, in contrast, was simply exhausted by politics.[8]

In this process of self-reform, there were also those who always followed the swings of the party, and now equally showed themselves to be very adaptive to the new conditions. One of them was Erwin Rohde. Still head of the area of international finance until June 1990, he believed that he could contribute to the framing of the new regime, considering his "privileged" knowledge of the West German market. In March 1990, he wrote on the question of ownership of public firms.[9] Anticipating that Western firms might take over many of the assets of East German firms, he argued that publically owned firms could be transformed into stock holdings, which would be distributed among the citizens as well as the workers. Each citizen would become owner of an investment certificate, thus sharing one out of sixteen million shares of the economic capital. Small firms could be bought by GDR citizens rather than sold to West German firms. Their sales revenues should be distributed equally among GDR citizens, which in

---

[6] Ibid.
[7] This could be seen as one of the origins of what was later called transformation studies, where several former economists found themselves after the fall of the socialist block. For a recent handbook on transformation studies, see Merkel, Kollmorgen, and Hans-Jürgen (2019).
[8] See interviews in *SED-Reformdiskurs*, TB Land, TB Will, TB Brie, TB Segert.
[9] See his manuscript "Volkseigentum in der DDR," in NR 46.

turn could be used for a "reconstruction fund" for infrastructure projects.

Rohde also took an active position in the debate about the currency reform in spring 1990. In a number of talk, he vigorously argued for an exchange rate of 1:1 for the East German and West German mark.[10] He took this position in light of the demand shock for Western products that resulted in a black market exchange rate of 1:20. In spite of the enormous debt of the GDR, such an exchange rate would not cause inflation, he argued. Only a selected number of industries that produced goods in high demand in East Germany (cars, tourism, and electronics) would be affected by monetary integration, while the rest of the economy could go on as usual. He argued for a quick depreciation of the liabilities of East German firms, which could lead to a quick economic boom. He submitted his position to the newspaper *Handelsblatt* in the form of a fictitious interview with the editor pretending that the newspaper had contacted him as an expert. He tried to convince the editor of the importance of his idea: "My suggestions could be *the* solution and the *Handelsblatt* brought them up first" (NR 48, 1). Rohde wished to partake in the public discussion as an expert, but his voice was hardly heard. The article was not published.

The end of the GDR came in a matter of months. At the central round table, the focus was on the illegality and violence exerted by the party regime that was strongly associated with the dismantling of the Ministry for State Security. On January 15, the main Stasi building in Berlin was occupied, which was one of the great reliefs and successes of the civil movement. While people requested access to their personal documents, the ministry managed to destroy several files, notably those of the HV A. It thus changed the history that would and will be written about the GDR. This applies, as we have seen, also to documents that could have been crucial for the preceding narrative. Possibly, we could have learned more about Erwin Rohde, Harry Maier, Dieter Klein, Ernst Strnad, and Arne Benary, and many others mentioned in this book.

In order to quickly fill the absence of power in the society, in January, Modrow agreed with the central round table on early elections in March instead of May. In response to a wave of massive withdrawals from the party, the SED-PDS acknowledged the need for a clearer cut with the past, and changed the name to PDS only. It was

[10] See NR 30, NR 48.

also then that public opinion about the future of the GDR changed rapidly, which was shocking to everyone who still believed in its future. Between mid-November and mid-February the belief in a reform of socialism sank from 86 percent to 56 percent, and support for reunification increased from 48 percent to 79 percent, according to opinion polls of the time (Sabrow 2010: 11). Though the voice of the people was not unified, there was less and less that could convince the population that the anarchic situation could be stabilized by its own institutions or forces – be it the round table, the People's Chamber that was not yet voted for, or the old party that was in an existential crisis. The class consciousness of the so-called party base dwindled away in a matter of weeks.

In this vacuum of power, the doors were open for international will to act upon the GDR. When Modrow came back from a visit to Gorbachev at the end of January, he changed course toward reunification, and accepted members of the round table into his transitional government. In February, at a conference in Ottawa, the first agreements were made for the so-called 2+4 negotiations between East and West Germany, on the one hand, and the United States, France, Great Britain, and the Soviet Union on the other. On March 18, the political direction was made offical through elections. With a turnout of 93 percent, 40 percent voted for the conservative party of Chancellor Helmut Kohl, 22 percent for the SPD, and 16 percent for the PDS. The "third way" of the PDS was indefinite and vague in terms of content, and considered an "embarrassing utopianism" with respect to the new stability that the West German conservative party promised (Sabrow 2010: 12). In the city of Berlin, however, the PDS received 30 percent while the CDU received only 18 percent of the votes. Once the conservative Lothar de Maizière was in charge of negotiating internationally the future of East Germany, it was only a question of time before the four superpowers would agree on reunification.

The central round table was active until the local elections early May. In just a few months, they not only dissolved the Stasi but also proposed a new constitution. Some of the ideas of the theory of modern socialism entered into this draft, notably through the presence of Rosemarie Will, who was the only former SED reformer accepted by the civil groups. On April 4, the draft constitution for the GDR was presented to the newly elected People's Chamber, but it was never discussed, be it in the form of a new GDR constitution or a new all-German constitution. The new conservative government, aligned to the politics of Chancellor Helmut Kohl, was ready to sign the unification treaty without any constitutional consequences for West Germany. The monetary union was decided by May 1990, in July Gorbachev agreed with the conservative's intention, and in August the reunification agreement was signed, coming into effect in September 1990. The hopes and enthusiasm that informed the attempts at self-reform were squashed.

Once the unification treaty came into effect, the new legislation would dismantle those institutions that were considered "close" to the party state – the profession of economics being one of them.

The Dismantling of East German Economics

The unification treaty defined the criteria for the extraordinary contract termination that was applied until October 1992 to all academics. Those who held public elective offices or special tasks in the party, and those detectably active as Stasi informants, were no longer employed. After the self-reforms had already made many leave, these terminations applied to 10 percent of the staff at Humboldt University, with the number of economists dismissed being below this average.[11] As most left without being forced, only some tried to get by. Rudolf Mondelaers, for example, made it into the restructuring commission for the new faculty before being identified as an informant of the Stasi.

Aside from individuals, more problematic was the question of what to do with entire institutions and disciplines that were considered to be too close to the party regime. The treaty demanded a so-called winding up (*Abwicklung*) – that is, they were to be closed with an incremental plan for replacing them, if necessary. For those that were not to be replaced, the change was radical but came relatively quickly. The Higher School of Economics, for example, was wound up without replacement. An evaluation committee set up by the Berlin Senate had proposed this in December 1990 since it was not considered to fit into the science system of the united Germany:

The Higher School of Economics was an expression of the centralism that had prevailed in the former GDR and its layout and size does not fit into

[11] See Ash (1999: 336), and Jarausch (2012).

Berlin's scientific landscape. It does not correspond to the federal structures that are now to be built up in the part of the Federal Republic that has joined. (Cited in Alisch 2010: 80)

Despite protests from the new rector, who compared the process unhappily with the National Socialist book burning, the Higher School of Economics was dissolved in October 1991. The staff were laid off collectively without individual evaluation, the remaining students were sent to other universities, and the building was used as an external campus of the Applied University for Technology and Economy (*Fachhochschule für Technik und Wirtschaft*). The former academic staff founded, in fall 1991, the "Karlshorst employment and qualification company" that was to organize qualifications measures to find jobs in the new Berlin. The higher the former qualification, the more difficult it was to find a job.[12]

The Academy of Sciences suffered a similar fate.[13] In June 1990, its legal status was suspended and it became a corporation under public law. That is, the elected positions were handed over to public servants. Once the West German mark was introduced, most of the contracted research with Eastern industry broke down. In July, the sixty institutes were evaluated one by one. Six out of fifty-five institutes were closed down, economics being one of them. The remaining large majority were newly founded as part of, or integrated into already existing, Western research institutes such as the Helmholtz Society of German Research Centers, the Fraunhofer Society, and the Max Planck Society. In addition, the Berlin Senate decided that the Academy of Sciences did *not* represent the tradition of Berlin's former Academy of Sciences. Thus, in 1992, the academy was formally dissolved. In accordance with the West German model of provincially based Academies of Sciences, the so-called Berlin-Brandenburg Academy of Sciences was founded (*Berlin-Brandenburgische Akademie der Wissenschaften*). More than a hundred former academy members, instead, felt that this new institution did not represent their tradition and founded the so-called Leibniz Society, a registered association without academic recognition. Observing the dismantling of his former institutions of the Academy of Sciences, as if still personally attacked, Harry Maier

---

[12] See Alisch (2010: 78–82).
[13] For the *Abwicklung* of the Academy of Sciences see in detail Mayntz (1994).

protested strongly. He wrote ardent articles in *Die Zeit* bemoaning the sellout of the Academy of Sciences.[14]

It was only in the case of the economics faculty at Humboldt University that the winding up was followed by a rebuilding of the institution rather than the closing of it. This is still remembered as a traumatic event. The Berlin Senate drew a precise line between ideology and science at the divisions between disciplines. Philosophy, history, education, law, and economics counted as faculties that were constitutive for the regime and thus had to be replaced, while all other disciplines received a free pass into the Western regime; recall that Marxism-Leninism was the foundation of all sciences in East Germany.[15] In the faculty of economics, in January 1991, all previously tenured contracts were converted into temporary contracts. This gave way to the possibility of applying for one's own post in competition with others. *De jure*, this showed a willingness to exploit the given potential, but *de facto*, this decision was equivalent to a layoff, because the requirements made it impossible for most professors to win back their positions. Evidently, publishing in a Western journal for East German economists was by no means encouraged, to say the least. Deterred, many left voluntarily, and took advantage of early retirement. The age limit was continuously reduced, which gave the entire hope generation the opportunity to retire.[16]

Erwin Rohde retired in this period, too. As an expert on Western finance, he thought until late on that he would play a role in the transition into the new regime of economics (NR 22, 21). He offered a class that aimed to prepare students for jobs in Western finance and that resembled his previous class without the political undertones. But this did not happen. In May 1991, the rector of the university, Heinrich Fink, informed him that an inquiry had been made regarding whether

---

[14] *Die Zeit*, 1991, 24 ("Gnadenlose Dampfwalze: Plädoyer für einen schonenderen Umbau der ehemaligen DDR-Forschung"), 1992, 44 ("Verunsichert, lahmgelegt, abgewickelt").

[15] Drawing this line was, according to Ash, one of the "hasty policy decisions" after the *Wende* (1999). It was not only a matter of trusting the higher virtues of real science but also a political matter. According to Fink, the president of the university, the institute for cultural science was spared being wound up because Kurt Hager had sought to close it down years before (*Die Zeit*, February 1, 1991).

[16] In 1990, two out of three of the professors of the entire Humboldt University were more than fifty years old, and thus had little incentive to adapt professionally to the new regime (Middell 2012: 383). More than half of all the professors who left the university between 1990 and 1994 – 215 of 417 – were cases of retirement (Jarausch 2012: 647).

Rohde was active for the Stasi, in which case he would not be allowed to be employed further.[17] Considering his role as a vice-rector, in charge of military finance, and then international finance, the anticipated result of such investigation might have made Rohde push for early retirement. He doubted the legality of the investigation since, as he argued, he did not reapply for his own job in public service. "I wish to be retired at the earliest possible occasion and have no intention to hold on my employment relationship," he wrote in response tó Fink on June 19, 1991. Before official retirement, he was on a sick leave because of high blood pressure.[18] Having quarrels about payrolls that he believed were unsettled, since July 1992, he received a disability pension, and then in September 1992, aged sixty-five, he officially retired.

Klein's Institute for Interdisciplinary Civilization Research was not considered suitable for the knowledge landscape of Germany's new capital. Already before reunification, an honorary commission at the university that evaluated further employability despite party functions or Stasi collaboration declared that Michael Brie, who did not hide his activities as a Stasi informant, was not suitable for further employment.[19] This did not help the further existence of the institute, and in June 1991, it was wound up because, as it was argued, it did not have the disciplinary structure of a (West German) political science institute. The chance of a "double transformation" that Klein and the other institute members envisioned for West Germany, Europe, and the entire globe was not seized upon. The system change in the East was a missed opportunity for the West to face its incapacity to solve an ever-increasing global crisis, he argued. The West remained in its old pattern.[20]

According to the reunification laws, Klein, as a former vice-rector and district secretary of the SED, should have left the university. However, Friedhelm Neidhardt, a liberal social democrat, head of

---

[17] See NR 13, "Einholung von Auskünften über eine eventuelle Tätigkeit von Mitarbeitern der Humboldt-Universität zu Berlin für den Staatssicherheitsdienst," 1991.

[18] See the letter in NR 21, and also NR 10 for more details on the payment quarrels.

[19] See the defense of Brie by Norbert Kostede, "Doktor Brie wird abgewickelt," *Die Zeit*, 28, July 5, 1991.

[20] See Brie and Klein (1993). For the global views of modern society after the fall of socialism, and the personal experiences regarding the wounding up of the institute, see the last publication of the Institute by Brie and Klein (1992).

the Berlin Social Science Research Center (*Wissenschaftszentrum Berlin für Sozialforschung*), and chairman of the restructuring commission at the department for social sciences, was well disposed toward Klein. After several positive reference letters from all around the globe, as well as from Egon Bahr in Hamburg, Klein received a so-called excess professorship between 1992 and 1996 for the "economic foundations of politics" at the department for social sciences. Due to a lack of personnel in this transition period, he had to carry out all sorts of administrative jobs as the head of the doctoral committee, the examination committee, and the undergraduate committee. Having contributed to the development of the new curriculum, when the new Western professors were appointed, it was accepted that he would stay. As late as 1997, he retired and continued teaching for another two years until 1999.[21] During these ten years after the fall of the wall, Dieter Klein published an astonishing number of articles and books. It was one of his most prolific periods. He described this period as the "liberating effect of a defeat," appreciating previously unknown liberty as a writer, as a person, and also as a voter.[22] However, at the same time, his previous views of capitalism were confirmed.

For the younger generation at Humboldt University, the reunification meant a harsh and humiliating end to their careers. Those who tried to survive in the new economics profession witnessed the most radical cleansing in the history of the faculty, more radical than in 1933 and 1945.[23] During the shortest period of time, Western research standards and teaching practices were enforced without considering the local potential of the previous regime. Hardly anyone from the previous regime was believed to fit into Western economics as they did not meet the new imperative of being "internationally competitive." For the younger generation in their mid-forties, the reform meant a

[21] His retirement speech is published in Klein (1997).
[22] See Brie and Klein (1993). For the list of his publications during the 1990s, see Klein (2009).
[23] Considering all disciplines, Ash states that "the number of politically caused dismissals between 1989 and 1994 in the universities alone was more than twice as high as the numbers of dismissals after 1933 and 1945 taken together" (1999: 335). There are several historical accounts of this reform, such as Rudder (1997) for the entire GDR, and Jarausch (2012) for Humboldt University. There are several first-person perspectives on the reform, most of which are critical; for the economics faculty see Kolloch (2001a); for a collection of essays of those having lost their elite status from one day to the other, see Bollinger and Heyden (2002).

radical rupture in their careers, falling from an elite status to being suspected of being politically inept. Some indeed sat in the lectures of West German visiting professors, to learn about shifting demand and supply curves, in preparation for competing some months later with economists who had received their PhDs in Bonn or Boston. They should have been given years to prove themselves, not a few months, according to one of the junior economic historians of the time (Frank Zschaler, personal communication).

The air became rarefied in the spring of 1991, when it became clear who would run the restructuring commission, and decide who would reobtain their jobs: Wilhelm Krelle. Krelle was a founding father of West German mathematical economics at the University of Bonn, and had brought up an entire generation of economists that held dominant positions in West German faculties.[24] Krelle, who was clearly against Marxism and a conservative in political terms, was one of those economists for whom method counted more than content, which contrasted starkly with the methodological eclecticism and pragmatic imperative prevailing in East Germany. He is quoted as saying that "no Marxist will put his foot over the threshold of this house as long as I am in charge."[25] Any other economist would have been more sensitive to the potential in Berlin. There were indeed several professors in the West who saw in the restructuring of East German universities a reform opportunity for the West German university system, but Krelle did not belong to that group. One spoke of a "clear-cutting" (*Kahlschlag*), a "human drama." "All attempts to rescue some of the ideas of the older education system that were worth keeping were futile," one of the members reported (Kolloch 2001a: 298).

In the midst of this process, Humboldt University as the only East German university sued the city Senate against the law of the wounding up (*Abwicklung*). In March 1992, the Higher Administrative Court indeed declared it illegal. The law required a closing down of the

---

[24] For Krelle's intellectual biography, see Düppe (2019).
[25] See *Der Freitag*, April 20, 2007. On June 26, 1996, Krelle wrote a justificatory note to the members of the commission: "[The commission] has never asked a candidate about his political beliefs or his party membership . . . However, it has refused to create a special chair for Marxism/Leninism . . . The severity that this change has brought for many former members of the Humboldt University was inevitable considering the fact that half of the posts were cut and former members of the faculty lacked professional qualifications" (Sibylle Schmerbach, personal correspondence).

institution followed by a reopening, in contrast to the practiced restructuring of one and the same institution. The problem of whether epistemic regimes could be reducible to one another, therefore, was also negotiated on a legal level. The restructuring commission was nonetheless allowed to continue working, now under a different title. As a consequence, all of the staff, if they had not already left the section, were reemployed. By then, however, it was already too late for many. In 1993, of all the former scientific staff only the economic historian Lothar Baar and two junior positions were still employed at the faculty.[26] The new faculty profile was supposed to be "quantitative" – that is, econometric – in contrast to the faculty at the Free University. Once Krelle left, his equally famous colleague from Bonn, Werner Hildenbrand, came as a visiting professor for a semester and, with the help of Wolfgang Härdle, attracted funds from the German Science Foundation, a so-called *Sonderforschungsbereich* – "Quantification and Simulation of Economic Processes." After the new faculty was built up, in 1994, Krelle was granted an honorary doctorate.

In 1996, this decision was revised once Krelle's past during National Socialism became public. Krelle suspected a smear campaign by former professors, though the hunt might have been launched by a former student of the faculty who asked a private detective to investigate, who in turn found a left-wing journalist, Andreas Förster, from the *Berliner Zeitung* to report about it.[27] Krelle had been a major in the German army (*Wehrmacht*) and served under Rommel in Africa. In August 1944, he was removed to the SS division Götz von Berlichingen, which had committed serious war crimes. The Senate appointed a committee and concluded: "SS-fighter yes, SS-member no. Posting to the Armed-SS yes, but not voluntarily. SS-major (*Sturmbannführer*) yes, but only on paper."[28] The humiliation was deep. If the denazification in West Germany had been carried out as strictly as in the East – which was a

---

[26] The case of Lothar Baar indeed shows that the reform could have taken place differently. After the fall of the wall, Baar did not shiver for fear of losing his job putting himself in the weaker position. Instead, he contacted Wolfram Fischer at the Free University to hold a joint colloquium that would turn out to be fruitful for all participants (Fischer and Zschaler 1998). Economic history, a subfield that was slightly less method-driven, stood for the possible cooperation between East and West.

[27] See *Berliner Zeitung*, February 6, 1996, "Wilhelm Krelle: 'Ich war nie SS-Mitglied' Schwere Vorwürfe gegen einen Professor."

[28] See *Berliner Zeitung*, May 13, 2004; for more details see Düppe (2019).

point of national pride for East Germans – Krelle could not have had an academic career at all. Combined with the personal disappointments of those who lost their jobs and social status from one day to another, Krelle's unearthed past cast a bad light on the reform at Humboldt University.

While for the young, reunification often meant a fall from the status of social elite to that of social welfare, the entire hope generation could retire jointly with their state. Without existential rupture, their retirement age often shows a remarkable continuity with their previous professional life. One of Rohde's colleagues, Johannes Gurtz, the last dean of the economics faculty, sought new professional opportunities in the unified Germany. Convinced that the practical skills the economics faculty represented were not limited to the system of the GDR, Gurtz launched his own private school outside the new academic regime, a teaching institution for local administrators called the Local Educational Institute (*Kommunales Bildungswerk*). With the knowledge of the old system, this was an advanced learning institute for channeling the old provincial administration into the new system. The same people who had previously been taught at the faculty would now be taught at the institute. Rohde and several other former professors of finance would occasionally give classes at this school. They helped each other out.

For Klein as a political economist of capitalism, there was a great deal of continuity between his professional career in East Germany and his retirement age in West Germany. Remaining true to the new party of which he shaped the foundations, the PDS, he took over official tasks. In 1997 and 1998, he was a member of the PDS Board of Executives, and in 1998 a member of the Commission of Principles of the PDS (*Grundsatzkommission*). He thus remained an important figure in the recreation of the party in a bourgeois parliamentary context. His ideas were still nourished by those developed in the project on modern socialism.[29] Later on, he became active in the *Rosa Luxemburg Stiftung*, the think tank of the PDS, later renamed *Die Linke*. Until 2008, he was the chair of the Future Commission of

[29] About the impact on the project of modern socialism on the later party, see Sturm (2000). In her interpretation, the question if or not Stalinism (as a system) was truly left behind – which was *the* ongoing question during the entire GDR period, continued haunting the party when trying to prove its political aptitude in the new German context.

the Foundation. Klein's intellectual career thus shows an astonishing, and for him happy, continuity as he never stopped analyzing the current state of capitalism from the socialist point of view. "I was back home again, as it were. Because this was the party [the PDS then *Die Linke*] which followed my ideal as it did before, and rejected the society which I always believed and still believe does not solve the great problems of humanity" (Klein interview 2021). Though he had been always skeptical of the discursive game of bourgeois parliamentarism, he accepted that he had to play it to some extent. In hindsight he would say that he was never against parliamentarism per se, but against parliamentarism as an element of capitalist power relations:

As a political form of capitalism, bourgeois democracy belonged to capitalism securing both its power and it positive development ... I have neither approved nor rejected bourgeois democracy. Democracy is good, but it is currently the form of the rule of power of the elite. Still, it must be defended as one step in the overall development. (Klein interview 2021)

Instead of reforming socialism, his goal is now, in contrast to a revolution, a long process of transformation. The victory of socialism will be the result of a profound *evolutionary* change rather than a series of national revolutions. This is clearly no longer the Marx of the Old Communists, but it is still the same tireless reform spirit that was critical for the stability of the GDR. On his 70th birthday, in 2001, Michal Brie wrote in *Neues Deutschland*, a newspaper that still exists today: "Neither Dieter Klein nor others were able to reform the socialism of the GDR in a way that render it viable, but he did help to keep the idea of a liberal and egalitarian socialism alive."[30] After the reform is before the reform.

* * *

The hopes of building up a socialist state failed. Hardly anyone from this generation, however, fell into melancholia. Some were interested in engaging with the new state, others lived out their retirement in quietude, but hardly anyone changed his or her mind. The two basic sentiments of their early careers, their gratitude toward the liberators, and the faith that socialism is the superior answer to the failure of

---

[30] "Dieter Klein zum 70. Geburtstag," *Neues Deutschland*, October 26, 2001.

Nazism, never left them. When speaking to those that are still alive, they show pride in their past, but are also willing to admit errors – both deeply ingrained in their generational being. They are ready to admit that they could have done better, and regret that they did not put the party regime into question earlier when there still was the chance to reform socialism from within.

We all know that it was highly problematic that one's own thinking would so easily be stamped as tribal factionalism and accused of deviation. Whenever we wanted to put forth decent ideas we faced collisions that were totally unnecessary. This sprang from the basic structure of a system with a ruling party. (Klein 2009)

The careers of the protagonists in this book began in gratitude, a feeling that transformed into loyalty, careerism, reform will, duty, and an unbroken hope for a truly democratic socialism to come. What prevails at the end of their careers, in contrast to the humiliation that the younger generation experienced, was again a feeling of gratitude. They show satisfaction with their careers, grateful for the historical chance they had. As Kolloch, the first elected dean at Humboldt University, said: "I am grateful that my professional activities under socialist relations of production could contribute to comradely cooperation and mutual assistance" (Kolloch 2009).

Since the new social reality in which the East German population found itself resembled what has been taught about capitalism, many aged with the confidence that one day socialism will prevail. Their socialist beliefs were not shaken but reinforced by the development they witnessed in East Germany, Europe, and the entire globe. As Klein commented, what remained was the "unbroken faith in the possibility of socialism in its original sense. I always had the hope that the GDR would be able to redeem a lot of it; but the GDR itself was not the object of my hope" (Klein interview 2021). When speaking to business leaders today, Klein is encouraged that they are becoming more sensitive and critical to environmental and social issues. But when speaking of actual social change, his point of view is considered naïve, a role that Klein knows well from his life in the GDR. Yet he knows better. Though little changed for a long time in his and his generation's lives, they learned twice, in 1945 and in 1989, that everything can change from one day to the next.

Appendix

Overview of Important Institutions Mentioned in Text

Foundation	Name	Renamed
1946	Party Academy Karl Marx (*Parteihochschule Karl Marx*)	
1946	Faculty of Economics Berlin University (*Wirtschaftswissenschaftliche Fakultät*)	1969: Section of Economics Humboldt University (*Sektion Wirtschaftswissenschaften Humboldt-Universität zu Berlin*)
1949	Marx-Engels-Lenin-Institute (*Marx-Engels-Lenin-Institut*)	1953: Marx-Engels-Lenin-Stalin-Institute; 1956: CC Institute for Marxism-Leninism
1950	Higher School for the Planned Economy (*Hochschule für Planökonomie*)	1956: Higher School for Economics (*Hochschule für Ökonomie*); 1972: Higher School for Economics Bruno Leuschner (*Hochschule für Ökonomie Bruno Leuschner*)
1951	CC Institute for Social Sciences (*Institut für Gesellschaftswissenschaften beim ZK der SED*)	1976: CC Academy for Social Sciences (*Akademie für Gesellschaftswissenschaften beim ZK der SED*)
1954	Central Institute for Economics at the Academy of Sciences of the GDR (*Zentralinstitut für Wirtschaftswissenschaften*)	
1965	CC Central Institute for Socialist Economic Governance (*Zentralinstitut für sozialistische Wirtschaftsführung beim ZK der SED*)	
1969–1973	Academy of Marxist-Leninist Organization Sciences (*Akademie der marxistisch-leninistischen Organisationswissenschaft*)	
1971	Institute for International Politics and Economy (*Institut für Internationale Politik und Wirtschaft*)	

References

Alisch, Steffen. 2010. "Die Hochschule für Ökonomie Berlin-Karlshorst (HfÖ): Eine wirtschaftswissenschaftliche Kaderschmieder der SED," *Arbeitspapiere des Forschungsverbundes SED-Staat*, 44. Freie Universität Berlin: Forschungsverbund SED-Staat.

Ash, Mitchell G. 1999. "Scientific Changes in Germany 1933, 1945, 1990: Towards a Comparison," *Minerva* 37: 329–354.

Autorenkollektiv. 1969. *Politische Ökonomie des Sozialismus und ihre Anwendung in der DDR*. Berlin: Dietz Verlag.

1997 (1955). *Lehrbuch der Politischen Ökonomie*. Offenbach: Olga Benario und Herbert Baum.

Alexeyeva, Ljudmila M., Paul Goldberg. 1993. *The Thaw Generation: Coming of Age in the Post-Stalin Era*. Pittsburgh: University of Pittsburgh Press.

Bahro, Rudolph. 1978. *The Alternative in Eastern Europe*. London: New Left Books.

Becker, Susanne, Heiko Dierking. 1989. *Die Herausbildung der Wirtschaftswissenschaften in der Frühphase der DDR*. Köln: Wissenschaft und Politik.

Beckert, Rudi. 1995. *Die erste und letzte Instanz: Schau- und Geheimprozesse vor dem Obersten Gericht der DDR*. Goldbach: Keip Verlag.

Behrens, Friedrich. 1948. *Alte und neue Probleme der politischen Ökonomie: Eine theoretische und statistische Studie über die produktive Arbeit im Kapitalismus*. Berlin: Dietz Verlag.

1957. "Zum Problem der Ausnutzung ökonomischer Gesetze in der Übergangsperiode," *Wirtschaftswissenschaft* 3 (Sonderheft): 105–140.

1958. "Die Planung und Leitung der Volkswirtschaft: eine Stellungnahme," *Wirtschaftswissenschaft* 1: 31–38.

1960. "Erklärung des Genossen Prof. Dr. Fritz Behrens," *Neuer Weg* 15 (9): 650–651.

1961. *Ware, Wert und Wertgesetz: Kritische und selbstkritische Betrachtungen zur Werttheorie im Sozialismus*. Berlin: Akademie-Verlag.

1968. "Kritik der politischen Ökonomie und ökonomische Theorie des Sozialismus," in Walter Euchner, Alfred Schmidt (eds.), *Kritik der politischen Ökonomie heute: 100 Jahre 'Kapital'*. Frankfurt a.M.: Europäische Verlagsanstalt, 288–299.

1992. *Abschied von der sozialen Utopie*. Berlin: Akademie-Verlag.

Behrens, Friedrich, Arne Benary. 1956. *Zur ökonomischen Theorie und ökonomischen Politik der Übergangsperiode*. Unpublished manuscript, private archive Gisela Eckstein.

Benary, Arne. 1957. "Zu Grundproblemen der politischen Ökonomie des Sozialismus in der Übergangsperiode," *Wirtschaftswissenschaft* 3 (Sonderheft): 62–94.

1960. "Erklärung des Genossen Arne Benary," *Neuer Weg 9*: 651–652.

Berger, Wolfgang. 1949. "Marx als Kritiker der modernen Betriebswirtschaftslehre," *Deutsche Finanzwirtschaft* 3 (10): 250–253.

Berger, Wolfgang, Otto Reinhold. 1966. *Zu den wissenschaftlichen Grundlagen des neuen ökonomischen Systems der Planung und Leitung*. Berlin: Dietz Verlag.

Bergien, Rüdiger. 2012. "Activating the 'Apparatchik': Brigade Deployment in the SED Central Committee and Performative Communist Party Rule," *Journal of Contemporary History* 47 (4): 793–811.

Berthold, Rudi et al. (eds.). 1960. *Die Humboldt Universität: Gestern, heute, morgen*. Berlin: Deutscher Verlag der Wissenschaften.

Bianchini, Mario. 2020. "Soldiers of Theory: German Economists and the Cold War," *German Studies Review* 43 (1): 41–58.

Bichtler, Karl. 1986. "Zur Gründungsgeschichte und Entwicklung des Zentralinstitutes für Wirtschaftswissenschaften an der Akademie für Wissenschaften der DDR," *Jahrbuch für politische Ökonomie*. Berlin: Akademie Verlag, 158–178.

Bichtler, Karl, Harry Maier. 1967. "Die Messung des Arbeitsaufwandes als politökonomisches Problem," *Probleme der politischen Ökonomie: Jahrbuch des Instituts für Wirtschaftswissenschaften bei der Deutschen Akademie der Wissenschaften zu Berlin* 10: 77–146.

Bichtler, Karl, Kurt Zieschang. 1958. "Revisionistische Konzeption oder einzelner Fehler?" *Wirtschaftswissenschaft* 1: 39–50.

Bleek, Wilhelm, Lothar Mertens. 1994. *DDR-Dissertationen: Promotionspraxis und Geheimhaltung von Doktorarbeiten im SED-Staat*. Wiesbaden: VS Verlag für Sozialwissenschaften.

Blum, Alain, Martine Mespoulet. 2003. *L'Anarchie bureaucratique: Statistique et pouvoir sous Staline*. Paris: La Découverte.

Bockman, Johanna. 2011. *Markets in the Name of Socialism: The Left-Wing Origins of Neoliberalism*. Stanford, CA: Stanford University Press.

References

Böhme, Hans-Joachim. 1986. *Studienplan für die Fachrichtung Finanzwirtschaft.* Zwickau: Ministerium für Hoch- und Fachschulwesen.

Bollinger, Stefan, Ulrich von der Heyden (eds.). 2002. *Deutsche Einheit und Elitenwechsel in Ostdeutschland.* Berlin: Trafo.

Borchert, Konstanze, Volker Steinke, Carola Wuttke (eds.). 1994. *Für unser Land: Eine Aufrufaktion im letzten Jahr der DDR.* Frankfurt a.M.: Iko-Verlag.

Bösch, Frank, Andreas Wirsching (eds.). 2018. *Hüter der Ordnung: Die Innenministerien in Bonn und Ost-Berlin nach dem Nationalsozialismus.* Göttingen: Wallstein.

Brie, Michael et al. 1989. *Studie zur Gesellschaftsstrategie.* Berlin: Dietz Verlag.

Brie, Michael, Dieter Klein. 1993. *Der Engel der Geschichte: Befreiende Erfahrungen einer Niederlage.* Berlin: Dietz Verlag.

Brie, Michael, Dieter Klein (eds.). 1992. *Zwischen den Zeiten: Ein Jahrhundert verabschiedet sich.* Hamburg: VSA Verlag.

Brockmann, Stephen. 2019. "Anna Seghers, Wolfgang Harich, and the Events of 1956," in Helen Fehervary et al. (eds.), *Anna Seghers: The Challenge of History.* Amsterdam: Brill, 197–222.

Buddrus, Michael. 1995. "A Generation Twice Betrayed: Youth Policy in the Transition from the Third Reich to the Soviet Zone of Occupation (1945–1946)," in Mark Roseman (ed.), *Generations in Conflict: Youth Revolt and Generation Formation in Germany 1770–1968.* Cambridge: Cambridge University Press, 247–268.

Bude, Heinz. 1987. *Deutsche Karrieren: Lebenskonstruktionen sozialer Aufsteiger aus der Flakhelfer-Generation.* Frankfurt a.M.: Suhrkamp.

Buthmann, Reinhard. 2003. "Die Arbeitsgruppe Bereich Kommerzielle Koordinierung," *MfS-Handbuch* III *(11).* Berlin: BStU.

Caldwell, Peter C. 2000. "Productivity, Value, and Plan: Fritz Behrens and the Economics of Revisionism in the German Democratic Republic," *History of Political Economy* 32 (1): 103–137.

2003. *Dictatorship, State Planning, and Social Theory in the German Democratic Republic.* Cambridge: Cambridge University Press.

Connelly, John. 1997. "Ulbricht and the Intellectuals," *Contemporary European History* 6 (3): 329–359.

2000. *Captive University: The Sovietization of East German, Czech and Polish Higher Education, 1945–1956.* Chapel Hill: University of North Carolina Press.

Croan, Melvin. 1962. "East German Revisionism: The Spectre and the Reality," in Leopold Labedz (ed.), *Revisionism: Essays on the History of Marxist Ideas.* London: George Allen and Unwin, 239–256.

Crome, Erhard, Lutz Kirschner, Rainer Land. 1998. "Der SED-Reformdiskurs der achtziger Jahre, Dokumentation und Rekonstruktion kommunikativer Netzwerke und zeitlicher Abläufe Analyse der Spezifik und der Differenzen zu anderen Reformdiskursen der SED," *Abschlußbericht zum DFG-Projekt CR 93/1-1*. Bonn: Deutsche Forschungsgemeinschaft.

Dale, Gareth. 2006. *The East German Revolution of 1989*. Manchester and New York: Manchester University Press.

Darnton, Robert. 2014. *Censors at Work: How States Shaped Literature*. New York: W. W. Norton.

Dittmann, Frank, Rudolf Seising (eds.). 2007. *Kybernetik steckt den Osten an: Aufstieg und Schwierigkeiten einer interdisziplinären Wissenschaft in der DDR*. Berlin: Trafo Verlag.

Dittmann, Frank. 2009. "Technik versus Konflikt: Wie Datennetze den Eisernen Vorhang durchdrangen," *Osteuropa* 59 (10): 101–119.

Donner, Otto. 1937. *Statistik*. Hamburg: Hanseatische Verlags Anstalt.

Douglas, Raymond M. 2012. *Orderly and Humane: The Expulsion of the Germans after the Second World War*. New Haven: Yale University Press.

Duller, Matthias. 2016. "Internationalization of Cold War Systems Analysis: RAND, IIASA and the Institutional Reasons for Methodological Change," *History of the Human Sciences* 29 (4–5): 172–190.

Düppe, Till. 2011. *The Making of the Economy: A Phenomenology of Economic Science*. Plymouth: Lexington.

2015. "Border Cases between Autonomy and Relevance: Economic Sciences in Berlin – A Natural Experiment," *Studies in the History and Philosophy of Science A* 51: 22–32.

2017. "The Generation of the GDR: Economists at the Humboldt University of Berlin Caught between Loyalty and Relevance," *History of the Human Sciences* 30 (3): 50–85.

2019. "Dealing with the Personal in the Contemporary History of Economics," in Till Düppe, E. Roy Weintraub (eds.), *A Contemporary Historiography of Economics*. New York: Routledge, 22–36.

2020. "War after War: Wilhelm Krelle, 1916–2005," *Journal of the History of Economic Thought* 42 (3): 307–334.

Düppe, Till, Harro Maas. 2017. "The Historical Epistemology of Economics: An Invitation," *Research in the History of Economic Thought and Methodology* 35 (A): 3–9.

Düppe, Till, Ivan Boldyrev (eds.). 2019. *Economic Knowledge in Socialism, 1945–1989*. Durham, NC: Duke University Press.

Düppe, Till, Sarah Joly-Simard. 2020. "Stalin's Pluralism: How Anti-dogmatism Serves Tyranny," *Research in the History and Methodology of Economics* 38 (B): 37–54.

Ehlert, Willi. 1976. *Geldzirkulation und Kredit in der sozialistischen Planwirtschaft*. Berlin: Die Wirtschaft.

Ehmann, Annegret. 2001. "Mischlinge," in Walter Laqueur, Judith Tydor Baumel (eds.), *The Holocaust Encyclopedia*. New Haven and London: Yale University Press, 422–423.

Ellman, Michael. 1973. *Planning Problems in the USSR: The Contribution of Mathematical Economics to Their Solution, 1960–1971*. Cambridge: Cambridge University Press.

Engelmann, Roger. 2011. "Politisch-ideologische Diversion," in Roger Engelmann, Bernd Florath, Walter Süß et al. (eds.), *Das MfS-Lexikon: Begriffe, Personen und Strukturen der Staatssicherheit der DDR*. Berlin: Ch. Links, 67.

Engelmann, Roger, Silke Schumann. 1995. "Der Ausbau des Überwachungsstaates. Der Konflikt Ulbricht-Wollweber und die Neuausrichtung des Staatssicherheitsdienstes der DDR 1957," *Vierteljahrsheft für Zeitgeschichte* 43 (2): 341–378.

Epstein, Catherine. 2003. *The Last Revolutionaries: German Communists and Their Century*. Cambridge, MA: Harvard University Press.

Erickson, Paul et al. 2013. *How Reason Almost Lost Its Mind: The Strange Career of Cold War Rationality*. Chicago and London: University of Chicago Press.

Fair-Schulz, Axel. 2009. *Loyal Subversion: East Germany and Its Bildbungsbürgerlich Marxist Intellectuals*. Berlin: Trafo.

Feige, Hans-Uwe. 1995. "Die SED und der 'bürgerliche Objektivismus' 1949/1950," *Deutschland Archiv* 10: 1074–1083.

Fischer, Wolfram, Frank Zschaler. 1998. "Wirtschafts- und Sozialgeschichte," in Jürgen Kocka, Renate Mayntz (eds.), *Wissenschaft und Wiedervereinigung: Disziplinen im Umbruch*. Berlin: Akademie Verlag, 361–434.

Florath, Bernd. 2004. "Das philosophische Argument als politischer Skandal: Die Herausforderung der SED durch Robert Havemann," in Martin Sabrow (ed.), *Skandal und Öffentlichkeit in der Diktatur*. Göttingen: Wallstein, 157–193.

Fulbrook, Mary. 1995. *Anatomy of a Dictatorship: Inside the GDR, 1949–1989*. Oxford: Oxford University Press.

Galbraith, John Kenneth. 1981. *A Life in Our Times*. Westminster: Ballantine Books.

Gebelein, Hans. 1943. *Zahl und Wirklichkeit: Grundzüge einer mathematischen Statistik*. Heidelberg: Quelle und Meyer.

Gerovitch, Slava. 2002. *From Newspeak to Cyberspeak: A History of Soviet Cybernetics*. Cambridge, MA: MIT Press.

2008. "InterNyet: Why the Soviet Union Did Not Build a Nationwide Computer Network," *History and Technology* 24: 335–350.

2009. "Die Beherrschung der Welt: Die Kybernetik im Kalten Krieg," *Osteuropa* 59 (10): 43–56.

Gieseke, Jens. 2000. *Die hauptamtlichen Mitarbeiter der Staatssicherheit: Personalstruktur und Lebenswelt 1950–1989/90*. Berlin: Ch. Links.

2015. *The History of the Stasi: East Germany's Secret Police, 1945–1990*. Oxford: Berghahn Books.

Granville, Johanna. 2006. "Ulbricht in October 1956: Survival of the Spitzbart during Destalinization," *Journal of Contemporary History* 41 (3): 477–502.

Grumbach, Detlef. 1989. "Es geht um handfeste Dinge: Gespräch mit Prof. Dr. Dieter Klein, Humboldt-Universität zu Berlin, über die Emanzipation von Schwulen und Lesben und die Rolle der Wissenschaft," *Dorn Rosa* (Dezember): 14–15.

Habermas, Jürgen. 1989. "Produktivkraft Kommunikation: Fragen von Hans-Peter Krüger," *Sinn und Form* 6: 1192–1206.

Hacking, Ian. 1990. *The Taming of Chance*. Cambridge: Cambridge University Press.

Hager, Kurt. 1971. "Die entwickelte sozialistische Gesellschaft: Aufgaben der Gesellschaftswissenschaften nach dem VIII Parteitag der SED," *Einheit* 26: 1203–1242.

Hahn, Erich. 2003. *Positionen zum SED/SPD-Dialogpapier von 1987: Nach-Lese in veröffentlichten und bisher unveröffentlichten Quellen*. Berlin: Gesellschaftswissenschaftliches Forum.

Hansen, Reimer. 2012. "Von der Friedrich-Wilhelms-zur Humboldt-Universität zu Berlin," in Rüdiger vom Bruch, Heinz-Elmar Tenorth (eds.), *Geschichte der Universität Unter den Linden 1810–2010, 3*. Berlin: Akademie Verlag, 17–123.

Harrison, Hope M. 2003. *Driving the Soviets up the Wall: Soviet–East German Relations, 1953–1961*. Princeton, NJ: Princeton University Press.

Haun, Horst. 1999. *Kommunist und "Revisionist": Die SED Kampagne gegen Jürgen Kuczynski (1956–1959)*. Dresden: Hannah-Arendt-Institut für Totalitarismusforschung.

Haustein, Heinz-Dieter. 1969. *Wirtschaftsprognose: Grundlagen, Elemente, Modelle*. Berlin: Die Wirtschaft.

Haustein, Heinz-Dieter, Harry Maier. 1979. "Basic Improvement and Pseudo-innovations and Their Impact on efficiency," Working Paper 79 (96). Laxenburg: IIASA.

1985. *Innovation and Efficiency: Strategies for a Turbulent World*. Oxford: Pergamon Press.

Haustein, Heinz-Dieter, Harry Maier, Jennifer Robinson. 1980. "Thinking about Appropriate Technologies: Criteria for Selecting Appropriate Technologies under Different Cultural, Technical, and Social

Conditions," in Antonio de Giorgio, Claudio Roveda (eds.), *Proceedings of the IFAC Symposium, Bari, Italy, 21–22 May 1979*. Oxford: Pergamon Press, 25–36.

Herzberg, Guntolf. 2006. *Anpassung und Aufbegehren: Die Intelligenz der DDR in den Krisenjahren 1956/58*. Berlin: Ch. Links.

Herzberg, Guntolf, Kurt Seifert. 2005. *Rudolf Bahro: Glaube an das Veränderbare*. Berlin: Aufbau Verlag.

Hesse, Jan-Otmar, Julia Laura Rischbieter. 2012. "Die Wirtschaftswissenschaften an der Humboldt-Universität zu Berlin 1945 bis 1990," in Rüdiger vom Bruch, Heinz-Elmar Tenorth (eds.), *Geschichte der Universität Unter den Linden 1810–2010, 6*. Berlin: Akademie Verlag, 255–276.

Heyck, Hunter. 2015. *Age of System: Understanding the Development of Modern Social Science*. Baltimore: Johns Hopkins University Press.

Hodos, George H. 1987. *Show Trials: Stalinist Purges in Eastern Europe, 1948–1954*. New York: Praeger.

Hoeft, Brigitte (ed.). 1990. *Der Prozess gegen Walter Janka und andere: eine Dokumentation*. Hamburg: Rowohlt.

Hornbogen, Lothar, Detlef Nakath, Gerd-Rüdiger Stephan (eds.). 1999. *Außerordentlicher Parteitag der SED/PDS: Protokoll der Beratungen 8./9. und 16./17. Dezember 1989*. Berlin: Dietz Verlag.

Jänicke, Martin. 1964. *Der dritte Weg: Die antistalinistische Opposition gegen Ulbricht seit 1953*. Köln: Neuer deutscher Verlag.

Jarausch, Konrad H. 2012. "Das Ringen um Erneuerung 1985–2000," in Rüdiger vom Bruch, Heinz-Elmar Tenorth (eds.), *Geschichte der Universität Unter den Linden 1810–2010, 3*. Berlin: Akademie Verlag, 555–690.

(ed.). 1999. *Dictatorship as Experience: Towards a Socio-Cultural History of the GDR*. New York and Oxford: Berghahn.

Jessen, Ralph. 1998. "Diktatorischer Elitewechsel und universitäre Milieus: Hochschullehrer in der SBZ/DDR (1945–1967)," *Geschichte und Gesellschaft* 24 (1): 24–54.

Judt, Matthias. 2000. "Review of André Steiner, Die DDR-Wirtschaftsreform der sechziger Jahre: Konflikt zwischen Effizienz- und Machtkalkül," *H-Net Reviews*, June.

2013. *Der Bereich Kommerzielle Koordinierung: Das DDR-Wirtschaftsimperium des Alexander Schalck-Golodkowski – Mythos und Realität*. Berlin: Ch. Links.

Kaemmel, Ernst. 1966. *Finanzgeschichte: Sklavenhaltergesellschaft, Feudalismus, vormonopolistischer Kapitalismus*. Berlin: Die Wirtschaft.

Kampfert, Karl. 1957. "Gegen das Aufkommen revisionistischer Auffassungen in der Wirtschaftswissenschaft," *Wirtschaftswissenschaft* 3 (Sonderheft): 1–19.

Kater, Michael. 2004. *Hitler Youth*. Cambridge: Cambridge University Press.

Keil, Johannes. 2015. "Militär(finanzökonomie) an der Universität: Eine Überlebensstrategie der Wirtschaftswissenschaften der DDR-Humboldt-Universität," *Die Hochschule: Journal für Wissenschaft und Bildung* 1: 34–47.

Keßler, Mario. 2005. "Jürgen Kuczynski: Ein linientreuer Dissident?," *Utopie kreativ* 171: 42–49.

2019. "... von gewissen Schwankungen nicht ganz frei..." *Josef Winternitz: Ein Leben zwischen Oxford, Prag, Berlin und London (1896–1952)*. Berlin: Trafo.

Klaus, Georg. 1958. "Zu einigen Problemen der Kybernetik," *Die Einheit* 13 (7): 1026–1040.

1964. *Kybernetik und Gesellschaft*. Berlin: VEB.

Klein, Dieter. 1967. "Der Konflikt zwischen Produktivkräften und kapitalistischen Produktionsverhältnissen heute," *Karl Marx: Das Kapital, 1867–1967, Sonderheft der Zeitschrift Marxistische Blätter*, 2.

1988a. "Dialog als Chance zu eigener Theorieentwicklung," *Weißenseer Blätter*, 1: 28–53.

1988b. *Chancen für einen friedensfähigen Kapitalismus*. Berlin: Dietz Verlag.

1989. "Beiträge marxistisch-leninistischer Theorieentwicklung zur Friedenssicherung," *Humboldt-Journal zur Friedensforschung* 5: 8–15.

1990. "Neues Denken und Entwicklungen in der marxistisch-leninistischen Theorie," in Peter Fischer-Appelt, Dieter S. Lutz (eds.), *Universitäten im Friedensdialog: eine Austausch-Vorlesungsreihe zwischen der Humboldt-Universität zu Berlin und der Universität Hamburg zum Thema Gemeinsame Sicherheit*. Baden-Baden: Nomos Verlagsgesellschaft.

1997. "Sozialwissenschaftliche Verantwortung angesichts globaler Handlungszwänge," *Berliner Debatte Initial* 8 (4): 75–87.

2009. *Zeitzeugen* (video series). Private Archive Roland Sender.

2014. "Die Arbeitsgruppe," *LuXemburg* 2: 88–95.

(ed.). 1972. *Futurologie und Zukunftsforschung: untaugliches Mittel einer überlebten Gesellschaft*. Berlin: Deutscher Verlag der Wissenschaften.

Klein, Dieter, Günter Hoell, Peter Hofmann, Alfred Lemmnitz, Hannelore Riedel, Karl H. Schwank, Gerhard Speer, Hans Wagner. 1986. *Politische Ökonomie des Kapitalismus: Lehrbuch*. Berlin: Dietz Verlag.

Klein, Dieter, Hannes Wunderlich. 1963. *Monopole, Integration Aggression: Die EWG – eine unheilige Allianz der Imperialisten gegen Frieden, Demokratie und Sozialismus.* Berlin: Dietz Verlag.

Klein, Dieter, Michael Brie. 1999. *Das Institut für Internationale Politik und Wirtschaft der DDR in seiner Gründungsphase 1971 bis 1974.* Berlin: Duncker und Humblot.

Kocka, Jürgen, Peter Nötzoldt, Peter Walther (eds.). 2003. *Die Berliner Akademien der Wissenschaften im geteilten Deutschland 1945–1990.* Berlin and Boston: Akademie Verlag.

Kohlmey, Gunther. 1956. "Einige Fragen der planmäßigen Ausnutzung der Wertformen und des Wertgesetzes in der Periode des Übergangs zum Sozialismus," *Wirtschaftswissenschaft* 3: 445–463.

1958. "Über politische und wissenschaftliche Verantwortung in der marxistischen wirtschaftswissenschaftlichen Forschungsarbeit: eine Stellungnahme," *Wirtschaftswissenschaft* 3: 367–370.

1968. "Planen als Regel und Steuern," *Probleme der politischen Ökonomie* 11, Berlin: Akademie Verlag.

1992. "Sozialismus-Utopie als Arbeitsaufgabe: Nachdenken über einen Nachlaßband von Fritz Behrens," *Utopie kreativ* 21–22: 88–94.

Kolar, Pavel. 2016. *Der Poststalinismus: Ideologie und Utopie einer Epoche.* Köln: Böhlan.

Kolloch, Klaus. 2001a. "Abwicklung und Neuaufbau der wirtschaftswissenschaftlichen Fakultät der Humboldt-Universität zu Berlin," in Friedrich Thießen (ed.), *Zwischen Plan und Pleite. Erlebnisberichte aus der Arbeitswelt der DDR.* Köln: Böhlau, 296–299.

2001b. "Humboldt oder Marx: Wirtschaftswissenschaftliche Forschung in der politisch-ideologischen Zwangsjacke," in Friedrich Thießen (ed.), *Zwischen Plan und Pleite: Erlebnisberichte aus der Arbeitswelt der DDR.* Cologne: Böhlau, 293–295.

2009. *Zeitzeugen* (video series). Private Archive Roland Sender.

Kopstein, Jeffrey. 1997. *The Politics of Economic Decline in East Germany: 1945–1989.* Chapel Hill: University of North Carolina Press.

Kotz, Samuel, Eugene Seneta. 1990. "Lenin as a Statistician: A Non-Soviet View," *Journal of the Royal Statistical Society* 153 (1): 73–94.

Kovács, Janos (ed.). 2018. *Populating No Man's Land: Economic Concepts of Ownership under Communism.* Lanham: Lexington.

(ed.). 2022. *Communist Planning versus Rationality: Mathematical Economics and the Central Plan in Eastern Europe and China.* Lanham: Lexington.

(ed.). forthcoming a. *Reforming Communism, Refusing Capitalism: Evolution of Market Concepts under Communism.* Lanham: Lexington.

(ed.). forthcoming b. *Ideas under (Self-)control: External Drivers of the Evolution of Economic Thought under Communism.* Lanham: Lexington.

Kowalczuk, Ilko-Sascha. 2009. *Endspiel: Die Revolution von 1989 in der DDR.* München: Beck Verlag.

2012. "Die Humboldt-Universität zu Berlin und das Ministerium für Staatssicherheit," in Rüdiger vom Bruch, Heinz-Elmar Tenorth (eds.), *Geschichte der Universität Unter den Linden 1810–2010, 3.* Berlin: Akademie Verlag, 438–553.

2013. *Stasi konkret: Überwachung und Repression in der DDR.* Munich: Beck Verlag.

Koziolek, Helmut (ed.). 1973. *Dialektische Wechselbeziehungen zwischen ökonomischer Theorie, Wirtschaftspolitik und Wirtschaftspraxis und die damit verbundenen Konsequenzen für die wirtschaftswissenschaftliche Forschung.* Berlin: Akademie Verlag.

1976. "The Systems Approach to Solving National Economic Problems," *IIASA Conference 10–13 May 1976.* Laxenburg: IIASA, 237–254.

(ed.). 1982. *Wirtschaftswissenschaftliche Forschungsaufgaben nach dem X. Parteitag der SED am 2.6.1981: Schlußfolgerungen für die wirtschaftswissenschaftliche Forschung, in Auswertung des X. Parteitages der SED am 2.6.1981.* Berlin: Akademie Verlag.

Krause, Günther. 1996. "Die Revisionismus Debatte in der DDR," *Arbeitsbericht* 2(96), Frankfurter Institut für Transformationsstudien.

1998a. "Economics in Eastern Germany, 1945–90," in Hans-Jürgen Wagener (ed.), *Economic Thought in Communist and Post-communist Europe.* London: Routledge, 264–328.

1998b. *Wirtschaftstheorie in der DDR.* Marburg: Metropolis.

Krüger, Hans-Peter. 1989. "Produktion und Kommunikation oder Marx und Habermas," *Sinn und Form: Beiträge zur Literatur* 41 (6): 1183.

Kučera, Jaroslav. 1992. "Die rechtliche und soziale Stellung der Deutschen in der Tschechoslowakei Ende der 40er und Anfang der 50er Jahre," *Bohemia* 33 (2): 322–337.

Kuczynski, Jürgen. 1947. "Soll ein Universitätslehrer Propaganda treiben," *Forum: Zeitschrift für das Geistige Leben an den Deutschen Hochschulen* 1 (2): 22–23.

1948. *Die Theorie der Lage der Arbeiter: Die Geschichte der Lage der Arbeiter unter dem Industriekapitalismus 7.* Berlin: Die Freie Gewerkschaft.

Kuhrt, Eberhard, Hannsjörg F. Buck, Gunter Holzweißig (eds.). 1999. *Opposition in der DDR von den 70er Jahren bis zum Zusammenbruch der SED.* Wiesbaden: VS Verlag für Sozialwissenschaften.

Kupferschmidt, Walter, Gernot Zellmer (eds.). 2013. *Hochschule für Ökonomie "Bruno Leuschner" 1950–1991: Leistungen und Defizite in Lehre und Forschung, persönliche Erfahrungen und Erinnerungen, Herausforderungen an die Wirtschaftswissenschaften.* Zielona Góra: Wydawnictwo Zakładu Controllingu i Informatyki Ekonomicznej.

Labedz, Leopold (ed.). 1962. *Revisionism. Essays on the History of Marxist Ideas.* London: George Allen and Unwin.

Laitko, Hubert. 2018. "Der lange Weg zum Kröber-Institut," in Wolfgang Girnus, Klaus Meier (eds.), *Wissenschaftsforschung in Deutschland: Die 1970er und 1980er Jahre.* Leipzig: Universitätsverlag, 13–154.

Land, Rainer (ed.). 1990. *Das Umbaupapier: Argumente gegen die Wiedervereinigung.* Berlin: Rotbuch Verlag.

2008. *Das 41. Jahr: Eine andere Geschichte der DDR.* Vienna, Cologne, and Weimar: Böhlau.

Land, Rainer, Ralf Possekel. 1994. *Namenlose Stimmen waren uns voraus: Politische Diskurse von Intellektuellen in der DDR.* Bochum: Winkler.

1998. *Fremde Welten: die gegensätzliche Deutung der DDR durch SED-Reformer und Bürgerbewegung in den 80er Jahren.* Berlin: Ch. Links.

Lange, Oskar. 1968a. *Einführung in die ökonomische Kybernetik.* Berlin: Akademie Verlag.

1968b. *Einführung in die Ökonometrie.* Berlin: Akademie-Verlag.

1969. *Politische Ökonomie. Band 1 und 2, Herausgegeben und mit einem Vorwort von Peter Hess und Harry Maier.* Berlin: Akademie Verlag.

Lemmnitz, Alfred. 1957. "Über die 'Administration' und die 'Ökonomie' im Sozialismus und in der Übergangsperiode," *Deutsche Finanzwirtschaft* 11 (2): 81–89.

Lenin, Vladimir Il'ič. 1947 [1909]. *Materialismus und Empiriokritizismus: kritische Bemerkungen über eine Reaktionäre Philosophie.* Moskau: Verlag für fremdsprachige Literatur.

Leonhard, Wolfgang. 1958. *Child of the Revolution.* Chicago: Regnery.

Levien, Roger E. 2000. "RAND, IIASA, and the Conduct of Systems Analysis," in Agatha C. Hughes, Thomas P. Hughes (eds.), *Systems, Experts, and Computers: The Systems Approach in Management and Engineering, World War II and After.* Cambridge, MA: MIT Press, 433–461.

Links, Christoph, Sybille Nitsche, Antje Taffelt. 2004. *Das wunderbare Jahr der Anarchie: Von der Kraft zivilen Ungehorsams 1989/90.* Berlin: Ch. Links.

Lönnendonker, Siegward. 1987. *Freie Universität Berlin: Gründung einer politischen Universität.* Berlin: Duncker und Humblot.

Luck, Herbert. 1957. "Bemerkungen zum Artikel von Behrens 'Zum Problem der Ausnutzung ökonomischer Gesetze in der Übergangsperiode'," *Wirtschaftswissenschaft* 3 (Sonderheft): 95–104.

Ludz, Peter C. 1972. *The Changing Party Elite in East Germany*. Cambridge, MA: MIT Press.

Luxemburg, Rosa. 1961. *The Russian Revolution and Leninism or Marxism?* Ann Arbor: University of Michigan Press.

Macrakis, Kristie. 2008. *Seduced by Secrets: Inside the Stasi's Spy-Tech World*. Cambridge: Cambridge University Press.

Macrakis, Kristie, Dieter Hoffmann (eds.). 1999. *Science under Socialism: East Germany in Comparative Perspective*. Cambridge, MA: Harvard University Press.

Maier, Harry. 1964. "Bildungsökonomie: Gegenstand, Aufgaben, Probleme," *Pädagogik* 9: 818–821.

1965. *Soziologie der Päpste: Lehre und Wirkung der katholischen Soziallehre*. Berlin: Akademie Verlag.

1967. *Bildung als ökonomische Potenz*. Berlin: Akademie Verlag.

1983. "Innovation and the Better Use of Human Resources," *Human Resources, Employment, and Development: Proceedings of the 6th World Congress of the International Economic Association Held in Mexico City*. London and Basingstoke: Macmillan.

1987. *Innovation oder Stagnation: Bedingungen der Wirtschaftsreform in den sozialistischen Ländern*. Cologne: Deutscher Instituts Verlag.

1994. *Bildungsökonomie: Die Interdependenz von Bildungs- und Beschäftigungssystem*. Stuttgart: Schäffer Pöschel Verlag.

Maier, Harry, Jürgen Wahse, Udo Ludwig. 1972. *Bildung als ökonomische Potenz im Sozialismus*. Berlin: Dietz Verlag.

Maier, Harry, Karl Bichtler. 1967. "Die Messung des Arbeitsaufwandes als politökonomisches Problem," *Jahrbuch des Instituts für Wirtschaftswissenschaften*, 10: 77–106.

Maier, Harry, Klaus Steinitz, Gerhard Schilling (eds.). 1968. *Zu Grundfragen der sozialistischen Wachstumstheorie*. Berlin: Die Wirtschaft.

Maier, Harry, Wolfgang Heinrichs (eds.). 1976. *Gesetzmässigkeiten der intensiv erweiterten Reproduktion bei der weiteren Gestaltung der entwickelten sozialistischen Gesellschaft*. Berlin: Akademie Verlag.

Malycha, Andreas. 2014. *Die SED in der Ära Honecker: Machtstrukturen, Entscheidungsmechanismen und Konfliktfelder in der Staatspartei 1971 bis 1989*. Oldenbourg: De Gruyter.

Mannheim, Karl. 1952 [1928]. "The Problem of Generations," in Paul Kecskemeti (ed.), *Essays on the Sociology of Knowledge*. London: Routledge, 276–320.

Marbach, Rainer, Volker Weiß (eds.). 2017. *Konformitäten und Konfrontationen: Homosexuelle in der DDR*. Hamburg: Männerschwarm Verlag.

Marchal, Jean. 1950. "Gegenstand und Wesen der Wirtschaftswissenschaft: Von einer mechanischen Wissenschaft zu einer Wissenschaft vom Menschen," *Zeitschrift für die gesamte Staatswissenschaft*, 106: 577–600.

Matern, Hermann. 1957. "Die Bedeutung der Werke von Karl Marx und Friedrich Engels für den gegenwärtigen Kampf der deutschen Arbeiterklasse," *Die Einheit* 2: 140–156.

Mayntz, Renate. 1994. *Deutsche Forschung im Einigungsprozess: Die Transformation der Akademie der Wissenschaften der DDR 1989 bis 1992*. Frankfurt a.M.: Campus Verlag.

McDonald, Alan. 1998. "Scientific Cooperation as a Bridge across the Cold War Divide: The Case of the International Institute for Applied Systems Analysis (IIASA)," *Annals of the New York Academy of Sciences* 866 (1): 55–83.

McDougall, Alan. 2008. "A Duty to Forget? The 'Hitler Youth Generation' and the Transition from Nazism to Communism in Postwar East Germany, c. 1945–49," *German History* 26 (1): 24–46.

Merkel, Wolfgang, Raj Kollmorgen, Hans-Jürgen Wagener (eds.). 2019. *The Handbook of Political, Social, and Economic Transformation*. New York: Oxford University Press.

Mertens, Lothar. 2004. *Rote Denkfabrik: die Akademie für Gesellschaftswissenschaften beim ZK der SED*. Münster: LIT Verlag.

Mespoulet, Martine. 2022. "Creating a Socialist Society and Quantification in the USSR," in Andrea Mennicken, Robert Salais (eds), *The New Politics of Numbers: Executive Politics and Governance*. London: Palgrave Macmillan, 45–70.

Meyer, Hansgünter. 1995. "Soziologie und soziologische Forschung in der DDR," in Bernhard Schäfers (ed.), *Soziologie in Deutschland: Entwicklung, Institutionalisierung und Berufsfelder, theoretische Kontroversen*. Opladen: Leske und Budrich, 35–49.

Middell, Matthias. 2012. "Die Humboldt-Universität im DDR Wissenschaftssystem," in Rüdiger vom Bruch, Heinz-Elmar Tenorth (eds.), *Geschichte der Universität Unter den Linden 1810–2010, 3*. Berlin: Akademie Verlag, 251–436.

Möller, Uwe, Bernd Preußer (eds.). 2006. *Die Parteihochschule der SED: Ein kritischer Rückblick*. Berlin: GNN.

Müller, Eva, Manfred Neuhaus, Joachim Tesch (eds.). 1999. *"Ich habe einige Dogmen angetastet": Werk und Wirken von Fritz Behrens*. Leipzig: Rosa-Luxemburg-Stiftung Sachsen.

Müller, Johannes. 1927. *Grundriß der deutschen Statistik: Ein Grundriß für Studium und Praxis*. Jena: Fischer.

Müller-Enbergs, Helmut et al. 2010. *Wer war wer in der DDR?* Berlin: Ch. Links.

Münkel, Daniela (ed.). 2014. *Herbst '89 im Blick der Stasi: Die geheimen Berichte an die SED-Führung.* Berlin: BStU.

Naumann, Friedrich. 2018. "Vom Tastenfeld zum Mikrochip: Computerindustrie und Informatik im 'Schrittmaß' des Sozialismus," in Dieter Hoffmann, Kristie Macrakis (eds.), *Naturwissenschaft und Technik in der DDR.* Berlin and Boston: Akademie Verlag, 261–282.

Naumann, Robert. 1953. "Stalin als Ökonom," *Wirtschaftswissenschaft* 1, 4–20.

1957. "Gegen die Gefahr der Entwicklung revisionistischer Anschauungen auf dem Gebiet der Politischen Ökonomie," *Einheit: Zeitschrift für Theorie und Praxis des wissenschaftlichen Sozialismus* 2: 157–167.

1959. *Theorie und Praxis des Neoliberalismus: Das Märchen von der freien und sozialen Marktwirtschaft.* Berlin: Die Wirtschaft.

Nick, Harry. 2003. *Gemeinwesen DDR: Erinnerungen und Überlegungen eines Politökonomen.* Hamburg: VSA.

2011. *Ökonomendebatten in der DDR.* Schkeuditz: GNN Verlag.

Nicolas, Marcel. 1952. *Wesen und Aufgabe der Statistik.* Berlin: Duncker und Humblot.

Niethammer, Lutz. 1994. "Erfahrungen und Strukturen: Prolegomena zu einer Geschichte der Gesellschaft der DDR," in Hartmut Kaelble, Jürgen Kocka, Harmut Zwahr (eds.), *Sozialgeschichte der DDR.* Stuttgart: Klett-Cotta, 271–294.

Nötzoldt, Peter. 1996. "Wissenschaft in Berlin: Anmerkungen zum ersten Nachkriegsjahr 1945/46," *Dahlemer Archivgespräche* 1: 115–130.

Oelßner, Fred. 1957. "Diskussionsrede auf der 30. Tagung des ZK der SED vom 30.1. bis 1.2. 1957," in Bruno Leuschner (ed.), *Unsere ökonomischen Probleme und die Verbesserung der Wirtschaftsführung.* Berlin: Dietz Verlag, 63–80.

(ed.). 1955. *Die Übergangsperiode vom Kapitalismus zum Sozialismus in der DDR.* Berlin: Akademie-Verlag.

Ohse, Marc-Dietrich. 2009. "Wir haben uns prächtig amüsiert: Die DDR, ein 'Staat der Jugend'?," in Thomas Großbölting (ed.), *Friedensstaat, Leseland, Sportnation? DDR-Legenden auf dem Prüfstand.* Berlin: Ch. Links.

Orlow, Dietrich. 2021. *The Parteihochschule Karl Marx under Ulbricht and Honecker, 1946–1990: The Perseverance of a Stalinist Institution.* Cham: Palgrave Macmillan.

Péteri, György. 1996. "Controlling the Field of Academic Economics: Hungary, 1953–1976," *Minerva* 34 (4): 367–380.

1997. "New Course Economics: The Field of Economic Research in Hungary after Stalin, 1953–1956," *Contemporary European History* 6 (3): 295–327.

Pfaff, Steven. 2006. *Exit-Voice Dynamics and the Collapse of East Germany: The Crisis of Leninism and the Revolution of 1989*. Durham, NC: Duke University Press.

Philby, Kim. 1983. *Im Secret Service: Erinnerungen eines sowjetischen Kundschafters. Ins Deutsche übertragen von Dr. Ernst Strnad*. Berlin: Militärverlag der DDR.

Pollock, Ethan. 2006. *Stalin and the Soviet Science Wars*. Princeton: Princeton University Press.

Posey, C. A. 1998. *Red Danube*. Toronto: Worldwide Library.

Praschek, Helmut. 2000. "Besonderheiten der amtlichen Statistik in der ehemaligen DDR," *Wirtschaft und Statistik* 1: 24–29.

Redaktionskollegium. 1956. "Über den Kampf gegen den Dogmatismus und über die Parteilichkeit in unserer wirtschaftswissenschaftlichen Arbeit," *Wirtschaftswissenschaft* 3: 21–33.

Richter, Helmut. 1957. "Wertgesetz und Spontaneität in der Übergangsperiode," *Wirtschaftswissenschaft* 3 (Sonderheft): 44–61.

Rieter, Heinz. 2010. "Die Anfänge der Wirtschaftswissenschaft an der Freien Universität Berlin: Personen, Institutionen, Konflikte," in Christian Scheer (ed.), *Studien zur Entwicklung der ökonomischen Theorie XXV: Die deutschsprachige Wirtschaftswissenschaft in den ersten Jahrzehnten nach 1945*. Berlin: Duncker und Humblot, 25–200.

Rindzevičiūtė, Eglė. 2016. *The Power of Systems: How Policy Sciences Opened up the Cold War World*. Ithaca, NY: Cornell University Press.

Riska-Campbell, Leena. 2011. *Bridging East and West: The Establishment of the International Institute for Applied Systems Analysis (IIASA) in the United States Foreign Policy of Bridge Building, 1964–1972*. Helsinki: Finnish Society of Science and Letters.

Rohde, Erwin. 1956a. "Zur Neuordnung des Haushaltsausgleichs," *Deutsche Finanzwirtschaft* 5.

1956b. "Zur Verbesserung des Wiwi Studiums," *Deutsche Finanzwirtschaft* 13.

1958. "Die Rolle des Staatshaushaltes bei der Verteilung und Umverteilung des Nationaleinkommens in der DDR," *Deutsche Finanzwirtschaft* 9.

1960. "Lenins Werke: Fundgrube der marxistischen Finanzwissenschaften," *Deutsche Finanzwissenschaften* 6.

1985. *Banken, Börsen, Währungen im gegenwärtigen Kapitalismus*. Berlin: Die Wirtschaft.

2009. *Zeitzeugen* (video series). Private Archive Roland Sender.

et al. 1951. "Die Stellung der Gemeinden und Kreise im Finanzausgleich," *Schriftenreihe der Deutschen Finanzwirtschaft* 16.

Rohde, Erwin, Helmuth Neltner, Dieter Reuschel. 1958. "Das einheitliche sozialistische Finanzsystem: Die gesellschaftliche Praxis und die Ansichten von Prof. Dr. Kohlmey," *Deutsche Finanzwirtschaft* 12: 187–193.

Rohde, Erwin, Gottfried Schneider, Heinz Siebenhaar. 1966. *Zur neuen Haushaltwirtschaft der Städte und Gemeinden. Finanzökonomisches Forschungsinstitut beim Ministerium der Finanzen.* Berlin: Staatsverlag der Deutschen Demokratischen Republik.

Rohde, Erwin, Heinz Fengler. 1959. *Der Staatshaushalt der Deutschen Demokratischen Republik: Eine Einführung.* Berlin: Die Wirtschaft.

Rohde, Erwin, Heinz Siebenhaar. 1972. *Haushalts- und Finanzwirtschaft der Städte und Gemeinden.* Berlin: Staatsverlag der Deutschen Demokratischen Republik.

Rosental, Mark. 1956. *Was ist marxistische Erkenntnistheorie?* Berlin: Dietz Verlag.

Ruben, Peter, Hans Wagner. 1980. "Sozialistische Wertform und dialektischer Widerspruch: Überlegungen zur entwicklungstheoretischen Auffassung des Arbeitswertes in der sozialistischen Produktion," *Deutsche Zeitschrift für Philosophie* 10: 1218–1230.

Rubin, Ernest. 1968. "Questions and Answers: The Statistical Approach of Karl Marx," *The American Statistician* 22 (2): 31–33.

Rudder, Helmut de. 1997. "The Transformation of East German Higher Education: Renewal as Adaptation, Integration and Innovation," *Minerva* 35: 99–125.

Sabrow, Martin. 2010. "Der vergessen dritte Weg," *Aus Politik und Zeitgeschichte* 11 (March): 6–12.

2013. "Der führende Repräsentant: Erich Honecker in generationsbiographischer Perspektive," *Studies in Contemporary History* 1: 61–88.

Sanderson, Paul. 1981. "East German Economists and the Path to the 'New Economic System' in the German Democratic Republic," *Canadian Slavonic Papers* 23 (2): 166–180.

Schalck-Golodkowski, Alexander. 2000. *Deutsch-deutsche Erinnerungen.* Reinbek: Rowohlt.

Scheler, Hermann. 1957. "Über das Verhältnis von Spontaneität und Bewußtheit," *Wirtschaftswissenschaft* 3 (Sonderheft): 20–43.

Schmerbach, Sibylle, Oliver Günter. 2010. "Deutsche Universitäten im Umbruch: 20 Jahre nach der Wende," in Frank Keuper and Dieter Puchta (eds.), *Deutschland 20 Jahre nach dem Mauerfall: Rückblick und Ausblick.* Wiesbaden: Gabler GWV, 401–417.

Schmidt, Johann Lorenz. 1954. "Die Planlosigkeit in der Übersetzung der Artikel von Sowjetökonomen und ein Vorschlag zu ihrer Überwindung," *Wirtschaftswissenschaft* 2: 308.

Schneider, Jürgen. 1997. "Marxistisch-leninistische Wirtschaftswissenschaften nach sowjetischem Modell an den Hochschulen der SBZ/DDR: Legitimation und Propaganda für Parteitage der SED," in Hans-Jürgen Gerhard (ed.), *Struktur und Dimension: Festschrift für Karl Heinrich Kaufhold*. Stuttgart: Franz Steiner, 214–265.

Scholz, Michael F. 1997. *Bauernopfer der deutschen Frage: Der Kommunist Kurt Vieweg im Dschungel der Geheimdienste.* Berlin: Aufbau Verlag.

Schorer, Hans. 1946. *Statistik: Grundlegung und Einführung in die statistische Methode.* Bern: Francke.

Schorlemmer, Friedrich. 1992. *Worte öffnen Fäuste: Die Rückkehr in ein schwieriges Vaterland.* Munich: Kindler.

Schrickel, Isabell. 2014. "Von Schmetterlingen und Atomreaktoren: Medien und Politiken der Resilienz am IIASA," *Behemoth* 2: 5–25.

2018. "International Institute for Applied Systems Analysis (IIASA)," in Frank Reichherzer, Emmanül Droit, Jan Hansen (eds.), *Den Kalten Krieg vermessen: Über Reichweite und Alternativen einer binären Ordnungsvorstellung.* Berlin and Boston: De Gruyter, 199–214.

Schüddekopf, Charles (ed.). 1990. *"Wir sind das Volk!" Flugschriften, Aufrufe und Texte einer deutschen Revolution.* Reinbek: Rowohlt.

Schüle, Annagret, Thomas Ahbe, Rainer Gries (eds.). 2006. *Die DDR aus generationengeschichtlicher Perspektive: Eine Inventur.* Leipzig: Leipziger Universitäts-Verlag.

Schulz, Tobias. 2010. *Sozialistische Wissenschaft: Die Berliner Humboldt-Universität (1960–1975).* Köln: Böhlau.

Schulze, Hans-Michael. 2003. *In den Villen der Agenten: Die Stasi-Prominenz privat.* Berlin: Quintessenz.

Segal, Jérôme. 2001. "Kybernetik in der DDR: Begegnung mit der marxistischen Ideologie," *Dresdener Beiträge zur Geschichte der Technikwissenschaften* 27: 47–75.

Shapin, Steven, Simon Schaffer. 1985. *Leviathan and the Air-Pump: Hobbes, Boyle, and the Experimental Life.* Princeton: Princeton University Press.

Sheynin, Oscar. 1998. "Statistics in the Soviet Epoch," *Journal of Economics and Statistics* 217 (5): 529–549.

Smirnov, Vladimir Ivanovič. 1954. Die Betriebsanalyse im Handel: *Übersetzungkollektiv unter der Redaktion von Ernst Strnad und Herbert Breitschneider.* Berlin: Die Wirtschaft.

Solomon, Peter. 2003. *Die Geschichte der Mikroelektronik-Halbleiterindustrie in der DDR.* Dessau: Funkverlag Bernhard Hein.

Stalin, Joseph V. 1950. "Marxism and Problems of Linguistics," in *Collected Works 16*. Moscow: Foreign Languages Publishing House.

1972 [1952]. *Economic Problems of Socialism in the USSR*. Peking: Foreign Languages Press.

Steiner, André. 1999. *Die DDR-Wirtschaftsreform der sechziger Jahre: Konflikt zwischen Effizienz- und Machtkalkül*. Berlin: Akademie Verlag.

2004. *Von Plan zu Plan: Eine Wirtschaftsgeschichte der DDR*. Munich: DVA.

2006. "Probleme mit der DDR-Statistik in der historischen Forschung," in André Steiner, Mitarbeit von Matthias Judt, Thomas Reichel (eds.), *Statistische Übersichten zur Sozialpolitik in Deutschland seit 1945: SBZ/DDR*. Bonn: Bundesministerium für Arbeit und Soziales, xiii–xxvii.

Steiner, Helmut. 1990. "Der aufrechte Gang eines DDR-Ökonomen: Fritz Behrens (1909–1980)," *Utopie konkret* 2: 80–84.

1992. "Fritz Behrens, Lebensbilanz eines sozialistischen Wissenschaftlers: Zum erstmaligen Erscheinen seiner Kritik des Staatssozialismus," *Deutschland-Archiv* 11: 1160–1168.

1996. "Prof. Dr. Gunther Kohlmey im Fadenkreuz der Revisionismus-Kampagne," *Utopie kreativ* 33/34: 82–86.

2000. "Das Akademie-Institut für Wirtschaftswissenschaften im Widerstreit wissenschaftlicher, ideologischer und politischer Auseinandersetzungen," *Sitzungsberichte der Leibniz-Sozietät* 36: 89–124.

Stibbe, Matthew. 2011. "Jürgen Kuczynski and the Search for a (Non-existent) Western Spy Ring in the East German Communist Party in 1953," *Contemporary European History* 20 (1): 61–79.

Streibel, Günter. 1975. "Umweltschutz und Umweltgestaltung als volks-wirtschaftliche Aufgabe," *Wirtschaftswissenschaft* 8: 1139–1156.

Strnad, Ernst. 1968. *Der kubanische Staatshaushalt vor und nach der Revolution*. Dissertation Universität Rostock (June 18).

1990. *Die Wirtschaft der Etrusker: Ausgewählte etruskologische Arbeiten*. Bernau: Eigenverlag.

Strnad, Walter, Ernst Strnad. 1990. *Der Befehl "ans Tor": Die authentische Geschichte eines Sonderkommandos im faschistischen Konzentrationslager Buchenwald*. Bernau: Eigenverlag.

Strohe, Hans G. 1996. "Statistik im DDR-Wirtschaftsstudium zwischen Ideologie und Wissenschaft," *Statistische Diskussionsbeiträge* 3. Potsdam: Universität Potsdam.

Sturm, Eva. 2000. '*Und der Zukunft zugewandt*'? *Eine Untersuchung zur 'Politikfähigkeit' der PDS*. Wiesbaden: VS Verlag für Sozialwissenschaften.

Sukrow, Oliver. 2019. "Die Akademie der Marxistisch-Leninistischen Organisationswissenschaft in Berlin: Geschichte und Kontext eines (vergessenen) sozialistischen Zukunftsorts," *Die Hochschule: Journal für Wissenschaft und Bildung* 28 (1): 113–126.

Süß, Walter. 1999. *Staatssicherheit am Ende: Warum es den Mächtigen nicht gelang, 1989 eine Revolution zu verhindern.* Berlin: Ch. Links.

Tenorth, Heinz-Elmar (ed.) (2010–2012). *Geschichte der Universität Unter den Linden 1810-2010*, Volumes 1–3. Berlin: Akademie Verlag.

Tippett, Leonard H. C. 1952 [1931]. *Einführung in die Statistik.* Vienna and Stuttgart: Humboldt-Verlag.

Ulbricht, Walter. 1957. *Grundfragen der Politik der Sozialistischen Einheitspartei Deutschlands: Referat auf der 30. Tagung des Zentralkommittees der Sozialistischen Einheitspartei Deutschlands am 30. Januar.* Berlin: Dietz Verlag.

1965. *Das neue ökonomische System der Planung und Leitung der Volkswirtschaft in der Praxis.* Berlin: Dietz Verlag.

Vaizey, Hester. 2014. *Born in the GDR: Living in the Shadow of the Wall.* Oxford: Oxford University Press.

Vaska, Tibor (ed.). 1987. *The Long-Wave Debate: Selected Papers from an IIASA International Meeting, Weimar, GDR, June 10–14, 1985.* Heidelberg: Springer.

Vogt, Annette. 2012. "Vom Wiederaufbau der Berliner Universität bis zum Universitäts-Jubiläum 1960," in Rüdiger vom Bruch, Heinz-Elmar Tenorth (eds.), *Geschichte der Universität Unter den Linden 1810–2010*, 3. Berlin: Akademie Verlag, 125–250.

Von der Lippe, Peter. 1996. "Die politische Rolle der amtlichen Statistik in der ehemaligen DDR," *Jahrbücher für Nationalökonomie und Statistik* 215 (6): 641–674.

Wagemann, Ernst. 1950 [1935]. *Narrenspiegel der Statistik: Die Umrisse eines statistischen Weltbildes.* Munich: Lehnen.

Wagener, Hans-Jürgen. 1997. "Second Thoughts? Economics and Economists under Socialism," *Kyklos* 50 (2): 165–187.

(ed.). 1998. *Economic Thought in Communist and Post-communist Europe.* London: Routledge.

Wagener, Hans-Jürgen, Maciej Tymiński, Piotr Koryś. 2021. *Sozialistische Ökonomie im Spannungsfeld der Modernisierung: Ein ideengeschichtlicher Vergleich DDR – Polen.* Wiesbaden: Springer.

Waugh, Albert E. 1952 [1938]. *Elements of Statistical Method.* New York: McGraw-Hill.

Will, Rosemarie. 1989. "Rechtsstaatlichkeit als Moment demokratischer Machtausübung," *Deutsche Zeitschrift für Philosophie* 9: 801–812.

Wille, Manfred. 1991. "Heimatvertriebene in den ersten Nachkriegsjahren in der sowjetischen Besatzungszone Deutschlands: Anmerkungen zur Statistik," in Manfred Wille, Karlheinz Lau, Jörg Bernhard Bilke (eds.), *Die Vertriebenen in Mitteldeutschland.* Bonn: Bund der Vertriebenen, 1–8.

Winternitz, Josef. 1950. "Von Stalin lernen," *Einheit* 2: 161–170.

Wirzberger, Karl-Heinz (ed.). 1968. *Aktuelle Probleme der Kybernetik, der elektronischen Datenverarbeitung und Operationsforschung.* Berlin: Humboldt-Universität zu Berlin.

Wolf, Dieter, Heinz Paragenings. 2004. *Zur Konfusion des Wertbegriffs: Beiträge zur "Kapital"-Diskussion.* Hamburg: Argument.

Wolle, Stefan. 1998. *Die heile Welt der Diktatur: Alltag und Herrschaft in der DDR 1971–1989.* Berlin: Ch. Links.

2006. "Revolte im Hörsaal: Die Berliner Humboldt-Universität im Jahre 1956," *Zeitschrift des Forschungsverbundes SED-Staat* 19: 3–26.

Wollmann, Hellmut. 2010. "Soziologie an der Humboldt-Universität unter dem SED-Regime und in der 'Wende' (1945–1991)," http://amor.cms.hu-berlin.de/~h0598bce/docs/HW-2010-HU-SED-Wende.pdf (accessed September 21, 2014).

Zatlin, Jonathan R. 2007. *The Currency of Socialism: Money and Political Culture in East Germany.* Cambridge: Cambridge University Press.

Zimmermann, Volker. 2010. *Eine sozialistische Freundschaft im Wandel: Die Beziehungen zwischen SBZ/DDR und der Tschechoslowakei 1945–1969.* Essen: Klartext.

Zschaler, Frank. 1984. *Die Geschichte der Wirtschaftswissenschaftlichen Fakultät der Humboldt-Universität zu Berlin und ihre Vorgängerinstitutionen von der Befreiung vom Faschismus bis zum Vorabend der sozialistischen Hochschulreform 1945–1945,* dissertation, Humboldt University, Berlin.

1997. *Vom Heilig-Geist-Spital zur Wirtschaftswissenschaftlichen Fakultät.* Berlin: Springer.

Zweynert, Joachim. 2019. "Shestidesyatniki Economics, the Idea of Convergence, and Perestroika," *History of Political Economy* 51 (Supplement): 277–299.

Personal Conversations

Apelt, Siegfried. July 2012, Humboldt University, Berlin.
Aßmann, Georg. July 2012, Humboldt University, Berlin.
Busch, Ulrich. June 2013, Humboldt University, Berlin.
Eckstein, Gisela (formerly Benary). June 2018, Berlin Grünau.
Fuchs-Kittowski, Klaus. May 2019, Berlin Rahnsdorf.
Gurtz, Johannes. July 2013, Kommunales Bildungswerk, Berlin.
Krause, Günter. August 2012, Humboldt University, Berlin.

Kuczynski, Thomas, June 2018, Berlin Pankow.
Loschinski, Hannamaria (née Behrens). June 2018, Berlin Petershagen-Eggersdorf.
Ludwig, Udo. June 2019, Halle.
Maier, Siegrid. June 2019, Berlin Dahlem.
Mechler, Siegfried. August 2012, Humboldt University, Berlin.
Paragenings, Heinz. June 2018, Berlin Treptow-Köpenick.
Radtke, Günther. August 2012, Humboldt University, Berlin.
Rambaum, Jürgen. August 2012, Humboldt University, Berlin.
Schmerbach, Sibylle. July 2012, Humboldt University, Berlin.
Sender, Roland. August 2012, Berlin Mahlsdorf.
Steinitz, Klaus. June 2019, Berlin Treptow.
Wilke, Jürgen. August 2012, Berlin Mitte.
Zschaler, Frank. September 2013, Skype.

Archives

Archiv der Berlin-Brandenburgischen Akademie der Wissenschaften (ABBAW), Jägerstr. 22/23, 10117 Berlin.
Archiv Demokratischer Sozialismus der Rosa-Luxemburg-Stiftung, Gesellschaftsanalyse und politische Bildung e. V., Historisches Zentrum Demokratischer Sozialismus, Straße der Pariser Kommune 8A, 10243 Berlin.
Bundesbeauftragte für die Unterlagen des Staatssicherheitsdienstes der ehemaligen Deutschen Demokratischen Republik (BStU), Karl-Liebknecht-Straße 31/33, 10178 Berlin.
Stiftung Archiv der Parteien und Massenorganisationen der DDR im Bundesarchiv (SAPMO), Finckensteinallee 63, 12205 Berlin, Postfach 450569, 12175 Berlin.
Universitätsarchiv der Humboldt-Universität zu Berlin (UA), Wagner-Régeny-Straße 81, 12489 Berlin.

Index

321

Other Books in the Series (*continued from page ii*)

Anthony M. Endres, Grant A. Fleming, *International Organizations and the Analysis of Economic Policy, 1919–1950* (2002)

David Laidler, *Fabricating the Keynesian Revolution: Studies of the Inter-War Literature on Money, the Cycle, and Unemployment* (1999)

Esther-Mirjam Sent, *The Evolving Rationality of Rational Expectations: An Assessment of Thomas Sargent's Achievements* (1998)

Heath Pearson, *Origins of Law and Economics: The Economists' New Science of Law, 1830–1930* (1997)

Odd Langholm, *The Legacy of Scholasticism in Economic Thought: Antecedents of Choice and Power* (1998)

Yuichi Shionoya, *Schumpeter and the Idea of Social Science* (1997)

J. Daniel Hammond, *Theory and Measurement: Causality Issues in Milton Friedman's Monetary Economics* (1996)

William J. Barber, *Designs within Disorder: Franklin D. Roosevelt, the Economists, and the Shaping of American Economic Policy, 1933–1945* (1996)

Juan Gabriel Valdes, *Pinochet's Economists: The Chicago School of Economics in Chile* (1995)

Philip Mirowski (ed.), *Natural Images in Economic Thought: "Markets Read in Tooth and Claw"* (1994)

Malcolm Rutherford, *Institutions in Economics: The Old and the New Institutionalism* (1994)

Karen I. Vaughn, *Austrian Economics in America: The Migration of a Tradition* (1994)

Lars Jonung (ed.), *The Stockholm School of Economics Revisited* (1991)

E. Roy Weintraub, *Stabilizing Dynamics: Constructing Economic Knowledge* (1991)

M. June Flanders, *International Monetary Economics, 1870–1960: Between the Classical and the New Classical* (1990)

Philip Mirowski, *More Heat Than Light: Economics as Social Physics, Physics as Nature's Economics* (1990)

Mary S. Morgan, *The History of Econometric Ideas* (1990)

Gerald M. Koot, *English Historical Economics, 1870–1926: The Rise of Economic History and Mercantilism* (1988)

Kim Kyun, *Equilibrium Business Cycle Theory in Historical Perspective* (1988)

William J. Barber, *From New Era to New Deal: Herbert Hoover, the Economists, and American Economic Policy, 1921–1933* (1985)

Takashi Negishi, *Economic Theories in a Non-Walrasian Tradition* (1985)

Printed in the United States
by Baker & Taylor Publisher Services